Renewed by the *Spirit*

365 daily meditations

Renewed by the *Spirit*
365 daily meditations

Ralph I. Tilley

LITS Books
PO Box 405
Sellersburg, Indiana 47172

ISBN: 10: 0990395030
ISBN: 13: 978-09903950-3-4

LITS Books
PO Box 405
Sellersburg, Indiana 47172

Bulk discounts are available; contact editor@litsjournal.org.

This book is available on Kindle and other devices.

For all books authored or edited by Ralph I. Tilley, go to litsjournal.org or amazon.com.

To
Emily,
my loving, devoted wife of fifty years;
and to
James R. Voyles,
who gave to me his daughter in marriage.

Preface

Since my conversion to Christ, over fifty years ago now, our gracious Lord has ministered to me daily through his sacred Scriptures. Additionally, my life and ministry have been immeasurably enriched as the Spirit has used the writings of men and women—past and present—who communicated a keen mind and a warm heart as they put pen to paper. In the words of the holy apostle, our merciful God is pleased to use both "parchments" (the Scriptures) and "books" (2 Tim. 4:13) in building up his people in the most holy faith.

One such book the Lord has favorably blessed to countless numbers of Christians is a book of daily devotionals. Personally, I have read for many years from at least one devotional each day and sometimes from more than one.

For the Christian to maintain a vibrant relationship in his or her walk with God, daily renewal is essential; a book of meditations can contribute toward that end. A devotional should not be a substitute for daily Bible reading; it should only serve as a supplement to the Word of God. Thus, I pray our Father will be pleased to use *Renewed by the Spirit* as an aid in one's walk with God. If that should be the case, to God alone belongs the glory.

A few notes about these meditations: Approximately one-third were selected and edited from some of my previous books and *Life in the Spirit Journal*. Furthermore, whenever a portion of a Scripture text is *italicized*, I have done so for the sake of emphasis. Also, each *unattributed* verse in this volume is my own composition. Additionally, where an asterisk (*) occurs, the reference material will be found in the Endnotes. Finally, I am indebted to my dear wife, Emily, for proofreading the entire manuscript in this current edition. Of course, I am responsible for any errors which may occur.

And now may "the grace of the Lord Jesus Christ and the love of God and the fellowship of the Holy Spirit be with you," as you read each day's meditation.

Ralph I. Tilley
Soli Deo Gloria
2016

Beginnings

In the beginning, God created the heavens and the earth.
Genesis 1:1

The one and only true God is alone capable of creating, for only God can bring something into being that had no prior reality; he is the God who "calls into existence the things that do not exist" (Rom. 4:17). God spoke the "heavens and the earth" into being. We believe this because we believe the inspired written record; it is a matter of faith; it is a matter of taking God at his word: "By faith we understand that the universe was created by the word of God, so that what is seen was not made out of things that are visible" (Heb. 11:3).

From the New Testament, we learn the second Person of the Triune God was the creative instrument: "For by him all things were created, in heaven and on earth, visible and invisible, whether thrones or dominions or rulers or authorities—all things were created through him and for him" (Col. 1:16). The heavens and the earth had a beginning; their beginning originated with our Creator-God.

As Christians, we, likewise, have been brought into existence through God's Son by the power of the Holy Spirit. This same God, who "created the heavens and the earth," is the God who established a higher creation: "For we are his workmanship, created in Christ Jesus" (Eph. 2:10).

As wonderful as God's entire universe is—from the smallest organism to the largest planet, from the majestic mountains to the prairies, deserts, rivers and oceans, and the creation of mankind—more magnificent still is the person who is enabled by God's Spirit to look up and call his Creator, "Father" (Gal. 4:6).

All created matter had a beginning; the same is true for spiritual beginnings. The Christian life has a beginning. When was your beginning? When were you born of God?

For me, I'll never forget the night when I went to a church service physically alive but spiritually dead. I left the church that same night with a new beginning: "if anyone is in Christ, he is a new creation" (2 Cor. 517).

Let us ever be thankful for both of God's creations—the material and the spiritual.

The Word

*In the beginning was the Word, and the Word
was with God, and the Word was God.*
John 1:1

The opening words in John's gospel are strikingly similar to those in Genesis 1:1: "In the beginning God." The heavens and the earth were not created from preexisting matter—"what is seen was not made out of things which are visible" (Heb. 11:3). The Second Person of the Triune God preexisted all matter: "he is before all things" (Col. 1:17).

As the Son of Man, Jesus had a human genealogy (see Matt. 1:1-17; Luke 3:23-38); as the Son of God, he eternally coexists with the Father ("was with God"), and is Deity himself ("the Word was God").

Jesus is called the "Word" by John. Words are speech expressions, communicating one's thoughts. John says of the Word, "All things were made through him, and without him was not any thing made that was made" (John 1:3). Before the Incarnation, God expressed himself through the Second Person of the Trinity—the Word—by creating all things. In Genesis 1, we have the record of God repeatedly speaking: "Let there be light ..."; "Let there be an expanse ..."; "Let the waters ..."; "Let the earth ..."; "Let us make man, ..." etc. All creation came into existence through the speaking Word, the Word of God.

God's ultimate and perfect manifestation of self-expression culminated in the Incarnation of the Word: "And the Word became flesh and dwelt among us" (John 1:14). In the Incarnation of Christ, God was not merely speaking words—he was speaking in and through a human body: "Long ago, at many times and in many ways, God spoke to our fathers by the prophets, but in these last days he has spoken to us by his Son" (Heb. 1:1-2).

The first time we see the Word made flesh, he is lying in a manger; the last time we see him called the Word, he is riding on a white horse, "clothed in a robe dipped in blood, and the name by which he is called is The Word of God" (Rev. 19:13).

To God be the glory for speaking!

Light from Above

Then God said, "Let there be light"; and there was light.
Genesis 1:3

Before God spoke light into existence, "The earth was without form and void, and darkness was over the face of the deep" (Gen. 1:2). The absence of light is darkness. It is impossible to imagine a universe without light.

One definition of light is, "the form of energy that makes it possible to see things." We cannot see without light. Where there is light—whether it is natural or artificial—one can see. Light makes the invisible visible.

Light is a biblical metaphor for the holiness of God: "God is light, and in him is no darkness at all" (1 John 1:5). What God's created physical light is to the universe, his holiness is to all mankind. His holiness makes visible to us what was previously invisible.

The world without God is like the primordial world: "without form and void, and darkness" (Gen 1:2). The prophet Isaiah saw a day when the "people who walked in darkness have seen a great light; those who dwelt in a land of deep darkness, on them has light shone" (9:2).

The light that Isaiah saw six centuries before the Incarnation was the "true Light, which gives light to everyone" (John 1:9). This true Light is none other than God in the flesh, the Lord Jesus Christ, who testified, "I am the light of the world. Whoever follows me will not walk in darkness, but will have the light of life" (John 8:12).

Philip P. Bliss (1838-1876) penned it beautifully:

The whole world was lost in the darkness of sin,
The Light of the world is Jesus!
Like sunshine at noonday, His glory shone in;
The Light of the world is Jesus!*

One who had seen the Light for himself, wrote, "if we walk in the light, as he is in the light, we have fellowship with one another, and the blood of Jesus his Son cleanses us from all sin" (1 John 1:7).

Have you seen the Light? Are you walking in the light of God's holiness?

The Mercy of God

Let us then with confidence draw near to the throne of grace,
that we may receive mercy and find grace to help in time of need.
Hebrews 4:16

Without a merciful God there is neither pardon for the sinner nor hope for the believer. Of the sinner, Paul writes, "But when the goodness and loving kindness of God our Savior appeared, he saved us, not because of works done by us in righteousness, but according to his own mercy ..." (Titus 3:4-5). Of the believer, Hebrews says, "Let us then with confidence draw near to the throne of grace, that we may receive mercy and find grace to help in time of need" (4:16). The Titus passage refers to repentant sinners, the Hebrews text, to believers.

While all Christians have confessed their need of God's mercy, when they first repented of their sins and received God's gracious forgiveness, not all Christians are persuaded they are continually in need of God's mercy. Additionally, not all Christians are convinced they fall short of God's glory (Rom. 3:23). So, if one does not believe he falls short of God's glory, it is only logical he does not feel the need of God's moment-by-moment mercy.

While sailing across the Atlantic to America with Mr. Oglethorpe, who was to be the governor of the new colony of Georgia, John Wesley (1703-1791) heard a noise in the governor's cabin. So Wesley went to the cabin, and the governor said, "I dare say you want to know what this noise is about, sir; I have good occasion for it. You know, sir, that the only wine I drink is Cyprus wine, and it is necessary for me; I put it on board, and this rascal, my servant, this Grimaldi, has drunken all of it; I will have him beaten on the deck, and the first ship of war that comes by, he shall be taken by press, and enlisted in His Majesty's service, and a hard time he shall have of it, for I will let him know that I never forgive." "Your honor," said Mr. Wesley, "then I hope you never sin."

The rebuke was so pointed, that the governor replied in a moment, "Alas, sir, I do sin, and I have sinned in what I have said; for your sake he shall be forgiven; I trust he will not do the like again."*

Only the self-righteous have nothing to confess.

The Father of Mercies

"And his mercy is for those who fear him
from generation to generation."
Luke 1:50

While meditating one day on the narratives in Luke 1, I was struck by the recurrence of the word "mercy." I shouldn't have been, I suppose, for after all, this passage recounts two resplendent, grace-filled events immediately preceding the miraculous birth of our Lord.

The first brief story informs us of an elderly Jewish couple who had no children. We are told the husband, Zechariah, served his Lord as a priest in the temple, and his wife, Elizabeth, was a descendant of Aaron, Israel's first high priest.

While Zechariah was ministering in the temple one notable day, he received a startling visit by an angel, informing him that not only would he and Elizabeth become parents in their old age, but that their son would play a special role in preparing God's people for the promised Messiah. Though he initially responded in disbelief to the angel's announcement, nine months later this righteous priest sang a Spirit-induced hymn, punctuated with the theme of mercy: "Blessed be the Lord God of Israel, for he has visited and redeemed his people ... to show the mercy promised to our fathers" (1:68, 72). Then, looking into the face of his newborn son, he sings: "And you, child, will be called the prophet of the Most High; for you will go before the Lord to prepare his ways, to give knowledge of salvation to his people in the forgiveness of their sins, because of the tender mercy of our God" (1:76-78).

The next story involves Mary, the mother of our Lord. Following Gabriel's incomparable announcement to the young virgin that she was to be the human bearer of the Christ child, she rushed to tell Elizabeth the good news. After greetings were exchanged, Mary burst forth in song, exulting in the mercy of God: "And his mercy is for those who fear him from generation to generation" (1:50). "He has helped his servant Israel, in remembrance of his mercy" (1:54).

Is it any wonder, then, that the early church's foremost persecutor, who was later surprised by God's mercy, calls this very same God "the Father of mercies" (2 Cor. 1:3)?

January 6

Christi is Greater (Part 1)

*"Are you greater than our father Abraham, who died?
And the prophets died! Who do you make yourself out to be?"*
John 8:53

Whenever we use the word *greater*, we are thinking in terms of comparison. The Spirit-inspired men of God often used this word in communicating to their readers the majesty and supremacy, the preeminence and unparalleled superlative uniqueness of the Lord Jesus Christ. Christ is greater!

The Scriptures compare Christ to several notable individuals in biblical history. By comparison, Jesus remains incomparable to anyone and anything; he always comes out first!

Christ is greater than Abraham. When asked by the Jewish leaders if he was greater than Abraham, Jesus replied, "Truly, truly, I say to you, before Abraham was, I am" (John 8:58). Jesus is the eternal, self-existent Son of God, greater than the father of the covenant people.

Christ is greater than Jacob. When the Samaritan woman asked Jesus if he was greater than Jacob, who provided the very well upon which he sat, Jesus responded, "Everyone who drinks of this water will be thirsty again, but whoever drinks of the water that I will give him will never be thirsty again" (John 4:13-14). As great as Jacob was in the minds of these ancient people, he was incapable of quenching any person's spiritual thirst. Only God through Christ can accomplish this.

Christ is greater than Moses. As great as Moses was among Israel's worthies, he paled in comparison to God's Son. Moses is commended for his faithfulness "in all God's house." However, since Jesus himself is the chief architect and builder and faithful overseer of the people of God, he is deemed greater, because he is God's Son. "For Jesus has been counted worthy of more glory than Moses—as much more glory as the builder of a house has more honor than the house itself.... Christ is faithful over God's house as a son" (Heb. 3:3, 6).

We run out of superlatives and comparisons when thinking of Jesus. Jesus is always and forever *greater*!

Christ is Greater (Part 2)

*"The men of Nineveh will rise up at the judgment with this
generation and condemn it, for they repented at the preaching
of Jonah, and behold, something greater than Jonah is here."*
Matthew 12:41

God the Father wants all mankind to know—and his people, in particular—that no Jewish patriarch, prophet or object exceeds his Son.
Christ is greater!

Christ is greater than Jonah. Jonah was the Old Testament
prophet God commissioned to preach the message of repentance to
Nineveh, a city notorious for evil. Though he was a reluctant
preacher, nevertheless, Jonah preached and the result was city-wide
repentance. However, when Jesus came to his own people, there
was no massive response (at the time) to his preaching: "For they
repented at the preaching of Jonah, and behold, something greater
than Jonah is here" (Matt. 12:41).

Christ is greater than Solomon. King Solomon was renowned
for his wealth, vast dominion, and wisdom. Many of the proverbs in
our Bible were authored by Solomon; his wisdom became known
throughout the world. Nonetheless, Christ exceeded Solomon in
wisdom: "The queen of the South will rise up at the judgment with
this generation and condemn it, for she came from the ends of the
earth to hear the wisdom of Solomon, and behold, something greater than Solomon is here" (Matt. 12:42).

Christ is greater than the temple. There was no building in
Jewish history that compared in beauty and sanctity with the temple. The temple was the central place of worship and sacrifice, the
place where Yahweh's very presence dwelt, the place where all devout Jews made a pilgrimage three times each year. However, to
many Jews, this place became a substitute for a Person. Thus Jesus
rebuked these people for turning a building into an idol: "I tell you,
something greater than the temple is here" (Matt. 12:6).

Every person and created thing,
Pales in comparison to Christ the King.
To him alone our worship bring—
The Lamb who made himself an offering.

"The Lord is Our Righteousness" (part 1)

*"And this is the name by which he will be
called: 'The Lord is our righteousness.'"*
Jeremiah 23:6

We are either trusting in our own righteousness or the Lord's. If we trust in our righteousness, we become legalistic, arrogant, hard, and disdain those we perceive less righteous than ourselves. The typical Pharisee in Jesus' day was the embodiment of self-righteousness. These men were socially aloof and detestably smug. In their presence the common man felt uncomfortable and unwelcome. They were without mercy and showed little compassion. They were men of the *letter*; they were devoid of the Spirit.

There was a time in the Apostle Paul's life when his confidence was in *whom* he perceived himself to be and in *what* he had achieved. He boasted of his religious pedigree and his external righteousness. Saul of Tarsus' warped belief system drove him to reject Christ and persecute his followers; self-righteousness always does that: "he who was born according to the flesh persecuted him who was born according to the Spirit, so also it is now" (Gal. 4:29).

The thing that prompted the Lord Jesus to share the parable of the Pharisee and tax collector was the nauseous self-righteousness of those whose religion had *spoiled*: "He also told this parable to some who trusted in themselves that they were righteous, and treated others with contempt" (Luke 18:9).

How we relate—or don't relate—to others is a good indication of the brand of our religion. What do we feel toward, how do we talk about, and how do we talk to *sinners*? The old adage is still true: "Love the sinner but hate the sin." Isn't it true for some of us, that we talk and act like we *hate* the sinner, treating sinners with contempt?

Pharisees act like they don't need God's mercy. Why? It is because self-righteous people trust in their righteousness. The person who claims no merit, identifies with Paul's desire to be found in Christ, "not having a righteousness of my own that comes from the law, but that which comes through faith in Christ" (Phil. 3:9).

January 9

"The Lord is Our Righteousness" (part 2)

Having begun by the Spirit, are you now being perfected by the flesh?
Galatians 3:3

It is possible to begin the Christian life in the Spirit, trusting in Christ alone as our Savior and our righteousness, but subsequently act in the flesh, thereby trusting in our righteousness. This can be done as an isolated act, or we can develop a pattern of self-righteous conduct.

The Apostle Peter is an example of one who acted in the flesh among Jewish brothers, and was rebuked by the Apostle Paul for his hypocrisy. Following the revelation he received from the Lord, that the Gentile Christians should not be considered "unclean," but received as equals in the body of Christ, Peter felt clear to eat with these brothers and sisters in Christ. But one day, as he was eating with Gentile converts, a delegation from the "circumcision party" arrived. Peter immediately distanced himself from the Gentile converts, fearing the scrutiny of the legalists. Paul rebuked Peter for his hypocrisy, because he—along with others he influenced—"were not straightforward about the truth of the gospel" (Gal. 2:14 NASB).

Furthermore, there were those among the Galatians who evidenced true Christian conversion, but because of false teaching, they added Law-obligations (circumcision) as necessary for one's acceptance before God. In other words, no one could be justified (declared righteous) before God apart from observing an Old Covenant rite. Paul knew better, because he had been taught better—by revelation from God.

So, the apostle asks these errant, misinformed believers: "Having begun by the Spirit, are you now being perfected by the flesh?" (Gal. 3:3). This is always a danger for Christians, especially those new in the faith. Young Christians are filled with zeal; they desire all that God wants for them. Then along comes a persuasive teacher, telling them, "You know if you really want to be right before God, you need to _____" (fill in the blank).

As Paul admonished Peter, such people need to be gently corrected with the truth of the gospel, so that "God may perhaps grant them repentance leading to a knowledge of the truth" (2 Tim. 2:25).

Coming to Jesus (part 1)

"Come to me, all who labor and are heavy laden, and I will give you rest."
Matthew 11:28

It has now been over a half-century since I preached my first sermon in my home church. The text chosen for that evening was Matthew 11:28-30. With much trepidation—and the saints praying—I managed to speak for some 15-20 minutes, as I recall. When the invitation was given at the close, a young boy knelt at the altar to receive Christ; the last I heard, Terry is still walking with the Lord.

I never read this text but what I am moved. Just this morning, feeling a bit anxious about a situation, the Spirit brought this passage to mind for the *umpteenth* time: "Come," Jesus said, "Come to me."

Jesus is addressing followers who are laboring—working hard, toiling—in their own strength. How often we go about life's duties and routines, working away without reference to God. In doing so, life becomes a grind, tense, wearisome. Moreover, those who are engaged in the work of God, often—without thinking—find themselves laboring without the strength of Christ. Is it any wonder men and women are leaving ministry by the droves? Why? For many, they say they left because they say they experienced *burn out*. Why is this so? They have not learned to come to Jesus—regularly, daily; they have not learned to minister in the strength of Christ.

The "heavy laden" are those who were oppressed by the legalistic system imposed by the Pharisees. These men burdened the common man and woman with a litany of rules they would not lift a finger to support. There are not too many second and third-generation Pharisees! Why is this? Because it is a burdensome way of life, sapping the joy and freedom from God's sincere and vulnerable followers.

God calls no man to be our master; God calls no man to rule our conscience. Christ's call is a call to spiritual life and freedom, not slavery and oppression.

Do you find yourself laboring in your own strength? Come to Jesus. Are you being oppressed by rigid manmade rules? Come to Jesus. If we do, he says, "I will give you rest."

Coming to Jesus (part 2)

*"Take my yoke upon you, and learn from
me, for I am gentle and lowly in heart."*
Matthew 11:29

Jesus never invites us to come to him without demanding something from us. A yoke, in Christ's day, was made from wood and joined two animals together, usually oxen; these yokes rested upon the necks of the animals. Among Jewish teachers, the yoke became a metaphor for the Law. Whenever a young man began to study the Law, he took the "yoke" upon himself.

Under Phariseeism, however, there were traditions and interpretations of the Law of Moses that became equivalent to the Law of God itself. By the time Jesus began his ministry, this religious system had become so ingrained and powerful in Judaism, that true shalom (peace) had disappeared. Peace and joy are nonexistent in a religious tyranny with 613 extrabiblical rules!

But unlike the rigid, chaffing yoke imposed by religious zealots, the person who comes to Jesus "learns from *him*." Sometimes we have to bypass people and doctrinal systems in order to get to Jesus—to the *real* Jesus!

I have often wondered about those who have made the way of Jesus into a burdensome system of statutes and regulations. God is much easier to get along with than these kinds of people. There is nothing attractive about Pharisees. Jesus is winsome!

We are right to cast off the "yoke" of Phariseeism; however, we must take care in doing so not to throw away the moral law of God. Jesus has a "yoke" as well. However, unlike the rigid, chaffing yoke imposed by strict fanatics, the person who comes to Jesus "learns from *him*." We are not to "learn" from those who love the praise of men more than the praise of God, lording over Christ's disciples.

When you read the Word of God, imagine yourself sitting at the feet of Jesus—listening to Jesus teach you by the Holy Spirit. Notice the difference with Jesus: "I am gentle and lowly in heart." He is not hard and harsh, not rigid and cruel, not proud and condescending; instead, Jesus is "gentle and lowly in heart"!

Come to Jesus.

Coming to Jesus (part 3)

"And you will find rest for your souls.
For my yoke is easy, and my burden is light."
Matthew 11:29-30

Jesus gives rest: "Come to me, all who labor and are heavy laden, and I will give you rest" (11:28). Furthermore, Jesus says we will discover a remarkable rest: "and you will find rest for your souls" (11:29). Without attempting to extrapolate some esoteric meaning from this text, it seems to me that Jesus is talking about two related but different dimensions regarding "rest."

First, to those who are striving in their own strength to serve God, and to those who are burdened with oppressive religion, Jesus invites these suffering people to come to him. To these worn, beleaguered souls, Jesus promises a deliverance from bondage, a cessation to slavery, a freedom from trying to earn God's favor. Jesus promises these faint souls "rest"! "Come to me ... and I will, give you rest."

Next, to those who accept Christ's invitation to take his yoke—meaning to accept his rule and teachings and commands, to enroll in his school of discipleship and learn from him (not merely being taught by him)—Jesus said these people "will find rest for your souls."

There is a rest that comes from experiencing a deliverance from religious bondage; there is a further rest we can experience after getting to know the living Jesus, through the Word and Spirit. Charles Wesley knew such a rest and wrote about it (though some hymnals have revised this verse):

Breathe, O breathe Thy loving Spirit,
Into every troubled breast!
Let us all in Thee inherit;
Let us find that second rest.*

If your experience of the Christian faith does not provide you with a soul-rest, you need to discover—or rediscover—Jesus. The yoke of Jesus is "easy"; the burden Jesus gives is "light."

Come to Jesus.

The Spirit of Orthodoxy

"And I will ask the Father, and he will give you another
Helper, to be with you forever, even the Spirit of truth."
John 14:16-17

Dr. Daniel Steele (1824-1914) served his Lord and the Methodist Church as a pastor, evangelist, college president (two colleges), professor (including Boston University), and as a writer to the church at large. He was the founding president of Syracuse University, Syracuse, New York.

Steele served on the committee assigned to create a charter for Syracuse, which was designed to be a Methodist-affiliated school. Upon reading the charter's first draft, he remarked later, it "would have suited a Muslim or Buddhist institution, for there was no reference to Christ."*

One of Steele's recommended corrections to the first draft was that the adjective "Christian" should be inserted at one point before the word "learning." A Methodist judge serving on the committee was asked by a colleague "whether an evangelical interpretation to 'Christian' could not be incorporated into this charter of the university, so that it could be forever held for orthodoxy as found in the Methodist standards."

Daniel Steele said he never forgot the judge's response: "There is no safeguard possible. Harvard went over to Unitarianism because the church itself apostatized from the faith. You cannot by legal documents prevent a denomination from drifting away from its creed. If Methodism backslides from orthodoxy, she will take her schools with her."

Steele later, in writing about this insightful remark, commented: "The lawyer taught the preacher an important lesson, which he has sought to teach others ever since: Orthodoxy can be conserved only by the Holy Spirit abiding in the consciousness of the individual members of the church. Then, and then only, are we safe."

Many Christians, churches, and institutions have betrayed the faith they once held fast, and they did it all while they preached and taught from the Bible!

The Holy Spirit—abiding in the hearts of God's people—is the sole conservator of orthodoxy.

Walking in the Truth

I have no greater joy than to hear that
my children are walking in the truth.
3 John 1:3

Disciples of the Lord Jesus Christ love the truth, because they love the God of truth and his Son who is the way and the truth and the life. God's people love all that God and his Son loves, and because the written Word of God is the Book of Truth, they love the Word—not as some magical, mysterious talisman—but as it is indeed—the Word of truth. Because the written Word of God came from God, through those who were inspired and moved by the Spirit of truth to write words of truth, lovers of truth love the Book of Truth.

When Christ's followers receive the gift of the Spirit, they receive the Holy Spirit of truth. Because they receive the Spirit of truth, each disciple will be led into all the truth necessary for his spiritual maturation (sanctification) and witness while here on earth. The means the Spirit uses to this end are varied. He primarily uses the written Word of God, through reading and preaching and teaching; he uses the wise and full-of-the-Spirit counsel given by the leadership in local churches, who live under the authority of the Word; he uses the fellowship of maturing believers, who wish to be guided by the Word; he uses the writings of both past and contemporary godly writers, who are men and women of the Word; he uses the hymns and songs written by Spirit-infused men and women who walk according to the Word. Whatever means God uses to aid his people in their walk with him, he uses the means that are always in harmony with his revealed written Word and never contrary to it.

Because this is so, everything the Word of God affirms to be true in matters pertaining to doctrine and life, each Christian will have an eager and earnest desire to pursue and obey—wherever that truth may lead. Conversely, every believer will avoid every lie, every falsehood, every teaching that does not harmonize with the plain teaching of God's Word.

Let us be people of Truth, who live under and by the Word of Truth.

January 15

The Generosity of God

"Am I not allowed to do what I choose with what belongs to me? Or do you begrudge my generosity?' So the last will be first, and the first last."
Matthew 20:15-16

We should neither question nor be surprised at our Lord's generosity toward undeserving mankind. We "all have sinned and fall short of the glory of God" (Rom. 3:23). None of our righteous deeds or good works can ever merit God's salvation: "For by grace you have been saved through faith. And this is not your own doing; it is the gift of God, not a result of works, so that no one may boast" (Eph. 2:8-9).

God does not justify those who view themselves as godly people; he justifies those who freely confess their ungodliness and acknowledge their unworthiness: "And to the one who does not work but believes in him who justifies the ungodly, his faith is counted as righteousness" (Rom. 4:5).

In the parable of the laborers in the vineyard (Matt. 20:1-16), Jesus makes a comparison that, on the surface, seems to cast God in a bad light. The vineyard keeper hired workers at different times of the day, promising to each of them a denarius at the end of the day. When it came time to pay the hired hands, the complaining began: "Now when those hired first came, they thought they would receive more, but each of them also received a denarius" (v. 10). The land owner's response was, "Friend, I am doing you no wrong. Did you not agree with me for a denarius? Take what belongs to you and go. I choose to give to this last worker as I give to you. Am I not allowed to do what I choose with what belongs to me? Or do you begrudge my generosity?" (vv. 13-15). What follows is Jesus' application: "So the last will be first, and the first last" (v. 16).

Salvation—both in this life and in the future life—is an expression of our God's wonderful generosity. Regardless as to what stage in life we trusted in the Lord Jesus, and no matter how long and hard his servants have worked in his "vineyard," we will all be abundantly rewarded according to his sovereign wisdom and pleasure on that Day.

How could we ever grumble at receiving such a gift?

Take Time

And he said to them, "Come away by
yourselves to a desolate place and rest a while."
Mark 6:31

J. Sidlow Baxter (1903-1999) relates that when he became pastor of a church in Scotland many years ago, he began to hear many appreciative remarks about a former deacon, who had died a few years earlier. Baxter heard how people said of this brother, "that it was almost impossible to think or speak unworthily in his presence." They said, "He always brought a sense of God's presence when he came into a room." This dear follower of Christ, Baxter said, made a difference in the church's board meetings: "If a discussion ever seemed to be getting edgy or uncharitable, he would quietly rise and lead the brethren in such a prayer, that afterward the discussion could only continue on a high spiritual plane."*

The man's name was William D. Longstaff. This British hymnist authored a hymn which provides us with the secret to his resemblance to the Lord Jesus Christ.

Take time to be holy, speak oft with thy Lord;
Abide in Him always, and feed on His Word.
Make friends of God's children, help those who are weak,
Forgetting in nothing His blessing to seek.

Take time to be holy, the world rushes on;
Spend much time in secret, with Jesus alone.
By looking to Jesus, like Him thou shalt be;
Thy friends in thy conduct His likeness shall see.

Take time to be holy, let Him be thy Guide;
And run not before Him, whatever betide.
In joy or in sorrow, still follow the Lord,
And, looking to Jesus, still trust in His Word.

Take time to be holy, be calm in thy soul,
Each thought and each motive beneath His control.
Thus led by His Spirit to fountains of love,
*Thou soon shalt be fitted for service above.***

Do you desire to reflect the likeness of the Lord Jesus?

A Product of Prayer

"For this child I prayed, and the Lord has
granted me my petition that I made to him."
1 Samuel 1:27

The Old Testament prophets were uniquely gifted by God. For one thing, prophets were *seers*. They were originally called such because they had insight and discernment unlike others. God had revealed to these men—and sometimes women—in sovereignly selected moments, the condition of nations and individuals, as well as the foretelling of events.

No man chose to be a prophet. They were called and commissioned by God. Kings and priests under the Old Covenant, and pastors and evangelists under the New Covenant, were called by God and set apart for ministry by constituted authority. Not so with the prophets. They were accountable to God alone. They could neither be hired nor fired. No man or organization employed them. They were on no institution's payroll; they stood for no election; they were God's special agents.

The life as a prophet could be lonely, because the masses and religious hierarchy often misunderstood his ministry. Inasmuch as his messages were convicting, they were mostly dreaded. After all, who enjoys hearing, "Thou art the man!" or being called a "generation of vipers"? These men weren't given "Preacher of the Year" awards or standing ovations at the annual church conferences. They were a different breed. Because of the nature of the prophet's role, it was vitally important that he walked closely with God—that he be a person of prayer. For without a praying heart, the prophet would become censorious and judgmental. With a praying heart, he could deliver his messages faithfully and courageously, and walk before God in joy and gratitude. Samuel was this kind of prophet—he was a praying prophet.

Samuel was a product of prayer: "For this child I prayed, and the Lord has granted me my petition that I made to him." Just as there would have been no Augustine without a praying Monica, so there surely would have been no Samuel without a praying Hannah.

Undoubtedly, all God-called ministers of Christ are a product of someone's prayers; I know I am one.

Study and Prayer

Devote yourselves to prayer, keeping alert
in it with an attitude of thanksgiving.
Colossians 4:2 NASB

Writers, like lawyers, will occasionally make what appears to be an exaggerated statement in order to drive home a point. Eugene Peterson—author of many devotional-theological books, as well as being the para-translator of *The Message*—once made such a remark: "We don't need more Bible studies," so said the pastor-preacher-theologian.

Having read after Peterson for many years, I'm quite certain he isn't opposed to studying the Bible—he himself studied and taught the Bible for many years. However, as I recall, the point he was driving home was that Christians and churches have lost their devotional balance—the balance between study and prayer.

If one is disinclined to agree with such an assertion, just take a serious look at your own prayer life and that of your church's. How much time are we giving to the study of the Scriptures in comparison to concentrated, meaningful prayer times? How often do we set aside time to be alone with God in undistracted communion? I'm not talking about hours in prayer, though that may occasionally occur.

We need to ask ourselves: What place does prayer have in my own life and my family's? For the church, what we call "Prayer Breakfast" is often ninety-eight per cent *breakfast* and two percent *prayer*. What we call midweek prayer meetings are regularly eighty-five percent Bible studies and singing and fifteen percent prayer—if that, and then much of the praying focuses on material and physical concerns.

While we are teaching many necessary things in our Sunday schools, Bible colleges and seminaries, who is teaching God's people how to pray?

God has always had a remnant throughout the centuries, who take his written words seriously. These saints take talking with God, communing with God, struggling with God, and pleading with God just as seriously—by means of this thing called *prayer*.

Effective Prayers

The effective prayer of a righteous man can accomplish much.
James 5:16 NASB

One cannot read about Enoch, Noah, Abraham, Hannah, David and Daniel, Anna and Mary, Stephen and Paul, John and James, Epaphras and Timothy—and a host of praying saints throughout the church's history—without being impressed with the importance that prayer played in their walk with God.

God's authentic people have always been praying people, following the supreme example of the Lord Jesus. Great works of God have been built through the intercessions of God's servants. God's work always moves most effectively when the people of God are on their knees as much as they are in business meetings. The church's wise men have unfailingly known this: "The effective prayer of a righteous man can accomplish much" (James 5:16 NASB).

Bishop Cassels (1858-1925) was the first Anglican bishop to China; he was schooled in the worth of prayer. He knew well that if peoples steeped in centuries of myths and superstitions were to be taken captive for the Kingdom, the walls of resistance could only be broken down by believing prayer. "We must advance upon our knees," said Cassels, in view of the needs and the possibilities of that vast country. "There must be a fresh taking hold of God in prayer.... I thank God that this mission lives upon prayer. But I say, God will do a new thing for us when there is a new spirit of prayer among us. God will do a new thing for us when there is a new spirit of consecration among us."*

Yes, "God will do a new thing for us when there is a new spirit of prayer among us"—the Spirit of prayer! When God breaths his Spirit within us, we will respond in prayer as naturally as breathing itself.

Much of the church does not believe this, because much of the church places a disproportionate emphasis on singing, Bible study, and preaching/teaching. Since this is so, we get what *man* can do instead of what *God* can do.

Changed Through Prayer

*"I have heard your prayer; I have seen
your tears. Behold, I will heal you."*
2 Kings 20:5

The Scriptures clearly teach God uses the prayers of his believing people, who pray according to his will to effect change. How else can one explain, for example, God answering the earnest cry of King Hezekiah when he became deathly ill? Isaiah delivered God's word to the king: "Thus says the Lord, 'Set your house in order, for you shall die; you shall not recover'" (2 Kings 20:1). But Hezekiah did not die and recovered. Why? Because God looked with favor upon the king's humble petition for healing. Following the king's fervent request for healing, God directed Isaiah to return to the king and inform him that his prayer was answered: "Thus says the Lord, the God of David your father: I have heard your prayer; I have seen your tears. Behold, I will heal you." On the one hand, God said the king would die; on the other hand—in answer to the king's prayer—God said the king would live.

Did God have a will in both Hezekiah's illness and his healing? Surely he did. Was God's will done? We must conclude it was. Within his will, does God invite his children to intercede sometimes so as to change his revealed and *apparent* will? It appears so.

Is there such a thing as God declaring a conclusion, an outcome, sealing the destiny of a person or peoples so as to never accept the prayers of even the godliest of people? Yes. God told Jeremiah on one occasion: "Then the Lord said to me, 'Though Moses and Samuel stood before me, yet my heart would not turn toward this people.'" (Jer. 15:1).

There are times when God is favorably disposed to answer the prayers of his servants and change a particular matter. At other times, God says that he will not change a situation, no matter if the most godly person on earth should pray.

Praying people will be given insight when to pray, what to pray for, and when not to pray. Only God can help us in these matters.

Learning from the Master

"Lord, teach us to pray."
Luke 11:1

Years ago I was privileged to develop a relationship with a veteran preacher and Bible scholar who later became a mentor to me in many ways. We first met while serving together on a Bible college faculty. Some years later, when he was serving on a local church board, he contacted me to inquire whether I would consider becoming their pastor, which I later did.

When it came to preaching on the major themes of Scripture, there was no one I enjoyed listening to more than S. I. Emery (1895-1977). He would soar in eloquence as he expounded upon the doctrine of Christ's atonement in particular. Blessed with a deep, bass voice, usually preaching without a note in front of him, this dear brother's passion for Christ and the Cross were both intense and genuine. Rarely did I hear him preach, but soon into his sermon he would have a handkerchief in hand, dabbing his nose, giving an occasional sniff, while his voice quivered as he tried to control his emotions.

As much as I enjoyed listening to Dr. Emery preach and teach the Word of God, I was blessed as well listening to him pray. He was as well-versed in the Scriptures as any person I've known, and when he prayed, he would recite appropriate Scriptures. And you could not listen to him pray without knowing he knew God. I loved to hear him pray.

After the disciples listened to Jesus pray one day, they urged him, "Lord, teach us to pray" (Luke 11:1). There is no record in the Gospels of any disciple requesting that Jesus teach them how to preach or teach, though we can be certain, he was a master at both. But, oh ... when the Twelve heard Jesus pray, they were deeply affected with the intimacy by which he spoke to his Father, and the utter simplicity and faith by which he offered his requests. Their prayers were lifeless and listless compared to Christ's. They knew their prayer-life was sorely deficient. "Lord, teach us to pray," they pleaded.

We would do well to repeatedly make the same request.

Christ Intercedes

For Christ has entered, not into the holy places made with hands,
which are copies of the true things, but into heaven itself,
now to appear in the presence of God for us.
Hebrews 9:24

What became of the Lord Jesus after he ascended into the heavens from the disciples' view some two thousand years ago? Where did Jesus go? What is he presently doing?

The Scriptures are clear: "After making purification for sins, he sat down at the right hand of the Majesty on high" (Heb. 1:3). In the language of Scripture, for the once crucified, risen Christ to be seated at the right hand of the Majesty on high depicts a position of the highest honor and authority.

Inasmuch as the Lord Jesus Christ defeated Satan at the Cross, with the empty tomb validating this victory, he was given a place of supreme glory and power: "Worthy is the Lamb who was slain, to receive power and wealth and wisdom and might and honor and glory and blessing!" (Rev. 5:12).

But just what is it that our triumphant Lord is doing now—this very moment in time at the Father's right hand? Hebrews 9:24 holds the answer: "For Christ has entered, not into the holy places made with hands, which are copies of the true things, but into heaven itself, now to appear in the presence of God for us." There you have it. What is our Lord and Savior engaged in at this very moment? He is in the presence of God the Father *for us*!

What God in Christ accomplished through the unique salvation events at the cross and the resurrection, the Lord Jesus mediates now for us in a position of ultimate power and authority with the Father. Furthermore, if Christ prayed while on earth that Simon Peter's faith would not fail, he surely intercedes now for the saints as well: "he always lives to make intercession for them" (Heb. 7:25).

Robert Murray M'Cheyne (1813-1843) once said, "If I could hear Christ praying for me in the next room, I would not fear a million enemies. Yet distance makes no difference. He is praying for me."*

God Uses Thorns

To keep me from becoming conceited because of the surpassing greatness
of the revelations, a thorn was given me in the flesh, a messenger
of Satan to harass me, to keep me from becoming conceited.
2 Corinthians 12:7

Once Martin Wells Knapp (1853-1901), the founding president of God's Bible School & College, Cincinnati, Ohio, was undergoing a painful trial. While in prayer, one day, he asked the Lord to remove the problem. In relating this painful encounter, Lettie Cowman (1870-1960) wrote, "As he waited before the Lord the vision of a rough piece of marble rose before him with a sculptor grinding and chiseling. Watching the dust and chips fill the air, he noticed a beautiful image begin to appear in the marble."

Cowman proceeds to relate how the Lord spoke to Knapp and said, "Son, you are that block of marble. I have an image in mind, and desire to produce it in your character, and will do so if you will stand the grinding; but I will stop now if you so desire." Knapp's resolute response was, "Lord, continue the chiseling and grinding."*

Years ago, I copied on the flyleaf of one of my Bibles the following words written by Francis Asbury (1745-1816), American Methodism's premier pioneer circuit rider and leader: "Dear Lord, if Thou seest Thy servant will miss the way, in tender pity send a thorn deep into his side to drive him to Thy Christ and Thy Calvary."

Free Church of Scotland pastor and hymn writer, George Matheson (1842-1906)—who is perhaps best known for his hymn "O Love That Will Not Let Me Go"—once confessed to his lack of gratitude for a most unpleasant providence (he became totally blind at age 20). While contemplating his ingratitude one day, he wrote, "My God, I have never thanked Thee for my thorn! I have thanked Thee a thousand times for my roses, but never once for my thorn."

Don't ask God to *remove* what he wants to *use*. In time, Paul understood how God wanted to use a "thorn" in his own life: "To keep me from becoming conceited because of the surpassing greatness of the revelations, a thorn was given me in the flesh, a messenger of Satan to harass me, *to keep me from becoming conceited.*"

Where Shall I Work Today?

Jesus said to him, "Feed my sheep."
John 21:17

Most of God's children are not called to perform *great* deeds, neither are they chosen to labor and minister for Christ in a prominent place. For them, much of life is routine and quite ordinary.

At times, we complain about our lot in life: *I'm not as gifted as that sister in Christ. My colleague has been called to a large church. Why am I never chosen to serve in positions of leadership? I am serving in such a small, unknown place.*

Pastor Mead McGuire must have been struggling one day about where he should serve and what he should do. He took pen to paper and wrote the following:

> *Father, where shall I work today?*
> *And my love flowed warm and free.*
> *Then He pointed out a tiny spot*
> *And said, "Tend that for me."*
>
> *I answered quickly, "Oh no, not that!*
> *Why, no one would ever see,*
> *No matter how well my work was done;*
> *Not that little place for me."*
>
> *And the word He spoke, it was not stern;*
> *He answered me tenderly:*
> *"Ah, little one, search that heart of thine.*
> *Art thou working for them or for me?*
> *Nazareth was a little place,*
> *And so was Galilee."**

The Scriptures are replete with individuals God used who were not seeking to be great. We have the names of some; however, many others remain anonymous—to us, but not to God.

Where has the will of God placed you? Wherever you are, whatever work you are engaged in, our sovereign Lord has called each of us to faithfully "tend" that field of labor for him and to his glory. Don't covet another's person's calling and position in life. Be faithful where you are.

January 25

Serving Christ as a Chimney Sweep

"It is enough for the disciple to be like his
teacher, and the servant like his master."
Matthew 10:25

At age seventeen, Peter Torjesen (1892-1939) signed his life away. During a church service in his native Norway, he listened to a passionate missionary talk about China. Following the sermon, an offering was received. His daughter later wrote, "He opened his wallet and poured out all the money in it. Then he realized he had to offer more than money, and found a piece of paper and wrote three words *Og mit liv* ('And my life')."

"The man who counted the collection that day," writes Kari Torjesen Malcom, "was Peter's Sunday school teacher. Immediately recognizing the handwriting, he decided to keep the note to see what would happen with this unusual promise."

Torjesen kept his promise. Eventually, he served effectively in China with his childhood sweetheart, Valborg. However, his life was cut short in 1939, when Japan bombed China; his wife remained to serve.

It is often the case with many God-called servants in ministry: Peter enjoyed a godly heritage; his parents were devout Christians. His father Torleif was employed as a chimney sweep in Kristiansand. And interestingly enough, he was "expected to read Scripture and pray in each home where he came to take care of a chimney." His granddaughter remarks, "So he was a chimney sweep that could also sweep the souls of his clients."

Upon interviewing one of Torleif's clients years later, the elderly woman said to Kari, "It was like peace came to the house when Torleif came. He would always conduct a prayer service in each home where he swept the chimney." Peter once wrote of his parents, "My parents were missionary-minded, and I got the impression from my childhood that to be a missionary was the greatest thing anyone could want to be."*

At the beginning of the nineteenth century, our Lord gave to China one of his devout servants. That servant was influenced by godly parents, with a father who served Christ as a chimney sweep.

Losing and Keeping

"Whoever loves his life loses it, and whoever hates his life in this world will keep it for eternal life."
John 12:25

One does not have to go to the ends of the earth in order to demonstrate a complete devotion to the Lord Jesus Christ. A stay-at-home mother can, and should be, just as consecrated to Christ as a missionary called to serve on foreign soil. That being said, we can thank God for those who have left their homeland to follow Christ's call to proclaim the gospel to peoples in far-away places.

David Livingstone (1813-1873) left his native Scotland for Africa on December 8, 1840, following his medical and missionary training. He poured out his life in sharing the gospel, and tending to the physical needs of people of another race and culture. Among his objectives: he purposed to open doors to the gospel for those who would follow him in years to come, and to bring to the world's attention the abominable slave-trade.

Livingstone had his critics. A biographer wrote, "Indeed, many regarded him as a failure. As a missionary, he brought only a couple of people to know Christ."

Regardless of the number of people coming to Christ under Livingstone's ministry of over thirty years, he left his mark for Christ. When he died, the native people insisted that his heart be buried in Africa. It was placed in a small tin box and buried beneath a Mpunjdu tree, where an inscription was carved into the tree: "Livingstone May 4 1873." The people wept. Then a small group of committed natives carried his body 1,500 miles to the coast, and shipped it to his homeland. When his body arrived in England, Livingstone was given a state funeral and buried in Westminster Abbey, the only pauper given such an honor.

Dr. Livingstone experienced unimaginable struggles as he served those made in God's image. Many thought he had failed in his efforts. However, years later an African said to a missionary about Livingstone, "He made a path through our land, and you his followers have come, God's lightbringers; and more come today."*

Livingstone gave his life away. Should you?

Loving God with Our All

"And you shall love the Lord your God with all your heart and with all your soul and with all your mind and with all your strength."
Mark 12:30

Jesus gave the above command in response to an inquiry: "Which commandment is the most important of all?" Jesus replied by citing Deuteronomy 6:4-5, from which the latter part is our text.

Question: While on earth, did the Lord Jesus ever exhort or command his followers to do anything they were incapable of doing? What is the answer? Yes and no.

What a cruel taskmaster the Lord Jesus would have been to tell his disciples to do anything they were incapable of performing. On the other hand, Jesus knew whenever he instructed his followers to do something, it exposed their own poverty and incapability. In other words, they would be driven to acknowledge their need for God's help, his strengthening grace. It is always grace.

One cannot love God with his all if he has not undergone a radical change of heart. If the love of God has not been "poured into our hearts by the Holy Spirit" (Rom. 5:5), and if our "double-mindedness" (James 4:8) has not been purified—then, of course, we cannot reciprocate God's love by loving him with our all. But let us not insult God by insisting that his grace cannot do for us what he has commanded us to do. Every command of his is accompanied by his power to perform.

Should any follower of Christ boast, "I love God with all of my heart, soul, mind, and strength"? Of course not! Can a follower of Christ say, "I believe God can help me to love him with everything I have?" Certainly! Because such a person has experienced God's purifying love. It is all of grace. It is God's grace "strengthening with all power through his Spirit in the inner man" (Eph. 16). It is God's grace enabling us to "work out [our] own salvation with fear and trembling, for it is God who works in [us], both to will and to work for his good pleasure" (Phil. 2:12-13).

Because we sometimes fall short in loving God with our all (Rom. 3:23), let no man tell us we can't. God doesn't use "carrot and stick" tricks in order to frustrate his people. If God commands, his grace will enable.

All for Jesus

And Jesus, looking at him, loved him, and said to him, "You lack
one thing: go, sell all that you have and give to the poor, and
you will have treasure in heaven; and come, follow me."
Mark 10:21

Mark 10 records one of the saddest narratives in all of Scripture.
Here was a man who refused to give his *all* in order to be a follower
of Jesus. Was the rich young man's response any different from
many of us? Have we given our *all* to Jesus in order that we might
be *all* for him? One of my favorite hymns of consecration was written by Mary D. James (1810-1883). Let this biblical truth sink deep
into your heart.

All for Jesus, all for Jesus!
All my being's ransomed powers:
All my thoughts and words and doings,
All my days and all my hours.

Let my hands perform His bidding,
Let my feet run in His ways;
Let my eyes see Jesus only,
Let my lips speak forth His praise.

Worldlings prize their gems of beauty,
Cling to gilded toys of dust,
Boast of wealth and fame and pleasure;
Only Jesus will I trust.

Since my eyes were fixed on Jesus,
I've lost sight of all beside;
So enchained my spirit's vision,
Looking at the Crucified.

Oh, what wonder! how amazing!
Jesus, glorious King of kings,
Deigns to call me His belovèd,
*Lets me rest beneath His wings.**

Walking in a woods one day with a friend, A. W. Tozer (1897-
1963) confided, "Junior, I want to love God more than anyone in my
generation."* What an aspiration!

Mighty in Faith

And through his faith, though he died, he still speaks.
Hebrews 11:4

George Müller (1805-1898) was great in faith and prayer, trusting God alone to supply the needs of orphans under his care. His biographer Roger Steer tells the following story about how God faithfully heard the prayers and honored his believing servant.

Early one morning Abigail was playing in Müller's garden on Ashley Down when he took her by the hand.

"Come see what our Father will do."

He led her into a long dining-room. "The plates and cups or bowls were on the table. There was nothing on the table but empty dishes. There was no food in the larder, and no money to supply the need." The children were standing waiting for breakfast.

"Children, you know we must be in time for school," said Müller. Then lifting his hand, he prayed, "Dear Father, we thank Thee for what Thou art going to give us to eat."

According to the account, a knock was then heard at the door. The baker stood there.

"Mr. Müller, I couldn't sleep last night. Somehow I felt you didn't have bread for breakfast, and the Lord wanted me to send you some. So I got up at two o'clock and baked some fresh bread, and have brought it."

Müller thanked the baker and praised God for His care.

"Children," he said, "we not only have bread, but the rare treat of fresh bread."

Almost immediately there came a second knock at the door. This time it was the milkman who announced that his milk cart had broken down outside the orphanage, and that he would like to give the children his cans of fresh milk, so that he could empty his wagon and repair it.*

George Müller set out in 1835 to prove to his fellow Christians and to the world, that God can and will meet the needs of his people without soliciting or advertising those needs. He trusted alone in the faithfulness of God. Repeatedly, God heard the cries of his trusting servant. Müller's name could well be added to the heroes of faith, recorded in Hebrews 11.

God Uses People to Accomplish His Purposes

You led your people like a flock by the hand of Moses and Aaron.
Psalm 77:20

It is an amazing thing—the ways and works of God among the children of men!

We often hear that the Lord God does not *need* people. In one sense that is true, for God is self-existent, almighty, and sovereign. However, when it comes to his kingdom work on earth, God has chosen to work his will and accomplish his purposes through people.

When God designed and created the animal and plant kingdoms, he gifted Adam to name the animals and care for Eden's garden. When God decided to cleanse the world of its evil and begin anew, he selected Noah to construct a vessel, saving his family, and began the task of repopulating the earth through him. When God chose to send his Son into the world through a select people, he began with Abram, a man living in Ur of the Chaldeans. When God initiated a plan to deliver his suffering people from Egypt's tyranny and slavery, he found an ineloquent, quick-tempered Hebrew by the name of Moses, and used his brother Aaron to be his spokesman: "You led your people like a flock by the hand of Moses and Aaron."

Whenever God wishes to accomplish something, he doesn't call perfect people; instead, he selects imperfect people and then begins working in them to perfect them. This work of God in a person often begins long before he sends them on a specific mission. And, of course, his perfecting work continues while they are engaged in mission.

One essential quality God looks for in calling any individual for a particular mission is this: a *listening* heart. God cannot mold and use a person who refuses to listen and obey. He rejected Saul because he refused to listen; he chose David because he learned to listen.

While Moses and Aaron experienced momentary failures, as we all will, their lives were characterized by listening, obeying, and following Yahweh. God could lead Israel because he had two men who would allow him to lead them. What does God wish to do through you? Will you listen?

A God-Reliant Life

*Indeed, we felt that we had received the sentence of death. But that was
to make us rely not on ourselves but on God who raises the dead.*
2 Corinthians 1:9

One characteristic marking the life and ministry of the Apostle Paul
was this: he lived a God-reliant life.

Ever after his life-transforming encounter with the living Christ
on his way to Damascus that one eventful day, Paul lived under the
guidance of God. At one time, his life was flesh-directed: making
choices generated from his sinful, fallen nature and will. However,
following his revelation of Christ and filling of the Spirit, the former
fire-breathing persecutor of Christians became the humble, obedient follower of the Lord Jesus Christ. Once a slave to the sinful passions of the flesh, in receiving a new heart, he became a willing slave
of the One who himself took on the form of a slave to offer himself
as an atoning sacrifice for the sins of all mankind.

Whether it is the Book of Acts—which records many of Paul's
works of ministry—or his thirteen epistles, one will search in vain to
find a hint in this man's life of anything but a total submission and
reliance on God.

For an example of his leading a God-reliant life, take this one
section from Paul's letter to the Corinthian Church (2 Cor. 1). At the
close of his exhortation on suffering, comfort and affliction (vv. 3-
8), he writes: "For we do not want you to be ignorant, brothers, of
the affliction we experienced in Asia. For we were so utterly burdened beyond our strength that we despaired of life itself. Indeed,
we felt that we had received the sentence of death. *But that was to
make us rely not on ourselves but on God who raises the dead*" (1:8
-9). Here Paul reveals his sensitivity to the providence of God, re-
minding him of his need for continual reliance upon God.

The all-wise God has called each of us to live a life of total reliance upon him, trusting him to make the critical choices for us, and
empowering us to walk in obedience to him.

All to Jesus, I surrender;
All to Him I freely give;
I will ever love and trust Him,
*In His presence daily live.**

February 1

The Fear of God (part 1)

*And he said, "I heard the sound of you in the garden, and
I was afraid, because I was naked, and I hid myself."*
Genesis 3:10

One of the consequences of experiencing the manifest presence of
God is the sensation of *fear*. The first record we have in the Scriptures of anyone experiencing the fear of God is in Genesis 3. Following the fall of Adam and Eve, they "hid themselves from the presence of the Lord God." When God came calling, "Where are you?"
Adam's response was, "I heard the sound of you in the garden, and I
was *afraid*, because I was naked, and I hid myself" (3:8-10). Adam
and Eve were fearful because they sensed the Lord God *walking*
toward them; our first parents were overcome with fear because
they knew they had sinned. It was the manifest presence of God that
caused Adam and Eve to fear.

Wherever sin is present—whether it lies in the heart of the sinner or saint—that person becomes very uncomfortable in the presence of pure holiness. When faced with the holiness of God, we will
either fall before God, confessing our sin and uncleanness; or we
will flee from God, clinging to our sin and defilement. Recall the
disparate reactions among the people when Jesus cast demons out
of a man (Luke 8:26-39). Following his healing, we find the restored man "sitting at the feet of Jesus, clothed and in his right
mind" (v. 35). On the other hand, all the onlookers asked Jesus "to
depart from them, for they were seized with great fear" (v. 37). Both
the healed Gadarene and all the people experienced fear in the presence of Jesus; however, only one person was healed while the others
left in their sins and sinfulness.

Following his sin, Adam "heard the sound" of God in the garden
and was immediately shaken with fear— "I was afraid." Lamentably,
the reason sinners and failing believers can leave many of our worship services week after week, without experiencing the pungent
fear of God is because God is *feelingly* absent from our meetings.

Where God is manifestly present, the fear of God is noticeably
apparent. When God shows up, we will either surrender to his holiness, or flee from it.

The Fear of God (part 2)

And awe [fear] came upon every soul.
Acts 2:43

The fear of God stimulates a response of reverence and awe in the hearts of those who embrace his words and surrender to his control. An awareness of awe and wonderment, and a sense of reverential fear envelop the hearts and minds of God's people when they come in contact with the powerful presence of God.

In 1970, Asbury College in Wilmore, Kentucky, experienced a mighty visitation of the refreshing presence of the Spirit of God. For a time, classes were suspended as day after day students, faculty, and visitors gathered in Hughes Auditorium to worship and to wonder. Spontaneous confessions of sin were heard from students, faculty and staff. Without a formal structure to the meetings, testimonies of God's saving and sanctifying grace were given; hymns were sung spontaneously. A renewed seminarian summed this fresh outpouring of the Spirit in one word: "Immanuel, God with us."

The glory of God was so palpably present during those days of divine visitation that "when three cultured ladies from Chattanooga walked into the back of Hughes Auditorium, one of them said, 'I must take off my shoes, for this is holy ground.'" A biographer of this revival, Robert Coleman, adds, "She did and her two companions did likewise. In their stocking feet, they walked forward and knelt at the altar for prayer."*

On that epochal Pentecost Day, full-of-the-Spirit apostles fanned out into the streets of Jerusalem, preaching a crucified, resurrected Lord; thousands were convicted of their sins and converted; lives were forever changed. As a result of the outpouring of the Spirit, these new disciples of the Lord Jesus "devoted themselves to the apostles' teaching and the fellowship, to the breaking of bread and the prayers" (Acts 2:42). Many of us love to quote that verse—and, of course it is great truth. However, we overlook the following verse: "And awe [fear] came upon every soul." Just as the cloud by day and the pillar of fire by night hovered over Israel during her wilderness journeys, now the awful sense of God's presence "came upon every soul."

Are we missing something—Someone?

The Fear of God (part 3)

*And great fear came upon the whole church
and upon all who heard of these things.*
Acts 5:11

At the close of Acts 4 and the beginning of Acts 5, we have two narratives: Barnabas' generous gift, and a couple's conspiracy to deceive church leaders. Barnabas sold a piece of property and contributed the entire proceeds to the church. Ananias and Sapphira sold property and *claimed* to have given all the proceeds to the church, though they were under no obligation to give anything.

The early church's leaders lived in contact with God; they were discerning individuals, given special insight on occasions when the Adversary approached to cause harm. Jesus said of Satan, he seeks "only to steal and kill and destroy" (John 10:10). Satan uses people—susceptible people—to make war against the church. He often uses the "tares" among the "wheat" to attempt to defeat God's purposes and cause havoc. He made such an attempt through a husband and wife when the church was yet young.

When Ananias brought his donation to Peter, claiming that his donation amounted to the total sale of his property, immediately the apostle detected duplicity and asked, "Why is it that you have contrived this deed in your heart? You have not lied to man but to God" (5:4). Suddenly, the man dropped dead. Three hours later, the wife came to Peter. When the apostle asked her about the sale of their property, she lied and fell over dead. Following these separate incidents, we read: "And great fear came upon all who heard of it" (5:5); and "great fear came upon the whole church and upon all who heard of these things" (5:11).

"Tares" and "wheat " will always exist side by side in the kingdom of God; however, where there are full-of-the-Spirit, discerning people in a local church, the damage Satan seeks to inflict can be overcome. God's judgment upon these early-church frauds served as a warning to the young church what he thinks of *pretenders*. News of what happened traveled among Christians far and wide; a holy fear was felt by all who heard. It is God's warning against living a lie, which, in reality, is lying to the Holy Spirit and fellow believers.

The Fear of God (part 4)

And walking in the fear of the Lord and in
the comfort of the Holy Spirit, it multiplied.
Acts 9:31

Have you ever heard anyone report that your local church is "walking in the fear of the Lord"? I wonder, why not? What does it mean to "walk in the fear of the Lord"?

By the time we come to Acts 9:31, much has occurred during the life of the young church: scores have been filled with the Holy Spirit, thousands converted, many signs and wonders performed by the apostles, physical healings, severe persecution of church leaders, an outpouring of generosity among believers, judgment of God upon a lying couple, the church's first martyr, and the appearance of Jesus to Saul of Tarsus. The Spirit of God worked mightily and freely in this new church—without hindrance in the hearts and lives of these God-thirsty people. And what was the attitude and sense surrounding these leaders and converts? What words might summarize the prevailing atmosphere these saints carried with them? Luke states it very succinctly: they were "walking in the reverential fear of the Lord and in the conscious presence of the Holy Spirit" (9:13 RIT).

With such an atmosphere pervading their hearts and homes, their fellowship and prayer gatherings, their council meetings and mission outreaches, and as they went about their daily chores and duties—they strove to please the Lord in all they did, and avoided committing sin at any cost. They were filled with joy inexpressible, delighted in fellowshipping with one another, esteemed their leaders highly, shared their possessions generously, witnessed to Christ's death and resurrection boldly, and expected Jesus to return at any moment.

Don't be mistaken in thinking this "fear of the Lord" produced "gloom and doom" among these enthusiastic saints. Not at all. Again and again, we find them rejoicing—at times after being beaten by their adversaries!

When people are "walking in the reverential fear of the Lord and in the conscious presence of the Holy Spirit," the church multiplies. How is that for a church marketing strategy?!

February 5

Abounding Hope

May the God of hope fill you with all joy and peace in believing,
so that by the power of the Holy Spirit you may abound in hope.
Romans 15:13

The Austrian neurologist and psychiatrist as well as a Holocaust survivor, Viktor Frankl, wrote about his years in Nazi concentration camps. In his book *Man's Search for Meaning*, Frankl says that without hope, survival in those camps was impossible.

Dr. Frankl tells about a prisoner that came to him one day, relating a dream he had the night before. In that dream, the prisoner said that on a certain date—which was about a month away—he saw he was to be released from prison. Frankl says that for the entire month that man's hope was vibrant with expectation. Sadly, the month came and went, and there was no release. Slowly, the man's hope declined, and was replaced by disappointment, then a lost hope.*

The Christian's hope is not based on some ephemeral dream and fantasy. Our hope is sure and certain, because it is founded on the fact of the resurrected Christ, who said before he ascended into heaven, "I go to prepare a place for you? And if I go and prepare a place for you, I will come again and will take you to myself, that where I am you may be also" (John 14:2-3).

Penetrating into the very Holy of Holies, the believer's hope is found where Jesus our Lord sits at the Father's right hand: "We have this as a sure and steadfast anchor of the soul, a hope that enters into the inner place behind the curtain, where Jesus has gone as a forerunner on our behalf, having become a high priest forever after the order of Melchizedek" (Heb. 6:19-20).

God wants his people to know that he is "the God of hope." He is the One who has freely provided for our salvation, who has prepared an eternal home for his people, and whose Son will return for his faithful Bride. He has promised never to leave or forsake his own. This God wants his people to "abound in hope." Regardless of trials, suffering, and tribulations, by the power of the indwelling Holy Spirit, each believer has every reason to overflow with a hope that is centered on the Man at God's right hand!

Are you abounding in hope today?

Christians Die Well

I have fought the good fight, I have finished the race, I have kept the faith.
2 Timothy 4:7

To die well, we must live well; to live well, we must live for Christ. "For to me to live is Christ, and to die is gain" (Phil. 1:21). The founder of Methodism, John Wesley (1703-1791), said often of the Methodists of his day, "Our people die well." He should have known, since he spent countless hours with dying saints.

When one is facing death, what fills one's mind in those days and hours is a transparent reflection of what filled the mind and heart during one's life. Some of the final words of dying saints serve as a beautiful testimony of a life lived well, no matter how long or brief that life may have been.

As a young man, Adoniram Judson (1788-1850) traveled to Burma to serve Christ and reach lost people. One day, he vowed, "I will not leave Burma, until the cross is planted here forever!" Years later, reflecting on his life and ministry, this American Baptist missionary said, "I am not tired of my work, neither am I tired of the world; yet when Christ calls me home, I shall go with the gladness of a boy bounding away from school."

Dwight L. Moody's (1837-1899) life was invested in gathering sheaves to place at his Master's feet. Whether in preaching to the lost in Chicago, Boston or London, this former shoe salesman, as his Lord did on earth before him, went everywhere proclaiming, "Repent and believe the gospel." And millions did. How was it with Moody in his dying hours? He turned to his son, and said with the utmost confidence, "Earth recedes; heaven is open before me. If this is what they call death, it is sweet. There is no valley here. God is calling me, and I must go. This is my coronation day; it is glorious!"

Just hours before she made the crossing, the saintly Susanna Wesley (1669-1742), mother of John and Charles, exclaimed with joy, "Children, as soon as I am released, sing a psalm of praise to God."

Are you living well—living for Christ? Then you can expect to die well. Christ has prepared the way, and there he waits to welcome you to your everlasting Home.

Unity of the Spirit

Then Abram said to Lot, "Let there be no strife between you and me,
and between your herdsmen and my herdsmen, for we are kinsmen."
Genesis 13:8

Inasmuch as there is only "one body and one Spirit ... one hope, one Lord, one faith, one baptism, one God and Father" (Eph. 4:4-5), the Spirit says Christians should be "eager to maintain the unity of the Spirit in the bond of peace" (Eph. 4:3). Only those who "in one Spirit ... were all baptized into one body" (1 Cor. 12:13) are equipped to "maintain the unity of the Spirit." Since "anyone who does not have the Spirit of Christ does not belong to [Christ]" (Rom. 8:9), such people are incapable of maintaining the unity of the Spirit. Only true believers, empowered by the indwelling Holy Spirit, are able to conserve the Spirit's unity in the body of Christ.

There are several causes for the Spirit's unity to be broken. Here are a few:

• The unity of the Spirit is broken when Christians do not submit to God's revealed, written Word. The apostolic injunction for such people is: "If anyone does not obey what we say in this letter, take note of that person, and have nothing to do with him, that he may be ashamed" (2 Thess. 3:14).

• The unity of the Spirit is broken when quibbling over morally indifferent issues: "As for the one who is weak in faith, welcome him, but not to quarrel over opinions" (Rom. 14:1).

• The unity of the Spirit is affected when we are more insistent in getting our own way than contending for the once-for-all delivered faith: "But the wisdom from above is ... open to reason [willing to yield]" (James 3:17).

• The unity of the Spirit is broken when Christians become apathetic regarding unity. God says we should be "eager to maintain the unity of the Spirit" (Eph. 4:3).

The patriarch Abram was a true peacemaker; he was eager to maintain fellowship with his nephew Lot. Abram graciously offered a solution to the developing friction: "If you take the left hand, then I will go to the right, or if you take the right hand, then I will go to the left" (Gen. 13:9). Let's strive to be people of peace, but not at the expense of God's revealed truth.

The Living One

"Fear not, I am the first and the last, and the Living One. I died, and behold I am alive forevermore, and I have the keys of Death and Hades."
Revelation 1:17-18

She went to the tomb before dawn, that one eventful morning over two thousand years ago, to care for the body of her crucified Lord. Instead of lovingly finishing the burial process, she received the surprise of her life: the body was missing! Mary Magdelene began weeping. Then she hears her name called by a familiar voice, "Mary." It is impossible to imagine the uprush of emotion she felt at that moment. Jesus was alive! Jesus called her name! After a brief exchange, Mary rushed to tell the disappointed and disillusioned disciples, "I have seen the Lord!" (John 20:18).

Mary Magdalene, the very woman out of whom the Lord Jesus had cast seven demons, was the first follower of Jesus to witness the living Christ on that great resurrection morning. She believed; she really believed! She saw the Living One. Within minutes, Peter and John were at the tomb; they witnessed the empty grave and saw the living Christ for themselves. Later, John wrote of this Word of Life: "we have heard ... we have seen with our eyes ... we looked upon and have touched with our hands ..." (1 John 1:1).

But what about those us who have never seen Jesus in his resurrected body? Are we less privileged? Present-day followers of Christ are also blessed, for Peter, who saw the Living One that first glorious morning, later wrote: "Though you have not seen him, you love him. Though you do not now see him, you believe in him and rejoice with joy that is inexpressible and filled with glory ..." (1 Pet. 1:8).

Do we believe? When rehearsing for a performance of *The Messiah*, a conductor was disturbed by the way the soloist began singing the refrain, "I know that my Redeemer liveth." He stopped the practice and asked the singer, "My daughter, do you really know that your Redeemer liveth?"

"Why, yes," she answered.

"Then sing it!" the conductor exhorted.

Do we really believe the Living One is presently alive? Then let's sing it; and let's live in such a way that our conduct reflects our faith.

Glad Service

Serve the Lord with gladness!
Psalm 100:2

We need to be careful lest our calling in life becomes a drudgery—whether that calling is as a homemaker, farmer, auto mechanic, engineer, vocational minister, or whatever it may be. Regardless of our respective station and vocation, God's desire for each of us is that we "Serve the Lord with gladness!"

When our vocation becomes drudgery, it is time to get alone with our Lord and receive his refreshing strength. Daily renewal by the Spirit is the sure antidote against life becoming humdrum and stale. When joy leaves, life becomes one constant headache. One who walks in daily intimacy with the Lord Jesus knows that his strength is in the "joy of the Lord" (Neh. 8:10).

Through the years I have been to many construction sites, and seen the hard and dirty work involved in plastering and dry-walling buildings. I've yet to see a joyful plasterer. But that was not the case with J. C. "Happy" Powers (1906-1986), the father of my friend Dr. Marvin Powers. Marvin said his father "was as happy as a Spirit-filled and Spirit-led man of God could be!" His early memory of his father, he said, "Takes me back to when, as a boy, I would see him in prayer each night before I went to bed. And then, upon waking in the morning, my first sight was my Dad in prayer." Marvin continues, "Once I found him standing by his truck, dressed in his work clothes, conversing with a chef from a nearby restaurant about the power of God to make changes in people's lives. When that exchange was over, Dad was beaming. He came to where I was standing and said to me: 'Marv, *that's* my business; I plaster in order to make a living.'"

No calling on earth has the power to rob a person of a glad heart. Whether it was the Levites serving in the temple, or a plasterer plying his trade, day after day, it is the privilege of God's people to serve the Lord with gladness. No matter what work we are engaged in, if we are not serving the Lord with gladness, we either need to change our vocation or let God change our heart (maybe both?). What a vibrant witness for Christ it is when one serves the Lord with gladness.

The Master's Minority

"Enter by the narrow gate. For the gate is wide
and the way is easy that leads to destruction, and those
who enter by it are many. For the gate is narrow and the way
is hard that leads to life, and those who find it are few."
Matthew 7:13-14

The Christian life begins by turning from the "wide gate" and entering the "narrow gate." The wide gate is the gate of moral permissiveness; it is the gate which the multitude enters to do evil, a gate of the world, the flesh, and the Devil. This gate is the popular gate. To enter this gate is to do what comes naturally: hate, retaliate, lust, take, condemn, get angry, swear, divorce—everything Jesus spoke against in the Sermon on the Mount.

Having entered eternal life through the "narrow gate," the Christian must make daily choices, affirming the narrowness of the path leading to life. The choices rarely reach the public eye; they are decisions made in the privacy of one's life. However, in making these decisions, we continually identify with either the narrow way or the wide way—life or destruction. The true Christian lives with an eye to please his Master. He is content to follow the voice of his Shepherd. He must turn a deaf ear to the shrill cries about him.

The narrow way can be a hard way; it is the way of courage instead of taking the most-traveled road. For example, the Spirit has repeatedly raised up courageous souls in the church's history to protect her against false teaching. Such was the case in the age of Athanasius (296-373). This man stood almost alone against doctrinal error. When it was said that the world was against Athanasius, this giant of faith boldly declared, "Athanasius *contra mundum*"; that is, "Athanasius against the world." He opposed popular opinion. To follow Jesus is to identify with the despised minority.

Let nothing now my heart divide,
Since with Thee I am crucified,
And live to God in Thee.
Dead to the world and all its toys,
Its idle pomp and fading joys,
Jesus, my glory be.*

The Great Sin

*"Are not Abana and Pharpar, the rivers of Damascus,
better than all the waters of Israel? Could I not wash in them
and be clean?" So he turned and went away in a rage.*
2 Kings 5:12

C. S. Lewis (1898-1963) called pride "the great sin."* One needs not travel far in searching for the cause of man's antagonism against God, as well as for a believer's failures; the reason is pride.

Naaman was a military commander in the Syrian army, who was afflicted with leprosy. Through the intercession of a Jewish servant, he learns about the prophet Elisha in Israel, whom God had used in miraculous healings. Naaman traveled to Israel and came to Elisha's house. Instead of personally greeting Naaman, Elisha sent word to Naaman, "Go and wash in the Jordan seven times, and your flesh shall be restored, and you shall be clean" (see 2 Kings 5 for the entire narrative). The proud commander was insulted: "Behold, I thought that he would surely come out to me and stand and call upon the name of the Lord his God, and wave his hand over the place and cure the leper. Are not Abana and Pharpar, the rivers of Damascus, better than all the waters of Israel? Could I not wash in them and be clean?' So he turned and went away in a rage." His wiser servants intervened and Naaman changed his mind, humbling himself, accepting God's word for a cure.

Years ago, when conducting revival services in western Michigan, I did something I had never done before or since. In the Sunday morning service before I preached to a full sanctuary, I felt impressed to invite the congregation to stand and march around the sanctuary's outside aisles, singing the chorus, "The Devil doesn't like it but I'm walking with the King." We had a joyful time, with all marching except one church member. In the Sunday evening service, when I rose to preach, Vernon stood and addressed me. "Brother Tilley, everyone knows I remained seated while everyone else marched this morning. I was too proud to join in. Now the Lord wants me to march by myself." He did, and the Lord was near.

If God chooses, he can use a Jordan River or marching saints to reveal one's pride. He can take what appears to be foolishness to man, and humble a proud heart.

Living Stones

*As you come to him, a living stone rejected by men but in the
sight of God chosen and precious, you yourselves like living stones are
being built up as a spiritual house, to be a holy priesthood, to offer
spiritual sacrifices acceptable to God through Jesus Christ.*
1 Peter 2:4-5

One day, I was reading the following words of C. S. Lewis (1898-1963); they have stayed with me ever since. "This world is a great sculptor's shop. We are the statues and there is a rumor going round the shop that some of us are some day going to come to life."*
With those words in mind, I penned the following.

*A room filled with statues:
all uniquely beautiful,
chiseled and hammered,
made out of stone.*

*There were ears and eyes,
hands and feet.
But they had no sight;
they did not feel or walk.*

*They were cold and lifeless stones;
they could not respond.
Void of love and devotion,
they stared, merely stared.*

*Then without notice
there came a gentle Wind blowing.
The stones became warm;
they could now hear and see.*

*Walking out of the room
into the loving embrace
of their Sculptor,
they cried, "Father!"*

Are you one of our Father's living stones? Have you come to life in Christ? Can you call God, "Father"?

Compassion

And when the Lord saw her, he had compassion
on her and said to her, "Do not weep."
Luke 7:13

Dr. Bob Pierce (1914-1978), founder of the Christian humanitarian organization World Vision, was on one of his trips to the interior of China. One day while visiting an orphanage, he noticed a sad little girl who had not been admitted. He asked why that was the case. The answer was, "We have no room."

Upset at the sister, Pierce responded, "Surely one child won't make that much difference. Couldn't you make room for just one more? Why isn't something being done?" Then the German sister swiftly picked the child up and thrust her into Pierce's arms. "What are *you* going to do about it?" Immediately Pierce reached into his pocket and gave the administrator enough funds to care for the little girl.

While walking among earth's needy people some two thousand years ago, the Lord Jesus never *felt* compassion without acting. So often we feel compassion and do nothing. To demonstrate compassion is to enter another's need with feeling, to suffer with another, to come alongside another, to help carry another's burden, to meet a need.

To feel compassion without acting on it produces hardness. Like the Levite and priest in the parable of the Good Samaritan, we look away and walk on the other side of the road instead of extending help. Our excuse: "We can't do everything!" God doesn't call us to do "everything"; he calls us to extend compassion toward the one he has providentially placed in our path, the one he calls our "neighbor."

We know John 3:16; do we know 1 John 3:16-18? "By this we know love, that he laid down his life for us, and we ought to lay down our lives for the brothers. But if anyone has the world's goods and sees his brother in need, yet closes his heart against him, how does God's love abide in him? Little children, let us not love in word or talk but in deed and in truth."

On a scale of 1 - 10, how compassionate do you think you are?

February 14

A Giver or Taker?

A woman came up to him with an alabaster flask of very expensive ointment, and she poured it on his head as he reclined at table.
Matthew 26:7

Why are we uncomfortable whenever we see a fellow Christian give his or her resources—extravagantly? Extreme giving to the glory of Christ convicts us of our self-centeredness; it reveals our poverty— our poverty of soul. Selfless service for Christ was fine for martyr Jim Elliott (1927-1956) and his ilk, but for us? Not on your life!

The woman who offered her gift in Matthew 26 (identified as Mary, the sister of Lazarus and Martha in John 12:3), withheld nothing from Jesus, unlike the rich young man who refused to sell everything to follow Jesus. Mary knew nothing about halfhearted discipleship. She was a giver—a worshiper and a giver. Her gift to Christ was accepted by him because she had first given herself. Our gifts to God without a whole heart first given to God mean nothing. Some of Christ's closest followers saw Mary's offering to Jesus as an expression of poor stewardship—"Why this waste?" (26:8). That is the inevitable reaction from those who live *measured* lives.

Mary was a giver. However, in stark contrast to Mary's benevolent spirit, a few verses later, we have the account of a *taker*. Judas had been exposed to the teachings and works of the Lord Jesus, just as Mary had. Even so, Judas' heart was left untouched. All those days he lived in the presence of Messiah, he remained unwhole and selfish. Judas never knew what it meant to surrender himself wholly to the Lord. Thus we see Judas, on the night of Jesus' arrest and betrayal, asking the Jewish leaders, "What will you *give me* if I deliver him over to you?" (26:15).

What a contrast: Mary gave; Judas took. Mary gave extravagantly, with no thought of sacrifice; Judas took, with every thought of himself.

We have a choice: to be a giver or taker. For those who have not only been forgiven, but have also wholly given themselves to the Lord, the decision is an easy one—they choose to be a giver to the glory of the Lord Jesus.

Which one are you?

Christ Loved the Church

Christ loved the church and gave himself up for her.
Ephesians 5:25

Without Christ's self-sacrificial offering for the church, the church would be unable to reciprocate such love, because the church would have been deprived of Christ's love manifested through his death and resurrection life. Love—*agape* love—originates in the person and heart of God, and has been eternally expressed between the members of the triune God. Unless it had been revealed to us through the Son by his voluntary death, we would be incapable of loving God and his Son. Jesus loved the church—in life and in death and forever.

Recalling his Lord's last hours before his death, while gathered with his disciples for a final meal, John writes, "when Jesus knew that his hour had come to depart out of this world to the Father, having loved his own who were in the world, he loved them to the end" (John. 13:1). Jesus loved the church in life; he loved the church in death.

Jesus' death not only provided an effective atonement for sin, but his sufferings and death provided an example of self-giving love to the church for all ages. In explaining the Ephesians 5 passage with respect to the self-sacrificial offering of Christ, H. C. G. Moule (1841-1920) wrote, "The business of this passage is with the Lord's Example, and it does not enter in detail into His Sacrificial work.... The supreme Act of self-devoting love for others which, as a fact, the Atoning Death was, is here used as the great Example of all acts of self-devoting love in the Christian church. As the Father has just been named as the Ideal for the forgiving Christian, so here the Son is named as the Ideal for the self-sacrificing Christian."*

What a sublime thought! What a glorious fact! "Christ loved the church and gave himself up for her"! What an Example of self-sacrificing love!

We are called to emulate our Lord. Can we aspire to anything less?

Momentary Afflictions

For this light momentary affliction is preparing for us
an eternal weight of glory beyond all comparison.
2 Corinthians 4:17

It was his love and devotion to Christ that compelled David Livingston (1813-1873) to return to his Lord the same love by investing his life as a medical missionary on the African continent for thirty-four years until the day of death.

Livingston's life and career were forever changed after hearing African missionary Robert Moffat (1795-1883), Livingston's future father-in-law, say in a service, "I have sometimes seen, in the morning sun, the smoke of a thousand villages where no missionary has ever been."*

For most of his years in Africa, Livingston's four children remained in England, with his wife often doing the same. The years of family deprivations and loneliness; constant bouts of illness; frequently under threat from hostile natives; at times accompanied by unfaithful co-workers; lacking the conveniences of modern life—all of these trials were counted as loss to Livingston for the sake of taking the love of Jesus to unreached and unsaved peoples. It was for the love of Christ that he taught and witnessed, translated and wrote, suffered and died.

Noting the fever he was suffering and many obstacles he faced, Livingston wrote to his friend Arthur Tidman on October, 12, 1855, "These privations, I beg you to observe, are not mentioned as if I considered them in the light of sacrifices. I think the word ought never to be mentioned in reference to anything we can do for him who, though he was rich yet for our sakes he became poor."* Writing once again to Tidman in 1856, Livingston reiterates his motive for passionate service for the Lord Jesus: "We still have a debt of gratitude to Jesus ... and there is no greater privilege on earth than, after having our own chains broken off, to go forth to proclaim liberty to the captives, the opening of the prison to them that are bound."**

How the indwelling love of Jesus compels his followers to live and to serve!

February 17

Listening Prayer (part 1)

*"Morning by morning he awakens; he awakens my ear to
hear as those who are taught. The Lord GOD has opened
my ear, and I was not rebellious; I turned not backward."*
Isaiah 50:4-5

In the third of Isaiah's Servant Songs, the prophet speaks of how
the coming Servant will carefully listen to the voice of the Sovereign
Lord: "Morning by morning he awakens; he awakens my ear to hear
as those who are taught. The Lord GOD has opened my ear, and I
was not rebellious; I turned not backward." From early childhood,
Jesus cultivated a listening ear. His Father awakened him to commune with him, to speak to him, to teach him. The Son never failed
to hear the voice; he looked forward to listening.

Listening is an essential component in prayer and possibly the
most important component. It must be assumed that since prayer
was a vital part of the life and ministry of the Lord Jesus, listening
prayer was integral to his prayer life. Since Jesus did nothing on his
own initiative, and since he always did those things that pleased his
Father, Jesus knew and loved his Father's voice and was careful to
listen to him.

The servant is not above his Lord. As disciples of the Lord Jesus, who wish to cultivate a close walk with him, the importance of
listening-prayer is essential for our growth in the knowledge and
grace of the Lord Jesus. Jesus said, "Whoever is of God hears the
words of God" (John 8:47). Again, "My sheep hear my voice, and I
know them, and they follow me" (John. 10:27). To listen is to pray;
to pray is to listen.

That seventeenth-century spiritual master, Brother Lawrence
(1614-1691), said it so well because he listened so well: "There is not
in the world a kind of life more sweet and delightful than that of a
continual conversation with God. Those only can comprehend it
that practice and experience it; yet I do not advise you to do it from
that motive. It is not pleasure which we ought to seek in this exercise; but let us do it from a principle of love, and because God would
have us."*

Is your ear tuned to hear the Master's voice?

Listening Prayer (part 2)

Then the Lord came and stood and called as at other times, "Samuel! Samuel!" And Samuel said, "Speak, for Your servant is listening."
1 Samuel 3:10 NASB

If listening is an integral part of prayer, the question that needs asking is, Where do we find this voice to listen to? What is the answer? We turn to the words of Jesus; we turn to the Word of God.

James Houston, founding principal and chancellor of Regent College, Vancouver, British Columbia, makes reference in one of his books to an old Scottish preacher by the name of John Brown. Houston says of Brown, he "used to pause now and again in his preaching, as if listening to a voice." Houston adds, "Prayer is a constant listening to the voice of Jesus, and then meditating on his words."*

Carefully listening to the *Voice* was the learned behavior and practiced discipline of all the Old Testament saints. While serving under the direction of Eli the priest, the young child Samuel was not yet familiar with the voice of the Lord. However, the Lord chose to call the child to a special vocational ministry to serve as his spokesman to his people. One night, when the boy was sleeping, the Lord spoke to him, though he did not recognize the voice. Samuel twice got up and went to Eli, thinking he had called. Soon the priest discerned the Lord was calling Samuel and instructed him how he should respond if the Lord spoke again. The Lord did speak again, and Samuel replied appropriately: "Speak, for your servant hears" (1 Sam. 3:10). This is the attitude of the true servants of God. Such servants soon learn to love their Master's voice.

While many of the Old Testament worthies, such as Samuel, received direct, personal communications from God, many did not—just as we do not. The Lord has primarily chosen to speak to his people through his written revelation—the Word of God. To repeat Dr. Houston, let us practice, "A constant listening to the voice of Jesus, and then meditating on his words."

The Word of God

The unfolding of Your words gives light;
It gives understanding to the simple.
Psalm 119:130 NASB

The Holy Spirit does not reveal any *new* truth to his church today; the written Word of God contains all revealed truth necessary for salvation and doctrine. With this in mind, J. I. Packer writes, "Once the Scriptures were written, and the prophetic and apostolic witness to Christ was complete, no need remained for private revelations of new truths."*

Nonetheless, even though special revelation is closed with the formulation of the Canon (66 books of the Bible), the true disciple of the Lord Jesus desires to *understand* the *old* truth, be led into all truth, and regularly experience the need for personal guidance. How can this be accomplished? By listening well.

In *A Quest for Godliness*, Packer explores why so many of the Puritan theologians and preachers were great men of God; he examines the thoughts and practices of one of his favorite Puritans, John Owen (1616-1683). On the subject as to how God communicates with his people, Packer distills Owen's thinking under four main headings:

"First, the Spirit imparts to the Scriptures the permanent quality of light.

"Second, the Spirit makes the Scriptures powerful to produce spiritual effects.

"Third, the Spirit makes Scripture impinge on the individual consciousness as a word addressed personally to each man by God himself, evoking awe, and a sense of being in God's presence and under his eye.

"Fourth, the internal testimony of the Holy Spirit, whereby the external testimony (Scripture) comes to be recognized and received, is not an inward voice, revealing facts otherwise unknown and unknowable (that is, a private revelation), nor is it an unreasoning conviction, objectively groundless, coming to us out of the blue; it is, rather, an activity of inward illumination, whereby a man's natural spiritual blindness is removed ..."*

"The unfolding of Your words gives light."

Discerning the Voice of God

"My sheep hear my voice, and I know them, and they follow me."
John 10:27

Impressions come from a variety of sources—the flesh (our fallen nature), Satan, one's own imagination, and the Spirit of God. I don't believe I have ever heard or read better advice on how to carefully discern the voice of Christ and ascertain his will, than that shared by the venerable and faith-filled George Müller (1805-1898). Here is Müller's advice:

"I seek at the beginning to get my heart into such a state that it has no will of its own in regard to a given matter. Nine-tenths of the trouble with people is right here. Nine-tenths of the difficulties are overcome when our hearts are ready to do the Lord's will, whatever it may be. When one is truly in this state, it is usually but a little way to the knowledge of what His will is.

"Having surrendered my own will, I do not leave the result to feeling or simply impressions. If I do so, I make myself liable to great delusions.

"I seek the will of the Spirit of God through, or in connection with, the Word of God. The Spirit and the Word must be combined. If the Holy Ghost guides us at all, He will do it according to the Scriptures, and never contrary to them.

"Next, I take into account providential circumstances. These often plainly indicate God's will in connection with His Word and Spirit.

"I ask God in prayer to reveal His will to me aright. Thus, through prayer to God, the study of His Word, and reflection, I come to a deliberate judgment, and if my mind is thus at peace, and continues so after two or three more petitions, I proceed accordingly. In trivial matters, and in transactions involving most important issues, I have found this method always effective."*

A prayer by William M. Runyan (1870-1957):

Lord, I have shut the door,
Speak now the word
Which, in the din and throng,
*Could not be heard.***

Obedient Love

"If you love me, you will keep my commandments."
John 14:15

The Lord Jesus equated love with obedience. Lest he be misunderstood, Jesus emphasized repeatedly in his Final Discourse with the Twelve, that obedience to his words was one of the spiritual laws of his kingdom. Jesus assumed obedience would be the expected result from those who truly loved him with *agape* love. He said, "If you love me, you will keep my commandments." A few verses later, he said, "Whoever has my commandments and keeps them, he it is who loves me" (John. 14:21).

In a book that greatly influenced the revivals in the eighteenth century, on both sides of the Atlantic, young Henry Scougal (1650-1678) wrote, "If we desire to have our souls moulded to this holy frame, to become partakers of the divine nature, and have Christ formed in our hearts, we must seriously resolve, and carefully endeavor, to avoid all ... sinful practices ..." He adds, "Every willful sin gives a mortal wound to the soul, and puts it at a greater distance from God and goodness; and we can never hope to have our hearts purified from corrupt affections, unless we cleanse our hands from vicious actions."*

C. S. Lewis (1898-1963) once rather crudely remarked on the subject of obedience to Christ: "The command 'Be ye perfect' is not idealistic gas. Nor is it a command to do the impossible. He is going to make us into creatures that can obey that command."**

"The missing note in Evangelical life today," observed Baptist minister and philosopher, Dallas Willard (1935-2013), "is not in the first instance spirituality but rather obedience." Then Willard laments, "We have generated a variety of religion to which obedience is not regarded as essential. I do not understand how anyone can look ingenuously at the contents of the Scripture and say that Jesus intends anything else for us but obedience."***

The entire teaching ministry of Christ becomes meaningless, unless we understand that Jesus expected his words to be obeyed by his disciples. This is truly loving Christ.

Quality Christians

"You are the salt of the earth, but if salt has lost its taste, how shall its saltiness be restored? It is no longer good for anything except to be thrown out and trampled under people's feet."
Matthew 5:13

Just because no disciple of Jesus has ever *absolutely* complied with his every command under all circumstances at all times, should not suggest that Jesus does not mean what he says. Furthermore, to say that *being* is more important than *doing* in the teachings of Jesus, doesn't absolve the disciples of Jesus from the *doing*. Certainly, *doing* must flow out of *being*. However, if language means anything, Christ *did* expect his followers to behave in specific ways under a given set of circumstances; otherwise, his commands make no sense at all.

Jesus desires that the conduct of his disciples be the result of having an intimate relationship with him. Such a life is not a matter of rule-keeping. The disciples of Jesus comply with his commands because they love him—because they have entered upon a love relationship with their Master and Teacher: "my yoke is easy, and my burden is light" (Matt. 11:30). This is not the religion of the Pharisees. "The Pharisee takes as his aim keeping the law," says a noted scholar, "rather than becoming the kind of person whose deeds naturally conform to the law."

The quality of Christians, and therefore, the church, would be elevated to a degree Christ intended if we only took his words *seriously*. William Law (1686-1761)—whose writings have had a significant impact on many earnest believers—looked at the dismal level of Christian living in his own day and wrote: "If the doctrines of Christianity were practiced, they would make a man as different from other people as a civilized man is different from a savage. If the doctrines of Christianity were practiced, it would be as easy a thing to know a Christian by the outward course of his life as it is now difficult to find a person who lives the Christian life."*

To be a Christian is to take Christ and his words seriously.

Serving with Humility

Clothe yourselves, all of you, with humility toward one another,
for "God opposes the proud but gives grace to the humble."
1 Peter 5:5

The renowned Scottish New Testament Greek scholar, William Barclay (1907-1978), related a little story about a missionary who arrived in the Congo years ago to share the gospel of the Lord Jesus. Two missionaries had preceded this particular one and had failed miserably. The former missionaries had been members of the Baganda tribe, for which menial work was reserved for women and slaves. When the native people refused to provide food for these two missionaries, they left because they were too proud to work.

Knowing about the failures of his predecessors, a man by the name of Apolo entered the area prepared to grow his own food. On his way to the village of his calling, he stopped to cut some hoe handles, so he would be able to work a patch of ground. When the ruler of the tribe saw Apolo entering their village carrying the hoe handles, he exclaimed, "Here is a man who is going to conquer." Apolo won the hearts of these villages because he went prepared to serve—in his example, with his hands.* This servant of Christ had learned well the advice given once by Bernard of Clairvaux (1090-1153): "Learn the lesson that, if you are to do the work of a prophet, what you need is not a scepter but a hoe."*

Our Lord is in the business of whittling us down until he can use us effectively. The famed London preacher Charles Spurgeon (1834-1892) was used mightily by God because he walked humbly before him. This is evident by what he recorded one day. "Today I saw as I went home some old crocks and broken bricks and pieces of all sorts of earthenware put by the side of the road because the road is going to be widened, and I thought to myself, 'If the Lord would only use me as an old broken crock to help to make a roadway for him to ride through London, so that he might be glorified, I would be glad to be thus honoured.'"**

"Clothe yourselves, all of you, with humility toward one another, for 'God opposes the proud but gives grace to the humble.'"

Works of Service

We give thanks to God always for all of you, ...
remembering before our God and Father your work of
faith and labor of love ... in our Lord Jesus Christ."
1 Thessalonians 1:2-3

On the subjects of spiritual gifts, Paul says the reason God has sovereignly distributed Spirit-gifts throughout his church is that every believer might serve their fellow believers effectively in Jesus' name to the glory of God: "To each is given the manifestation of the Spirit for the common good" (1 Cor. 12:7).

The Apostle Peter in commenting on the same subject, wrote, "As each has received a gift, use it to serve one another, as good stewards of God's varied grace" (1 Pet. 4:10). Even in Heaven, we are informed that God's people will be engaged in loving works of service: "Therefore they are before the throne of God, and serve him day and night in his temple" (Rev. 7:15).

The range to which Christians are called to serve is as wide and unique to the individual believer's giftedness and field of ministry as there are gifts and needs. For example, in 1 Corinthians 12:8-10, Paul identifies eleven gifts, which are to be used in the service of God and for the edification of believers. There are also references in which the good works and service of a particular believer, or a group of believers, are noted. Acts 9 records the account of a believer by the name of Dorcas, who "was full of good works and acts of charity" (Acts 9:36). Following her death, and in hope that the Apostle Peter could somehow miraculously intervene, the mourners showed Peter some of the results of this lady's service to others: "All the widows stood beside him weeping and showing tunics and other garments that Dorcas made while she was with them" (Acts 9:39).

The Thessalonian believers were an example of those who were commended by the apostle for their good works. Paul wrote to these Christians: "We give thanks to God always for all of you, ... remembering before our God and Father your work of faith and labor of love ... in our Lord Jesus Christ."

Christians should be faithfully engaged in loving works of service—to the glory of God.

A Slave for Christ

*Paul, a slave of Christ Jesus, called to be
an apostle, set apart for the gospel of God.*
Romans 1:1 RIT

We discover in the pages of the New Testament, that the concept of service and servanthood for Christians is found on practically every page. This is picturesquely revealed, for example, by the use of the Greek word *doulos* (i.e., "servant," "slave"). In commenting upon the meaning of this word, Marvin Vincent (1834-1922) says the "word involves the idea of belonging to a master, and of service as a slave." He says the former use is employed by Paul, "since Christian service, in his view, has no element of servility, but is the expression of love and of free choice."*

While Christian service has "no element of servility," Murray Harris would go further than Vincent did in explaining the New Testament meaning of *doulos*. When he was serving on the faculty at Trinity Evangelical Divinity School in 1987, Harris heard Dr. Josef Tson, a Romanian pastor speak. He said Tson asked to be introduced as "a slave of Jesus Christ." Tson said, "There aren't many people willing to introduce me as a slave. They substitute the word 'servant' for 'slave.'" Then Harris added an insightful observation: "In twentieth-century Christianity, we have replaced the expression 'total surrender' with the word 'commitment,' and 'slave' with 'servant.' But there is an important difference. A servant gives service to someone, but a slave belongs to someone. We commit ourselves to do something, but we surrender ourselves to someone, we give ourselves up."** The late Beeson School of Divinity professor Calvin Miller (1936-2012) agreed: "A *doulos* is a slave; the word emphasizes the servant's accountability to his master."***

The Apostle Paul often introduced himself to listeners and readers as a *slave* of Jesus; for example, "Paul, a *doulos* of Christ Jesus, called to be an apostle, set apart for the gospel of God."

The implications of being a slave of the Lord Jesus are immense. What does it mean in your life?

February 26

Imitate Their Faith

*Remember your leaders, those who spoke to you the word of God.
Consider the outcome of their way of life, and imitate their faith.
Jesus Christ is the same yesterday and today and forever.*
Hebrews 13:7-8

David Brainerd (1718-1747) was a missionary to the American Indians in the Northeastern part of the United States, especially in New York, New Jersey, and eastern Pennsylvania. He was a man who served God night and day with his tears for the conversion of Native Americans, and preached faithfully for their salvation. Although he fought chronic battles with illness and inclement weather, Brainerd never tired of sharing the saving grace of the Lord Jesus Christ.

As an example of his labors, Brainerd records in his journal on October 1745 about his ministry in Crossweeksung, New Jersey: "When I first came into these parts in June, I found not one man at the place I visited, but only four women and a few children. But before I had been there many days, they gathered from all quarters, some from more than twenty miles distant. When I made them a second visit in August, some came more than forty miles to hear me." Then he says of these congregants: "And these were almost as soon affected with a sense of their sin and misery, and with an earnest concern for deliverance, as they made their appearance in our assembly. After this work of grace began with power among them, it was common for strangers of the Indians, before they had been with us one day, to be much awakened, deeply convinced of their sin and misery, and to enquire with great solitude, 'What shall we do to be saved?'"*

Although he lived but a brief time, Brainerd has cast a long shadow through the publication of his journal by Jonathan Edwards (1703-1758). *The Life and Diary of David Brainerd* has impacted the lives of countless men and women, who have wanted to serve God faithfully and zealously.

There was only one David Brainerd; however, we can emulate his passion for Christ and his zeal to share the gospel.

Don't Grow Weary

*And let us not grow weary of doing good, for in
due season we will reap, if we do not give up.*
Galatians 6:9

Kenneth N. Taylor (1917-2005) is best known for his writing and publishing ministries, and particularly as the author of a paraphrase of the Bible, *The Living Bible*. Taylor was for many years the editor of *His* magazine. While serving with *His*, he joined the staff at Good News Publishers, which at the time emphasized tract translation and foreign distribution. He later joined the editorial staff at Moody Bible Institute, and eventually became director of Moody Press.

It was while he was serving at Moody that the seminal thought occurred to Taylor for the publication of a Bible that would be understandable for younger children. Having been blessed with twelve children, Taylor and his wife Margaret were very careful that these gifts from God would receive a godly upbringing.

As a father who faithfully led the family in worship, Taylor did his best to make the stories and teachings of God's Word meaningful to the children. It was with this thought in mind that he began to paraphrase the Bible. Taylor says, "We had read over and over again to our youngest children ... all the available books of Bible stories geared to three-and-four-year-olds.... But I could not find a book that covered the entire Bible for very young children." Then Taylor says, "Finally the thought occurred to me to try writing such a book myself." Taylor said as he began his disciplined pursuit: "At some point it occurred to me that other families might be similarly helped if they had this easier text to read."*

Taylor attempted to publish his paraphrase. Following a series of rejections from publishers, he finally was offered the generous help of a local printer, who only asked for payments as copies of *Living Letters* were sold. When Billy Graham saw a copy of *Living Letters*, he endorsed it in 1963, and sales began to soar.

*He who in His righteous balance
Doth each human action weigh,
Will your sacrifice remember,
Will your loving deeds repay.**

February 28

Pride and Humility

Humble yourselves, therefore, under the mighty hand
of God so that at the proper time he may exalt you.
1 Peter 5:6

"Grant us to sit, one at your right hand and one at your left, in your glory" (Mark 10:37).

Such a request would have been out of place on any occasion, but that it was made shortly after Jesus foretold his impending death was outrageous (see Matt. 20:17-19). However, regardless of the occasion, the request of James and John revealed their inherent self-centeredness, which is the essence of sin.

With Jesus facing desertion, arrest, mockery, flogging, and crucifixion, two of his disciples were striving for superiority over their fellows. They sought the limelight, positions of power and authority. Frederick Bruner insightfully reminds us of the particular temptations one faces in life's three major seasons: "It has been observed that the typical temptation of the young is lust, of the middle-aged ambition, and of the elderly bitterness." Then he writes, "Actually, all three drives are similar and related: ambition is a refined lust, bitterness a disappointed one. In addition, ambition is a drive that (like sexual desire), precisely because it is not wholly evil, is so difficult to tame." Bruner then asks, "When are desires to do well legitimate desires for the glory of God and the service of others, and when are desires to do well illegitimate and for one's own glory?" Bruner answers: "Disciples never know exactly. They can only pray—constantly—to be delivered from temptation."*

James and John were ambitious—*sinfully* ambitious. Because of their innate sinfulness, and without any apparent embarrassment, they requested Jesus to provide them with positions of influence in order to promote themselves above the other disciples.

What a change Pentecost produced in these men. It was Peter who later wrote: "Humble yourselves, therefore, under the mighty hand of God so that at the proper time he may exalt you."

What a contrast!

Misplaced Focus

Looking to Jesus, the founder and perfecter of our faith.
Hebrews 12:2

There is a pitfall every disciple of the Lord Jesus Christ must constantly guard against. This pitfall is so well disguised that the new convert, as well as a mature believer, may imperceptibly fall into its trap: the danger of a *misplaced focus*—loving Christ's *gifts* instead of loving Christ *himself*.

Jesus detected this deadly flaw among many of those who followed him during his earthly ministry. For example, after the feeding of the five thousand, Jesus and his disciples crossed the Sea of Galilee. The following day, many of the beneficiaries of that miracle traveled miles in search of Jesus. When they found him, he intuitively knew why they had come: they were in search of Christ's gifts instead of seeking Christ himself. They only came to Jesus for what he could do for them: "Truly, truly I say to you, you are seeking me, not because you saw signs, but because you ate your fill of the loaves" (John 6:26).

The same ulterior motive pervades much of the church's landscape today. Many uninstructed, immature believers are lusting after the next miracle, blessing, dynamic worship service. These zealous souls are so preoccupied with what they want Christ to do *for* them that they give little or no thought about getting to *know* Christ himself, through the Word and Spirit.

The language of the apostle is foreign to these uninformed souls: "Indeed, I count everything as loss because of the surpassing worth of *knowing* Christ Jesus my Lord" (Phil. 3:8). For Paul, the Lord Jesus was always at the center; everything else was the circumference.

The living Christ never comes to an honest, seeking heart without also bringing with him those moral qualities and spiritual gifts he chooses to sovereignly distribute to his children. However, let the maturing disciple learn to concentrate on Christ and not his gifts.

Let us always be "Looking to Jesus, the founder and perfecter of our faith."

March 2

Pleading for the Spirit

*And when they had prayed, the place in which they were gathered
together was shaken, and they were all filled with the Holy Spirit
and continued to speak the word of God with boldness.*
Acts 4:31

The same disciples, who were filled with the Holy Spirit on the Day
of Pentecost, were some of the same ones spoken of in our text, who
experienced a fresh filling of the Spirit.

Sanctification produces Christlike character; the filling of the
Spirit has to do with effective service. God calls every Christian to
separate himself from all ungodliness, uncleanness and sin, conse-
crating himself to live only and always to the glory of God. Furthermore, it is God's will to purify—and keep pure—every believer who
has totally surrendered himself to the sovereign lordship of Jesus
Christ. This is sanctification.

However, the level of God's manifest power, operating in the
heart and life of a consecrated, sanctified Christian, ebbs and flows.
The Christian is called to walk in the Spirit and to live a Christlike
life, but he will not always have the necessary power to minister effectively, unless he takes time to plead for a fresh anointing of the
Spirit. Effective service requires fresh fillings.

Faced with severe opposition, Peter and John chose to gather
with their fellow believers to plead with the sovereign Lord to pour
out his Spirit afresh. The Lord answered the pleadings of his servants, and the work of God surged forward.

How often has the work of God been defeated in and through
us, because we failed to get alone and plead with God for a fresh
filling of the blessed Holy Spirit? These noble men and women did
not rely on a previous experience of the Spirit—as remarkable as it
was—to equip them to face a present crisis and challenge. They
knew they needed a fresh touch from above.

You and I are no different. Is the Spirit calling you even now to
get alone, or possibly with a small group, and to plead for a fresh
move of God's Spirit, so that the work of God might move forward
in power?

Knowing Christ

That I may know him.
Philippians 3:10

A person who views God as only a curious object to be studied, instead of the infinite Father desiring fellowship with each member of the human family, thinks it foolhardy when hearing Christ's disciples speak of *knowing* Christ. After all, wasn't Jesus of Nazareth killed and buried two thousand years ago? How can one know a dead man whom they never met?

Saul of Tarsus must have thought the same thing before his life-changing Christ-encounter on the Damascus Road. However, that one personal revelation of the resurrected, living Christ immediately transformed the mistaken theology of this radical rabbi, thrusting him into a lifelong quest. He saw Christ with his own eyes; he heard Christ with his own ears. Now he must seek to know this one who knows this chief of sinners so well.

Thirty years after Paul's meeting the Lord Jesus, he is sitting in a Roman prison, dictating a letter to the Philippian Christians. By now a seasoned veteran of the Cross, his love for Christ is undiminished. However, he longs to know Christ in a deeper reality. Paul writes, "that I may know him." Think of it, here is the church's foremost apostle, apologist, and evangelist confessing his one paramount, driving desire: "I want to know Christ." A. W. Tozer (1897-1963) called this the "soul's paradox of love." He wrote: "To have found God and still pursue Him is the soul's paradox of love, scorned indeed by the too-easily-satisfied religionist, but justified in happy experience by the children of the burning heart."*

The same word Paul used for "know" in Philippians 3:10 is a form of the Greek word rendered "knew" in the Septuagint (Greek version of the Hebrew Old Testament) in Genesis 4:1: "Now Adam *knew* his wife Eve." The physical intimacy expressed between husband and wife is analogous to the spiritual knowledge and intimacy every thirsty-hearted disciple longs for in his relation to the living Christ.

Let our passion always be to *know* Christ—intimately and increasingly.

A Book of Remembrance

*Then those who feared the Lord spoke with one another. The Lord
paid attention and heard them, and a book of remembrance was written
before him of those who feared the Lord and esteemed his name.*
Malachi 3:16

There have always been tares and wheat among the visible church of
God; this was true in the early church, and such is the case today.

During the time of the prophet Malachi, many in Israel had
turned away from following Yahweh. The priesthood became corrupt, the people married idolaters, the poor were neglected, and
they were not honoring God with their tithes and offerings. While
some may not have overtly deserted the faith of their fathers by
worshiping idols and committing adultery, the faith they held to
had become a dead faith, a dead orthodoxy. True religion had got-
ten so bad during these times, that the prophet lamented, "Oh that
there were one among you who would shut the doors, that you
might not kindle fire on my altar in vain! I have no pleasure in you,
says the Lord of hosts, and I will not accept an offering from your
hand" (Mal. 1:10).

Through the centuries, the earnest people of God have always
searched for the like-minded. They look for those who are true to
and practice the faith. Saints need the fellowship of the saints—they
even crave it. This was the scene in Malachi's day. There were still
those left in Israel, who possessed an awesome regard and a reverential fear of God. They found one another and enjoyed mutual fellowship. God was impressed. "The Lord paid attention and heard
them, and a book of remembrance was written before him of those
who feared the Lord and esteemed his name."

True Christian fellowship is necessary for the health of the individual Christian as well as for the local church, and it is sorely lacking in many places.

Blest be the tie that binds
Our hearts in Christian love;
The fellowship of kindred minds
Is like to that above.*

March 6

Flesh or Spirit?

But I say, walk by the Spirit, and you will not gratify the desires of the flesh.
Galatians 5:16

When the Apostle Paul uses the term "flesh," he uses it as a metaphor to describe man's thinking and acting as a *mere* man. The "flesh" consists of attitudes, thoughts, and behavior contrary to the Spirit. But the "flesh" is more than attitudes, thoughts, and behavior; it is what we essentially are, apart from the active presence of the Spirit of God.

In describing the human condition prior to the Flood, the Lord announced his verdict for that age: "My Spirit shall not strive with man forever, because *in his going astray, he is flesh*" (Gen 6:3; literal translation in italics). That pre-flood generation was so dominated by its animal appetites that God called fallen mankind "flesh."

The Apostle Paul, under the inspiration of the Spirit, submits a partial list of the "works of the flesh"—those attitudes and behaviors that characterize a variety of people who are not living life in harmony with the Spirit: "Now the works of the flesh are evident: sexual immorality, impurity, sensuality, idolatry, sorcery, enmity, strife, jealousy, fits of anger, rivalries, dissensions, divisions, envy, drunkenness, orgies, and things like these ..." (Gal. 5:19-21).

Before the Spirit invaded his own life, the Apostle Paul's ultimate confidence was in the "flesh"—religious works. Paul said if he chose to, he could boast about his religious pedigree: "circumcised on the eighth day, of the people of Israel, of the tribe of Benjamin, a Hebrew of Hebrews; as to the law, a Pharisee; as to zeal, a persecutor of the church; as to righteousness, under the law blameless ..." (Phil. 3:5-6).

As God's people, we have a moment-by-moment choice to either walk in the flesh or walk in the Spirit. It is only by the Spirit's indwelling power that we are enabled to fulfill the latter and spared the former. "But the fruit of the Spirit is love, joy, peace, patience, kindness, goodness, faithfulness, gentleness, self-control ..." (Gal. 5:22-23).

Unashamed

He is not ashamed to call them brothers.
Hebrews 2:11

I experienced an epiphany some years ago while sitting in a local restaurant, watching my four-year-old grandson entertain himself in the adjoining play area. Luke had quickly made friends with another boy, while the two frolicked on an assortment of play equipment designed for small children. After the boys made their way a number of times up the steps and down the slide, they ran over to the glass panel, which separated the booth where I was sitting. Pointing to me, while wearing a big smile, Luke said to his new friend, "That's my Papa!" I returned the smile, and then the two were off to play again.

Being the young child he was, Luke undoubtedly never gave that spontaneous, affectionate interlude another thought. But I did; days later I was still basking in its glow. However, I was left to wonder. With my mind filled with cascading thoughts—thoughts of the love and affection I felt for this boy, and the affection he had instinctively and publicly expressed for his grandfather in the presence of a stranger—my mind went back to one of the most remarkable statements spoken about the Lord Jesus in all of God's Word: "He is not ashamed to call them brothers."

Quoting selections from Psalms and Isaiah, the Spirit-inspired writer of the Letter to the Hebrews says the Lord Jesus exults in his solidarity with his "brothers" (the ancient Greek term often included both genders, and is used three times in this passage: verses 11, 12, 17). The Son of Man, who "was made like his brothers in every respect, so that he might be a merciful and faithful high priest," is not ashamed to identify with his Father's children, because all those "he ... sanctifies and those who are sanctified ... have their origin in one Father" (2:17, 11).

If a little boy, without inhibition, hesitation or embarrassment, proudly announced his relationship to a man almost six decades older, how much more will the Lord Jesus announce his relationship to his Father's children before a watching universe one day. He will not be ashamed to call them his brothers!

A Parable of Grace

Jonathan, the son of Saul, had a son who was crippled in his feet.... And his name was Mephibosheth.
2 Samuel 4:4

Grace, God's grace, is the outpouring of his kindness toward the undeserving—undeserving sinners, undeserving saints. That takes us all in!

Whenever Evangelicals think of grace, our minds turn instinctively to passages like Ephesians 2:8, "For by grace you have been saved through faith. And this is not your own doing; it is the gift of God"; and Titus 2:11, "For the grace of God has appeared, bringing salvation for all people." Hymns like "Amazing Grace" by John Newton (1725-1807) also come to mind. How we love these Scriptures and hymns about grace—for good reasons.

The salvation doctrines that are clearly delineated in the New Testament are often demonstrated in the lives of people in the Old Testament. This is true for the doctrine of grace.

We would probably never have heard of a man by the name of Mephibosheth, if it had not been for King David's benevolence toward him. Mephibosheth was five years old when his father and grandfather (Saul and Jonathan) died in battle. Upon receiving this tragic news, his nanny hurriedly picked up Mephibosheth, and fled for his protection. But she stumbled; the child fell, and as a result the child was crippled for life. After Jonathan died, David wanted to do something to show kindness toward one of Jonathan's offspring. He learned that his crippled son was still living.

David had Mephibosheth brought to him, and announced, "I will show you kindness for the sake of your father Jonathan, and I will restore to you all the land of Saul your father, and you shall eat at my table always" (2 Sam. 9:7).

What had Mephibosheth done to deserve such treatment by the king? Not a thing! What have we done to deserve the outpouring of God's kindness toward us? Nothing! It is all grace.

Surely, there was not a day passed but this crippled man was reminded of the king's kindness. What about us?

Knowing Christ Personally

*Indeed, I count everything as loss because of the
surpassing worth of knowing Christ Jesus my Lord.*
Philippians 3:8

Noted evangelical theologian J. I. Packer, wrote: "I walked in the sunshine with a scholar who had effectively forfeited his prospects of academic advancement by clashing with church dignitaries over the gospel of grace. 'But it doesn't matter,' he said at length, 'for I've known God and they haven't.'"* Packer said the man's remark caused him to do a great deal of thinking. Such thinking resulted in his writing *Knowing God*, a book now considered a classic in its field.

No one, including the greatest of the church's saints, has ever been able to comprehend God fully—the finite is incapable of fully comprehending the Infinite. However, the Bible affirms that God can be known—not perfectly, not absolutely, but he can be known by those to whom he reveals himself—to those who cultivate a healthy spiritual appetite for him.

So while God cannot be known exhaustively, nonetheless, he can be known—known personally. God has chosen through the centuries to grant a limited knowledge to man by revealing himself in a number of ways—through natural creation, the law and the prophets, signs and miracles, and the conscience. However, God's ultimate revelation of himself culminated in the Incarnation—"the Word became flesh and dwelt among us" (John 1:14).

In the coming of the Lord Jesus Christ, God's Son walked among men and women to more perfectly reveal what God is like. Thus, to see Christ was to see God—in a limited measure, but the most limited measure man had ever experienced until that point in history. As the apostle would later write, "For in him all the fullness of God was pleased to dwell" (Col. 1:19). And as Jesus himself once explained to an inquiring disciple who asked to see the Father: "Have I been with you so long, and you still do not know me, Philip? Whoever has seen me has seen the Father" (John 14:9).

Do you know Christ personally? Are you seeking to know him more intimately?

The Love of Christ

May you experience the love of Christ,
though it is too great to understand fully.
Ephesians 3:19 NLT

Of all the prayer requests I've heard in more than half-a-century in ministry, I have heard few requests quite like the Apostle Paul's. I have listened to a litany of health-related requests. I have heard requests for physical protection and job promotions. I have heard requests for passing tests and for material success. However, a prayer request for someone to experience the love of Christ is rare.

Why is this so? It is because we are so material-conscious. The average twenty-first century Christian in the Western world is pre-occupied with earning a living, making investments, saving for retirement, acquiring the latest gadgets—that if and when he does show up for a prayer meeting, he instinctively thinks in material terms when requests are solicited. Why? Because he is consumed by the material.

We cannot experience the love of Christ if our hearts are filled with the love of the world and the things in the world. It is one thing for us to possess things; it is another for things to possess us. Christ earnestly desires to possess us. Christ wants to fill our hearts with his very own love.

My greatest ongoing need is to experience the love of Christ—the pure, selfless love of Christ. For in experiencing the love of Christ, I am enabled to think of others more highly than I think of myself; I am empowered to bear with my brother's and sister's short -comings and failures. By being filled with Christ's love, life's petty annoyances and irritations are almost nil. What would normally frustrate and exasperate me is borne with ease when experiencing the love of Christ.

How often we have fallen short, because we failed to wait in God's presence until our heart was replenished with Christ's love.

Prayer: *Too often, O Christ, I have tried to do your work without experiencing your all-consuming love. Grant to your servant such an appetite for you, that nothing less than your love will satisfy. This I plead in the name of your Son. Amen.*

The Daily Tryst

*Behold what manner of love the Father has bestowed
on us, that we should be called children of God!*
1 John 3:1 NKJV

Just as there is a reciprocation of romantic love between a husband and wife, so there is an exchange of *agape* love between the heavenly Father and all of his children.

When the repentant sinner comes alive to God in regenerating grace, the love of God is poured into the new believer's heart (see Romans 5:5). Consequently, such a one can testify with the beloved apostle, "We love Him because He first loved us" (1 John 4:19 NKJV).

For those lovers who love one another on the human and natural level, they must meet often and take time with one another in order for their love to deepen and grow. These couples demand regular appointed places of meeting—*trysts*, if you will.

The word "tryst" is a noun and a verb. When used as a noun, it means an agreement (as between lovers) to meet; when used as a verb, it means to make or keep a tryst. The word derives its source in Scandinavia and originally meant "trust."

The new believer soon learns the value of keeping a daily tryst with his Divine Lover. He or she would rather go without food and drink than to miss spending time alone with the Father. This tryst does not spring from law and duty; it is born and maintained by love—*agape* love—the very same love that led Christ to get alone with his Father.

Continuous communion is to be the experience and goal for every growing Christian, but continuous communion must be maintained and renewed through the daily tryst. It is there the Lover speaks to the loved one through his Word and the loved one speaks to his Lover in prayer.

Lovers enjoy spending time together. Even when they part they're really together—in each other's thoughts. They look forward to the next tryst.

Do we love the Father? Do we carefully guard our daily tryst with him? Can God trust you to keep your trysts?

Psalm 19 (part 1)

The heavens declare the glory of God....
The law of the Lord is perfect, reviving the soul.
Psalm 19:1, 7

David writes of two revelations in Psalm 19: God's revelation in creation and God's written revelation; he addresses the former in verses 1-6, the latter in verses 7-11.

Revelation through creation. In reference to God revealing himself to mankind through his creation, David says this revelation declares God's glory; is daily speaking to mankind (v. 2); and is universal as to its extent (vv. 3-6).

In writing to the Roman Church, Paul argues that pagan peoples had been exposed to God's revelation through his creation: "For what can be known about God is plain to them, because God has shown it to them. For his invisible attributes, namely, his eternal power and divine nature, have been clearly perceived, ever since the creation of the world, in the things that have been made. So they are without excuse" (Rom. 1:19-20).

Written revelation. From revelation through creation, David proceeds to speak of God's revelation through written words—undoubtedly a reference to the Torah. He says of the Word of God: it is perfect, sure, right, pure, clean, and true. Furthermore, he says of this Word: it revives the soul makes wise the simple, rejoices the heart, enlightens the eyes, endures forever, and is altogether righteous. Then, emphasizing the preciousness of God's instructions, David writes: "More to be desired are they than gold, even much fine gold; sweeter also than honey and drippings of the honeycomb" (v. 10). In Germany, around the twelfth century, a custom developed among Jews that when a boy began the study of the Torah, a rabbi would write on a slate the Hebrew alphabet. Then, the rabbi would place a little honey on the slate, from which the child would lick the honey from the letters. This was done to impress upon the boy the sweetness of the words of God.

God has revealed himself through his creation and written words; however, he ultimately revealed himself through the incarnation of his Son, the Lord Jesus Christ. How sweet God's words are! Let us *eat* them, and act accordingly.

Psalm 19 (part 2)

Who can discern his errors? Declare me innocent
from hidden faults. Keep back your servant also from
presumptuous sins; let them not have dominion over me!
Then I shall be blameless, and innocent of great transgression.
Psalm 19:12-13

The psalmist begins by asking a question, which implies a negative answer: "Who can discern his errors?" Because the writer knows God and understands the weaknesses of fallen humanity, he realizes that apart from the illumination of the Spirit, no one is capable of judging his own failures. Under the Old Covenant, when a person suspected he may have contracted leprosy, he went to the priest for a diagnosis. So it is with the believer: our "errors" and "hidden faults" must be taken to our High Priest to be diagnosed, cleansed, and then declared "innocent."

I like Adam Clarke's (1760-1832), remarks on "errors" and "hidden faults": "From those which I have committed, and have forgotten; from those for which I have not repented; from those which have been committed in my heart, but have not been brought to act in my life; from those which I have committed without knowing that they were sins, sins of ignorance; and from those which I have committed in private, for which I should blush and be confounded were they to be made public."*

Furthermore, David prayed to be protected against "presumptuous sins." We sin presumptuously when we sin with our eyes open, when we knowingly act contrary to God's revealed moral law, when we deliberately cross a proscribed line. Repeatedly committing "presumptuous sins" enslaves a person; therefore, David prays that they will not "have dominion over me." If he is thereby protected and obedient, the psalmist will be "blameless, and innocent of great transgression." The inevitable consequence of persisting in presumptuous sins is defection and apostasy. We do well to join the psalmist in making such a request.

The man who prayed this prayer was kept from persisting in "presumptuous sins." For when he was confronted by the prophet in his sin against Bathsheba, he immediately confessed.

We would profit by reading this psalm often.

Psalm 19 (part 3)

O give thanks unto the Lord, for he is good:
for his mercy endureth for ever.
Psalm 107:1 KJV

I have purposely chosen the KJV's wording for the above verse for a reason. When I was fifteen years of age, my sister Dorothy was married to Joe, who was a farmer. In the summer, following their marriage, my father took me out to the farm and told my brother-in-law in these precise words: "Show this boy how to work." For the next five summers—while in high school and college—I worked on the farm (one of the best experiences in my life). Joe was an excellent teacher, and I tried to be a good learner.

Joe was raised in a German-Lutheran family. In their home, prayer was offered both before and after the meals. The prayer prior to a meal was prayed in unison by all, one of Martin Luther's table prayers: "Come, Lord Jesus, be our guest, and let Thy gifts to us be blessed. Amen." The prayer following a meal was prayed by the head of the household (and no one was to leave the table until the prayer was prayed). That prayer was Psalm 19:14, repeated in the language of the King James Version of the Bible.

The psalmist knew that what one spoke, and what one thought about, were important in our walk with God. After all, kings had a lot to think about; and verbal communication came with the territory of being a king. Being a godly person, David desired to say the right things and think the right thoughts. He wanted Yahweh to approve of both, thus his request.

How often we would have been spared speaking, or using the wrong words, or saying the right words inappropriately, if we had prayed this prayer beforehand—I know I would have. Addressing this challenge of how to use our words graciously, James wrote, "For we all stumble in many ways. And if anyone does not stumble in what he says, he is a perfect man" (3:2). And who is the "perfect man" in this matter? Could it be if we were more prayerful, we would be more careful in our speech? The answer is obvious.

Let us pray often: "Let the words of my mouth, and the meditation of my heart, be acceptable in thy sight, O Lord, my strength, and my redeemer."

The Disciple's One Essential

*"Martha, Martha, you are anxious and troubled about
many things, but one thing is necessary. Mary has chosen the
good portion, which will not be taken away from her."*
Luke 10:41-42

I have heard a number of comments through the years about this Mary-Martha narrative that could be summarized in a few words: "The work of the church could not survive without Marthas." Of course, it is usually a "Martha" making such a remark. Amazing isn't it, how we are wiser than Jesus!

Martha was a "distracted," "anxious," and "troubled" disciple of Jesus, feverishly engaged in doing what she thought was the work of the Lord. I wonder, who told Martha to prepare a meal for the Lord and his disciples? Martha had "welcomed Jesus into her house" (10:38), and then hurried off to do her own thing. Self-initiated service inevitably frays our nervous system, and causes friction and complaints in the body of Christ: "Lord, do you not care that my sister has left me to serve alone? Tell her then to help me" (10:40).

Do we not often hear in our local churches, leaders pleading and complaining because of a lack of volunteers for a "ministry" that may not have been *birthed* by the Spirit? We have many "Marthas"—and they're not all females—running around, making quite a scene, thinking they are doing God's work when they are merely following an echo of their own voice.

Jesus commended Mary, not Martha. No one is prepared to serve Christ, who does not first sit at his feet, listening to his word. We are in a rush to get busy, and to be active in the work of the Lord. Unless we learn to sit and listen, we are ill-prepared to serve. Mary chose the better way; she listened before she ministered: "Mary has chosen the good portion, which will not be taken away from her."

Jesus said, "but one thing is necessary." Are you modeling your life after this truth? Or are you in such a hurry to work for Christ that you have neglected to block off extended time to sit and listen to his teaching in the Word, by the illuminating Spirit?

March 15

Christian Modesty

I desire then that in every place ... that women should
adorn themselves in respectable apparel, with modesty ...
1 Timothy 2:8-9

Some years ago, a retired Methodist minister's wife said to me, "You know, Ralph, one never hears from our pulpits anymore anything about modesty in dress." When a church I once pastored was searching for a youth minister, I scheduled an appointment to meet with the candidate at a local restaurant. Not having met him before, he described the vehicle he would be driving, so I would know when he arrived. I saw the vehicle arrive, with his wife accompanying him. As they walked toward the entrance, I noticed her abbreviated attire; I said to myself, "I will be gracious in the interview; however, they have already disqualified themselves for consideration." One would have thought this lady should have known how to clothe herself, inasmuch as she and her husband were Bible college students and from Christian homes.

The above words of Scripture were written to a pastor. Pastors are to teach the people; they are to teach what was first written. Pastors are to teach women to dress modestly, and the spiritually mature women in the church are to model Christian modesty. The wives of pastors, deacons, and elders should be role models for the women in the congregation with regard to modesty in dress.

The body is the temple of the indwelling Holy Spirit (1 Cor. 6:19). When these bodies are consecrated as living sacrifices to God (Rom. 12:1), we are under the Spirit's control. We are no longer conforming ourselves to the world, but we are being transformed by the Spirit, so that by "testing [we] may discern what is the will of God, what is good and acceptable and perfect" (Rom. 12:2).

If the Spirit of God prompted a previously demon possessed man to clothe himself after meeting Jesus (Luke 8:35), surely the same Spirit teaches Christian women to clothe themselves modestly.

Let the beauty of Jesus be seen in me,
All His wonderful passion and purity;
O Thou spirit Divine, all my nature refine,
*Till the beauty of Jesus be seen in me.**

Hearing the Word

*"Take care then how you hear, for to the one who has,
more will be given, and from the one who has not,
even what he thinks that he has will be taken away."*
Luke 8:18

Those of us, who are in the habit of reading our Bibles daily, face an ongoing challenge: it is possible to read printed words without *hearing* the Word. The habit of reading the Word of God is a good and necessary habit, and one to be practiced regularly. However, unless the Word enters our hearts, our reading is useless, a waste of time, just as would be the case if we only took bites of food without swallowing.

Jesus knew this; thus he warned: "Take care then how you hear." He addressed these words to people who were listening to the spoken Word of God. We must heed his words, whether we are reading or listening to the Word of God. Following his address to each of the seven churches of Revelation, Jesus admonished, "He who has an ear, let him hear what the Spirit says to the churches." How should we read and listen to the Word of God?

Prayerfully. Lift your heart to God before you read and often while you read and listen. Remember, the Word of God is like seed, Jesus said, and it only flourishes in prepared soil. Listen to the voice of the Spirit as you read.

Slowly. We should *masticate* what we read. Stop often and think about what you are reading. Re-read the text. Young children hurriedly eat their food, anxious to rush away from the table. Take time; don't be concerned about how many verses or chapters you read. Allow the Word of God to sink into your inner ear.

Obediently. One day a woman in the crowd, following Jesus, thought she was paying him a compliment when she cried out, "Blessed is the womb that bore you, and the breasts at which you nursed!" While Jesus never questioned the woman's sincerity, he knew that there was a class of people who were far more blessed than his earthly mother. Jesus replied, "Blessed rather are those who hear the word of God and keep it!" (Luke 11:27-28).

We will never go astray, as long as we *hear* as we read and listen to the preached Word of God.

Hell

*"You serpents, you brood of vipers, how are
you to escape being sentenced to hell?"*
Matthew 23:33

It is not a pleasant thought, this subject of Hell. While we naturally shrink from thinking about it, we cannot avoid the subject when reading the Word of God. What are we to believe about Hell? It should be assumed by those who believe the written Word of God to be inspired and trustworthy, that we are only free to believe about Hell what the Bible affirms. What does the Bible say?

• Hell is a literal place. Repeatedly, Jesus and the apostles spoke of Hell as a *place*. We don't know where that place is, but we can rely on the words of Christ that Hell is a specific location. The Apostle Peter declared of the fallen angels, "God did not spare angels when they sinned, but cast them into hell ..." (2 Pet. 2:4).

• Hell is everlasting separation. In speaking of the destinies of Lazarus and the rich man, Jesus quoted Abraham, who said to the rich man in Hell, "Between us and you a great chasm has been fixed, in order that those who would pass from here to you may not be able, and none may cross from there to us" (Luke 16:26).

• Hell is a place of torment. While our finite, fragile minds are incapable of comprehending such a place, by faith we accept the fact. To those whose lives are characterized by wickedness, Jesus said a day will come when he says to them, "Depart from me, all you workers of evil! In that place there will be weeping and gnashing of teeth, when you see Abraham and Isaac and Jacob and all the prophets in the kingdom of God but you yourselves cast out" (Luke 13:27-28).

• Hell is not the destiny for those who are trusting in Christ. For those who are believing in Christ as Savior and Lord, the Word says, "For God has not destined us for wrath, but to obtain salvation through our Lord Jesus Christ" (1 Thess. 5:9).

Hell—the Word of God teaches there is such a place; however, the one who trusts in and walks with Christ will never be found there!

March 18

Near to God's Heart

One of his disciples, whom Jesus loved,
was reclining at table at Jesus' side.
John 13:23

It was the last time the apostles were to observe Passover with their Lord. Jesus had informed them that one of his chosen ones would defect and betray him; the shadow of suffering permeated the air. John, who five times in his Gospel refers to himself as one whom Jesus loved, is reclining at table, near to God's heart. He can't comprehend what his Lord has said about leaving them.

There is something about suffering and uncertainty that should draw intimate followers of the Lamb closer to his side. Such was the case with Presbyterian pastor and college professor Cleland B. McAfee (1866-1944). From his heartbreak, following the deaths of two nieces, he wrote the following words, which have ministered to the people of God ever since. In time, God wants to use our pain to bring comfort to others.

There is a place of quiet rest,
Near to the heart of God.
A place where sin cannot molest,
Near to the heart of God.

Refrain
O Jesus, blest Redeemer,
Sent from the heart of God,
Hold us who wait before Thee
Near to the heart of God.

There is a place of comfort sweet,
Near to the heart of God.
A place where we our Savior meet,
Near to the heart of God.

There is a place of full release,
Near to the heart of God.
A place where all is joy and peace,
Near to the heart of God.*

Are you allowing God to use your sufferings to draw you nearer to him?

God's Perspective

"For what is exalted among men is an abomination in the sight of God."
Luke 16:15

The pride of man keeps him from viewing life from God's vantage point. When one's heart is fixed on himself and temporal concerns, he will naturally applaud what appeals to his own sensibilities and appetites.

The religious elite in Jesus' day projected a radical devotion for Yahweh. They were obsessed with appearances. And yet while wanting others to think they were loyal followers of Yahweh—fully loving and obeying him—Jesus knew that in their hearts they "were lovers of money" (Luke 16:14). These people were experts in condemning others while rationalizing their own behavior: "You are those who justify yourselves before men, but God knows your hearts" (Luke 16:15). What was in their hearts mattered little with these self-righteous zealots; what others thought of them was of primary concern.

What the natural man exalts, God condemns. The fact is, Jesus declared, "For what is exalted among men is an abomination in the sight of God" (Luke 16:15). Throughout Scripture, God employed the word "abomination" when he wanted to reveal to us his utter distaste toward certain kinds of unacceptable behavior and attitudes.

It would serve us well as Christians to take a regular inventory of our lives in the light of God's holiness. We should ask ourselves if what we are placing a high value on harmonizes with what God esteems. Is our lifestyle being shaped by the ungodly or by the Word? Are we more concerned with what man thinks about us or what God knows about us?

Since mine eyes were fixed on Jesus,
I've lost sight of all beside;
So enchained my spirit's vision,
Looking at the Crucified.*

Slothfulness

Go to the ant, O sluggard; consider her ways, and be wise.
Proverbs 6:6

More than twenty years ago, a friend of mine said of his son-in-law, "Ralph, he is absolutely lazy!" What a sad commentary. From the earliest Christian centuries, sloth was classified among the seven deadly sins. The church included it with lust, gluttony, greed, wrath, envy, and pride. Someone has defined sloth as "failing to do things that one should do." This is a good working definition for every facet of life for the Christian.

For the disciple of the Lord Jesus, there should be no distinction between the *secular* and the *sacred*. Every aspect of life is holy for the believer. Wherever duty calls us, whatever our daily responsibilities may be—every task is to be done faithfully and diligently to the glory of God.

Each of us has our "down" moments. But we can't allow these moods to last long, or they will paralyze us, stalling our productivity. The last of the nine fruits Paul mentions in Galatians 5 is the fruit of "self-control" (v. 23). How often tensions are created in some homes because the husband or wife is indolent. House chores are left undone simply because one or the other is too slothful to do what needs to be done. Some families suffer because the father is irresponsible; he won't work or he can't keep a job. The apostle had no sympathy for such: "If anyone is not willing to work, let him not eat" (2 Thess. 3:10). Paul presented himself as a model to the early Christians as a person of industry, one with an excellent work ethic: "For you yourselves know how you ought to imitate us, because we were not idle when we were with you ..." (2 Thess. 3:7).

No one could rightfully charge the Son of Man with being a lazy person; he was always engaged in his Father's business. Hopefully, others will witness the same about you. The wise man calls us to look to the tiny ant as an example of diligence and industriousness. Some things won't get done, unless we do them. Idleness will kill God's life in us. God calls us to redeem the time, not waste it. Some of us need to confess the sin of slothfulness.

"Not What My Hands Have Done"

*But when the goodness and loving kindness of God our Savior
appeared, he saved us, not because of works done by
us in righteousness, but according to his own mercy, by the
washing of regeneration and renewal of the Holy Spirit, whom
he poured out on us richly through Jesus Christ our Savior.*
Titus 3:4-6

Horatius Bonar (1808-1889) was called "the prince of Scottish hymn writers." At his memorial service, a minister said of Bonar's hymn writing: "His hymns were written in very varied circumstances, sometimes timed by the tinkling brook that babbled near him; sometimes attuned to the ordered tramp of the ocean, whose crested waves broke on the beach by which he wandered; sometimes set to the rude music of the railway train that hurried him to the scene of duty; sometimes measured by the silent rhythm of the midnight stars that shone above him."* Whenever and wherever he wrote, this minister, author, and poet was continually thinking God's thoughts.

*Not what my hands have done can save my guilty soul;
Not what my toiling flesh has borne can make my spirit whole.
Not what I feel or do can give me peace with God;
Not all my prayers and sighs and tears can bear my awful load.*

*Your voice alone, O Lord, can speak to me of grace;
Your power alone, O Son of God, can all my sin erase.
No other work but Yours, no other blood will do;
No strength but that which is divine can bear me safely through.*

*Thy work alone, O Christ, can ease this weight of sin;
Thy blood alone, O Lamb of God, can give me peace within.
Thy love to me, O God, not mine, O Lord, to Thee,
Can rid me of this dark unrest, and set my spirit free.*

*I bless the Christ of God; I rest on love divine;
And with unfaltering lip and heart I call this Savior mine.
His cross dispels each doubt; I bury in His tomb
Each thought of unbelief and fear, each lingering shade of gloom.*

*I praise the God of grace; I trust His truth and might;
He calls me His, I call Him mine, my God, my joy and light.
'Tis He Who saveth me, and freely pardon gives;
I love because He loveth me, I live because He lives.***

Dependence

"Whoever abides in me and I in him, he it is that bears
much fruit, for apart from me you can do nothing."
John 15:5

The disciple of the Lord Jesus needs the constant reminder that
"apart from me you can do nothing." Our strength is in Christ alone;
apart from him, fruitfulness is a mere mirage. He who trusts in himself will, in time, discover an alien presence, as did the Apostle Peter. Our only safety is found in Jesus Christ; he is our security; he is
our strength. With this in view, William Cowper (1731-1800) wrote
the following hymn titled "Dependence."

To keep the lamp alive,
With oil we fill the bowl;
'Tis water makes the willow thrive,
And grace that feeds the soul.

The Lord's unsparing hand
Supplies the living stream;
It is not at our own command,
But still derived from Him.

Beware of Peter's word,
Nor confidently say,
"I never will deny Thee, Lord,"—
But,—"Grant I never may."

Man's wisdom is to seek
His strength in God alone;
And e'en an angel would be weak,
Who trusted in his own.

Retreat beneath his wings,
And in His grace confide!
This more exalts the King of kings
Than all your works beside.

In Jesus is our store,
Grace issues from His throne;
Whoever says, "I want no more,"
Confesses he has none.*

Is your life characterized by a total reliance on Christ alone?

The Sunrise from on High

*"Blessed be the Lord God of Israel ... with which
the Sunrise from on high will visit us ..."*
Luke 1:68, 77-78 NASB

My family knows how much I enjoy viewing sunrises. Whether the sun rises to a cloudless or cloudy sky, I enjoy them all, in every season of the year. I have seen sunrises on the Atlantic Ocean, Mediterranean and Galilean Seas, and the Superior, Michigan and Huron lakes. I have exulted in the beauty of God's creation as I have watched the sun rise over the Canadian and American Rockies, and in many other sites. I always make it a point when traveling, to view the sunrise, and it is a rare day that the sun ever rises before I do.

It was only recently that it dawned on me why I enjoyed sunrises. It is because Jesus himself is called the "Sunrise" in Zechariah's prophetic song. The NASB translators rightly capitalized the word, for it specifically refers to the Sunrise as the Messiah and coming Lord as a person, the Lord Jesus Christ. What a meaningful metaphor and description of God's visible revelation and incarnation of himself—"the Sunrise from on high."

• A sunrise means a new beginning. Darkness has fled; a new day has arrived. "Blessed be the Lord God of Israel, for He has visited us and accomplished redemption for His people ..." (Luke 1:68). With the Incarnation of Jesus Christ, a new day dawned for man's redemption.

• A sunrise brings with it God's mercy. We are undeserving people, who have turned away from our Creator and Redeemer. Nonetheless, our God causes "the sun to rise on the evil and good" (Matt. 5:45). And it is "because of the tender mercy of our God" that the Sunrise has visited us with salvation (Luke 1:78).

• A sunrise portends hope. Zechariah's song is replete with anticipation and expectancy. The Sunrise will visit fallen man! There is Hope! There is a future! God will come!

• A sunrise is accompanied by light. The sun itself is light. Jesus is the light. God has given us his Sunrise "to shine upon those who sit in darkness and the shadow of death, to guide our feet into the way of peace" (Luke 1:79).

Has the Sunrise risen in your heart?

Gethsemane

*And they went to a place called Gethsemane. And he said to his
disciples, "Sit here while I pray." And he took with him Peter and
James and John, and began to be greatly distressed and troubled.*
Mark 14:32-33

When we contemplate what our Lord felt and prayed in Gethsemane, it makes one remove his shoes, for here we are on holy ground.

The word Gethsemane is derived from two Hebrew words, meaning "a place for pressing oil (or wine)." Since Gethsemane was located on the Mount of Olives, it likely had at least one olive press there, a machine which squeezed harvested olives into oil.

Before he reached Calvary, the Son of Man bore the weight of man's sin on his heart. Moreover, God's Son knew the time was at hand when he would experience momentary darkness, an hour when he could not see his Father's face nor sense his Father's presence. Soon he would cry out, "My God, my God, why have you forsaken me?" (Mark 15:34). He was facing the cross: "it was the will of the Lord to crush him" (Isa. 53:10).

In Gethsemane, our Lord was being crushed. In describing that night, the Evangelists use the words "greatly distressed"; "troubled"; "very sorrowful even to death"; and "agony." Luke records that Jesus at that hour, "being in an agony he prayed more earnestly; and his sweat became like great drops of blood falling down to the ground. Samuel Stennett (1727-1795) had it right when he wrote,

*No mortal can with Him compare
Among the sons of men.**

Frederick W. Faber (1814-1863) urged believers to remember Gethsemane when facing temptation.

*Ever when tempted, make me see,
Beneath the olives' moon pierced shade,
My God, alone, outstretched, and bruised,
And bleeding, on the earth He made;
And make me feel it was my sin,
As though no other sins there were,
That was to Him Who bears the world
A load that He could scarcely bear.***

The Cross (part 1)

For the word of the cross is folly to those who are perishing,
but to us who are being saved it is the power of God.
1 Corinthians 1:18

The cross of Christ is at the very heart of the gospel and the Christian faith. Without the cross, there is no salvation. Without the cross, there is no forgiveness of sins. Without the cross, there is no reconciliation. Without the cross, we have no gospel to proclaim.

If we remove the cross from the pulpit, our theology, and the hymnal, we are left with nothing but human wisdom and a religion of self-righteousness—the foolishness and stumbling block with which the Greeks and unbelieving Jews of Paul's day were afflicted: "For Jews demand signs and Greeks seek wisdom, but we preach Christ crucified, a stumbling block to Jews and folly to Gentiles, but to those who are called, both Jews and Greeks, Christ the power of God and the wisdom of God" (1 Cor. 1:22-24).

If we glory in anything but what God did in and through the cross, we are glorying in ourselves and what man can do through self-effort and human works. The Apostle Paul's religious credentials were as impressive as anyone's—credentials he once boasted in, credentials in which he at one time trusted (see Phil. 3:3-11). However, there came a day when this self-righteous religious fanatic met the Christ of the cross. Suddenly, he was stripped of self-achievements and his own righteousness. So radical was his transformed change of thinking after meeting the living Christ, he would later write, "But far be it from me to boast except in the cross of our Lord Jesus Christ, by which the world has been crucified to me, and I to the world" (Gal. 6:14).

What God in Christ did on that unique cross over two thousand years ago changed human history. And it will change every person who embraces the One who offered himself as the sinner's substitutionary sacrifice.

The message of the cross is God's power at work—to those "who are being saved." Let's believe it, preach it, and sing it!

The Cross (part 2)

In Christ God was reconciling the world to himself,
not counting their trespasses against them, and
entrusting to us the message of reconciliation.
2 Corinthians 5:19

God took the religious community by surprise when he used a cross, the death of Christ, to provide atonement for man's sins. There were veiled hints, coming through the Old Covenant prophets, as to what God's ultimate and perfect *instrument* of salvation would look like—for example, in passages like Isaiah 53:5: "But he was pierced for our transgressions; he was crushed for our iniquities; upon him was the chastisement that brought us peace, and with his wounds we are healed."

However, we now have the advantage of looking back at Isaiah's prophecy of the Suffering Servant. For those who heard and read about this Suffering Servant, a veil covered their eyes, a veil of unbelief: "For to this day, when they read the old covenant, that same veil remains unlifted, because only through Christ is it taken away. Yes, to this day whenever Moses is read a veil lies over their hearts. But when one turns to the Lord, the veil is removed" (2 Cor. 3:14-16).

The unbelieving Jews were always in search of some miraculous sign: "for Jews demand signs" (1 Cor. 1:22). Their history was well-known and well-rehearsed for generations. They gloried, and often repeated, how Yahweh delivered their forefathers from Egyptian bondage by miraculously opening the Red Sea. They exulted in Yahweh's appearance on Sinai, providing them with the Ten Holy Words. And, of course, there were the manna and quail that sustained their ancestors for forty years in the wilderness. These were amazing signs—signs of their uniqueness as the people of God, signs that Yahweh was present among them.

But a cross, a death—the death of their promised Messiah as the means of their salvation? Incomprehensible! Unimaginable!

And yet, it was so. This was God's method; this was God's plan: God's Son, nailed to a cross; Christ's blood, shed on a cross. "In Christ God was reconciling the world to himself."

This is the "message of reconciliation."

The Cross (part 3)

For Christ did not send me to baptize but to
preach the gospel, and not with words of eloquent
wisdom, lest the cross of Christ be emptied of its power.
1 Corinthians 1:17

Early in his ministry, Billy Graham returned to his room after preaching to a large audience in the city of Dallas. He felt defeated; there had not been the usual response at the close of the service he was used to seeing. When sharing his concerns with one of his crusade partners about the apparent meager results, the man said to the famed evangelist: "Billy, you failed to take the people to the cross; you failed to preach the cross."

Our adversary Satan hates the cross, despises the cross. He hates and despises the cross because of what took place there—the redemption of mankind. Satan did his best to keep Christ from going to the cross, even speaking through one of Christ's disciples. Jesus, having announced his intention to go to Jerusalem and be killed at the hands of the Jewish leaders, Peter responded, "Far be it from you, Lord! This shall never happen to you." Jesus immediately discerned Satan using one of his disciples and rebuked Peter: "Get behind me, Satan! You are a hindrance to me. For you are not setting your mind on the things of God, but on the things of man" (Matt. 16:22-23). Satan despises the cross!

The Apostle Paul understood that it was not only necessary that he preach the cross, but it was important as to *how* he preached it. The Greeks of Paul's day exulted in human oratory. *How* these men delivered their orations was as important as *what* they spoke. Paul was not a polished speaker. He neither depended on human wisdom nor studied orations in presenting the gospel message. He preached the cross with simplicity and power. In writing to the Thessalonian Church, he said, "Our gospel came to you not only in word, but also in power and in the Holy Spirit and with full conviction" (1 Thess. 1:5).

There is a kind of preaching that impresses the unregenerate, but is empty of God's power. When the preacher *trusts* in his own eloquence, delivery, and research, the cross of Christ is "emptied of its power." We are in need of power!

Called to Holiness

As obedient children, do not be conformed to the passions of your former
ignorance, but as he who called you is holy, you also be holy in all your
conduct, since it is written, "You shall be holy, for I am holy."
1 Peter 1:14-16

God is holy—in his total personhood, and in all his ways and works. In using the metaphor "light" for God's holiness, the beloved apostle wrote, "God is light and in him is no darkness at all" (1 John 1:5). God is absolutely and perfectly holy: "in him is no darkness at all."

Because God is who he is—a holy God—he calls his people in every age to a holy life. The Holy Spirit, through the Apostle Peter, delivered this call to the first-century believers, citing God's call to Israel centuries before: "As obedient children, do not be conformed to the passions of your former ignorance, but as he who called you is holy, you also be holy in all your conduct, since it is written, 'You shall be holy, for I am holy.'"

God is calling each of us to be a wholehearted, totally devoted disciple of the Lord Jesus Christ—from the inside out. Atonement has been made by the once-for-all sacrificial death of Christ on the cross; our Lord has risen from the dead and is presently interceding for us as our Great High Priest; and the Holy Spirit has been given to indwell all born-from-above believers.

Sin is the only barrier to this call to holiness being effectively realized in our heart and conduct. If we are in earnest about being a follower of the Lord Jesus, we must be willing to confront and put away everything that impedes our walk with God: "let us also lay aside every encumbrance and the sin which so easily entangles us" (Heb. 12:1 NASB). And we must actively and daily pursue God's call: "walk by the Spirit, and you will not gratify the desires of the flesh" (Gal. 5:16).

According to the Apostle Peter, to "be holy" is to walk in non-conformity to sinful passions: "do not be conformed to the passions of your former ignorance."

Are you pursuing your high calling in Christ Jesus?

Forsaking All

*"If anyone would come after me, let him deny
himself and take up his cross and follow me."*
Mark 8:34

In the allegory of John Bunyan's (1628-1688) *Pilgrim's Progress*,
we meet an unconverted man living in the "City of Destruction"
with his family, holding "a Book in his hand with a great Burden on
his back." When he began to read the Book "he wept and trembled."
Not knowing what to do, he goes home and gathers his family, announcing, "O, my dear wife, ... and you the children of my bowels, I,
your dear friend, am in myself undone by reason of a burden that
lieth hard upon me; moreover, I am certainly informed that this our
city will be burnt with fire from heaven; in which fearful overthrow,
both myself, with thee my wife, and you my sweet babes, shall miserably come to ruin, except (the which yet I see not) some way of
escape can be found whereby we may be delivered."

Believing her husband, and the father of her children, was delu-
sional, his wife quickly put him to bed. However, that night and following days did not alter the man's internal trauma. In the kind
providence of God, he finally meets an evangelist of the gospel one
day, and inquires as to what he should do. Whereupon the evangelist gave the seeker a "Parchment Roll, and there was written within, "'Fly from the wrath to come.'" Wishing to know where he
should flee to, "Evangelist, (pointing with his finger over a very
wide field,) 'Do you see yonder wicket-gate?' The man said, 'No.'
Then said the other, 'Do you see yonder shining light?' He said, 'I
think I do.' Then said Evangelist, 'Keep that light in your eye, and
go up directly thereto, so shalt thou see the gate; at which, when
thou knockest, it shall be told thee what thou shalt do.'"

Immediately the man, though carrying a heavy load upon his
back, "began to run." Even so, he had no sooner left his house when
"his Wife and Children perceiving it, began to cry after him to return; but the Man put his fingers to his ears, and ran on crying,
'Life! Life! Eternal Life!'"

The cross of Christ is our only safety. Let us flee to Christ and
be saved. Christ is our life; only Christ is our security.

Just Forgiven?

To the church of God that is in Corinth, to those
sanctified in Christ Jesus, called to be saints.
1 Corinthians 1:2

Christians in every age have to grapple with the ethical implications of being a follower of the Lord Jesus Christ. Authentic disciples of Christ are taught both by Word and Spirit, that there is an ongoing price to be paid to walk in fellowship and obedience to the Lord Jesus: the "gate is narrow" (Matt. 7:13). But repeatedly church-goers are told in effect, by the pulpit, "Dear friends, our loving and merciful Father in heaven doesn't expect you to be holy, to live holy. Be careful that you don't take your Christianity too seriously. After all, there was only one Person who ever walked this earth who was perfect, and that wasn't you. You're not perfect—just forgiven!" Having heard this repeatedly from a shepherd of the sheep week after week, the average believer understandably leaves the church affirmed in his or her sinning.

In commenting on the folk theology slogan that "Christian's aren't perfect—just forgiven," the late Southern Baptist philosopher and writer, Dallas Willard (1935-2013), wrote, "Well, it certainly needs to be said that Christians are forgiven. And it needs to be said that forgiveness does not depend on being perfect. But is that really what the slogan communicates? Unfortunately, it is not. What the slogan really conveys is that forgiveness alone is what Christianity is all about, what is genuinely essential to it.

"It says that you can have a faith in Christ that brings forgiveness, while in every other respect your life is no different from that of others who have no faith in Christ at all. This view so pleasingly presented on bumpers and trinkets has deep historical roots. It is by now worked out in many sober tomes of theology, lived out by multitudes of those who sincerely self-identify as Christians."*

Our Adversary has insidiously and pervasively deluded many of our pulpits and pews into believing the only difference between Christians and non-Christians is that they have been forgiven: "Don't trouble yourselves about a so-called biblical call to holiness. Who do you think you are—a *saint*?!"

A Sanctified Heart

Now may the God of peace himself sanctify you completely, and may your whole spirit and soul and body be kept blameless at the coming of our Lord Jesus Christ. He who calls you is faithful; he will surely do it.
1 Thessalonians 5:23-24

It is a terrible neglect within the church when many of her teachers and scholars relegate the doctrine of sanctification to only a matter of *consecration*. It is true that all believers—at the moment of re-generation—have been "sanctified in Christ Jesus" (1 Cor. 1:2), that is, set apart by God to live a holy life. It is also true that all believers should make a full consecration of themselves to God (see Rom. 12:1-2). However, Paul is speaking of something more than conse-cration in 1 Thessalonians 5:23. Here, it is not God setting us apart to live a holy life, or us making a total consecration to the Lord. Paul is speaking of what God himself desires to perform in the *heart* of each believer: "Now may the God of peace himself sanctify you com-pletely." One of our modern versions has interpreted its meaning correctly: "Now may the God of peace make you holy in every way" (NLT).

The Greek word for "completely" is found only here in the New Testament. It is a compound of two Greek words (*holos*, whole, en-tire; and *telos*, end). Paul's prayer for believers "means that the di-vine sanctification extend to every part of their being, leaving no area untouched by the pervasive power of divine holiness."*

How can any Christian be satisfied with a heart that is less than made completely holy? How can a thirsty-hearted follower of the Lord Jesus continue to reserve pockets in his life that are off-limits to the sanctifying Spirit of God? It is God's desire to make holy all interior parts of our being—intentions, imaginations, desires, voli-tions—the very fountain of our personhood: our *heart*. No, this does not imply that we cannot fail and sin; but it does mean that we are empowered to live a life that is characteristically pleasing to God— the God of peace. When the God of peace makes the interior of our life holy, this peace will displace within us disunity and disharmony, disintegration and moral disease. Holiness is spiritual health and vitality. Have you asked the Lord to give you a heart that is holy— through and through?

Clouds and Shadows

And a cloud overshadowed them, and a voice came
out of the cloud, "This is my beloved Son; listen to him."
Mark 9:7

In the Scriptures, "clouds" often accompany an epiphany, a visitation of God. Clouds appeared on Mount Sinai when Moses was given the law of God. We are told clouds will accompany the second coming of the Lord Jesus Christ. In the Mark 9 account of the transfiguration of Jesus, a cloud "overshadowed" the disciples, and "a voice came out of the cloud."

God will often come to us in a cloud; and he will speak to us in the cloud, if we will but listen. God does not intend for the clouds to harm us; he does not wish to oppress us by *cloudy* visitations. No, as our merciful Father in Heaven, he desires to use these providential clouds to speak to our situation, our turmoil, our condition, our affliction, our bewilderment, our suffering, and, yes, even to our disobedience. These clouds are not meant to crush us. God wants to use the clouds to guide us, form us, make us, and establish us. "After you have suffered for a little while, the God of all grace, who called you to His eternal glory in Christ, will Himself perfect, confirm, strengthen and establish you" (1 Peter 5:10 NASB).

Are you allowing God to speak to you in the cloud that is now overshadowing you? Remember, God brought this cloud to you for a purpose; don't waste it, listen to his voice.

We must take care that the cloud is not of our own making. In grieving the Spirit, we cause our own clouds and shadows. God's clouds produce refreshment; our clouds produce grief. The hymn writer prayed:

O may no earthborn cloud arise
To hide Thee from Thy servant's eyes. *

Whenever we are visited by a cloud, we need to ask God its source: was it sent by God, or was it caused by me and my sin? Either way, let us give attention to the voice of God speaking to us "out of the cloud."

The Fruit of Love (part 1)

But the fruit of the Spirit is love.
Galatians 5:22

The love the apostle speaks of in Galatians 5 is *agape* love, a quality of thought and action that finds its source in God alone. One does not enter this world possessing this kind of love. Only those born of God's Spirit know *agape* love and are capable of expressing the same: "God's love," writes the apostle, "has been poured into our hearts through the Holy Spirit who has been given to us" (Rom. 5:5).

Immediately before he pens his "Ode to Divine Love" in 1 Corinthians, Paul addresses the subject of spiritual gifts. There was great turmoil in the Corinthian Church on this subject. The lesser gifts were being exalted out of proportion to greater gifts. Paul gently, but candidly, informs his readers that each member of Christ's church is Spirit-gifted, and the gifts should be exercised with humility, without becoming tools for division. As important a role as spiritual gifts had in the church, Paul informed the believers, "I will show you a still more excellent way" (1 Cor. 12:31). Then he proceeds to write of that "more excellent way" in the following chapter.

Agape love, God's love, is the more excellent way. That is so because it will outlast faith and hope. It is greater than possessing the gift to speak with "prophetic powers." It is greater than having the ability to understand the mysteries of God's Word, and to exercise mountain-removing faith. Even if I'm the most benevolent person in the world and die as a martyr, if I do not demonstrate the love of Jesus, as far as God is concerned, I'm nothing, an absolute *zero*.

Agape love excels all gifts and all facets of human love, because it is not of this world. It is other-person-minded, with an eye fixed on the Lord Jesus Christ. It neither quarrels nor struts; it doesn't boast nor seek to be the first and the greatest; it serves with humility and faithfulness; it's not concerned with who gets the credit; it freely admits when in error, and graciously honors others; it believes itself to be the most unworthy of all the saints. *Agape* love is the greatest of all the gifts and graces. *Lord, fill me daily with this love, the very love of Christ.*

The Fruit of Joy (part 2)

But the fruit of the Spirit is ... joy.
Galatians 5:22

At one of our prayer services in the church I pastored a number of years ago, a seasoned Christian asked, "Pastor, where has the *joy* gone among God's people?" This dear brother grew up in the church; his parents were godly people. Then, well into his 70s, he was wondering at the absence of joy.

Approximately forty-five years after my godly mother died, I was back home visiting a neighboring church one Sunday morning. After I had preached, Bill, a former member of my home church, approached me, and said this about my mother, "Ralph, I have never known a Christian with as much joy as your mother had."

The Book of Acts is a record of joy-filled followers of the risen Lord Jesus Christ. You couldn't keep those early Christians from rejoicing. They never lost their joy because they suffered and were persecuted. The fact is, right after Paul and Barnabas were driven out of a city because of preaching Christ, Luke writes, "And the disciples were filled with joy and with the Holy Spirit" (Acts 13:52).

Full-of-the-Spirit disciples are disciples filled with the joy of the Lord. Spirit-cleansed disciples are full disciples—full of the fruit of joy. If God's people are not living with the fullness of joy, it could be they need to make some adjustment in their lives. You cannot be full of the Spirit without being full of joy. The writer of the Book of Hebrews says of God's Son, "You have loved righteousness and hated wickedness; therefore God, your God, has anointed you with the oil of gladness beyond your companions" (Heb. 1:9).

"The oil of gladness"! That is precisely what the church needs. And that is what the church will experience when she quits making excuses for her sinning. Sin and joy are antithetical to each other; where sin lives joy must leave.

What is the answer we can give to the brother who asked, "Pastor, where has the joy gone among God's people?" The answer is simple: "The joy left when we chose to sin. The joy left when we failed to walk in the Spirit."

Does Christ's joy permeate your life? It can't be manufactured, you know.

The Fruit of Peace (part 3)

But the fruit of the Spirit is ... peace.
Galatians 5:22

The Bible speaks of the "peace with God" and the "peace of God." The first peace occurs when the repentant sinner enters a new relationship with God: "Therefore, since we have been justified by faith, we have peace with God through our Lord Jesus Christ" (Rom. 5:1). Enmity between God and the new convert is gone, made possible by the atoning death of Christ. The second peace spoken of is a result of the indwelling of the Holy Spirit. All believers experience this peace at the point of their spiritual birth, but as with each of the Spirit's fruits, it is not as fully developed in the hearts of many of God's people as it could be. That is why we have a prayer like this of the apostle: "Now may the Lord of peace himself give you peace at all times in every way" (2 Thess. 3:16).

Christians can be robbed of their peace because of fretting and worrying. Anxiety is a real emotion, and one experienced by many believers. But does God want us to be anxious? Of course not. When anxiety overtakes us, peace leaves. What should we do when troubling thoughts enter our mind? Embrace the apostle's exhortation: "Do not be anxious about anything, but in everything by prayer and supplication with thanksgiving let your requests be made known to God. And the peace of God, which surpasses all understanding, will guard your hearts and your minds in Christ Jesus" (Phil. 4:6-7).

Imagine that—peace as a "guard"—God's peace guarding our hearts and minds! How can Christian's weather life's storms? By worrying about nothing, praying about everything, and giving God thanks in all circumstances.

I love the words of Haldor Lillenas (1885-1959).

Oh, the peace that Jesus gives
Never dies; it always lives.
Like the music of a psalm,
Like a glad, eternal calm,
Is the peace that Jesus gives,
Is the peace that Jesus gives.*

May this fruit abound more and more in Christ's Church!

The Fruit of Patience (part 4)

But the fruit of the Spirit is ... patience.
Galatians 5:22

When our daughter Julie was quite young, she had for a playmate one of our neighbors. Whenever they were playing together and Julie acted impatiently, the little boy would tell Julie, "Patience is a virtue." It is that and more. The patience the Bible speaks of is a product of the Holy Spirit. The Scriptures speak of patience in a variety of ways; the following are a few examples.

We are to be patient with one another. Paul urges Christians to "walk ... with all humility and gentleness, with *patience*, bearing with one another in love" (Eph. 4:2). Patience is required when we disagree with each other, when provoked by others, and when another's perceived or real weaknesses are annoying to us. Anger aimed at another person in the body of Christ is a failure to exercise the patience of Christ toward our brother and sister. No matter how hurtful and unpleasant another's behavior is toward us, if we fail to respond with genuine patience, we have failed in our witness.

We are to imitate the patience of former saints. The writer of Hebrews encouraged his readers to remember the lives of the Old Covenant worthies, who demonstrated remarkable patience as they awaited the fulfillment of God's promises: "so that you may not be sluggish, but imitators of those who through faith and *patience* inherit the promises" (Heb. 6:12). Human nature wants to intervene when God wants us to wait his time. Abraham did not "waver concerning the promise of God, but he grew strong in his faith as he gave glory to God" (Rom. 4:20).

Pastors are to minister with patience. Those who oversee the spiritual life of the local church, sometimes forget that not all believers are living spiritually mature lives. Furthermore, there will be those who need to be confronted over conspicuous sinful attitudes and behavior. Paul's advice to Timothy was "preach the word; be ready in season and out of season; reprove, rebuke, and exhort, with complete *patience* and teaching" (2 Tim. 4:2).

God will grow the fruit of patience in us—with our cooperation; he often uses trials in order to perfect our patience.

The Fruit of Kindness (part 5)

But the fruit of the Spirit is ... kindness.
Galatians 5:22

To be kind is to be sympathetic and forbearing in spirit, to be thoughtful and considerate.

Inconsiderate Christianity is not only a paradox and possibility, but too often a *reality*. Christians don't always act like they love each other, and possibly they don't! Francis A. Schaeffer (1912-1984) once wrote: "I have observed one thing among true Christians in their differences in many countries: What divides and severs true Christian groups and Christians—what leaves a bitterness that can last for 20, 30 or 40 years ... is not the issue of doctrine or belief which caused the differences in the first place. Invariably, it is a lack of love—and the bitter things that are said by true Christians in the midst of their differences. These stick in the mind like glue."*

Yes, a lack of observable love will always "stick in the mind like glue." If the Lord Jesus behaved toward others in any way while he walked upon this earth, it was in a loving consideration toward others.

Kindness is shown in the choice of words we use in speaking to one another, and the attitude in which they are spoken. I recall my godly mother singing a little jingle whenever she heard children quarrel—which was often:

Kind words will never die, never die, never die.
Kind words will never die, no never die.

In 1965, my father died suddenly of a heart attack. Following my conversion in 1961, I made necessary apologies to my stepmother for the bitter feelings I had harbored toward her. However, when my father passed away, I was tempted to think unkindly about her again. I'll never forget the Scripture the Holy Spirit used to check this temptation: "Be kind to one another, tenderhearted, forgiving one another, as God in Christ forgave you" (Eph. 4:32).

Instead of unkindness, may the fruit of kindness characterize our words and our actions. When the Spirit is in control, kindness will inevitably prevail.

The Fruit of Goodness (part 6)

But the fruit of the Spirit is ... goodness.
Galatians 5:22

I recall hearing one of my theological mentors say that before his conversion to Christ, while still a young man, he possessed a strong desire to be *good* but didn't know how. Without Christ indwelling us by his Spirit, all appearances of goodness are merely superficial, because they don't spring from a good heart. I think we forget this sometimes, when making references to a variety of people in our respective circles. Only a heart made good by God is capable of performing deeds that he counts as good—a goodness untainted by selfishness and impure motives.

When unsaved people perform works that can be called good, it is only because the image of God has not been completely effaced in them. Yes, the sinner is totally depraved—*extensively*, but not *intensively*. Meaning, every faculty of his being has been affected by the fall; however, he is not totally depraved *intensively*, for a sinner is capable of behaving civilly and even admirably (of course, any good the sinner does is without merit, as well as any good a Christian performs).

Luke noted that Barnabas was a "good man" (Acts 11:24). Because we have reason to believe that Luke knew Barnabas personally, and because he had a close friendship with those who also knew Barnabas well, including the Apostle Paul, Luke could make such a claim.

In the Book of Acts, Luke joins Paul at some point in Philippi (Acts 16:10). By this time, Barnabas and Paul had a strong disagreement with regard to taking Mark with them on a missionary expedition, and as a result initiated separate campaigns (Acts 15:36-41). Nonetheless, when Luke writes the Acts' story, whatever occurred between the two, never tainted Barnabas' reputation. Because writing years later, Luke calls Barnabas "a good man, full of the Holy Spirit and of faith." A man can disagree strongly with a brother in Christ, and yet maintain a reputation for being a good person, one who is full of the Holy Spirit and faith.

The church and the world need more people like Barnabas—good people, from the inside out.

April 8

The Fruit of Faithfulness (part 7)

But the fruit of the Spirit is ... faithfulness.
Galatians 5:22

To be considered *faithful* means to loyally carry out the responsibilities assigned to us—whether going about our daily duties or fulfilling our obligations to the Lord in Kingdom work. God calls each of us to be true—to him and to one another. In John Bunyan's (1628 -1688) *Pilgrim's Progress*, the one companion soon joining Christian after he fled the City of Destruction was a man by the name of Faithful. Sadly, Christian did not always prove to be faithful in his journey toward the Celestial City, as is the case with many of us. However, by the grace of God, he did persevere.

God commends the grace of faithfulness in his people. Peter called Silvanus "a faithful brother"; Paul said Timothy was "his faithful child," and that Tychicus and Epaphras were faithful ministers of the Lord Jesus Christ; and Onesimus was a "faithful and beloved brother" (1 Pet. 5:12; 1 Cor. 4:17; Eph. 6:21; Col. 1:7; 4:9). The writer of the Book of Hebrews says of Jesus, that he "was faithful to him who appointed him, just as Moses also was faithful in all God's house" (Heb. 3:2).

Mennonite minister, educator, and author John M. Drescher shared the following poignant anecdote on the fruit of faithfulness. Peter Ainslie III (1867-1934) writes: "I shall never forget the first time I saw Poynter's great picture 'Faithful unto Death' in the Walker Art Gallery in Liverpool. There stood the Roman guard on duty while the palace was falling into ruins during the destruction of Herculaneum. The dead were lying in the background; others were falling onto the pavement amid the red-hot eruptions of Vesuvius; everyone who could was fleeing for his life. The Roman guard might have made his escape, but there he stood like a marble statue, preferring to remain at his post faithful unto death. The picture clung to me like an individual—not simply the man standing at his post of duty but the expression of faithfulness that showed in his countenance. I have thought of it a hundred times since, and I have felt its influence as I have felt that of a living person."*

God's challenge to each of us is: "Be faithful unto death, and I will, give you the crown of life" (Rev. 2:10).

The Fruit of Gentleness (part 8)

But the fruit of the Spirit is ... gentleness.
Galatians 5:22, 23

The Apostle Paul exhorts believers in Colossians 3:12 to "put on ... *gentleness*" (NASB). He uses the same word in Galatians 6:1, where he directs mature believers to restore failing believers "in a spirit of *gentleness*." Earlier in Galatians, he informs us that *gentleness* is a product of the Spirit (5:23).

Sometimes it is easier to see the meaning of a word by looking at its opposite in action. The late New Testament Greek scholar, William Barclay (1907-1978), in commenting on the essence of the grace of gentleness shares an anecdote describing what it is not. "Sir Joshua Reynolds said of Dr. Johnson: 'The most light and airy dispute was with him a dispute in the *arena*. He fought on every occasion as if his whole reputation depended upon the victory of the minute, and he fought with all his weapons. If he was foiled in an argument, he had recourse to abuse and rudeness.' After a vivid night at the Crown and Anchor, Johnson said contentedly to Boswell: 'Well, we had a good talk.' To which Boswell dutifully replied: 'Yes, sir, you tossed and gored several persons.'"

Clearly, Samuel Johnson (1709-1784) and the grace of gentleness were strangers to each other. However, by keeping our eyes fastened on Jesus, and being filled with the very presence of Christ himself, we will become more and more gentle people. By our doing so, the church and the world will be the beneficiaries. The Master himself is our perfect example of gentleness: "Take my yoke upon you, and learn from me, for I am *gentle* and lowly in heart, and you will find rest for your souls" (Matt. 11:29).

A Bible scholar said of a certain prominent minister, that he much preferred hearing the man disagree with others on a conference floor, rather than listening to some other people with whom he happened to agree. Why? He said it was because of the *gentle* way in which the brother disagreed.

April 10

The Fruit of Self-Control (part 9)

But the fruit of the Spirit is ... self-control.
Galatians 5:22, 23

Before the gospel arrived at Crete, the island was inhabited by typical pagans. We catch a glimpse of the average kind of person Titus dealt with in his ministry there by reading Paul's letter addressed to him. The Cretans generally were anything but self-controlled people: sexual immorality and depravity in every degree were commonplace. Noting the pervasive moral degradation of these people, the apostle quotes one of their own authors that acknowledged the "Cretans are always liars, evil beasts, lazy gluttons" (1:12). Paul immediately follows up by writing, "This testimony is true" (1:13). The Cretans and the modern world appear to have a lot of similarities.

Many lives had been wonderfully transformed by God's saving grace by the time Paul wrote to Titus. The apostle directs Titus to appoint men as spiritual overseers of the church, and he is very specific about the character qualities and behavior each man must possess. One attribute a leader must have is the fruit of *self-control*: "For an overseer, as God's steward, must be above reproach. He must not be arrogant or quick-tempered or a drunkard or violent or greedy for gain, but ... *self-controlled*, upright, holy, and disciplined" (1:7-8). Imagine—from this godless culture, there were soon candidates for eldership.

However, the fruit of self-control is not only essential for church leaders; it is to be actively present and growing in the life of every believer. God calls each of us to be self-controlled in every area of our life: sexual conduct, eating habits, and the use of time and money; the way we speak, act, react, and interact; how we use our leisure time, and how we control every natural passion and desire. One of the most striking analogies we have in Scripture of the grace and fruit of self-control is Paul's reference to an athlete: "Every athlete exercises self-control in all things. They do it to receive a perishable wreath, but we an imperishable" (1 Cor. 9:25).

God will use us in remarkable ways, as the Spirit enables us to live a life of self-control.

The Fruit of the Spirit—in Summary (part 10)

But the fruit of the Spirit is ...
Galatians 5:22

It is important that we keep a few things in mind as we think and discuss the fruit of the Spirit Paul speaks of in Galatians 5:22-23.

We need to remember the context in which this was written. Paul begins this Spirit-fruit passage with the conjunction "but." He contrasts the fruit of the Spirit with "the works of the flesh" (5:19), which are produced when the "desires of the flesh" are gratified (5:16). He identifies many of these fleshly works and concludes the list by adding, "things like these" (5:19-21). In other words, this list is not exhaustive. These expressions of the "flesh" (man's fallen sinfulness) Paul calls "works." They are *self*-produced; they are actions, which result from *self*-centeredness, gratifying our fallen passions instead of walking in the Holy Spirit.

God's answer to self-producing sinful attitudes and behavior is to walk—one step after another—under the control of the Holy Spirit. Impossible? Not with God. Do you belong to Jesus? By the strength of God, have you crucified the flesh? Following the list of the fruit of the Spirit in verses 22-23, Paul adds in verse 24, "And those who belong to Christ Jesus have crucified the flesh with its passions and desires."

Having said that, we must say also if we fail to "keep in step with the Spirit" (5:25), we disappoint God and grieve the Holy Spirit; repentance will return us to keeping in step.

A final thought: This fruit should not be viewed in isolation from each other; they belong together. We should think of them like a cluster of grapes. When the Holy Spirit enters his temple (our body), he immediately goes about producing his fruit in and through us—after all, this fruit is called the fruit of the *Spirit*. As we yield to the Holy Spirit's control—in his cleansing, sanctifying, refining, disciplining ministries—he will increasingly transform us into the image of Christ (see 2 Cor. 3:18).

Both the church and the world are in need of Christians, who are beautiful, symmetrical products of the Spirit's own making. Surrender to the heavenly Vinedresser if you desire to be one of them.

April 12

The Valley of Baca

As they go through the Valley of Baca they make it a place of springs.
Psalm 84:6

We have to make some critical choices in life. One of those recurrent decisions will involve how we respond to difficulties, trials, suffering, and affliction.

The valley the psalmist speaks of has been lost to history; we don't know its particular geographical location. What we do know is that it was generally an arid place, a waterless location. Only infrequently did the rains fall in the Baca Valley.

The Valley of Baca is a metaphor for life's spiritually *difficult times.* Anyone who has walked with God knows all about this *valley.* In visiting this valley, one may be plagued with doubts, as John the Baptist once was. Or, while there, the pilgrim may be given a "thorn" that will accompany him for the remainder of his life, which was the case for Paul. For some, they lose everything that is near and dear to them, as Job did. For others, Yahweh will take them to the "backside" of the desert, until his glory can be revealed, as he did with Moses.

The question is not, Will there be valleys? The question is: How will we respond to these valleys?

I recently read again a biographical account of the venerable Jonathan Edwards (1703-1758), one of God's instruments in the Great Evangelical Awakening during the eighteenth century. Following years of a fruitful pastoral ministry in Northampton, Massachusetts, Edwards was dismissed from his pulpit by a congregational vote of 200 to 23. Though he was offered attractive pulpits, he felt called to labor as a missionary among the Housatonic Indians. It was during those six years, among these Native Americans, serving in a little noticed place, that Edwards wrote some of his greatest works. Under God, Jonathan Edwards chose to make his Valley of Baca "a place of springs."

What are you walking through today? Is it a *valley*? If so, God wants you to find your strength in him and be renewed and refreshed. Don't let the valley break you; allow God to make you.

 April 13

Power, Faith, Accomplishments

To this end we always pray for you, that our God may ... fulfill every resolve for good and every work of faith by his power, so that the name of our Lord Jesus may be glorified in you, and you in him, according to the grace of our God and the Lord Jesus Christ.
2 Thessalonians 1:11-12

Everywhere the Apostle Paul's ministry took him, every sermon he preached, and every prayer he prayed, his primary objective was that God's name would be glorified. What holds your attention? What is your supreme objective in life? No, you're not an apostle, and you may not be engaged in a vocational ministry. No matter. What does God desire for each one us?—"That the name of our Lord Jesus may be glorified in you, and you in him ..."

How might the name of the Lord Jesus be glorified in our life, and our life be glorified in him? Within the context of 2 Thessalonians 2, the apostle provides the answer: We bring glory to Christ, and we are glorified in him, when we are given the power to accomplish all the good things which our faith prompts us to do. Paul desires this for each Thessalonian Christian; not only for the leaders, but for each person.

What is your faith prompting you to do? What are you waiting for? God wants his people to venture, to step out in faith. There are so many works of service needing to be done; and they won't get done without acting on faith and relying on the power of God.

Does God have you in a place where he can speak to you? Are you in a condition in which God can use you? Or do you first need a soul-cleansing? God can't use dirty hands and a divided heart. Sin stifles faith; sin obscures vision; sin prevents God's power from flowing through us.

Paul was always praying for believers; here he prays that "good things" would be accomplished to the glory of Christ, by the grace of God: "May he give you the power to accomplish all the good things your faith prompts you to do. Then the name of our Lord Jesus will be honored because of the way you live, and you will be honored along with him. This is all made possible because of the grace of our God and Lord, Jesus Christ" (NLT).

What is your faith prompting you to do?

April 14

Washing Feet

"If I then, your Lord and Teacher, have washed your feet, you also ought to wash one another's feet. For I have given you an example, that you also should do just as I have done to you."
John 13:14-15

While we should not quibble with those who believe Jesus institut-ed an ordinance of washing feet in John 13, we must take care lest we miss its most profound meaning: stooping to serve our brothers and sisters in Christ, no matter how menial the task.

Sin-tainted egos keep us from serving one another as Jesus served. We don't mind serving those we perceive to be great or im-portant or prominent. But to wash Simon Peter's feet? Never! After all, he denied he had any relationship with Christ. Shall we wash Thomas' feet? We can't do it, for he doubted the resurrection of Christ. What about Judas Iscariot? No way! He goes down in histo-ry as the infamous betrayer.

And yet, Jesus stooped to serve Simon Peter, Thomas and Ju-das, along with nine others. All had dirty feet. All were imperfect believers. All had sinned and were falling short of the glory of God.

We can't "pick and choose" the one we should serve—at least we should not. Our sovereign Lord brings into our circle those he wants us to serve. Do we resist? Are pride and a hard heart keeping me from stooping? Is it beneath us to inconvenience ourselves to take the time?

While our spiritual gifts vary, each gift is given by God to be used in service of others: "As each has received a gift, use it to serve one another, as good stewards of God's varied grace" (1 Pet. 4:10). Oswald Chambers (1874-1917) said, "The real test of the saint is not preaching the gospel, but washing disciples' feet; that is, do-ing the things that do not count in the actual estimate of men but count everything in the estimate of God."*

Who was it who washed feet in John 13? Our Lord and Teacher! If our Lord and Teacher stooped to serve, the servant is not above his Lord. Whose feet is the Spirit calling you to wash? Let's serve the servants of Christ with joy, as Jesus did.

Aspirations for Old Age

So even to old age and gray hairs, O God, do not forsake me, until I proclaim your might to another generation, your power to all those to come.
Psalm 71:18

As one approaches the sunset years of life, an assortment of concerns compete for attention: financial security, health, children and grandchildren, etc. As he reflects on end-of-life concerns in Psalm 71, the writer expresses two matters close to his heart.

First, the psalmist desires Yahweh's presence: "O God, do not forsake me." He expresses the same sentiment in verse 9: "Do not cast me off in the time of old age; forsake me not when my strength is spent." Frequently in the declining years, some saints become anxious about God's nearness—whether or not he is present with them. The truth written by John Rippon (1751-1836) has cheered the hearts of many doubting saints. It is the promise contained in Isaiah 46:4: "Even to your old age I am he, and to gray hairs I will carry you."

> *Even down to old age all My people shall prove*
> *My sovereign, eternal, unchangeable love;*
> *And when hoary hairs shall their temples adorn,*
> *Like lambs they shall still in My bosom be borne.*

Second, the author is thinking of others. Often as people grow older, their world becomes quite small; the tendency is to turn inward, thinking of ourselves. Such was not the case with the psalmist as he thought about his future. He was thinking of a future generation, of those who would follow him: "O God, do not forsake me, *until* I proclaim your might to another generation, your power to all those to come."

Because the psalmist was accustomed to talking about God's mighty works—"O God, from my youth you have taught me, and I still proclaim your wondrous deeds"—we have good reason to assume that his aspirations were fulfilled in old age.

What fills your mind as you think about old age? Do you desire God's nearness? Do you desire to proclaim God's might and power to all who will listen?

Reconciled Brothers

But Esau ran to meet him and embraced him and
fell on his neck and kissed him, and they wept.
Genesis 33:4

It grieves the Holy Spirit whenever a fissure occurs between broth-ers and sisters in Christ. Soon before he offered his life as a ransom for all, our Lord's prayer-burden was that his church would be char-acterized by oneness in love, truth, and fellowship. Jesus said such unity reflected that of the One-in-Three God: "that they may be one even as we are one" (John 17:22). There never has been a time when any member of the holy Trinity was out of harmony with another member; they have been one from eternity past, and will remain one into all eternity future.

Jacob and Esau had problems from the start. Their father Isaac preferred Esau over Jacob, and their mother doted on Jacob. Early on the boys began to squabble, with Jacob eventually stealing Esau's birthright. Receiving Isaac's greater blessing, Esau becomes enraged; Jacob flees for his life. Then some twenty years pass when Jacob has a sudden encounter with God—and begins to think seri-ously about Esau, his estranged brother. God was working on Esau as well, for the angelic messengers informed Jacob: "We came to your brother Esau, and he is coming to meet you, and there are four hundred men with him" (Gen. 32:6).

Jacob is fearful because he thinks Esau is planning revenge, so he goes to prayer, wrestling with God. Jacob is changed. He leaves that holy event and meets his brother, not knowing what the out-come will be. However, God has been working on Esau as well. When the formerly alienated brothers meet, they don't rehash the past; they don't argue who was right and who was wrong. They em-brace and weep, and try to outdo one another with generosity. The once conniving Jacob insisted: "Please, if I have found favor in your sight, then accept my present from my hand. For I have seen your face, which is like seeing the face of God, and you have accepted me" (Gen. 33:10).

In the words of the psalmist, "Behold, how good and pleasant it is when brothers dwell in unity!" (Psa. 133:1). Is God calling you to initiate reconciliation with someone?

April 17

Paths of Righteousness

He leads me in paths of righteousness for his name's sake.
Psalm 23:3

While recently walking past a department store, I noticed at the rear of the clothing section a large sign which read, "Find the path." There was an immediate response in my soul, "Glory be to God; I have found the *path*, for my God has shown to me the *right path*."

I read some time ago where a popular new-age motivational speaker said, "Most of the people who come to me for coaching on finding their purpose and having more passion in their lives, are stuck because they are trying to choose the *right* path. If this is true for you too, then let me let you off the hook: There is no *right* path."

This is the kind of philosophy to life being promoted in our fallen culture, and the advice millions are falling prey to. The counsel of a marketing campaign is to "Find the path"; the pathetic advice of a life coach—a coach who advocates deadly advice instead of life-giving counsel—is to tell his audience and followers: "There is no *right* path."

Followers of him who said, "I am the way" know better. Having been redeemed and rescued by the Lamb of God who takes away the sin of the world, even our sin, we are no longer groping in the darkness, trying to find the right path. Jesus is the Light, the Light who leads us "in paths of righteousness for his name's sake." The Lord Jesus fills his followers with his light and holiness, and then sets them on the right paths, righteous paths.

The Bible says, "The god of this world has blinded the minds of the unbelievers, to keep them from seeing the light of the gospel of the glory of Christ, who is the image of God" (2 Cor. 4:4). In the words of Philip Bliss (1838-1876), we invite those who have yet to discover the Lord Jesus Christ:

Come to the light, 'tis shining for thee;
Sweetly the light has dawned upon me.
Once I was blind, but now I can see:
The Light of the world is Jesus!*

April 18

Our Blessed Hope

Looking for the blessed hope and glorious appearing
of our great God and Savior Jesus Christ.
Titus 2:13 NASB

"Looking," in the above text, carries with it the idea of "an eager expectation." Let's face it: It is a rare Christian in the twenty-first century who longs for the return of the Lord Jesus Christ. I should qualify that: It is a rare Christian in the *Western World* who eagerly longs for Christ's return to earth.

How long has it been since you heard a sermon on the second coming of Christ? When was the last time you were in conversation with a fellow believer that he or she said, in effect, "Won't it be wonderful when Jesus returns?" Or, "How I eagerly anticipate the return of my Lord and Savior."

Why is this? Why don't we have a passionate desire for our Lord to return for his Bride, the church? The answer should be obvious: We love this world more than we love our Lord and Savior. Those who love Christ want to be with Christ. Those whose love is cold or lukewarm, are essentially unmoved by the thought of seeing Jesus; they are too attached to this world.

The church is populated with "thorny believers"—those who have heard the Word, "but the cares of the world and the deceitfulness of riches choke the word, and it proves unfruitful" (Matt. 13:22). Jesus once warned his disciples: "But watch yourselves lest your hearts be weighed down with dissipation and drunkenness and cares of this life, and that day come upon you suddenly like a trap. For it will come upon all who dwell on the face of the whole earth. But stay awake at all times, praying that you may have strength to escape all these things that are going to take place, and to stand before the Son of Man" (Luke 21:34-36).

We are "weighed down"; we are using so much of our time and resources on foolishness, interested primarily in fleeting pleasures (the meaning of "dissipation"); we have intoxicated ourselves with the things of time.

If this is true of you, ask the Spirit of God to shake and awake you, until you count yourself among those who love the thought of "the appearing of our great God and Savior Jesus Christ."

Dark Light

"Therefore be careful lest the light in you be darkness."
Luke 11:35

"Light" in Scripture represents the holiness of God. For example, John writes, "God is light, and in him is no darkness at all" (1 John 1:5). The opposite of light is darkness; the opposite of holiness is evil. There is no evil in God. God is absolutely holy.

What a healthy eye is to our body, God's light is to our spirit. When God's holiness pervades our being, we are capable of seeing ourselves and this world with clarity. However, if our spirit is dark, our vision is corrupted; everything we see is affected. In our text, Jesus issues a warning: "Therefore be careful lest the light in you be darkness."

It sounds rather strange, doesn't it, that light—God's holiness and truth—is in fact "darkness" (falsehood and unreality) in some people. Such people have been exposed to the light; they have heard and seen the light, and some may have at one time embraced the light. However, at some point, light became darkness.

It makes me think of King Saul. As a young man, he was selected by God to be Israel's leader. Scripture informs us that after meeting with and being anointed by the prophet Samuel, "God changed his heart" (1 Sam. 10:9). Here was a devoted follower of Yahweh, who led Israel to great victories on the field of battle. Eventually, however, pride and impatience, disobedience and jealousy, hatred and envy, overcame the light in Saul. Darkness displaced the light; evil expelled holiness. Sadly, he fell so low that he sought a witch's counsel, when years before he tried to destroy all witches.

Though it grieves God's people, we should not be shocked whenever we hear the news of someone, who once was stalwart in the faith and evidenced a true devotion to Christ and his Word, departing from the faith and now advocating evil. How did this happen? They failed to walk in the truth of Jesus: their light is now darkness.

The antidote to light becoming darkness is to always "walk in the light as he [God] is in the light" (1 John 1:7). Are you walking in God's light, God's holiness, today?

April 20

Faith and Vision

*But Caleb quieted the people before Moses and said, "Let us go up
at once and occupy it, for we are well able to overcome it." Then
the men who had gone up with him said, "We are not able to go
up against the people, for they are stronger than we are."*
Numbers 13:30-31

Numbers 13 is the account of Moses—upon God's instructions—
selecting and sending twelve men to explore the land of Canaan, the
land promised by God to Israel as an inheritance. We are told in
Leviticus 25:38 the reason for which God delivered his people from
Egypt's bondage: "I am the Lord your God, who brought you out of
the land of Egypt to give you the land of Canaan, and to be your
God."

These enslaved people had cried to Yahweh for deliverance, and
he heard their agony, raising up a leader and performing mighty
wonders. Now they are in the wilderness, at the very threshold of
entering their promised territory. However, after surveying their
future possession, the twelve spies return with a divided verdict as
to what they saw. Ten of the men reported that indeed the land
flowed with "milk and honey," but there was a problem: they described the men they saw as "giants" and themselves as
"grasshoppers" by comparison. To them, the cities were incapable
of being defeated.

The other two men—Joshua and Caleb—saw the same people
and the same cities. However, their report was vastly different from
the majority. Caleb and Joshua said, "We are well able." The ten
protested, "We are unable" (v. 30). Here were twelve men who saw
two different realities: one was a false reality (which, in essence,
was not *real*); the other saw the *true* Reality. The ten saw as they
did, because they lacked faith in God. Caleb and Joshua saw as they
did, because they believed the God who promised.

What do you see? Are you looking through the eyes of faith or
unbelief?

Faith, mighty faith, the promise sees,
And looks to that alone;
Laughs at impossibilities,
And cries, "It shall be done!"*

Genuine Concern

For I have no one like him, who will be genuinely concerned for your
welfare. For they all seek their own interests, not those of Jesus Christ.
Philippians 2:20-21

One of the immediate results of man's fall in the Garden was a pre-occupation with himself: "they knew that they were naked. And they sewed fig leaves together and made themselves loincloths" (Gen. 3:7). Sin does that. Sin turns us inward, causing us to be primarily self-interested.

I believe it is more than coincidental that our Philippians 2:20 text is located just below the classic self-humbling passage of the Incarnate God, the Lord Jesus Christ. The apostle says of Jesus, "And being found in human form, he humbled himself by becoming obedient to the point of death, even death on a cross" (2:8). We have no greater example of servanthood and humility than the Incarnation and self-sacrifice of the Lamb of God. Without any thought of self-interest, he bore our griefs and carried our sorrows. Similarly, the Spirit exhorts believers to serve one another: "Do nothing from selfish ambition or conceit, but in humility count others more significant than yourselves" (2:3).

Paul is sitting in a Roman prison as he dictates this letter. Instead of "licking his wounds," he is thinking of the saints in Philippi, the first church he founded in Europe. He carried all the churches on his heart, but this church was especially dear to him because, as he said, "no church entered into partnership with me in giving and receiving, except you only" (4:15).

In thinking how he might encourage this church further, Paul's mind instinctively turns to his son in the gospel, Timothy, his loyal companion in Christ. "I hope in the Lord Jesus to send Timothy to you soon,.... For I have no one like him, who will be genuinely concerned for your welfare. For they all seek their own interests, not those of Jesus Christ" (2:19-21).

How many church leaders are "genuinely concerned" for the flock of God? Are you a self-centered person? Or are you genuinely concerned about others—and show it?

Why Do We Ask?

"Is the Lord among us or not?"
Exodus 17:7
"Where is the Lord, the God of Elijah?"
2 Kings 2:14

Questions—we all have them. Sometimes I think I have too many. In reading God's Word through the years, I have been intrigued by the many questions raised by men and women. I have especially been fascinated with what prompted the inquiries, what motives lay behind the questions. God is concerned why people raise questions as well.

In Exodus 17, we read the account of the recently delivered people camped at Rephidim. There is no water in sight; they begin to complain to Moses. Faulting him for leading them out of Egypt, they are on the verge of stoning him! God's patience was tested, for the people asked, "Is the Lord among us or not?" This question was asked after God sent the ten plagues, delivered the people from slavery, opened the Red Sea, provided food for them, and gave them a sign of his presence with a cloud by day and pillar of fire by night. The people thought they needed one more miracle from God to *prove* he was with them. It was a question of unbelief; they questioned whether God was really with them. They were a quarrelling and grumbling people.

On the other hand, there is Elisha, standing on Jordan's bank. After following his mentor on a lengthy journey, suddenly Elijah is taken from him. Elisha witnessed many miracles while accompanying Elijah, and he was promised by the prophet that if he was present at his departure, a "double portion" of Elijah's spirit would rest on Elisha. Elisha was there; he saw Elijah ascend into heaven. Then, taking the cloak that fell from Elijah, Elisha stands at the river bank, crying out, "Where is the Lord, the God of Elijah?" Whereupon, Elisha struck the water, and it parted. He asked the question, not in unbelief, but in faith, knowing the power of God. He knew "where" God was. He wanted the sons of the prophets looking on (2:15) to witness God's mighty power.

Are our questions asked out of unbelief or faith? It makes a difference, you know.

April 23

Walking and Running

But those who wait on the Lord shall renew their strength;
they shall mount up with wings like eagles, they shall run
and not be weary, they shall walk and not faint.
Isaiah 40:31 NKJV

When I was a much younger man, I did quite a bit of running. However, I gradually changed to walking for exercise and have been a walker for years.

The Scripture often employs these two forms of mobility as metaphors for particular aspects of the Christian life. We frequently see "walk" and its cognates used as descriptions of a quality of conduct a Christian should be engaged in. By comparison, the metaphor "run" is used to depict perseverance and endurance.

The above text uses both terms. In giving comfort and encouragement to fainthearted and weary people, God reminds them their Creator-God never faints or grows weary, and that he gives power to the weak. When even the children and young men's strength is spent, renewed strength is given to those who "wait on the LORD." The fact is such people will be so energized by the Spirit that they will run without becoming tired; they will walk without growing unsteady.

Note some additional texts on these two spiritual metaphors.

"Walk by the Spirit, and you will not gratify the desires of the flesh" (Gal. 5:16).

"And walk in love, as Christ loved us and gave himself up for us, a fragrant offering and sacrifice to God" (Eph. 5:2).

"Walk as children of light" (Eph. 5:8).

"But if we walk in the light, as he is in the light, we have fellowship with one another, and the blood of Jesus his Son cleanses us from all sin" (1 John 1:7).

"Do you not know that in a race all the runners run, but only one receives the prize? So run that you may obtain it" (1 Cor. 9:24).

"And let us run with endurance the race that is set before us" (Heb. 12:1).

God desires to make "walkers" and "runners" out of all of his people. Are you "running" and "walking" today?

The World's Hatred

*"I have given them your word, and the world has hated them
because they are not of the world, just as I am not of the world."*
John 17:14

The "world," as it is used in its ethical sense by Jesus and the apostles, refers to systems and people who are opposed to true holiness and righteousness. Any person, movement, and organization, which does not identify with God and his Son are of "this world," according to the Word of God. Even fallen, unsanctified desires find their origin in the "world": "For all that is in the world—the desires of the flesh and the desires of the eyes and pride of life—is not from the Father but is from the world" (1 John 2:16).

For newly born converts, who expected that all would be a "bed of roses" following their conversion, a revelation of reality will eventually awaken them to their true identity: to follow Christ involves a cross; to follow Christ antagonizes the Adversary and his minions.

While Jesus was *friendly* to sinners, he was never a *friend* of the world. He never joined in its evil, nor sought to win its approval. Jesus neither felt intimidated by the ungodly, nor compromised God's truth to gain followers. The apostle James learned this lesson well and taught it to the first Christians: "You adulterous people! Do you not know that friendship with the world is enmity with God? Therefore whoever wishes to be a friend of the world makes himself an enemy of God" (James 4:4).

Christians are always in danger of being squeezed into the world's mold (see Rom. 12:2). We are called to be transformed people, not people shaped by the world's appetites and passions, mindset and behavior. To be a Christian is to follow him whom the world hated. To be a Christian is to carry a cross—a cross that identifies us with the Crucified one.

Jesus, I my cross have taken, all to leave and follow Thee.
Destitute, despised, forsaken, Thou from hence my all shall be.
Perish every fond ambition, all I've sought or hoped or known.
Yet how rich is my condition! God and Heaven are still mine own.
Let the world despise and leave me, they have left my Savior, too.
Human hearts and looks deceive me; Thou art not, like them, untrue.
And while Thou shalt smile upon me, God of wisdom, love and might,
Foes may hate and friends disown me, show Thy face and all is bright.*

April 25

A Solemn Assembly

"Blow the trumpet in Zion; consecrate a fast; call a solemn assembly."
Joel 2:15

All was not well in Zion when the prophet Joel penned his little but powerful oracle. Both the land and the hearts of the people were ravished by the Destroyer: "What the cutting locust left, the swarming locust has eaten. What the swarming locust left, the hopping locust has eaten, and what the hopping locust left, the destroying locust has eaten" (1:4). The man, whose name means "Yahweh is God" sounds an alarm, calling God's backslidden people to wake up, weep, lament, and mourn. To the priests, he exhorted, "Put on sackcloth and lament, O priests; wail, O ministers of the altar. Go in, pass the night in sackcloth, O ministers of my God!" (1:13).

Why was the prophet so disturbed? Because Yahweh was disturbed. The prophets spoke Yahweh's words, not their own. The prophets stayed close to the heart of Yahweh, listening to his voice and writing his words. As their covenant God looked upon Zion in those days, he saw devastation instead of fruitfulness; he saw indifference instead of a passion for truth and righteousness; he saw impending judgment and anguish: "For the day of the LORD is great and very awesome; who can endure it?" (2:11).

What should Israel do? Yahweh's prescription for revival was not attractive—it never is: "Return to me with all your heart, with fasting, with weeping, and with mourning; and rend your hearts and not your garments" (2:12-13).

We want the easy way, the quick way; however, with God, desperate times call for desperate measures. But we would rather sing praise choruses and clap our hands (of which neither is wrong in its place); we would rather leave our gatherings feeling good, when spiritual death and moral sickness may be inundating the pews.

Where God's remedies are applied, God's grace abounds. "And it shall come to pass *afterward*, that I will pour out my Spirit on all flesh" (2:28). *After* what? *After* we have seen our condition as God sees it; after we have turned completely away from our wicked ways; after we have torn our hearts. Only then can we expect "a fountain [to] come forth from the house of the Lord" (3:18).

Moses Strikes Back

"Hear now, you rebels: shall we bring water for you out of this rock?"
And Moses lifted up his hand and struck the rock with his staff twice ...
Number 20:10-11

How often I have heard through the years that it is entirely permissible for Christians to display anger because Jesus did. Yes, the Bible records occasions in which Yahweh in the Old Testament, and the Lord Jesus in the Gospels exercised anger. However, we need to keep in view *why* God becomes angry.

God's anger is always a holy and righteous anger. When Jesus "overturned the tables of the money-changers and the seats of those who sold pigeons" (Mark 11:15), he didn't take this action because he was personally offended or slighted; nor was his own *pride* wounded. Jesus took action because of the holy jealousy he had for his Father's House. It is right to be angry whenever we see the things of God being desecrated, especially his temples—the church and bodies meant for his indwelling Spirit.

With that being said, it is a rare person—even a Christian man or woman—who can manifest anger for the right reason, at the right time, in the right amount. When the reason and occasion are right, we need to take heed to the biblical admonition: "Be angry and do not sin" (Eph. 4:26). Because anger is such a volatile emotion, it is possible to cross a line.

Moses crossed that line. He became so frustrated with those complaining, hardhearted people, that he directed his anger at them. God severely disciplined him: "for you did not believe in me, to uphold me as holy in the eyes of the people of Israel" (20:12).

I remember hearing an evangelist tell the story years ago, how one Sunday morning he walked to his pulpit with his pockets filled with "rocks." He intended to let his people "have it"! God said to him, "Empty your pockets." He kept walking. God repeated, "Empty your pockets." He said before he got to the pulpit his pockets were empty, but his heart was full. The apostle wrote, "The anger of man does not produce the righteousness of God" (James 1:20).

Do you have an anger problem? Do you become angry for the wrong reasons? Talk to God about it, and possibly a wise Christian friend.

The Lord Uses Our Surrendered Resources

And Elisha said to her, "What shall I do for you?
Tell me; what have you in the house?" And she said,
"Your servant has nothing in the house except a jar of oil."
2 Kings 4:2

It remains to be seen what God can do through the life of a person who surrenders his finite resources to our Father's infinite, loving, and wise control. God always takes what we surrender to him, and multiplies it to bless us and others.

During the 1970s, it was my privilege to serve Tom Clark and his family as pastor, in the northern regions of the lower peninsula of the state of Michigan. When I first met Tom, he was in his mid-60s, and had owned and operated a saw mill since 1944. Tom died in 2003, at 94 years of age.

Tom was a plain-spoken person; some would even say he was gruff at times. However, he had the heart of a child and a worldwide compassion for the needy and lost, beginning at home. I never knew Tom and his family to come to church in just one car. They always drove two, stopping along the way to pick up adults and children. It made no difference to Tom if he had just recently purchased a new vehicle (he always drove a Buick); he was more concerned about taking people where they could hear the gospel than maintaining a clean car.

The Lord prospered Tom. The Lord prospered Tom because he had surrendered himself and his business to the Lord as a young man. From a little operation, beginning in 1944, to his death, Tom gave hundreds of thousands of dollars to the work of God. Tom and his family always lived frugally, but he always gave lavishly.

The widow in 2 Kings 4 only possessed "a jar of oil." However, God used that surrendered oil to fill many vessels, blessing her and her two children, and millions since who have read the account and trusted God with what they had. Tom Clark only had "trees," but he surrendered every tree to the God of Elisha, and God prospered him, making him a blessing to countless people, of whom many are still being blessed because of his gifts and their memories of Tom.

You say you don't have much. It makes no difference. The question is, Have you surrendered to the Lord what you do have?

A Monumental Task with a Blessed Assurance

"Have I not commanded you? Be strong and courageous.
Do not be frightened, and do not be dismayed, for the
Lord your God is with you wherever you go."
Joshua 1:9

As the Lord's designated successor to Moses, Joshua was given an unenviable position and assigned a monumental task: he was appointed Israel's leader, charged to lead them into the Land of Promise. No man could serve in that position and accomplish such a task without God's strength.

Evidently, there were qualities Joshua possessed that caught Moses' attention early on, because the first time we meet Joshua, he is Moses' assistant, and chosen to lead a military campaign against Amalek (Ex. 17). Having led Israel to victory in battle, we later see Joshua accompanying Moses up to Mount Sinai, where God confirms his covenant with his people. Leaving everyone else behind, including Aaron and the seventy elders, Moses takes Joshua with him, ascending higher.

Joshua was allowed to see and hear things few others had. We catch a glimpse of his privileged position in Exodus 33. Here we have the account of how Moses used to meet with God often in "the tent of meeting." Israel observed Moses whenever he approached the tent. It was a wonderful sight: God descended on the tent (signified by a cloud), when Moses entered, and the cloud rose, when the man of God left. Then note this: "When Moses turned again into the camp, his assistant Joshua the son of Nun, a young man, would not depart from the tent" (v. 11).

By the time of Moses' departure, Joshua was prepared to lead Israel. However, God's leaders are not always assured of success—as God counts success—apart from continued renewal and obedience: "This Book of the Law shall not depart from your mouth, but you shall meditate on it day and night, so that you may be careful to do according to all that is written in it. For then you will make your way prosperous, and then you will have good success" (Josh. 1:8). Only by heeding God's words could Joshua claim God's promise: "Just as I was with Moses, so I will be with you. I will not leave you or forsake you" (Josh. 1:5).

The Song of Moses

"Now therefore write this song and teach it to the people of Israel."
Deuteronomy 31:19

Early in my Christian pilgrimage, I discovered that in addition to reading my Bible during quiet times, it was also helpful to have at least one hymnal close at hand (of course, in our Bible, we have a built-in hymnal, such as the 150 Psalms). A good hymnal is important, because God has moved many saints through the years to write "hymns and spiritual songs" (Eph. 5:19), which minister grace to the hearts of his worshiping people.

There is something about words set to poetry that makes for easier memorization than prose. In my own experience, I have found myself during prayer times quoting verses from a hymn that I memorized years before, some biblical truth set to verse.

Israel was about to enter the Land of Promise, while temporarily stationed in the plains of Moab at the end of their 40-year wilderness wanderings. It was there Moses reiterated God's laws and urged the people to obedience as they were about to cross the Jordan and possess the land "flowing with milk and honey." But Yahweh knew Israel would soon turn to other gods and break his covenant. Therefore, God directs Moses to write a song, then teaching it to the people, "that this song may be a witness for me against the people of Israel" (31:19). Verse 22 reads: "So Moses wrote this song the same day and taught it to the people of Israel." The first forty-three verses of chapter 32 record the song of Moses. Thus, going into Canaan, Yahweh was in the midst of his people; the Ten Commandments resided in the Ark of the Covenant; the Book of the Law lay beside the ark (31:26); and Moses' song was on everyone's lips.

Unfortunately, it wasn't long before Israel broke her covenant with Yahweh and forgot Moses' song. Have we done the same? Have we forgotten God's holy laws? Have we lost our song?

Sing them over again to me,
Wonderful words of life,
Let me more of their beauty see,
Wonderful words of life;
Words of life and beauty
*Teach me faith and duty.**

"Oh That Thou Wouldest Rend the Heavens"

Oh that thou wouldest rend the heavens, that thou wouldest come down, that the mountains might flow down at thy presence.
Isaiah 64:1 KJV

I chose to use the *King James Version* for the above text, since I memorized this Scripture as a young preacher; and I must say, the cadence sounds better to my ear than the modern versions. It was also as a fledgling pastor that I first read the story of the 1904 Welsh Revival, led by an evangelist by the name of Evan Roberts, who was God's principal mouthpiece in that revival.

When the Spirit of God anointed Evan Roberts (1878-1951) with his cleansing and energizing grace, he was employed in the south of Wales, working long hours in the local coal mine. One of the deacons at Moriah Chapel in Loughor, where Evan attended, said to Evan after prayer meeting one evening, "Evan, you don't want to miss it when the Holy Ghost comes." What William Davies meant was that the church and Wales were in desperate need of revival, and it just could be that such a fresh move of the Spirit would commence in one of their own prayer services.

Evan was one of God's thirsty-hearted servants. The Spirit of God drove into his heart the words of the deacon that day, and thereafter he attended at least five prayer meetings a week—after working all day in the mine! For thirteen years, Evan prayed for a fresh visitation of God to the churches and his beloved country. The landlady, from whom he rented a second-floor apartment, often heard him pacing back and forth in prayer. The prayer he prayed repeatedly was, "O Lord, bend me, bend me, bend me!"

The Lord did "bend" Evan and thrust him out to proclaim the saving and sanctifying ministries of the crucified, risen Christ. Thousands came to Christ through his ministry; many Christians were renewed as well.

While in England, in 2007, I traveled to Wales and located Moriah Chapel, where the "fire of God" fell in 1904. As I stood outside the gated courtyard before the small stone structure, I read the memorial plaque, honoring Evan Roberts. I offered a brief prayer, thanking God for his obedient servant, who had witnessed with his own eyes an answer—in a measure—to Isaiah's prayer.

Always Grace!

For we are the aroma of Christ to God among those who are being saved.
2 Corinthians 2:15

From beginning to end the Christian life is a product of divine grace. We are debtors, and will always be, to our Creator-Redeemer, who formed us in our mother's womb, birthed in us our first thoughts of him, drew us to Calvary's cross, enabled us to trust in his Son, and sustains and preserves us as we run this race.

God is a debtor to no man, but the saved will be forever indebted to God. For the one who was lost and is found, was blind but now can see, was dead and now is alive—this man knows his salvation was not manufactured or self-generated. This salvation came from above; like manna, it is a gift from our merciful Father. And like the heavenly bread which was freely given to the complaining rebels in the wilderness centuries ago, God's benevolent favor descends upon all his imperfect and needy children today.

There is never an earthly moment—from spiritual conception and regeneration to our parting breath—when the follower of the Lord Jesus can take credit for anything. Everything we have is a gift; everything has been received. We simply open our hands.

While man does not remain passive in receiving God's grace, he knows even the ability to receive is a gift from God. It is all of grace; hence, there is no room for boasting.

It is so easy for us to forget this. We are naturally prone to pride, self-adulation, and self-absorption. We tend to be fiercely independent, often falling into the trap of self-reformation. However, only a broken and contrite heart makes room for grace, stripping us of our arrogance and self-righteousness.

Many of us are well-informed that initial salvation is all of grace; we may not be so sure that sanctification is by grace as well—God's process of conforming believers to the likeness of Christ.

The growing, maturing believer learns, and is often reminded, that he is wholly dependent upon the God of all grace in all things, for all things, all the time, and for all time.

Conversion

*"Go home to your friends and tell them how much the Lord
has done for you, and how he has had mercy on you."*
Mark 5:19

Christian conversion is an event as well as a process. By "event," we mean there is a point in time when one is regenerated by the Spirit of God and justified by faith. By "process," we mean one continues to change (sanctification) more and more into the likeness of Christ, as he and she grows in the grace and knowledge of God.

The man from Gadara is a case in point of a conversion event. Prior to his conversion to Christ, this man lived in a cemetery, was possessed by an unclean, violent and mean spirit, impossible to reason with, and abused his body. Upon encountering Jesus, he fell at his feet, and Jesus cleansed him of his moral impurity and cast the demons from him. There was an immediate observable change to all who witnessed this event: "And they came to Jesus and saw the demon-possessed man, the one who had had the legion, sitting there, clothed and in his right mind, and they were afraid" (Mark 5:15).

While every Christian does not have—nor is expected to have—the kind of dramatic conversion the Gadarene did, nonetheless, according to God's Word, all who are "in Christ Jesus" have been changed (Acts and Paul's Epistles are replete with supporting witnesses).

However, all change does not occur at the moment when one is born from above. To the Corinthians, Paul wrote, "And we all, with unveiled face, beholding the glory of the Lord, are being transformed into the same image [the image of Christ] from one degree of glory to another" (2 Cor. 3:18).

Spiritual transformation is an ongoing process—or should be—in the life of every disciple of the Lord Jesus. Our likeness to Jesus will only be *approximated* in this life. However, the New Testament writers expected a growing resemblance to Christ to appear in their converts.

For all those who are "in Christ," the challenge is to become more like Christ. This can only occur through a moment-by-moment loving obedience through the Spirit's power.

The Pure in Heart

"Blessed are the pure in heart, for they shall see God."
Matthew 5:8

The pure in heart have been to the holy mount and have gazed upon the face of the exact representation of God, the Lord Jesus Christ. They do not behold the Jesus of history, they contemplate the living Christ of eternity—the Christ who said, "I am ... the Living One; I was dead, and behold I am alive for ever and ever!" (Rev. 1:17-18, NIV).

The pure in heart have seen God. Not in his full revelation, but in Jesus: "Whoever has seen me has seen the Father" (John 14:9). To see God is not to see God with the physical eye, but to see God with the eye of faith: "Though you have not seen him, you love him; though you do not see him, you believe in him and rejoice with joy that is inexpressible and filled with glory" (1 Pet. 1:8).

The pure in heart have seen a God who is glorious in holiness: "in him is no darkness at all" (1 John. 1:5). God's holiness is absolute. That is why neither man nor beast were permitted to touch Mount Sinai when the Law was given. Only Moses and Joshua were allowed to ascend the mountain—men who had consecrated themselves wholly to God (see Ex. 19).

The pure in heart will one thing—they will the will of God. However imperfectly they may perform that will, however far short they fall in resembling the Lord Jesus Christ, nevertheless they aspire to do the will of God.

The pure in heart are always conscious of their own shortcomings, failures in performing the will of God perfectly, and their unlikeness to the Lord Jesus Christ. They habitually confess their need for God's holiness. They know apart from Christ they are altogether sinful and unclean.

The pure in heart experience a continuous cleansing, through a grace that enables them to obey God freely, though not absolutely. The language of their spirit is, "Yes, Lord."

"Blessed are the pure in heart, for they shall see God"—today, right now. The pure in heart enjoy a *heaven* on their way to Heaven.

A Vessel for Noble Purposes

In a large house there are articles not only of gold and silver,
but also of wood and clay; some are for noble purposes and some
for ignoble. If a man cleanses himself from the latter, he will be
an instrument for noble purposes, made holy, useful to
the Master and prepared to do any good work.
2 Timothy 2:20-21 NIV

After many years of carefully observing the ways of God with the children of men, the venerable John Wesley (1703-1791) wrote: "From long experience and observation, I am inclined to think that whoever finds redemption in the blood of Jesus—whoever is justified—has the choice of walking in the higher or lower path. I believe the Holy Spirit at that time sets before him the 'more excellent way' and cites him to walk therein—to choose the narrowest path in the narrow way—to aspire after the heights and depths of holiness—after the entire image of God. But if he does not accept this offer, he insensibly declines into the lower order of Christians; he still goes on in what may be called a good way, serving God in his degree, and finds mercy in the close of life through the blood of the covenant."*

Methodism's founder was simply reiterating in his own words the same truth affirmed in the Scripture above. The church of the Lord Jesus Christ consists of two categories of believers: the "vessels for ignoble purposes" and the "vessels for noble purposes." The ignoble vessels are likened to wood and clay; the noble vessels resemble the precious metals of gold and silver.

The apostle informs us the ignoble vessels can become noble if they choose. However, there is a price to pay. If the ignoble vessel becomes totally dissatisfied with his lowly condition, he must take resolute, radical measures in order to change his status; he must rid himself of all the "wood" and "clay" in his life.

Sadly, the church is populated with too many ignoble vessels. Who among us will hear the voice of the Spirit calling us to a noble life, a holy life? Who will cleanse himself from all that contaminates the body and spirit? Who will consecrate himself totally to the Lord? Will you purpose to be a noble vessel—to the glory of God in the power of the Spirit?

God's Dwelling Place

Or do you not know that your body is a temple of the
Holy Spirit within you, whom you have from God?
1 Corinthians 6:19

That the Lord God should choose to dwell in man is utterly incomprehensible. That he who is high and lofty, holy and infinite, perfect in all he is and does—that such a God should bend to inhabit fallen man cause even angels to wonder.

Where God dwells often creates disruption. When the Lord Jesus walked into the temple one day, he overthrew tables of greed and covetousness, driving from that consecrated place all wickedness and selfishness. Before Christ can fill a temple with himself, he must drive out all adversaries to his rightful reign.

The city of Corinth was notorious for sexual impurities. It was a city of twelve temples. One of the most infamous of these was dedicated to Aphrodite, the goddess of love, whose worshipers practiced religious prostitution. At one time, one thousand prostitutes served in this temple. Sexual immorality was so rampant in Corinth that the Greek verb "to Corinthianize" came to mean "to practice sexual immorality."

We also live in a day when sexual impurity is pervasive. No popular medium of communication is exempt from Satan's evil creations and devices to lure the curiosities of God's people to explore the impure and licentious. The printed page, television, the Internet, and videos are all being exploited by our Adversary to destroy the love and faith of God's people.

How are we to respond to this Niagara of sexual depravity?

- Consecrate our body to the Lord Jesus Christ (Rom. 12:1).
- Remember that such property—our body—is the sacred temple of the Lord Jesus Christ in which he dwells (1 Cor. 6:19).
- Seek daily to walk in the Spirit so as not to engage in the acts of the flesh (Gal. 5:16).
- Remember at what cost we were purchased and that we are Another's property (1 Cor. 6:20).
- Habitually honor God with our body (1 Cor. 6:20).

Our body ... God's dwelling place! What God expects from us his Spirit will enable our wills to perform.

Praying the Will of God

And this is the confidence that we have toward him,
that if we ask anything according to his will he hears us.
1 John 5:14

That God has a will, and the disciple of the Lord Jesus is always to pray in harmony with our Lord's will, is a teaching clearly taught in the sacred Scriptures.

John tells us, "And this is the confidence that we have toward him, that if we ask anything according to his will he hears us. And if we know that he hears us in whatever we ask, we know that we have the requests that we have asked of him" (1 John 5:14-15). The Lord Jesus instructs us to pray, "Your will be done," and exemplifies what he taught by praying in Gethsemane, "My Father, if it be possible, let this cup pass from me; nevertheless, not as I will, but as you will" (Matt. 26:39).

Since the Bible teaches that it is imperative for the believer to offer his prayers according to the will of God, can we actually know we are offering our petitions in God's will? Yes. If the matter for which we are petitioning God is clearly covered in the Scriptures, then the believer has been supplied through God's written revelation what his will is. On the other hand, if a believer asks God if he should resign job "A" to take job "B," the Scriptures will not tell the believer what to do, but does furnish him with many "pointers" (principles) in ascertaining God's will in matters of personal guidance. We must search the Scriptures in order to identify these pointers.

If as followers of the Lord Jesus, we are to pray in the will of God, it is essential that we live in the will of God. James declared, "The prayer of a righteous man is powerful and effective" (James 5:16 NIV). Only those who are living in a right relationship with God—"a righteous man"—can offer prayers in the will of God.

If we do not know how to pray about a particular matter, we can at least groan: "For we do not know what to pray for as we ought, but the Spirit himself intercedes for us with groaning too deep for words. And he who searches hearts knows what is the mind of the Spirit, because the Spirit intercedes for the saints according to the will of God" (Rom. 8:26-27).

May 7

Asking for Bread

"Give us this day our daily bread."
Matthew 6:11

The Son of God was also very much the Son of Man—a *real* man. Because he was a man, he experienced the same physical needs of every other human being. He needed air to breathe, water to drink, clothes to wear, shelter to retire to, and food to eat. During his earthly sojourn, the Lord Jesus expressed the heart of the Father in many ways. One of those ways was the care he showed toward hungry people—people who were in need of daily food.

Many Christians, who sincerely aspire to live wholly for God, forget in their quest to be Christlike that the Father is vitally interested in the whole person—including the human body.

While God's design for Christians is for them to live a morally clean life, it is also God's design and desire to care personally for the material and bodily needs of his children. As a loving and merciful heavenly Father, who created the lilies of the field and sees every fallen sparrow, and who knows us so intimately that the hairs of our head are numbered, this same Father wants to furnish my every material need.

Thus, in addition to teaching us to pray for the complete and universal reign of his kingdom, and to pray for the forgiveness of our trespasses, our Lord also taught us to look to him for our daily physical needs.

When Jesus taught his disciples to pray, "Give us this day our daily bread," he suggested not only were they dependent on the Father to meet their needs, but also that the Father would answer such a petition. The Father will answer this petition of his children in a variety of ways, including giving us the strength and ability to *earn* bread. And while the Father is answering our own petition for bread, let us not forget to share bread, as we are able, with others who are less fortunate. Jesus looked upon the crowds and saw they were hungry—*and did something about it.*

Is God using you to be his hands in helping meet the physical needs of someone?

Brilliant Luminaries

Do all things without grumbling or questioning, that you may be blameless and innocent, children of God without blemish in the midst of a crooked and twisted generation, among whom you shine as lights in the world.
Philippians 2:14-15

The inspired writer, in describing the moral climate of his own generation, said it was both "crooked and twisted" (Phil. 2:15). They were "crooked," with regard to their behavior; they were "twisted," with respect to their mindset. Unlike today's typical philosopher and counselor, Paul believed in a revealed, moral objective standard of thinking and conduct; otherwise such descriptions would be meaningless—behavior and worldviews can't be considered "crooked" and "twisted" unless there is a straight and right standard of thinking and conduct.

But the issue is not how bad the world is; the question for Christians is, How are we to live in such a world of moral blight? The first-century apostle exhorted the Philippian believers to counter their fallen culture by walking cautiously and reverentially before God. Such a walk would impact even their speech—a speech that would be characterized by an absence of "complaining," and "questioning." The one speaks of ingratitude, the other of unbelief.

By living such a grace-filled lifestyle, Paul says these believers are blameless before God, morally unadulterated, and walking in such purity that they will look like true children of God. Such transformed individuals stand out. The apostle says they will "shine as lights in the world."

This world is in desperate need of brilliant luminaries. With its crooked and twisted views of everything God has ordained and commanded, the Christian is called to *shine*. We are to *shine* in our attitudes, speech, and conduct. We are called to a life of Christlike integrity. God has not called us to be rude and inconsiderate. We are not called to be obnoxious and thoughtless. We are called by a holy God to merely *shine*—with the life and light of Jesus.

We don't have to *force* the light. Just be Christian ... and you will *shine* to the glory of God!

May 9

Believing Prayer (part 1)

*"Therefore I tell you, whatever you ask in prayer,
believe that you have received it, and it will be yours."*
Mark 11:24

At first glance, the title of this meditation may appear redundant. After all, is there such a thing as praying without believing? Surely we need to go no further to obtain an honest answer to this question than to make a candid appraisal of our own prayer-life (assuming that yours is no different than mine).

How much of our praying is half-hearted—lacking earnestness, passion, fervency and faith? How often do we go to our knees (Does anyone actually kneel anymore?) with the subliminal thought: Will God actually answer my petition? Is Jesus Christ truly the same yesterday, today, and forever? Is God indeed a rewarder of those who earnestly seek him? Did Jesus really mean, "Everyone who asks receives" (Mt. 7:12)?

Prior to his conversion to Christ, Charles Finney (1792-1875)—who later was God's instrument in revival in upstate New York in the nineteenth-century—frequently attended a midweek prayer service in Adams, New York. A young attorney at the time, Finney reports that during one of these services, he was asked if he wished the Christians there to pray for him. In his own words, here is his rather audacious reply: "I suppose I need to be prayed for, for I am conscious I am a sinner; but I do not see that it will do any good for you to pray for me; for you are continually asking, but you do not receive."* What an indictment! Happily, later that church's prayer-life was transformed as well as Finney's.

Does your prayer-life need to be transformed until you believe God will actually answer your requests, according to his will? If so, believingly pray this prayer until you *feel* what you pray: Lord, *transform my prayer-life, until I pray with true faith in you. In the name of your Son I offer this earnest request, believing you will answer. Amen.*

Believing Prayer (part 2)

"Therefore I tell you, whatever you ask in prayer,
believe that you have received it, and it will be yours."
Mark 11:24

In the early part of the twentieth century, a young Lutheran pastor by the name of Armin Gesswein was doing his best to plant a new church on Long Island, New York. Things weren't going well for this fledgling minister. Writing about it, years later, Gesswein says his ministry was transformed when he began to pray differently.

There was a blacksmith in this little church by the name of Ambrose Whalen. Whalen had the reputation of getting his prayers answered. Desperate for help himself, Gesswein asked Whalen one day if he could join him in prayer. He was invited to the blacksmith's home. Once there, Gesswein says they went to Whalen's barn and climbed to the hayloft. The young pastor prayed first. Then the old blacksmith prayed. After he finished, Gesswein asked, "You have some kind of secret in praying. Would you share it with me?" "Young man," said the blacksmith, "learn to plead the promises of God."* The old man was kneeling between two bales of hay. On each bale was an open Bible. As he prayed, he prayed believing God meant what he said—each hand on a promise of God.

The Lord Jesus maintained an implicit confidence in his Father; he knew that whatever he asked of his Father he would be heard; his Father would provide the answer. The words Jesus prayed outside Lazarus' tomb epitomized his relationship with his Father: "Father, I thank you that you have heard me" (John 11:41). Our Father in Heaven desires that we develop a similar intimacy and prayer-relationship with him that his Son enjoyed.

Too much of our praying is formal, just words—empty words. The Spirit desires to take us to a deeper place in our prayer-life, a place where when we pray we know we have been heard. It may be we will have to persist in our requests for a time before the answer comes; nonetheless, did Jesus mean what he said or not?— "Therefore I tell you, whatever you ask in prayer, believe that you have received it, and it will be yours."

Real prayer, prayed in faith, prayed in the will of God, expects an answer from Heaven.

The Blessed Person

Blessed is the man ...
Psalm 1:1

Inherent in the very character of God is a perfect hatred of evil and a perfect love for righteousness—the one assumes the other. One existing without the other would not be the God, Creator, and Redeemer revealed through both the written and living Word, but a caricature. The Eternal God is beautiful in holiness, because he is perfectly symmetrical in all his attributes and ways. He always acts and reacts in *character*—because of who he is.

To pursue a life of holiness is to avoid sin and embrace righteousness. It is to have the mind of Christ; it is to imitate God as revealed in the person of his Son, through the power of the indwelling Christ.

True holiness involves a negative as well as a positive. The follower of the Lord Jesus Christ is characterized by both what he does as well as by what he avoids; what he embraces as well as by what he shuns.

Much of contemporary Christianity ignores the description of the balanced believer recorded in Psalm 1. But it is there just the same. The psalmist says the truly happy Christian is blessed by God because of what he does as well as by what he doesn't do; the blessed person lives differently from all those surrounding him. And because his life is unlike his wicked surroundings, his everlasting habitation will be dissimilar to those who are not blessed by God.

The truths of both Psalm 1:1 and 1:2 should characterize all Christians: the negatives and the positives: "The person who does not order his life on the basis of ungodly advisors, nor hang out with God-rejecters, nor has fellowship with the profane—this person is blessed by God and is truly happy. This blessed and truly happy person gets more excited over the truth and wisdom of God than anything else in life. He delights in God's truth so much that he ponders it again and again" (RIT).

Are you living a blessed and truly happy life?

Thirsting for God

On the last day of the feast, the great day, Jesus stood up and
cried out, "If anyone thirsts, let him come to me and drink.
Whoever believes in me, as the Scripture has said,
'Out of his heart will flow rivers of living water.'"
John 7:37-38

Water has always been a precious natural resource. Whenever a severe hurricane or earthquake strikes, cutting off the affected area's power supply, one of the first calls for help is for water.

All plant and animal life depend on water for their daily sustenance. Where there is no water, there is no life. One can travel for hundreds of miles through a desert wasteland without a sign of life, because of the absence of water; when the signs of life appear, there is sure to be the presence of water.

Water is used in Scripture as a symbol of the essential life-giving sustenance of God. Jesus said that he is the source and fountainhead of spiritual life (see Rev. 21:6). Without Christ, we live in a desert; with Christ, we enjoy an eternal oasis.

Some of God's final words of written revelation are in the form of an invitation—an invitation offered to the thirsty: "And let the one who is thirsty come; let the one who desires take the water of life without price" (Rev. 22:17). Here, "desires" is used to underscore the intensity of the appetite of "the one who is thirsty." Both "thirsty" and "desires" are present participles. Thirst and desire should culminate in a deliberate, decisive action—"take" (aorist tense).

The Lord Jesus is both the source and object of such thirst. We drink from him—and are satisfied. He is our salvation—we are satisfied; he is our life—we keep on drinking. "To have found God and still to pursue Him is the soul's paradox of love," observed A. W. Tozer (1897-1963).* Every God-thirsty Christian is a witness to such a reality. Bernard of Clairvaux (1090-1153) captured this truth when he wrote the following words:

We taste Thee, O Thou Living Bread,
And long to feast upon Thee still:
We drink of Thee, the Fountainhead
*And thirst our souls from Thee to fill.**

The Day of Christ

So that in the day of Christ I may glory
that I did not run in vain or labor in vain.
Philippians 2:16

In his classic volume *Purity of Heart is to Will One Thing*, Danish theologian Søren Kierkegaard (1813-1855) offers this sobering insight regarding the Day of Christ: "In eternity you as an individual will only be asked about your faith and your faithfulness. There will be absolutely no asking about whether you were entrusted with much or little, whether you were given many talents of silver to work with or whether you were given a hundred-pound weight to carry. But you will be asked only about your faith and your faithfulness."*

I have been repeatedly impressed that the Apostle Paul possessed an intense desire that his converts remain loyal to Christ and the gospel until the Day of Christ. Moreover, he not only wanted his converts to be faithful and persevere to the end, so that they would be able to give a good accounting at the Day of Christ, but he also wanted them to remain faithful so that his own labors among them would prove not to have been worthless.

Faithfulness for the Philippians—and for all Christians—involved, on the positive side, obedience: "Therefore, my beloved, as you have always obeyed ..." (2:12). On the negative side (in the Philippian Letter), faithfulness is marked by the absence of grumbling and questioning: "Do all things without grumbling or questioning ..." (2:14).

Paul is not only concerned that these believers will remain faithful to Christ; he is also anxious how his own ministry among the Philippians will be viewed at the Day of Christ: "so that in the day of Christ I may glory that I did not run in vain or labor in vain" (2:16).

If Paul's converts remain faithful until the Day of Christ, his ministry in Philippi will have proved to be successful. According to God, if our efforts fail to produce changed and fruitful disciples—shining lights in this world—all the time, energy, and funds we have expended will be for naught.

The High and the Low

*"All the trees of the field will know that I am the LORD; I bring down
the high tree, exalt the low tree, dry up the green tree and make the dry
tree to flourish. I am the LORD; I have spoken, and I will perform it."*
Ezekiel 17:24 NASB

Fallen man is preoccupied with where he perceives himself to be on
"Life's Ladder of Success." Regardless of one's economic status, social standing, occupation, educational attainments, or giftedness,
prideful man intuitively compares himself to those above and below.

Living in Babylon among his exiled people some 2600 years
ago, Ezekiel, the prophet-priest, was God's messenger to proud
kings and people. Because Judah's arrogant king had stubbornly
refused to listen to the prophets, God would bring him "low." In his
place another would be elevated—given a "high" place—effectively
fulfilling God's ultimate purposes for his people.

It's tough being a "high tree" and remain humble. With his usual insight, C. S. Lewis (1898-1963) offers this comment on the subject of pride: "A proud man is always looking down on things and
people: and, of course, as long as you are looking down, you cannot
see something above you"* (see Matt. 5:8). Lewis notes that the
"something above" is, in reality, God. We cannot see God, as long as
we think of ourselves as a "high tree." To see God is to be pure in
heart.

One should not be surprised that the world is full of "high
trees." We expect that. However, to its shame, the contemporary
church has rolled out the carpet to the "high trees." We feverishly
parade our successes and flaunt our statistics. With blaring trumpets and rolling drums, we heap honors upon one another while
turning a deaf ear to the honor of God. We love being "tall trees";
we're in love with ourselves!

When does spiritual renewal (revival) begin? Renewal begins
when the "high" tree bows low before God. How does renewal and
revival continue in the heart and life of the believer? By living as a
"low tree": "God opposes the proud, but gives grace to the humble" (James 4:6).

Weakness and Strength

*So to keep me from becoming conceited because of the surpassing
greatness of the revelations, a thorn was given me in the flesh, a
messenger of Satan to harass me, to keep me from becoming conceited.*
2 Corinthians 12:7 NIV

One of those paradoxical principles of the Kingdom of God is that
we are only made strong by first becoming weak—and staying weak.

Unsanctified humanity seeks to be strong—a strong politician, a
strong parent, a strong professor, a strong pastor, a strong leader, a
strong person, a strong Christian. In our desire and need to be
strong, we manipulate people in order to advance our objectives and
achieve our goals. Our arrogant impatience with people and Providence are obstacles to overcome while we get on with our more important agenda for success. Our fallen and diseased egos are intolerant of those we view as rivals, and dismissive of those we perceive as
inferior to us. A dominant *self* rules and doesn't easily bow—to God
or men.

Whether such an individual is in the church or outside matters
little. Inside his heart, he is the same. He may consider himself to be
an Evangelical Christian or a Protestant liberal or a Catholic conservative. Whatever his label, he lives like he is ultimately in command; a self-ruled, man-managed, autonomous, sinful ego is at the
helm. Such a person pays merely lip service to the lordship of Jesus
Christ, and acts as though he never heard of the Holy Spirit.

The Spirit of God can only effectively work through the weak—
those who have become powerless enough to die to self-rule, self-
interest, self-promotion, and self-sovereignty. Such a person was
Jacob of old. Facing a real and present crisis, this Old Testament
patriarch went down by a brook to pray and wrestle. But Jacob was
strong—too strong for God to use mightily. He must become weak;
he must acknowledge his sinfulness, his vulnerabilities, and his failures. He must confess who he was *essentially*—a deceiver.

Jacob wanted to be blessed; God knew he first needed to be
bruised and broken. How we Christians want to be blessed—to be
strong.

Only those weakened by God are strong. This is God's way.
Shall we go down to the *brook*?

Pruned to Produce

"And every branch that bears fruit, He
prunes it so that it may bear more fruit."
John 15:2 NASB

Anyone would have to be a sadomasochist to enjoy being cut on. I have only undergone a surgeon's knife once in my adult life, and then, of course, I had the benefits of modern-day anesthesia. I didn't *feel* a thing. It has been quite the contrast in my walk with Christ for over a half-century. Often my Vinedresser has taken up his knife and deftly removed what would hinder growth and fruitfulness. Unlike physical surgery, accompanied by anesthesia, I have *felt* my heavenly Vinedresser's incisions—sometimes through tears.

I am told that before pruning, an average grapevine may have 200-300 buds, all of which are capable of producing fruit. However, if left unpruned, the number of grape clusters would be excessive; the vine would be incapable of producing a large crop or sustaining adequate vegetative growth.

The reason the vinedresser prunes his vine regularly is to obtain maximum yields of high-quality grapes, and to allow adequate vegetative growth for the following season. Therefore, pruning is essential.

Pruning takes both knowledge and wisdom. It must be done by skilled experts and at the proper season. And the vinedresser must be thoroughly acquainted with his vines in order to prune his plants with balance. One university horticulture department says: "The degree or extent of pruning is dictated by vine vigor. Vine vigor is determined by estimating the amount of the previous season's growth. This concept is called 'balanced pruning.'"* The expert vinedresser knows what to cut away, what to leave, and when to cut.

So it is with the Christian's Vinedresser. Desiring that we may produce luscious fruit to his praise and glory, our Father in Heaven wants to excise from our life everything that hinders us from being a fruitful branch. And he can be trusted to remove from our heart and lives only what is necessary in order to achieve maximum growth.

A Friend to the Lost

"For the Son of Man came to seek and to save the lost."
Luke 19:10

Zacchaeus was lost and didn't know it, not unlike most lost people in every age. It usually takes some time before a person discovers that he or she is lost. That is true geographically speaking, as well as spiritually.

I can remember the day, as though it just happened. When in our teens, my friend Dennis and I were taking a hike through a dense forest. It was a beautiful summer day in the Brown County woods. We laughed, ran, investigated—just like any two boys would do. We were enjoying the forest and our time together. But then it happened—we suddenly realized we didn't know where we were or how to get back to his aunt's house. We were lost! And then we became fearful, for the sun was about to set.

I'm sure neither Dennis nor I—before or since—have ever talked to a dog as much as we did in the evening twilight that day. It so happened that his aunt's dog, Yeller, went with us on that eventful hike. After learning of our plight, we started talking to Yeller in animated tones: "Yeller, show us the way home! Show us the way back! Come on, Yeller, show us! Show us the way home!" And Yeller never failed those two scared kids. He led us back home.

The Lord Jesus Christ was, and is, a compassionate friend to lost people. Zacchaeus was lost—lost from God. Oh, God knew where this wandering Jew was, but Zacchaeus didn't. Jesus went to find him. That's why he came—to seek and to save lost people. He came to lead people back to the Father, back to their true Home.

God has called you and me to seek the lost and bring them to Jesus, bring them Home to their true resting place. Augustine of Hippo's (354-430) mother, Monica, followed her prodigal son for years—with her tears. After finally coming *Home*, Augustine wrote: "Thou hast made us for Thyself, O God, and we are restless until we find our rest in Thee." The lost was found.

Let us join with the Son of Man in being a real friend to lost people.

Seven Channels

"This is the word of the LORD to Zerubbabel: 'You will never be adequate to fulfill my mission, while depending on your own abilities and resources, or putting your trust in the influence and abilities of other people. Look to me alone, the all-sufficient source for your every need.'"
Zechariah 4:6 RIT

Our Father in Heaven yearningly desires each of his children be a channel of grace and blessing in this dark, fallen world. Is his desire your desire?

The only way God's desire can be effectively approximated in our lives is that we make a conscious and total surrender to his Son, the Lord Jesus Christ, and then walk day-by-day, keeping in step with the blessed Holy Spirit.

If we desire to be a conduit of mercy and grace, but fail to walk in obedience and fellowship with our Lord, then our desires are tainted with a sinful pride and self-centered ego. With such a spiritual handicap, if we do accomplish anything—even in the church— while it may result in the applause of men, it is incapable of bringing true glory and honor to Christ. We cannot promote ourselves and Christ at the same time.

As he surveyed the awesome assignment to rebuild the house of worship, Zerubbabel felt completely inadequate. Seeing his inadequacy, a vision of God's sufficiency was given to the prophet-priest Zechariah to share with Zerubbabel. It was a vision of two olive trees, furnishing an abundant supply of oil to a menorah—a lampstand with seven channels.

Just like many in the church today, the prophet didn't understand the meaning of the vision. Thus, the Lord gave the interpretation: "This is the word of the LORD to Zerubbabel: 'You will never be adequate to fulfill my mission, while depending on your own abilities and resources, or putting your trust in the influence and abilities of other people. Look to me alone, the all-sufficient source for your every need'" (Zech. 4:6 RIT).

Do you wish to be a channel of blessing, dear reader? Cast yourself totally upon the Lord. Let your complete dependence be upon him alone, and then receive his supply of fresh *oil*.

Wholeheartedness

*"For the eyes of the LORD move to and fro throughout the earth
that He may strongly support those whose heart is completely His."*
2 Chronicles 16:9 NASB

King Asa died in the forty-first year of his reign. That is a long time to be king—even a longer time to be a godly king. And that was the problem. Asa failed to persevere in godliness. Out of a total of some four decades on the throne, Asa served the Lord with a whole heart only ten years.

For ten years, this king was a righteous reformer. He cleansed the land of its foreign altars and gods. He led the way in seeking the Lord and observing the law and commandments. He constructed fortified cities throughout Judah's territories. Asa was a builder, a leader. And he was very successful, successful as God counts success. For ten years he "did good and right in the eyes of the LORD his God" (2 Chron. 14:2).

It is a rare person who can handle large success (large success given as a result of God's blessing)—successfully. While millions of our contemporaries have prayed the prayer of Jabez, "Oh that you would bless me" (1 Chron. 4:10), I wonder how many of them realize that God can't trust them with his blessing—not yet.

At the pinnacle of Asa's success and blessing, he failed miserably. What had characterized his life and reign for ten years—total reliance upon God—he forfeited in a moment of fleshly weakness. He chose to rely on man—himself and others.

The renowned evangelist of the Hebrides Revival, Duncan Campbell (1898-1972), knew the heights of God's blessing as well as the depths of personal powerlessness. After being used mightily by God, he wrote years later, "For 17 years, I moved in [a] barren wilderness." Why? Because he started enjoying the sound of being introduced as "Campbell of the Mid Argyll Revival."* Thankfully, he repented of his prideful heart, and God once more could bless his minister and ministry.

By the sanctifying power of the blessed Holy Spirit, there is one thing each of us can render to the Lord by his grace—a heart which is "completely His."

A Promised Rest

So then, there remains a Sabbath rest for the people of God.
Hebrews 4:9

The writer of the Letter to the Hebrews clearly saw Canaan as a destination to be entered and enjoyed in this present life. It was a land rich in natural resources, described eight times in the Old Testament as a "land flowing with milk and honey."

Canaan was God's promised gift to people who had been delivered from Egyptian slavery. It was a gift Yahweh intended his covenant family to enter within a few weeks following their miraculous Red Sea crossing. However, because of unbelief, Israel turned away from her promised inheritance and wandered aimlessly for forty years in the Arabian Peninsula. Those years were characterized by defeat, disappointment, disillusionment, and frequently despair. And yet, God was gracious to his people and mercifully provided for them. Under Joshua's leadership, Israel entered Canaan.

Speaking through the author of Hebrews, God views Canaan—the land he promised to Israel—as a prototype of the inheritance he wishes to give his people in every age. This inheritance is available in this life, not some distant eschatological future, following death.

This Canaan Land inheritance is called a "rest" in Hebrews 4. "Therefore, while the promise of entering his rest still stands, let us fear lest any of you should seem to have failed to reach it" (v. 1). Remember, these words were addressed to Christians, but Christians who had not yet entered into this promised rest.

Israel, under Joshua's leadership, never experienced the fullness of this promised rest. The rest under Joshua was essentially material and physical. The rest spoken of in Hebrews 4 is a spiritual, a Sabbath rest, an inner rest. "For if Joshua had given them rest, God would not have spoken of another day later on. So then, there remains a Sabbath rest for the people of God, for whoever has entered God's rest has also rested from his works as God did from his" (Heb. 4:8-10).

Some years ago, a minister friend of mine told me he had been living much of his ministerial life laboring in his own strength, until God opened his heart to this "Sabbath rest."

Have you rested from your works?

Wind of God

And suddenly there came from heaven a sound like a mighty rushing
wind, and it filled the entire house where they were sitting.
Acts 2:2

It was a crisp October morning as I sat in the car overlooking beautiful Montagu Bay. My vehicle was provided to my wife Emily and me by our gracious hosts, Sir Durward (the first Olympic gold medal winner from the Bahamas) and Lady Holly Knowles, during my week of ministry among the dear people at the Nassau Ebenezer Methodist Church.

As I viewed the wide assortment of commercial and pleasure boats on the bay that day, I was struck by the sight of the sailboats being pushed gently along by the wind. Tilting slightly to the side, these motorless vessels—each majestic in its own right—made no sound, except that caused by nature, as they effortlessly pursued their destinations.

The power propelling these sailboats was unseen and unheard, but the effects were real and observable. Vessels, which apart from the wind would remain motionless and useless, were traveling according to plan. They were fulfilling the very purpose of their respective creators.

Of the several symbols for the Spirit of God in the Scriptures, wind is one. Interestingly enough, both the Hebrew and Greek words for "Spirit" are also two of the same words rendered as "wind." Wind is a mysterious force, providing energy and power, motion and refreshment, evoking awe among its respectful witnesses. So is the Spirit of God.

Just as the mysterious, sovereign Spirit generates life in men and women dead in their sins (see John 3), so this same Spirit empowers Christ's thirsty-hearted disciples with energy to do the will of the Father in this world: "And suddenly there came from heaven a sound like a mighty rushing wind.... And they were all filled with the Holy Spirit" (Acts 2:2-4).

It is one of God's axioms: Whoever by God's grace will hoist his *sail* to catch the *Wind*, the Spirit of God will fill that person, achieving his purposes in and through such a life.

True Greatness

"But whoever would be great among you must be your servant,
and whoever would be first among you must be slave of all."
Mark 10:43-44

As fledgling followers of the Lord Jesus, the Twelve did not understand what true greatness was all about. Greatness to them was about position, prestige, titles, being first, and authority. They still loved the praise of men more than the praise of God. To serve others was to be done—as long as they were seen and got credit for it. Silent service, unnoticed service, lowly service—these were not on their respective horizons.

When James and John on one occasion expressed their desire to be given prominent positions in Christ's future reign, they vented their natural desires: they wanted to "rule," they wanted to be "great," they wanted to be "first."

It was a teaching moment. Jesus responded that leadership in his kingdom was just the opposite of worldly leadership: "But whoever would be great among you must be your servant, and whoever would be first among you must be slave of all."

True greatness, as Christ views it, is an attitude before it becomes an action—a servant attitude. A true servant doesn't serve for what praise he or she will receive from men. Christian servants perform their loving acts of service, striving for faithfulness and excellence. They serve with an eye to please their Master in Heaven. They don't seek to do great things; they seek to do small things in a great way. They seek to do their duty.

One of the most poignant poems George MacDonald ever penned was written for one of his young sons by the name of Willie. Willie evidently aspired to do something *great*. Knowing of his son's youthful, misplaced aspirations, the wise father wrote a poem (sixty-three verses!) to remind the boy what true greatness was all about. One stanza reads:

The man who was Lord of fate,
Born in an ox's stall,
Was great because he was much too great
*To care about greatness at all.**

Ego

I have been crucified with Christ. It is no longer I who live,
but Christ who lives in me. And the life I now live in the flesh I live
by faith in the Son of God, who loved me and gave himself for me.
Galatians 2:20

I once heard a renowned evangelist say, "While the sins of the *flesh* have slain its thousands, the sins of the *spirit* have slain its tens-of-thousands." Of course the evangelist wasn't using the term "flesh" in Paul's ethical usage of the word; he was speaking of overt acts of sin. Strictly speaking, the "flesh," as Paul employs the term in his letters, encompasses sins of the "spirit" (unchristlike attitudes) as well as every other action contrary to a life lived in the Spirit.

What is the answer to unchristlike attitudes and actions among Christians? Paul provides the solution in his own personal testimony in Galatians 2:20: "I have been crucified with Christ. It is no longer I who live, but Christ who lives in me. And the life I now live in the flesh I live by faith in the Son of God, who loved me and gave himself for me."

Crucifixion is both objective and subjective—something done *for* us, and something done *in* us. Christ took Paul with him to the cross. Christ not only died for Paul, Paul died with Christ. But Paul had to appropriate that redemptive event through faith—which he did. However, there's more. Paul said, "It is no longer *I* (Greek: *ego*) who live." Here's one of the essential keys to successful Christian living: something fundamentally and radically happened to Paul's *ego* when he affirmed his death with Christ on the cross—his *ego* was forever altered; his unsanctified/uncrucified *ego* no longer dominated his life. But we can't live the Christian life successfully merely with a crucified ego. Paul says his ego not only died with Christ, but that Christ himself moved in and became a dynamic presence: "Christ lives in me."

Such a life was transformative and radically different in contrast to the life Paul previously lived: "And the life I now live ..."—right now in this present world. "No more do I exult in my self-righteousness. I have ceased to be governed by a sinful, fallen, driven, self-centered ego." A crucified person, indwelt by the living Christ, is the church's greatest force and the world's greatest need.

Daily Renewal

Though our outer self is wasting away,
our inner self is being renewed day by day.
2 Corinthians 4:16

As I write this, the North American continent is undergoing its perennial renewal. Springtime has arrived once more. Trees and fields are awaking from their season of dormancy and sleep. Renewed life is everywhere present.

In nature, the seasons are cyclical, with months intervening between spring and the following winter. In one's walk in the Spirit, daily renewal is every Christian's privilege, and should be every believer's desired goal.

Day-by-day renewal is made possible by the Spirit's presence in the life of every regenerated Christian, but it is often a neglected privilege. How Christ longs to be refreshingly near to every follower. And yet we regularly allow the mundane and trivial to crowd out what is primary and essential.

For forty years in their wilderness wanderings, the Old Covenant people of God were daily sustained by bread from Heaven each morning and given meat every evening. In order for their physical needs to be met, God instructed them to gather the manna early. For those who rose too late, they discovered the manna was gone. The provisions for physical renewal had been forfeited.

To experience daily renewal means more than to survive. To be renewed by the Spirit day-by-day is to thrive.

Was not daily spiritual renewal the key to the Apostle Paul's abounding joy and passionate love for the Lord Jesus Christ? How could he claim he was constantly "afflicted in every way, but not crushed; perplexed, but not driven to despair; persecuted, but not forsaken; struck down, but not destroyed"? How? Because he also testified, "Though our outer self is wasting away, our inner self is being renewed day by day" (2 Cor. 4:7-18).

We suffer because of the failure to allow the Spirit to renew our daily strength. Instead of rising up with wings like eagles, we run and are weary; we walk and are faint.

God's manna awaits us. Let us gather our portion daily.

Habakkuk's Faith

*"Though the fig tree should not blossom ... yet I will rejoice
in the LORD; I will take joy in the God of my salvation."*
Habakkuk 3:17-18

An uninformed person might conclude that a person who is filled
and walking in the Spirit's power will always see the kind of Kingdom successes that he or she so earnestly desires. Such is not necessarily the case.

Some of our Lord's most godly followers never saw—and never
see—in this world, large numerical results from their faithful, Spirit-
filled labors and ministries. Whether as a pastor, evangelist, Sunday
school teacher, elder or deacon, or one who simply attends the
means of grace faithfully—having no leadership role in the local
church—God has on record the innumerable company of choice
saints who love the Lord God with all their heart, soul, mind, and
strength—and yet from man's vantage point their fruit is little.

It is true to the Word of God to believe that God desires his people to bear much fruit; this was the burden and vision Jesus shared
with his disciples in John 15. However, we must remember that God
does not use man's yardstick in measuring spiritual results.

Habakkuk was a prophet who, from all appearances, saw little
fruit from his ministry. The fact is most of the prophets never
gained mega-followings. But Habakkuk was God's man and God's
mouthpiece to his generation, and to those who followed. His faith
was so rock-solid in the God he served, that he knew God's grace
would be sufficient for him, even though Judah eventually was
plundered and laid waste by the Babylonians. This didn't take place
until after the prophet's death, but when he offered his prayer (Hab.
3:17-19), he had no idea what God's prophetic timetable was.

By the strength of the Spirit, Habakkuk was given a resolute
faith and prepared to face the *whatever*. It is one thing to exercise
faith in God when the harvest is large and the stalls are full, but
what about the opposite? Preaching seven centuries before Christ,
this Old Testament prophet lived what he taught: "The righteous
will live by his faith" (2:4).

Gazing on Jesus

And when they lifted up their eyes, they saw no one but Jesus only.
Matthew 17:8

The Lord Jesus can only be seen through the eyes of loving faith. Such loving faith causes his disciples to experience a heavenly and incomprehensible joy: "Though you have not seen him, you love him. Though you do not now see him, you believe in him and rejoice with joy that is inexpressible and filled with glory" (1 Pet. 1:8). However, our vision of Jesus can be blurred. When this is the case, our faith becomes weak and our love grows cold. Then the joy wanes, and the glory fades.

When the vision of the Lord Jesus begins to grow dim in the Christian's walk, the Holy Spirit is gently present to renew clarity, discernment, and assurance. No God-thirsty believer will be content to go a long distance with an impaired vision of Jesus. We need the regular touches of the Spirit in order to maintain a fresh vision of Jesus.

The gaze of the disciples of Jesus should always to be directed toward him: "looking to Jesus, the founder and perfecter of our faith" (Heb. 12:2). But what are we to do when our vision of Jesus grows dim—a vision of his love, mercy, and compassion; his holiness, righteousness, and truth; his power, gentleness, courage, and perseverance? What are we to do?

This is what we should do: Let Jesus take us aside and touch us anew. Let us bow before him, waiting in his presence, being still. And let us stay there until we begin to see him clearly once again.

In the words of George MacDonald (1824-1905):

I waited for the Master
  In the darkness dumb;
Light came fast and faster—
  My light did not come!
I waited all the daylight,
  All through noon's hot flame:
In the evening's gray light,
  *Lo, the Master came!**

Deepened by Deserts

"For I give water in the wilderness, rivers in the desert."
Isaiah 43:20

Deserts are neither for novices nor tourists. Deserts are for maturing saints.

A desert is a place—both geographically and spiritually—which is essentially barren. It is a region with very little or no rainfall. The vegetation, if any, is sparse and rarely does one see any species deserving of the name tree.

Deserts are usually uninhabited. Normal people don't choose to live in deserts, unless of course, there is a ready supply of air conditioning by day and heat by night. Deserts can be tough—tough on bodies, tough on souls.

There were men, who came to be known as "Desert Fathers," who in the fourth century chose geographically arid regions of Egypt, Palestine, and Syria to isolate themselves from the general population in order to concentrate completely on God. Normally, no Christian would choose a "dry place" as a place to stimulate spiritual fruitfulness. Nevertheless, God chooses to lead his thirsty-hearted saints periodically to travel into desert places—not to *break* them, but to *make* them.

Deserts are meant not for talking. Deserts are quite places, places intended for listening—listening to God.

Deserts are not made for harvests; harvests are for another season. Deserts are meant to destroy—destroy our dependencies on things, our *toys*, and our autonomous selves.

Deserts are one of God's favorite and most effective instruments of mercy in producing in us his holiness and wholeness, his symmetry and beauty. The desert is intended to make us real, authentic, and genuine. The Holy Spirit burns intensely in the desert.

It was in a desert that Moses heard God's call. John the Baptist was shaped in the desert. Deserts inevitably precede fruitfulness.

Don't resist the deserts. Embrace them. In time, you will learn to bless God for them.

God cannot make saints without deserts. Don't search for a substitute. There is none.

Glancing Over Our Shoulder

When Peter saw him, he said to Jesus, "Lord, what about this man?"
John 21:21

There is a temptation we have all yielded to at one time or another—the temptation to compare ourselves or our ministry to another brother or sister in Christ or to another ministry.

Some years ago, I was perusing an excellent Christian periodical that had come across my desk. I noticed in the credits' section that the magazine had a circulation of over 40,000 subscribers. Although this paper has been in circulation for over forty years and is sent free to its readership, nevertheless, almost involuntarily I began to wonder why it would have such a larger readership than *Life in the Spirit* journal, of which I was the editor.

Dipping his pen into the inkwell of divine inspiration, the Apostle Paul wrote that those who compare themselves among themselves are not wise (see 2 Cor. 10:12). How is that so? Why is it unwise to make comparisons in the family of God? It is unwise to make comparisons between ourselves and other ministries, because ...

• *Our gifts differ*. The Spirit distributes gifts in the church according to his sovereign will. Moses is not to be compared with Elijah; neither is Paul to be compared with Timothy. God gives different gifts in order to build a balanced church.

• *Our callings are unique*. Some are called to leadership roles, others to supportive ministries. Some have one unique gift to share with the body of Christ; others are multi-gifted.

• *It can engender envy*. If we are comparing our gifts to one we perceive to be more gifted, it can cause us inwardly to wish we had the same gift.

• *Dissatisfaction will occur*. To accept and be content with the gifts we have been given by God is a beautiful thing. Otherwise, we are questioning the goodness and wisdom of God.

• *Pride will overtake us*. If we compare our gifts to those we perceive as having inferior gifts, it will inevitably foster pride.

Let us ask God to help us not to look over our *shoulder*. Instead, let us keep our eyes fixed on Jesus.

Moral Acuity

Try to discern what is pleasing to the Lord.
Ephesians 5:10

Because one's moral acuity is a major factor in spiritual integrity and holiness, it is critical to the Christian's growth that he is always learning what brings great pleasure to the heart of his God. The Apostle Paul knew this, thus he writes to the Ephesian believers: "try to discern what is pleasing to the Lord."

This apostolic exhortation was directed toward those who had been converted to Christ out of paganism, and who lived in a society which lacked a moral compass. While our particular conversion environment may have differed from that of these Ephesians, the moral climate we live in is not far removed from theirs, thus the need for moral discernment.

How does the Christian develop moral acuity (i.e., the ability to perceive what pleases the Lord when facing moral issues)? Let's look at the immediate context of Ephesians 5 for our answers.

- *Walk in love* (v.1). It is only as we are continually filled with *agape* love for God and other people that we are prepared to make moral judgments.
- *Stay clear of impurity* (vv. 3, 5). We live in a dirty age. Many Christians are being told from some pulpits that sexual purity is an ideal which cannot be realized in this world—that it is normal (for a Christian) to lust, etc. Paul says purity is expected of all saints—true believers.
- *Guard your tongue* (v. 4). Profanity, obscenity, and vulgarity have no place in the language of Christians; off-color jokes are totally unbecoming. Rather, let the tongue be employed in giving thanks to God.
- *Walk as children of light* (vv. 8-17). One cannot exercise keen moral judgment while walking in darkness. We are to walk in the light—holiness and righteousness—of God.
- *Be always filled with the Spirit.* (vv. 18-21). To be filled with the Spirit is to live under the Spirit's control. As we live under the Spirit's control, the Spirit sharpens our moral insight, which in turn brings great pleasure to the heart of our Father in Heaven.

Am I a Soldier of the Cross?

Be watchful, stand firm in the faith, act like men, be strong.
1 Corinthians 16:13

The Christian is called to be a valiant soldier for the Lord Jesus Christ. From the moment of conversion onward, the disciple of Christ is engaged in warfare against the world, the flesh, and the Devil. This is no pilgrimage for the faint of heart.

One of the church's greatest hymn writers was Isaac Watts (1674-1748); he was also a pastor. Watts once preached a sermon from 1 Corinthians 16:13, a text filled with militant terminology. In preparation to preach his sermon, he composed a hymn titled "Am I a Soldier of the Cross?"

In the hymn, Watts asks the congregation to consider seriously a series of searching questions. The first question addresses the matter of living as a witness for Christ before a watching world.

Am I a soldier of the cross, A follower of the Lamb,
And shall I fear to own His cause, Or blush to speak His Name?

The second question addresses the subject of total consecration.

Must I be carried to the skies On flowery beds of ease,
While others fought to win the prize, And sailed through bloody seas?

The next series of questions consider our response to a hostile world.

Are there no foes for me to face? Must I not stem the flood?
Is this vile world a friend to grace, To help me on to God?

What was the pastor's answer?

Sure I must fight if I would reign; Increase my courage, Lord.
I'll bear the toil, endure the pain, Supported by Thy Word.*

What are your answers? Are you a faithful soldier of the Cross?

Friendship

A friend loves at all times, and a brother is born for adversity.
Proverbs 17:17

True Christian friends are a gift from God; by the very nature and demands of friendship, friends are few. Because we are a part of the family of God, everyone who is in Christ is our brother or sister, but not necessarily a close friend.

None of us has many friends, and that's the way it should be. We have a host of acquaintances and contacts, but only a few friends. Why is this so? Because genuine friendship requires compatibility, flexibility, availability, and unconditional acceptance.

• *Compatibility.* Just as a couple in a healthy marriage, genuine friends are compatible. They are not "carbon copies" of one another, but they have the ability to relate to each other with a high degree of harmony. Their dissimilarities don't get in the way of a growing, loving relationship.

• *Flexibility.* True friends give each other space; they are not demanding; they don't force themselves on each another. One cannot be possessive and develop a true friendship.

• *Availability.* Genuine friendships require time. It takes time to grow a friendship, and it takes time to maintain a friendship. Friends want to be with each other. There are some relationships, which could blossom into beautiful friendships, if the two parties simply took the time to invest in each other. Of course, it takes two. One person can't be the one always initiating the contact.

• *Unconditional acceptance.* Authentic friends are non-judgmental. One can be totally transparent with a friend without fear of endangering the friendship. Candor is one of friendship's traits. Friends don't wear masks.

We all need friends. I pray you are blessed, as I am, with a few genuine Christian friends.

Prayer: *Father, I thank you for the gift of friendship. Grant me the necessary sensitivity and wisdom to be a true friend to all of my friends. Amen.*

God's Tests

They were for the testing of Israel, to know whether Israel
would obey the commandments of the Lord, which
he commanded their fathers by the hand of Moses.
Judges 3:4

When the people of Israel entered Canaan under the leadership of Joshua, the Lord God displayed his mighty power among them by enabling his people to conquer their enemies. In city after city, territory after territory, God's people were victorious. Before long, however, some leaders in Israel grew weak and failed to completely conquer their adversaries. We read in Judges 1 that Manasseh, Ephraim, Zebulon, Asher, and Naphtali, failed to "drive out" their respective enemies.

Because Israel began making alliances with her enemies instead of conquering them, God announced, "I will not drive them out before you, but they shall become thorns in your sides, and their gods shall be a snare to you" (Jdg. 2:3). Again, we read in Judges 3:4, that God left pagan nations among the people, "for the testing of Israel, to know whether Israel would obey the commandments of the Lord, which he commanded their fathers by the hand of Moses."

It is God's will for his people to conquer, to overcome sin; nothing less pleases the Lord. When we fail to conquer sin, sin will conquer us. Repeatedly, Israel failed the test, marrying foreign wives and serving foreign gods.

However, something else needs to be said. Sidlow Baxter (1903-1999) used to tell the story about two friends meeting years after their conversions to Christ. Both men had been alcoholics prior to their conversions. Inquiring as to how each other handled his appetite for alcohol through the years, the one said he had been delivered from the desire for drink; the other said there had not been a day he didn't want a drink, but never yielded.

There are some appetites that will remain with the Christian all his life. God will use these to test us. He may not deliver us from them, but he will make us stronger each time we say, "No." God will deliver us from sin, but not necessarily from the natural appetites which can lead to sin.

Are you passing the test?

Our Part (part 1)

But you, beloved, building yourselves up in your most holy faith and
praying in the Holy Spirit, keep yourselves in the love of God, waiting
for the mercy of our Lord Jesus Christ that leads to eternal life.
Jude 1:20-21

Jude 1:20 is a text in contrast—contrasting what is stated in the prior verses. In verses 17-20, the writer reminds his readers about certain "predictions" the apostles made: "In the last time there will be scoffers, following their own ungodly passions" (1:18). Jude says of the scoffers: "It is these who cause divisions, worldly people, devoid of the Spirit" (1:19). Jude says believers are to be altogether different from the scoffers. In what way is this true?

The main clause in verses 20-21 is "keep yourselves in the love of God." This clause is modified by three participles: "building," "praying," "waiting." The writer is appealing here to our *will*. There are some things God cannot do for us; he insists on our cooperation. Those who constantly repeat Romans 8:39, about nothing separating us from the love of God, should balance it with Jude 1:20: "keep yourselves in the love of God." God does not keep those who don't *behave like* they want to be kept! Of course, we can't "keep ourselves in the love of God" without God infusing us with the desire and power to *want to* be kept.

How are we to keep ourselves in the love of God? Jude mentions three ways in these two verses.

"Building yourselves up in your most holy faith." We do this by giving attentive obedience to the Word of God—applying what we hear and read.

"Praying in the Holy Spirit." We pray in the Holy Spirit as we pray according to the will of God. When we don't know how to pray "the Spirit himself intercedes for us with groanings too deep for words" (Rom. 8:26).

"Waiting for the mercy of our Lord Jesus Christ that leads to eternal life." This is not a passive, inactive waiting until Christ returns. This "waiting" involves active engagement in witness and service.

The Christian lives in contrast to false believers. Are you keeping yourself in the love of God, as defined by Jude?

Keep and Kept (part 2)

Keep yourselves in the love of God....
Now to him who is able to keep you ...
Jude 1:21, 24

In our walk with God, we do well to remember the relationship between what God does for us and what he requires us to do. God cannot do for us that which he calls us to do for ourselves. On the other hand, we cannot do for ourselves that which only God can do. And we must say up front: Whatever God requires of us, can solely be accomplished through the grace he supplies.

We are exhorted by the Spirit in Jude 1:21, to "keep yourselves in the love of God." This expression is the main clause in verses 21-22; it is modified by three participles: "building," "praying," and "waiting." God says that we are enabled to keep ourselves in his love by "building [ourselves] up in [our] most holy faith and praying in the Holy Spirit." Furthermore, we keep ourselves in God's love by "waiting for the mercy of our Lord Jesus Christ that leads to eternal life." These are all action words: "building," "praying," "waiting." This is what *we* are to do—by the strength of the Spirit.

The expression—"keep yourselves in the love of God" is Jude's equivalent of Jesus' "abide in me" in John 15. God's desire for his people is that they live in intimate union with him; nothing must be permitted to enter their hearts contrary to his holy love. Such a life can only be maintained as we allow the Spirit of God to empower us to live out the three participles in verses 21-22.

As we live out these three participles, keeping ourselves in the love of God, God is also keeping us: "Now to him who is able to keep you from stumbling and to present you blameless before the presence of his glory with great joy ..." (v. 24). In all of our "keeping," we need to be "kept." None of us is strong enough, wise enough, or obedient enough to outsmart our Adversary. If Jesus had not prayed for Simon Peter, he would have been hopelessly lost. Unless the Lord keeps us from "stumbling," we also will fall. But we have a vital role to play: we must "keep [ourselves] in the love of God." Don't expect God to do for you what he requires you to do for yourself by his grace. However, you can fully expect God to do for you what you cannot do for yourself.

Sin Was the Exception

*David did what was right in the eyes of the Lord and
did not turn aside from anything that he commanded him
all the days of his life, except in the matter of Uriah the Hittite.*
1 Kings 15:5

It appears from reading biblical and church history, that few leaders totally escape acquiring some *stain* before they complete their earthly pilgrimage. The Scriptures chronicle one person after another wavering in his faith and devotion toward God. From Cain to David to Peter to Demas, many men and women have faltered in their walk with God. Some repented, returning to the path of obedience and righteousness; others did not.

David was a man—a man who sinned, and a man with human shortcomings. David fathered twenty children; Adonijah was his fourth son. As with many fathers, David did not always use sound wisdom in rearing his children, including Absalom and Adonijah. Of Adonijah, the Word says, "His father had never at any time displeased him by asking, 'Why have you done thus and so?'" (1 Kings 1:5). One pays a price for parental neglect, as did David and Adonijah.

As important as it is to be a wise parent—and it is—it is just as significant—if not more so—to walk in purity before the Lord. By God's grace, some successfully do so, others have not. For those who have not, their failure was momentary (like David's)—they repented and recovered. Others did not. With some, their moral failure became public; with others, it was private: "The sins of some people are conspicuous, going before them to judgment, but the sins of others appear later" (1 Tim. 5:24).

Teachers who say that *willful* sin is inevitable for the Christian, that a Christian can't help but live a *sinning* life, should read again what God said about David. God said that sin was an *exception* in David's life: "David did what was right in the eyes of the Lord ... *except* in the matter of Uriah the Hittite."

The Lord did not overlook David's failure, but in mentioning it he wanted us to know that he recovered from it and thereafter lived a commendable life. While sin is not to be excused, it need not be the final word for the sincerely repentant.

A Pertinent Question

*And Gideon said to him, "Please, sir, if the Lord is
with us, why then has all this happened to us?"*
Judges 6:13

The children of God have every right to expect that when God is
with his people, there will be observable tokens of his presence. Before his departure, the Lord Jesus told his disciples, "Whoever has
my commandments and keeps them, he it is who loves me. And he
who loves me will be loved by my Father, and I will love him
and *manifest* myself to him" (John 14:21).

Yahweh's angel appeared to Gideon, announcing, "The Lord is
with you, O mighty man of valor" (Judges 6:12). Gideon's response
suggests at least two things: he either misunderstood the angel; or,
he believed God's presence among his people meant blessing and
victory.

First, did Gideon misunderstand the angel? The angel said,
"The LORD is with *you*." He didn't say, "The LORD is with *Israel*."
Israel once again had fallen away from Yahweh. Instead of prevailing over her enemies, she was serving other gods, living in defeat.
The people were hiding in dens, mountains, caves, and their crops
were ravished by Israel's enemies. Even Gideon was in hiding when
the angel appeared to him. While Israel was unfaithful, Gideon remained faithful.

Second, Gideon believed God's presence among his people
would result in blessing and victory: "Please, sir, if the Lord is with
us, why then has all this happened to us? And where are all his wonderful deeds that our fathers recounted to us, saying, 'Did not the
Lord bring us up from Egypt?' But now the Lord has forsaken us
and given us into the hand of Midian."

Gideon believed, and so should we, when God is present among
his people, there will be manifest signs of his presence. When these
tokens are absent, God's people should ask as did Gideon, "Where
are all his wonderful deeds that our fathers recounted to us?"

God's blessing may rest on an individual—as it did with Gideon—without his blessing upon those in the community he worships
with, as was the case with Israel. However, God can take an individual to bless an unblessed people, as was the case with Gideon.

Stirring Up One Another

And let us consider how to stir up one another to love and good works.
Hebrews 10:24

Human nature tends to discouragement. For some, discouragement comes more readily than it does with others. God calls his people to be characterized by *agape* love and good works. However, in the routine of living—even Christian living—one can become spiritually fatigued and disheartened. This was true for the first-century believers to whom the Letter of Hebrews was addressed. Some of these early followers of Christ were shrinking back, losing their confidence; they were growing weary and sluggish, apparently no longer meeting together with the saints regularly. Thus the exhortation: "And let us consider how to stir up one another to love and good works."

It is a fact—Christians need to be frequently *stirred up*. How can this be done? How can we continually stir one another up to love God with our all and love one another, and be a person full of good works? Note some of the following ways.

• Share with others what God has shared with you—from his Word. As we keep a fresh devotional life and are sensitive to the Holy Spirit, God will help us to speak words of grace to others.

• Pray with one another. Unfortunately, our Bible studies far outnumber meaningful prayer times. When we do study the Bible together, more time is given to study than to prayer. Praying with one another can bring creative thoughts to our mind.

• Read excellent Christian biography, asking God to help you emulate men and women of faith. Read about the life and labors of William Carey, George Whitefield, John Newton, Amy Carmichael, David Brainerd, Jonathan Edwards, Fanny Crosby, Kenneth Taylor, Robert Murray M'Cheyne, David Livingstone, the biographies by Warren Wiersbe, and so many more.

• Be an example of love and good works. Nothing has been a greater stimulant in my own life, than observing how God uses other believers who are full of the Spirit. Such men and women not only talked the talk—they walked the walk.

God is exhorting us today: "consider how to stir up one another to love and good works."

Life and Light (part 1)

*And this is the testimony, that God gave us
eternal life, and this life is in his Son.*
1 John 5:11

There are two Greek words translated "life" in the New Testament: *bios* and *zoe*. *Bios* pertains to physical life; *zoe* is primarily used in reference to spiritual life. All human beings experience *bios*, physical life; only those born of the Spirit enjoy spiritual life, eternal life. Of all the occurrences of the word *zoe* in the New Testament, more appear in John's writings than any other, a total of 64 times (Gospel of John, 36; First Epistle of John, 13; Revelation, 15).

John testifies he witnessed God's incarnation of life in the person of the Lord Jesus Christ: "We have seen with our eyes, which we looked upon and have touched with our hands, concerning the Word of Life—the life was made manifest, and we have seen it, and testify to it and proclaim to you the eternal life, which was with the Father and was made manifest to us" (1 John 1:1-2). Jesus Christ was *life* in the flesh! John said, "we have seen Life; we have touched Life"!

It is only through the Lord Jesus Christ that anyone can experience eternal life: "And this is the testimony, that God gave us eternal life, and this life is in his Son. Whoever has the Son has life; whoever does not have the Son of God does not have life" (1 John 5:11-12).

Since the Fall of man in the Garden, he has been plagued with death: "but of the tree of the knowledge of good and evil you shall not eat, for in the day that you eat of it you shall surely die" (Gen. 2:17). Man ate the forbidden fruit, and ever since death—physical and spiritual—has been his destiny. It is only through Christ that this vicious cycle of death can be broken. Because Jesus died and arose from the dead, triumphing over sin, death, and Hell, all who trust him will experience eternal life in this world and the next: "I am the resurrection and the life. Whoever believes in me, though he die, yet shall he live, and everyone who lives and believes in me shall never die" (John 11:25-26).

Have you received this *zoe* life—the very life of Christ?

Life and Light (part 2)

In him was life, and the life was the light of men.
John 1:4

I am moved each time I read the above declaration by the Apostle John. The natural, unconverted man is looking everywhere but the right place for life—real life. The natural man is walking in darkness because there is no life in him—*zoe* life. And because he has no indwelling *life*, the natural man is without *light*—moral and spiritual insight and discernment.

The very *zoe* life, which indwelt the Lord Jesus Christ, was *light*—everywhere he walked and taught. When Christ was present, sinners were conscious of their moral wickedness and innate sinfulness. When Christ was present, people were aware of pure holiness, perfect righteousness, and absolute goodness. Thus, we hear Peter exclaiming, "Depart from me, for I am a sinful man, O Lord" (Luke 5:8).

As a young boy, I recall how I enjoyed turning over a log or a stone, and then watching all the creatures of darkness scamper away, having been exposed to sunlight. This is a good picture of how sinful man often reacts when the light of Christ shines onto his wicked heart: he runs from the light instead of embracing the light. Jesus said, "The light has come into the world, and people loved the darkness rather than the light because their works were evil. For everyone who does wicked things hates the light and does not come to the light, lest his works should be exposed" (John 3:19-20).

We cannot have Christ's life unless we welcome his light; one presupposes the other. The light of Christ is the truth and holiness of Christ; the light of Christ comes to us through the Word of Christ, through the presence of Christ. When we receive Christ's light, we are filled with Christ's life. One cannot follow Christ without walking in his light: "I am the light of the world. Whoever follows me will not walk in darkness, but will have the light of life" (John 8:12).

Without the Lord Jesus, there is no light. Without the Lord Jesus there is no life. With Christ indwelling us, there are both life and light.

June 9

Our Prowling Adversary

Be sober-minded; be watchful. Your adversary the devil
prowls around like a roaring lion, seeking someone to devour.
1 Peter 5:8

To be "sober-minded" in the New Testament sense is not to be *somber-minded*, but to take one's walk with God seriously, and to take our adversary seriously as well. The Christian is to be always alert against the prowling enemy; to let down our guard is to become ready prey for Satan. George Heath's (1745-1822) hymn has been one of my favorites through the years, with regard to the need for Christian vigilance.

My soul, be on thy guard;
Ten thousand foes arise;
The hosts of sin are pressing hard
To draw thee from the skies.

O watch, and fight, and pray;
The battle ne'er give o'er;
Renew it boldly every day,
And help divine implore.

Never think the victory won,
Nor lay thine armor down;
The work of faith will not be done,
Till thou obtain the crown.

Fight on, my soul, till death
Shall bring thee to thy God;
He'll take thee, at thy parting breath,
*To His divine abode.**

The Apostle Peter knew well how the insidious adversary of the soul can take advantage of a weak moment. Christ had warned Peter of his imminent failure. However, when the test presented itself one night in Caiaphas' courtyard, Peter's self-confidence obscured his estimate of the adversary's strength—he denied his Lord three times.

We should never underestimate our prowling enemy.

Possessing Our Possessions

But in Mount Zion there shall be those who escape, and it shall be
holy, and the house of Jacob shall possess their own possessions.
Obadiah 1:17

The prophet Obadiah was given a vision of the Day of the Lord. The Day of the Lord in the Old Testament pointed to either relatively near judgments by God, or the ultimate Day when God judges all peoples and nations. The Day Obadiah speaks of is "near" (1:15).

When this Day arrives, the Lord says through the prophet that Israel will "possess their own possessions." He elaborates on this in verses 19-20, identifying who shall do the possessing, and what territories will be possessed.

As with many individuals, Israel did not always possess her possessions. When God's people crossed the Jordan River and entered the Land of Promise, under both Joshua's leadership and his successors, Israel was to conquer and take possession of the entire territory. She never did. Hence, we have lamentable comments regarding Israel's failures. Note these from the Book of Joshua: "Yet the people of Israel did not drive out the Geshurites or the Maacathites, but Geshur and Maacath dwell in the midst of Israel to this day" (Josh. 13:13). "But the Jebusites, the inhabitants of Jerusalem, the people of Judah could not drive out, so the Jebusites dwell with the people of Judah at Jerusalem to this day" (Josh. 15:63).

Israel did not completely drive out the seven pagan nations in Israel because she would not. With some, she chose to make alliances without consulting the Lord. With others, in stark disobedience to God's instructions, she spared some of her enemies. She was defeated by some enemies who were stronger than she was, because she failed to cry out to God for his wisdom.

The Christian, often like Israel of old, fails to possess his possessions in Christ Jesus. We limp along, suffering defeat after defeat, all because we choose not to walk in total obedience. There are no excuses. "Canaanites" will remain with us until we rise up against them in the strength of God, driving them out.

Are you possessing your possessions in Christ, or are you making alliances with the Enemy?

Power in the Blood (part 1)

And they have conquered him by the blood of the Lamb and by the word of their testimony, for they loved not their lives even unto death.
Revelation 12:11

When I was a Bible college student in the 1960s, one of my classmates was from the country of Haiti. Alex loved to sing hymns and testimony songs as he played the piano. Many years later, I can still hear him playing and singing, "There is Power in the Blood."

Would you be free from the burden of sin?
There's power in the blood, power in the blood;
Would you o'er evil a victory win?
There's wonderful power in the blood.

Chorus:
There is power, power, wonder working power
In the blood of the Lamb.
There is power, power, wonder working power
In the precious blood of the Lamb.

Would you be free from your passion and pride?
There's power in the blood, power in the blood;
Come for a cleansing to Calvary's tide;
There's wonderful power in the blood.

Would you be whiter, much whiter than snow?
There's power in the blood, power in the blood;
Sin stains are lost in its life giving flow;
There's wonderful power in the blood.

Would you do service for Jesus your King?
There's power in the blood, power in the blood;
Would you live daily His praises to sing?
There's wonderful power in the blood. *

In Revelation 12, the saints who were accused by Satan "day and night" before God overcame their adversary. How? They overcame "by the blood of the Lamb and by the word of their testimony."

God's Lamb died; we trust in the Lamb alone for our salvation! That equals victory! There is power in the blood!

Power in a Testimony (part 2)

*And they have conquered him by the blood of the Lamb and by the word
of their testimony, for they loved not their lives even unto death.*
Revelation 12:11

In the previous meditation, we spoke briefly about the power inherent in the blood of Christ, the power of the Lamb's sacrificial death. Revelation 12 also says the saints conquered Satan "by the word of their testimony." "Testimony" can be translated in this verse either as testimony or witness; the Greek word is *martyrias*, from which the word "martyr" is derived.

Satan fears the testimonies of God's saints. That is, our Adversary is defeated when he hears the Christ-exalting, God-glorifying witness of God's people. And let it be said, the best testimonies are *not* given in a prayer meeting, but in life's public square.

The voice which the Apostle John heard, when a prisoner on Patmos Island, said these saints conquered Satan by the "*word* of their testimony." In the heat of the battle, waging war with the enemy of their bodies and souls, these followers of the Lord Jesus Christ were not content to be silent witnesses to their faith. They spoke up; they let it be *heard* whose side they were on, and to *whom* they belonged, and for *whom* they were willing to die—"for they loved not their lives even unto death."

We either love Christ or ourselves—there is no middle ground. The deacon Stephen did not have to think twice when he was threatened by death at the hands of self-righteous religious fanatics. If you are full of the Holy Spirit, and see Jesus standing at the right hand of God while you are being pummeled to death, who is there to fear? Stephen's witness was loud and clear. No one listening to him that day had to question whose side he was on. Among others, Saul of Tarsus got the message. It was Stephen's testimony, Stephen's witness that the Holy Spirit used to convict and convert the church's foremost persecutor.

So many Christians are trusting in some experience instead of Christ. There is no power in an experience apart from Christ; however, there is great power in Christ's blood; there is power in a crystal-clear witness to Christ's saving power.

Are you conquering?

June 13

When the Light is Gone

*"Remember therefore from where you have fallen; repent, and
do the works you did at first. If not, I will come to you and
remove your lampstand from its place, unless you repent."*
Revelation 2:5

The figure of the lampstand in biblical literature was well known to the people of God. Among the few pieces of furniture within the Holy Place in the OT tabernacle/temple was the lampstand (menorah); it consisted of seven candles. These lights were kept burning day and night by the Jewish priest, who entered both morning and evening to trim the wicks.

The Ephesian Church had a wonderful history; they were taught by some of the early church's foremost apostles, evangelists and teachers: Paul and Silas, Priscilla and Aquila, Apollos and Timothy. Many had come to faith in Christ at Ephesus, turning from idolatry and immorality until "the word of the Lord continued to increase and prevail mightily" (Acts 19:20).

However, something happened to the Ephesian believers by the time the Lord Jesus addressed them in Revelation 2. While the church remained busily engaged in good works, and was orthodox in the faith, Christ was no longer the focus of their living and worship: they had abandoned their first love; they had fallen.

It is the greatest of all tragedies whenever a church loses the very purpose for her existence. Years ago in Washington D.C., a sign was placed on the front door of a church building: "Gone Out of Business; Didn't Know What Our Business Was."

The Head of the church, the Lord Jesus Christ, warned the Ephesian Church, that unless she repented, "I will come to you and remove your lampstand from its place." In other words: "You will cease to be a church; the light will be totally removed." Many churches are numbly unaware. Christ has gone, but they continue to go through the motions. In the words of the Elizabethan bard, they are "full of sound and fury, signifying nothing."

Repentance is the only answer to lost first love. Unless a church repents, her light is removed, the lampstand is gone. Pray that your church will not suffer such a lamentable demise. By the strength of God, let us keep our love fresh and passionate.

June 14

Extravagant Devotion

*"Why do you trouble the woman? For she
has done a beautiful thing to me."*
Matthew 26:10

It is instinctive in human nature to wish to return a favor with a favor, a good deed with a good deed, a gift with a gift.

The peaceful and wholesome Bethany home had been shattered by death. Where joy had once reigned, gloom filled the atmosphere. The sisters of Lazarus, Mary and Martha, were convinced if Jesus had been present, their brother would never have died; they had at least that much faith in their Lord.

But Jesus had not been present; their brother did die. However, four days later Jesus came, Jesus was present, and Jesus raised their brother from the grave.

I wonder if this was not what prompted Mary to anoint the Lord Jesus with her precious and expensive gift. She wanted to honor Jesus for what he had done in restoring their brother to life. She wished to present something of immense value to Jesus.

We should spend our lives in giving back to our Lord for what he has done for us—through his death, the forgiveness of sins, and so much more. Sylvanus Phelps (1816-1895) said it well:

Savior, Thy dying love Thou gavest me.
Nor should I aught withhold, dear Lord, from Thee.
In love my soul would bow, my heart fulfill its vow,
Some offering bring Thee now, something for Thee.

Give me a faithful heart, likeness to Thee.
That each departing day henceforth may see
Some work of love begun, some deed of kindness done,
Some wanderer sought and won, something for Thee.

All that I am and have, Thy gifts so free,
In joy, in grief, through life, O Lord, for Thee!
And when Thy face I see, my ransomed soul shall be
*Through all eternity, something for Thee.**

While others criticized Mary for her extravagant act of devotion, Jesus commended her: "Why do you trouble the woman? For she has done a beautiful thing to me" (Matt. 26:10).

Godly Courage

When Daniel knew that the document had been signed, he went to his house where he had windows in his upper chamber open toward Jerusalem. He got down on his knees three times a day and prayed and gave thanks before his God, as he had done previously.
Daniel 6:10

Daniel lived in an environment that was antagonistic to the true God and his devoted followers. There were only a handful of God-fearing men and women, whose piety was conspicuous in Daniel's day. It was unpopular to take a public stand for Yahweh, when all around there was idol worship, desecration of the holy, and intolerance toward those who held an exclusive loyalty toward the one and only true God. The world has never been a friend of grace and godliness. It wasn't in Daniel's day; it isn't in our day.

When a crisis comes to test our devotion to God, whether we pass the test or not will depend on our prior commitments and habits. It will depend on whether or not we have been faithful to God in the small things, in life's unobservable duties. The tests will inevitably come. The question is, *Will we pass the test?* Tests to our loyalty and devotion to God often come without warning, as they did in Simon Peter's case. The Lord Jesus had warned Peter he would be tested, but Peter didn't know how the test would occur. When the test did come, he failed the test.

Daniel was prepared when the test came. He developed an important habit when living in Israel—the habit of prayer. When Daniel, along with many others was taken to Babylon, Daniel never altered his prayer life. He continued to pray—three times a day. For Daniel, prayer was more than a religious exercise; it was a true expression of his dependence on Yahweh.

When the edict was announced that death would result for anyone who offered a petition to any god or man other than the king, Daniel didn't waver: "He got down on his knees three times a day and prayed and gave thanks before his God, as he had done previously."

Our inconspicuous acts of devotion toward God will serve us well whenever the tests come. We don't trust in exercises of devotion; however, through grace God uses them to keep us strong.

Possessed to Serve

*"For this very night an angel of the God to whom
I belong and whom I serve stood before me, ..."*
Acts 27:23 NASB

One of the first discoveries that the child of God makes following his conversion to Christ is that he now belongs to Another. Whereas he once was the subject of the ruler and god of this world, a great transference has occurred: "He [God] has delivered us from the domain of darkness and transferred us to the kingdom of his beloved Son, ..." (Col. 1:13).

Satan, the enemy of God and true righteousness, is a thief. He has stolen those who by right of creation and redemption were God's, and made them slaves of wickedness and unrighteousness: "The thief comes only to steal and kill and destroy" (John 10:10).

However, at the moment of his new birth, the Father's child, who has been purchased by the blood of the Lord Jesus Christ, now belongs to God and his Son. This is a revelation to the infant in Christ Jesus: we were "called to belong to Jesus Christ" (Rom. 1:6).

Can you imagine how an American slave must have felt following the news that he was now free to leave his slave owner and pursue a life of freedom? He was no longer owned by a human master; he was free to leave. Where this analogy breaks down, however, in making a spiritual application is this: Whereas the freed slave left the ownership of the slaveholder, he then became his own master. Not so with the Christian: "Do you not know that if you present yourselves to anyone as obedient slaves, you are slaves of the one whom you obey, either of sin, which leads to death, or of obedience, which leads to righteousness? But thanks be to God, that you who were once slaves of sin have become obedient from the heart to the standard of teaching to which you were committed, and, having been set free from sin, have become slaves of righteousness" (Rom. 6:16-18).

We have become "slaves of righteousness" because we now belong to God and serve him. That is precisely what Paul announced to his fellow passengers on that storm-tossed sea some two thousand years ago. He testified for all to hear that he belonged to God, and that he was his servant.

A Diamond-Hard Heart

They made their hearts diamond-hard lest they should hear the
law and the words that the Lord of hosts had sent by his Spirit.
Zechariah 7:12

Each one of us has a decision to make whenever God's truth comes
to us, whether in public worship, small-group Bible studies, or during our quiet times alone with God. We cannot hear/read the Word
of God without being confronted with truth. It matters not who the
human instrument may be in delivering God's message; it is what
God has said that is important.

We have a choice to live with either a heart of *flesh* or a heart of
stone. God told Ezekiel that a day would come when "I will remove
the heart of stone from their flesh and give them a heart of
flesh" (Ezek. 11:19). God wants to give us a soft heart; he wants us to
maintain a willing, obedient heart to all that he speaks. It is possible
for a heart once softened to become hardened toward what God has
spoken.

Zechariah was one of God's faithful messengers. As a prophet, it
was his duty to take God's words to God's people, and deliver them
without addition or subtraction. Not all responded favorably to
God's words, just as many people fail to listen today: "But they refused to pay attention and turned a stubborn shoulder and stopped
their ears that they might not hear" (7:11).

There is something that takes place in the heart of a man who
hears the Word of God but fails to act on what he hears. It may be
imperceptible at first, but slowly a hardening process occurs unless
it is checked. This happened to some under Zechariah's ministry:
"They made their hearts diamond-hard lest they should hear the
law and the words that the Lord of hosts had sent by his Spirit" (7:12).

The Christian's only safeguard against forming a hard heart is
to embrace the Word of God every time he hears/reads it. "But exhort one another every day, as long as it is called 'today,' that none
of you may be hardened by the deceitfulness of sin" (Heb. 3:13).

The Necessary Link

And Jesus said to him, "'If you can'!
All things are possible for one who believes."
Mark 9:23

During the earthly ministry of our Lord, he was especially drawn to those undergoing dire difficulties. We see this when the multitudes were hungry, when Simon Peter was in danger of drowning, when Jesus reached out to the lepers and the blind and diseased. We notice the moving compassion of Christ in restoring life to a little girl, a young man, and to a brother who was dead for four days. When he looked upon those who suffered, the Lord Jesus was indeed, "a man of sorrows, and acquainted with grief" (Isa. 53:3).

Following the revelation of his glory in the Transfiguration Event, Jesus descends the mountain with his disciples. There they encounter a desperate father with his afflicted son. Thinking Christ's disciples could help his son, the father pled with them to cast the unclean spirit out of the boy. However, they were powerless. Relentless in his pursuit for a cure, the father finds Jesus and makes a plaintive plea, "if you can do anything, have compassion on us and help us" (9:22).

Jesus knew he could do "anything" that was in harmony with his Father's will; after all, he was the Father's Son. Jesus also knew before God can act in some situations, it is necessary for man to exercise faith in God. Jesus corrected the father's statement by putting the responsibility on him: "'If you can'! All things are possible for one who believes."

This text has special meaning for me. One afternoon I awoke from a brief nap with this very Scripture on my mind—Mark 9:23. I asked myself, *What does this mean? What does Mark 9:23 really say?* I had never had this happen before nor since. I immediately took my Bible and turned to the text and read it. I was amazed; I was humbled. I had been praying for a long while about a particular need. God revealed to me that day that his words in Mark 9:23 held the key to my need: "If you can!"

When faith is joined to God's omnipotence, the impossible becomes possible.

A Triad of Graces

So now faith, hope, and love abide,
these three; but the greatest of these is love.
1 Corinthians 13:13

At least seven times in his letters, the Apostle Paul joins a triad of
Christian graces: faith, hope, and love (Rom. 5:1-5; 1 Cor. 13:13; Gal.
5:5-6; Eph. 4:2-5; Col. 1:4-5; 1 Thess. 1:3, 5:8). While he states in
his first letter to the Corinthian Church that love is the greatest of
the three, he certainly doesn't discount the importance of the other
two, since they are often mentioned in his correspondence.

Faith. Without this gift of grace from God, we cannot believe
God exists (Heb. 11:6); we cannot be justified (Rom. 5:1); we cannot
please God (Heb. 11:6); we cannot believe God will answer our petitions (Heb. 11:6); we cannot accomplish God's purposes through us
(see Heb. 11). Faith in God is as essential to our daily walk with God
as the air we breathe is necessary for our physical existence. It is the
Christian's shield (Eph. 6:16), as he wages war against his Adversary; it makes the impossible possible, because of its object (Mark
9:23).

Hope. This Christian grace has reference to the future, and is
anchored in both what God has done through Christ and what he
has promised to do in the future. More is said about hope in the
Letter of Hebrews than any other New Testament book, undoubtedly because of the severe opposition these early believers were experiencing. The writer encouraged these suffering believers to "hold
fast the confession of our hope without wavering, for he who promised is faithful" (10:23). Without evangelical hope, we are left with
discouragement and despair.

Love. Paul calls this the greatest of the three graces. It is superi-
or to faith and hope, because a day is coming when faith and hope
will no longer be necessary. However, the very love of God will forever be present. For where God is, there is always love.

In the meantime, as we continue our journey here below, we are
to "put on love, which binds everything together in perfect harmony" (Col. 3:14).

The more we abound in love, the more we will abound in faith
and hope.

The New Birth

*"Truly, truly, I say to you, unless one is born
again he cannot see the kingdom of God."*
John 3:3

For one to experience and enjoy *physical* sight in this world, a biological birth must occur. A person cannot see the world about him without the faculty of sight. Sight can only happen when it is preceded by birth. Before a person can experience *spiritual* sight (insight), something deep within him must take place. Jesus likened this something to a *birth*.

Nicodemus was a man who was well-versed in the Law of Moses. He held to the strict tradition of the elders, for he was a member of the Pharisees, the most conservative group of the Jewish parties. And he was not just any Pharisee—he was a "ruler of the Pharisees" (John 3:1). Being a Pharisee, he prayed to Yahweh and fasted regularly. No doubt he committed to memory many passages in the Torah and the Psalms. He faithfully attended and observed all the Jewish holy days in the temple. Even so, he felt a need, a lack in his soul. He hungered for something more.

It was this God-implanted hunger that caused Nicodemus intentionally to search for the Lord Jesus one night. He acknowledged that Jesus was a teacher sent by God; he believed the miracles Jesus performed were of God (John 3:2), and yet he was still blind—spiritually blind.

Jesus immediately went to the heart of this Pharisee's need: "Truly, truly, I say to you, unless one is born again he cannot see the kingdom of God." Nicodemus was confused: "How can a man be born when he is old? Can he enter a second time into his mother's womb and be born?" (John 3:3-4). Nicodemus didn't understand; his eyes were yet closed.

The new birth—being born again, being born from above—is a mystery: "The wind blows where it wishes, and you hear its sound, but you do not know where it comes from or where it goes. So it is with everyone who is born of the Spirit" (John 3:8). It is an amazing mystery, but it is also an amazing reality and necessity if we are to experience the rule and reign of God in our lives—"see the kingdom of heaven." Have you been born from above?

Desperate Times Call for Desperate Action

As soon as I heard these words I sat down and wept and mourned for
days, and I continued fasting and praying before the God of heaven.
Nehemiah 1:4

Nehemiah never forgot the day when he was told about Jerusalem's
desperately sad plight. He was in the city of Susa; it was November/
December, 445 B.C., the twentieth year of Artaxerxes' reign. Nehemiah was anxious to learn from a recently arrived delegation from
Jerusalem as to the welfare of the people and the condition of the
city. He was informed: "The remnant there in the province who had
survived the exile is in great trouble and shame. The wall of Jerusalem is broken down, and its gates are destroyed by fire" (Neh. 1:3).

Though Susa (located in present-day Iran) was a great distance
from Jerusalem, Jerusalem to Nehemiah and the Jewish people was
the city of God. The temple was there, God's dwelling place. Jerusalem was full of history and memories; three great pilgrimages were
taken to the city by God's people annually. Her people often sang:
"If I forget you, O Jerusalem, let my right hand forget its skill! Let
my tongue stick to the roof of my mouth, if I do not remember you,
if I do not set Jerusalem above my highest joy!" (Psa. 137:5-6).

But bad times came to Jerusalem. Her walls were in disrepair;
her gates were destroyed; ruin and destruction were everywhere. An
air of despair and hopelessness filled the air.

Whenever God desires to bring revival/renewal to a people, he
entrusts to a caring, God-sensitive person a prayer burden. He
found such a person in Nehemiah: "As soon as I heard these words
I sat down and wept and mourned for days, and I continued fasting
and praying before the God of heaven" (Neh. 1:4).

Mission always results from earnest prayer. It was out of days
of fasting and prayer that Nehemiah discovered the method of approach in seeing Jerusalem renewed. God heard; God gave wisdom.

Genuine renewal does not occur without a foundation of prayer.
Mission is the inevitable result of earnest prayer. What God has
joined together, let not insensitive leaders put asunder.

A Whole Heart

And he did what was right in the eyes
of the Lord, yet not with a whole heart.
2 Chronicles 25:2

It is possible to serve the Lord with less than a *whole* heart. We can be engaged in doing the right thing from God's perspective, yet fail to do the right with a *whole* heart. Moreover, we see in the Scripture that a believer can start walking with God with a whole heart, but end up with a divided heart.

Language means something, and the language God used to communicate his words through Spirit-inspired men of old was precisely chosen for a reason. When God chose to speak of a person who did or did not serve him with a whole heart, God was saying to them and to us, that person was either walking fully according to his revealed will, or he was not. It was a matter of the heart. A whole heart will serve the Lord wholly; a divided heart will serve the Lord halfheartedly.

God's desire for all of his people is that they have whole hearts, so they can serve him wholeheartedly. Knowing this, Israel's sweet singer prayed, "Teach me your way, O Lord, that I may walk in your truth; unite my heart to fear your name" (Psa. 86:11). One can read through the Psalms, taking note of what the psalmists did with their whole heart: giving thanks, rejoicing, seeking God, obeying God's word, praying, and praising God.

Some of Israel's and Judah's kings served the Lord with their whole heart; most did not. Amaziah reigned as a king for twenty-nine years, doing many things that were right and won many victories. However, the Lord said of him, "he did what was right in the eyes of the Lord, yet not with a whole heart" (2 Chron. 25:2).

Realizing that any service less than wholehearted service is unacceptable to God, David charged his son Solomon to serve God with wholehearted devotion: "And you, Solomon my son, know the God of your father and serve him with a whole heart" (1 Chron. 28:9).

God's antidote for an incomplete heart is a pure heart: "purify your hearts, you double-minded" (James 4:8).

Have you asked God to give you a whole heart, a pure heart?

June 23

Perfect Peace

You keep him in perfect peace whose mind is
stayed on you, because he trusts in you.
Isaiah 26:3

Peace is more than the absence of conflict; it is the presence of tranquility, a sense of security. When one enjoys God's peace, he experiences internal harmony and quietness, serenity and unity.

When one is justified by faith, the enmity between God and man disappears, reconciliation occurs—at God's initiative through the cross of Christ. "Therefore, since we have been justified by faith, we have peace with God through our Lord Jesus Christ" (Rom. 5:1). "And you, who once were alienated and hostile in mind, doing evil deeds, he has now reconciled in his body of flesh by his death" (Col. 1:21-22).

A Christian may be right with God while living with internal discord, fear, and strife. God wants to give us his peace, perfect peace. Isaiah says it comes by focusing on God, trusting in God. One who came to a place of perfect peace, Frances R. Havergal (1836-1879), wrote about it so beautifully.

Like a river glorious, is God's perfect peace,
Over all victorious, in its bright increase;
Perfect, yet it floweth, fuller every day,
Perfect, yet it groweth, deeper all the way.

Refrain
Stayed upon Jehovah, hearts are fully blest
Finding, as He promised, perfect peace and rest.

Hidden in the hollow of His blessed hand,
Never foe can follow, never traitor stand;
Not a surge of worry, not a shade of care,
Not a blast of hurry touch the spirit there.

Every joy or trial falleth from above,
Traced upon our dial by the Sun of Love;
We may trust Him fully all for us to do.
*They who trust Him wholly find Him wholly true.**

I pray you will know this perfect peace that both the prophet and the hymn writer wrote about.

June 24

Faith in the Dark

"Oh that my words were written! Oh that they were
inscribed in a book! Oh that with an iron pen and
lead they were engraved in the rock forever!"
Job 19:23-24

In all of Scripture, we have no greater declaration of faith in God by a man than those recorded in Job 19:23-27. All of Job's possessions and livelihood were taken from him; his sons and daughters were killed by a wind storm; his body was afflicted with boils "from the sole of his foot to the crown of his head" (2:7). In the midst of all of his pain and anguish, his wife said to him, "Do you still hold fast your integrity? Curse God and die" (2:9). If all this were not enough, three miserable *comforters* provide anything but comfort to God's suffering servant.

Here was a man who was "blameless and upright, one who feared God and turned away from evil" (1:1). Yet he suffered! He experienced devastating loss!

Satan didn't know Job as well as God did, for Satan told God, "You have blessed the work of his hands, and his possessions have increased in the land. But stretch out your hand and touch all that he has, and he will curse you to your face" (1:10-11). God knew better. What does God know about you? How will you respond in a crisis, when all around your soul gives way?

Job's faith in God was so strong that he wanted his words preserved in a book and engraved in rock—for all to read:

"Oh that my words were written!
  Oh that they were inscribed in a book!
Oh that with an iron pen and lead
  they were engraved in the rock forever!
For I know that my Redeemer lives,
  and at the last he will stand upon the earth.
And after my skin has been thus destroyed,
  yet in my flesh I shall see God,
whom I shall see for myself,
  and my eyes shall behold, and not another" (19:23-27).

When Job spoke these words, he had no idea what his earthly future held. He only knew that he knew God and that God knew him. That was enough!

Praying for Laborers

*And he said to them, "The harvest is plentiful, but
the laborers are few. Therefore pray earnestly to the Lord
of the harvest to send out laborers into his harvest."*
Luke 10:2

As I write this, in our part of the country most of the grain fields have been harvested of wheat, corn and soy beans. From mid-summer to late fall—day after day—farmers have been busily employed in their fields reaping grain. Large combines have gone back and forth, field after field, then unloading their product into trucks, which in turn take the fruit of the farmers' labor to grain elevators to be sold. Harvesting is intensive work; it is tiring work; it is fruitful and rewarding work.

There is no harvest without farmers; there is no harvest without laborers. The Lord Jesus and his disciples were familiar with the farming culture; they lived in a day and in a land that was surrounded with fruit trees, vineyards, and grain fields. Much of Israel was populated by men and women who were people of the soil—people who sowed, tilled, and harvested. They knew the fruit of their labors would spoil and rot unless it was harvested. All the soil preparation, planting and cultivating would be in vain unless the grain and fruit were gathered.

Jesus called the Twelve and commissioned them as apostles (lit., "sent ones"). In Luke 10:1, Jesus "appointed seventy-two others and sent them on ahead of him, two by two, into every town and place where he himself was about to go." In commissioning these laborers—these *sent ones*—he shares a specific prayer request: "pray earnestly to the Lord of the harvest to send out laborers into his harvest."

I wonder if much of the church has not forgotten this prayer-burden of her Lord. Of all the requests we hear in our public prayer times, how often do we hear someone request, "We need to pray earnestly—earnestly—that the Lord would send men and women into the harvest fields to labor for him"?

The Lord of the harvest *depends* on the prayers of his church to plead with him to call and send out laborers. Are we praying?

A Proven Weapon

Whenever Moses held up his hand, Israel prevailed,
and whenever he lowered his hand, Amalek prevailed.
Exodus 17:11

One of the wonders of God's ways among men is that he uses the intercessions of his people to further his work on earth. And one of the wonders of the church is that she doesn't engage more faithfully in doing God's work in God's way.

The church has tried every available substitute in advancing God's cause here below. Mega dollars have been invested in one endeavor after another. Hours have been spent in training and equipping her workers to go forth wearing *Saul's armor*. Depending on the wisdom and expertise of the corporate world, the church often remains powerless and ineffective; she is content to build with "wood, hay, and straw" (1 Cor. 3:12).

Moses knew better, for Moses had been schooled and disciplined in the ways of God, long before he engaged in God's mission. He who would become Israel's great leader, at one time suffered embarrassing defeat, all because he attempted to do God's work in his own way. However, Moses had a transforming encounter in the desert; it forever altered his life and future ministry. Thereafter, he aspired to do God's work in God's way.

Hence, when we come to Exodus 17, and read the account of Israel waging war against her enemy, we see Moses interceding for the people of God on top of a hill with the "staff of God in his hand," while Joshua is on the field of battle below. We don't have a more striking picture in all of Scripture as to the efficacy of prayer than we have in this narrative: "Whenever Moses held up his hand, Israel prevailed, and whenever he lowered his hand, Amalek prevailed" (17:11).

Moses grew weary; he needed help: "so they took a stone and put it under him, and he sat on it, while Aaron and Hur held up his hands, one on one side, and the other on the other side" (17:12). He persisted in prayer, "until the going down of the sun" (17:12). What was the result on the field of battle? "And Joshua overwhelmed Amalek and his people with the sword" (17:13).

Will we ever learn this lesson?

June 27

Complete Consecration

*Then you shall take part of the blood that is on the altar,
and of the anointing oil, and sprinkle it on Aaron and his
garments, and on his sons and his sons' garments with him.*
Exodus 29:21

What we see fulfilled through Christ under the New Covenant, we find an array of salvation themes and their respective antitypes under the Old Covenant. The same holds true for Christian experience: What God expects from his people under the New Covenant, he provided us with types and descriptions in the Old Covenant, including the doctrine of total consecration.

When God calls us to himself, he never expects us to become a *partial* disciple of Christ; he calls us to complete renunciation of the world and ourselves, and a total consecration of our being to him. Such a calling is expressed by both the Lord Jesus and the Apostle Paul: "If anyone would come after me, let him deny himself and take up his cross and follow me" (Mark 8:34). "I appeal to you therefore, brothers, by the mercies of God, to present your bodies as a living sacrifice, holy and acceptable to God, which is your spiritual worship" (Rom. 12:1).

This total consecration of oneself to God is foreshadowed in Exodus 29. There we have the account of the consecration of Aaron and his sons as priests. Following the designated animal sacrifices on their behalf, the blood from the animals was to be sprinkled on Aaron and his sons, including "the tips of the right ears of his sons, and on the thumbs of their right hands and on the great toes of their right feet" (29:20). Then in verse 29:21, Aaron and his sons are anointed with holy oil.

Here we have a vivid picture of total consecration: every extremity of the person is to be consecrated to the Lord. Every part of our being is to be covered with the blood of Christ and the oil of the Holy Spirit. We are to make a total surrender of ourselves to God; we are to give ourselves to God—without reservation. Have you given your all to Christ? Are you affirming this daily?

*Take my life, and let it be
Consecrated, Lord, to Thee.**

Jealous With God's Jealousy

Then Phinehas stood up and intervened, and the plague was stayed.
Psalm 106:30

God's work on earth progresses to the degree that it is preserved and conserved by his Spirit working through godly men and women. The church, since its inception, has waged war on two fronts: those without and those within. The design of Satan, God's adversary and ours, is to seek to "steal and kill and destroy" everything that is of God. He does this overtly and covertly, seductively and boldly, persistently and relentlessly. He constantly stalks his prey as a roaring lion.

Moral and spiritual integrity cannot be bought in the world's marketplace, but it can be sold through worldly pressure. The church of God, purchased with the blood of Christ, is constantly under attack by her enemies on the outside. And the truth of God is often wounded in the house of her friends as well.

When evil marched into the midst of God's people one day, through the sexual liaison between a pagan woman and an Israelite male, a man by the name of Phinehas saw it and was morally outraged. He strode right into the bedroom and killed both. And how did God view this priest's action? "And the Lord said to Moses, 'Phinehas the son of Eleazar, son of Aaron the priest, has turned back my wrath from the people of Israel, in that he was jealous with my jealousy among them, so that I did not consume the people of Israel in my jealousy'" (Num. 25:10-11).

Phinehas was intolerant of rivals to God's words and truth. He was jealous with God's jealousy. God commended him for what he did.

Of course, God does not call us to pick up worldly swords to kill his enemies, but he does call us to guard his truth—on local church boards, business meetings, and from pulpits. A failure to stand up for truth results in disaster for the church. As Aleksandr Solzhenitsyn (1918-2008) has reminded us, "Just as a shout in the mountains can start an avalanche, so a word or stand for truth that does God's work in God's way in God's time can have an incalculable effect."*

Of Inestimable Value

"Fear not, therefore; you are of more value than many sparrows."
Matthew 10:31

Our Father-God has assured—and reassured—his people throughout biblical history that his loving care for them is beyond human measure. From the Garden of Eden in the Book of Genesis, to the New Jerusalem in Revelation, the Lord our God demonstrates his unfathomable kindness and generosity toward the saints.

• *God demonstrates his care for us through his creation.* While we don't worship created matter, we certainly honor the Creator by thanking him for his creation and treating it with respect. From the farthest star in the universe to the smallest creature of earth—the Lord God made them all. Every river, lake, and ocean; every flower, shrub and tree; every beast, bird, and insect—from the sky above to the soil below—God has given them all for our needs and pleasure.

• *God demonstrates his care for us through the Incarnation.* That "the Word became flesh and dwelt among us" (John 1:14) is God's revelation of grace, love, and kindness. He would not allow us to go through life alone; he sent his one and only Son to this fallen, sin-soaked world to show us how to live, how to love, how to treat other people.

• *God demonstrated his care for us at the Cross.* John 3:16 is more than a verse to be memorized; it is a fact to be pondered, a truth that should cause us to bow our heads in wonder and amazement. Jesus offered himself for our sins, that we might be redeemed and reconciled to God is a revelation of God's ultimate regard for us; he loves us that much!

• *God demonstrates his constant care for us by his material provisions.* Before Jesus sent out his disciples on mission, he knew the human tendency—fear of adversaries, and anxiety because of need. He assured them their sovereign God was in control, caring for each of them. Their Father in heaven sees each sparrow when it falls to the ground. "Fear not, therefore; you are of more value than many sparrows" (Matt. 10:31). Again, "Look at the birds of the air: they neither sow nor reap nor gather into barns, and yet your heavenly Father feeds them. Are you not of more value than they?" (Matt. 6:26). God cares!

Unworthy Servants

*"So you also, when you have done all that you were commanded, say,
'We are unworthy servants; we have only done what was our duty.'"*
Luke 17:10

I remember reading about a pastor who stood in the vestibule of the church following each Sunday morning sermon; there he would greet the people as they left the sanctuary. One after another, parishioners expressed their appreciation for his fine sermon. However, the pastor began to struggle with pride—too many nice things were being said; he didn't know how to handle all the kind words of affirmation. So he decided he would no longer greet the people as they left.

Following her years of imprisonment in Nazi Germany, Corrie ten Boom (1892-1983) began traveling around the world, telling how Christ's love can conquer in the darkest of circumstances. Everywhere Corrie went, hosts and listeners would heap praise after praise upon her. How was she to cope with such adulation? She decided on this response, which she used throughout her years of ministry. Upon returning to her room following a speaking engagement, she would go to her knees, taking all the kind remarks, and lay them at the feet of Jesus like a bouquet of flowers. She refused to keep the "flowers"; she passed them on to Jesus.

Because he knew all people, and their propensity to pride and self-exaltation, Jesus told us how we are to combat pride whenever we are congratulated by others in the performance of Christian service: "when you have done all that you were commanded, say, 'We are unworthy servants; we have only done what was our duty.'"

We cannot represent Jesus and ourselves at the same time. We are either servants of Christ or slaves to our ego. God knows the difference; and so will discerning people who have listened to us for any length of time. It is an awful and abominable thing to insinuate ourselves into taking credit for something that was presumably done in Jesus' name. How many acts of service have been spoiled because we have subtly stolen God's glory!

"The crucible is for silver, and the furnace is for gold, and a man is tested by his praise" (Prov. 27:21).

An Encouraging Word

Anxiety in a man's heart weighs him down,
but a good word makes him glad.
Proverbs 12:25
Gracious words are like a honeycomb,
sweetness to the soul and health to the body.
Proverbs 16:24

As a little boy, while attending elementary school, I well remember a song our chorus teacher taught us one day. It's a western ballad that most American school children learned at one time or another—"Home On the Range." There is a line in this song that should serve as a standard of speech for all Christians: "And never was heard a discouraging word."

Words—how powerful they are; how motivating and inspirational they can be. Impressionable words, spoken by a significant person, can even chart the course for the rest of one's life.

Benjamin West (1738-1820) tells how he became a great artist. One day, his mother went on an errand, leaving young Benjamin responsible for his little sister Sally. In his mother's absence, Benjamin discovered some bottles of colored ink and decided to try to paint a portrait of his sister. However, in doing so, he made quite a mess of things and ink blots ended up all over the room.

After some time, his mother returned. She quickly surveyed the mess, but said nothing. She picked up the piece of paper and saw Benjamin's drawing. "Why," she exclaimed, "It's Sally!" And she stooped to kiss her son. Ever afterward, Benjamin West used to say, "My mother's kiss made me a painter."* Words—and kisses!—matter.

While a Christian should avoid flattery—insincere complimentary words—he will search out ways in which he can bring comfort and encouragement, inspiration and affirmation, to God's dear children.

In a different context, the apostle wrote, "Let your speech always be gracious, seasoned with salt, so that you may know how you ought to answer each person" (Col. 4:6).

"Seasoned with salt"! Often that *seasoning* means giving an encouraging word.

Christ in You (part 1)

Christ in you, the hope of glory.
Colossians 1:27

Years ago, the Scottish evangelist Dr. John S. Logan was at a meeting of pastors where Watchman Nee (1903-1972), the saintly Chinese evangelist, was present. Logan gave the following account of the impression Nee left upon that gathering of ministers: "After speaking, Watchman Nee was fielding questions from the crowd, and one pastor asked if he could define holiness. Nee said, 'It is the Spirit of Christ in me, plus ...' and he began to move around the room placing his hands on each pastor in succession and saying, 'the Spirit of Christ in you, plus the Spirit of Christ in you, plus the Spirit of Christ in you, plus ...'"

"The pastors," Dr. Logan said, "were all nodding in consent. Holiness is personal in its reformation of our character into the increasing likeness of the character of Christ, plus it has a definite relational dimension—primarily in how we react and respond to one another.

"When Nee had moved all around the room and arrived back on the platform, the pastors were ready for the next question, but Nee was not finished, yet.

"He then proceeded around the room again, saying, 'Less the self in me, less the self in you, less the self in you, less the self in you, less the self in you ...'"*

God is calling each disciple of the Christ to be increasingly transformed into his Son's likeness (2 Cor. 3:18). It is one thing to be *in* Christ; it is quite another to *live out* the implications of Christ living *in* me.

The Lord Jesus Christ indwells every believer in the person of the Holy Spirit, and as we grow in the grace and the knowledge of the Lord Jesus, we will reflect more and more of Christ and less and less of self—by the power of the Holy Spirit.

Is this your desire and aspiration?

"Christ *in* you, the hope of glory"!

July 3

Christ in You (part 2)

Christ in you, the hope of glory.
Colossians 1:27

In the fall of 2007, my wife Emily and I traveled to Canterbury, England, to attend my graduation exercises. One of the several places I wanted to visit while in England was Westminster Chapel, where the famed Dr. Martyn Lloyd-Jones (1899-1981) ministered for some thirty years.

On the Sunday morning following our stay in Canterbury, we attended a worship service at the Chapel, with four of my family members accompanying us. Before entering the sanctuary, I was struck by the church's signboard, which displayed at the bottom the favorite verse of the deceased pastor: "Christ in you, the hope of glory" (Col. 1:27). Think of it—"Christ *in* you"!

It was the gift of the Father that sent the Son into the world. It was the gift of the Father and Son that sent the Spirit to the church. That gift—the gift of the Holy Spirit—brings Christ to us and *in* us.

The New Testament writers repeatedly affirm this truth about the indwelling of Christ. Here are two examples: "Christ lives in me" and "if anyone does not have the Spirit of Christ, he does not belong to Christ. But if Christ is *in* you ..." (Gal. 2:20; Rom. 8:9-10). Christ *in* you!

Jesus Christ is both a historical as well as contemporary Person. Historical: He died, arose, ascended, and was exalted to serve as our Mediator. But inasmuch as he is also "the Living One" (Rev. 1:18), he desires to be vitally and dynamically present in the life of every believer: Christ is present in his glorified body at the Father's right hand, where he sits as our Mediator. However, Christ is also present in every Christian by indwelling believers in the person of the Holy Spirit.

Do we actually believe this same Jesus—the crucified, risen, ascended Lord is, in reality, inhabiting every believer this very moment—even you?

"Christ *in* you, the hope of glory"!

July 4

The Living Reality

God ... was pleased to reveal His Son in me.
Galatians 1:15-16 NASB

As a young English pastor, Samuel Chadwick (1860-1932) became so dissatisfied—that's the *key*—with his lack of spiritual reality and authenticity, his lack of passion for Christ, his lack of power in the pulpit, his lack of love for people, his lack of fruitfulness. Chadwick took drastic action: he burned all of his sermons (!) and set out to seek the Lord of the church to satisfy his thirsty heart, which Christ did, purifying his ego and filling him with the Holy Spirit.

R. W. Dale (1829-1895), pastor for thirty-six years at Carrs Lane Chapel, Birmingham, England, testified to the reality of the Spirit's deep work in him. One day, while sitting at his desk writing an Easter sermon, suddenly the Holy Spirit made the "Living One" *real* to this thirsty-hearted pastor.

In recounting this event in Dale's life, Dr. Joe Brice, once president of Cliff College, England, writes, "At first it seemed strange, but at last the truth dawned in a burst of glory. The preacher rose and paced about his study repeating, 'Christ is living! Christ is living! Yes, Christ is living!' Dale said this experience had the nature of a new discovery. 'I thought that all along I believed it, but not until that moment did I feel sure about it.' Then Dale exclaimed, 'All my people shall know it. I shall preach it again and again until they believe it as I do now.'"*

What R. W. Dale and Samuel Chadwick experienced was not unlike what Paul experienced in the home of Ananias, or what the disciples experienced on the day of Pentecost, or what a myriad of other thirsty-hearted believers have experienced. Christ is the Son, the Lord of glory, who wishes to fill his people with the dynamic knowledge and present reality of himself.

In speaking of his indwelling fullness, William Warren (1833-1929) penned these words:

With Thee each day is Pentecost,
*Each night Nativity.***

July 5

Saved

"You will call his name Jesus, for he will save his people from their sins."
Matthew 1:21

Of the scores of occurrences of the word "save" (and its cognates) in both the Old and New Testaments, and of the many occurrences of the word "salvation"—they have reference primarily to God through Christ saving the repentant sinner from his or her sins. The angel said to Joseph, "You will call his name Jesus, for he will save his people from their sins." He did not say, "in" their sins, but "from" their sins. There is a difference!

While he had a godly Christian father and mother, and attended a Church of England's chapel from the day of his infant baptism; and while he was a graduate of Oxford University, where among other subjects, he studied theology; and while he could read the sacred Scriptures in their original languages, and was ordained to be a Christian minister; and while he labored a few years in the United States in the state of Georgia as a missionary—it wasn't until he was thirty-one years of age, as he read Martin Luther's commentary on Galatians, that Charles Wesley (1707-1788) saw himself as a sinner and trusted at that moment in God through Christ to *save* him. Writing later of that experience, he wrote,

Long my imprisoned spirit lay,
Fast bound in sin and nature's night;
Thine eye diffused a quickening ray—
I woke, the dungeon flamed with light;
My chains fell off, my heart was free,
I rose, went forth, and followed Thee. *

"My chains fell off"!

Have your "chains" fallen off, dear reader, or are you still "Fast bound in sin and nature's night"? The angel announced, "You will call his name Jesus, for he will save his people from their sins." Religion will not suffice; only Jesus saves—and he saves us from our sins and sinning!

Converted Language

"For out of the abundance of the heart the mouth speaks."
Matthew 12:34

The Apostle Paul exhorted believers of his day, "Let there be no filthiness nor foolish talk nor crude joking, which are out of place ..." (Eph. 5:4). Christians don't tell risqué jokes. Christians don't use profanities, vulgarities, obscenities, or hang around people who do (if they can prevent it). Christians don't share salacious stories, or laugh at those who do. Why is this? Because their once defiled hearts have been purified. And purified hearts—hearts enthroned by the pure Christ—do not use their consecrated tongues for filthy purposes.

Now, lest Satan should take advantage of a recent convert, allow me to provide this note of caution. The old language—the language of "Egypt"—may not necessarily leave overnight, but it will leave.

E. Stanley Jones (1884-1973), who served Christ in India for more than fifty years, speaks to this point from personal experience. He said the morning following his conversion, "I walked out into a new world. The trees seemed to clap their hands; the sky was never so blue, and nature was never so alive and radiant." Jones said he was feeling so good, "I walked up to my chum, Ras, slapped him on the back, and said, 'My, what a d____ fine day!'" Jones amusingly adds, "The angels must have smiled and said: 'He's trying to say "Hallelujah," but he doesn't know the language yet.'"*

Paul not only said what God's people should not speak with their tongues, but what they should speak: "but instead let there be thanksgiving" (Eph. 5:4). Let there be continual gratitude to God from the lips of Christians. "I thank you, Father" (Matt. 11:25) characterized the life of Jesus. It did the same in the life of Paul; so it should do for us. It will, if the heart is good and pure and growing in the knowledge of God and the grace of the Lord Jesus.

How my heart is filled with praise
And thanksgiving to my God—
The God who walks with his child,
Each step of every day.

Not Because of Our Righteousness

He saved us, not because of works done by us in righteousness.
Titus 3:5

Dr. D. James Kennedy (1930-2007), longtime pastor of Coral Ridge Presbyterian Church in Fort Lauderdale, Florida, related how our gracious and merciful God stepped into his life and stripped him of his cloak of self-righteousness.

While employed in 1953 as an Arthur Murray dance studio instructor on Florida's West Coast, Kennedy was awakened one Sunday morning by his radio alarm clock. The station happened to be tuned to the broadcast of Philadelphia's 10th Presbyterian Church, with long-time pastor Dr. Donald Gray Barnhouse preaching. The first words Kennedy heard from the preacher were in the form of a question: "Young man, if you were to die tonight and stand before Almighty God, and he was to say to you, 'What right do you have to enter my Heaven, what would you say?'"

Kennedy's response in that bedroom, alone by himself, was: "Well I've tried to live a good life, and I've done the best I could. I've kept the Ten Commandments, and I've followed the Golden Rule." Then Kennedy added: "And Dr. Barnhouse said to me, or at least, it seemed that way, 'Young man, if you had had the audacity to say such a thing as that to the All-Holy God who knows your every thought and deed, he would have instantly plunged you into the Lake of Fire!'"

Kennedy, lying in his bed, said he was shocked by the preacher's words. Kennedy thought: "Well, my entire toothpick castle of theology collapsed to the floor, and I realized that I didn't have any hope. For the first time in my life, I was lost. I didn't know how to get home. Now, I had been lost for 23 years; I just never knew it before. He went on to tell the Gospel, and he said the most astonishing thing. He said that eternal life was a free gift, that Jesus Christ had paid for it with his own suffering and blood on the Cross, and God offered it graciously, freely to all of those who would trust in Christ."*

That's Good News!

Paul reminds Titus as to how we are *not* saved: "he saved us, not because of works done by us in righteousness ..."

The Spirit's Training School

*For the grace of God has appeared, bringing salvation for all
people, training us ... to live godly lives in the present age.*
Titus 2:11-12

Christians should be known more for what they *do* than what they
don't do. One who knew him most intimately, said of the Lord Jesus, he was "full of grace and truth" (John 1:14). Godliness covers
the entire spectrum of living for the Christian. Christians are to be
people of grace and truth.

The Spirit trains us how to walk in humility before God and one
another. He shows us how to walk in love with the people of God
and our neighbors. The Spirit teaches us to live in peace with all
people, how to be forbearing and forgiving, patient and longsuffering, merciful and compassionate, thoughtful, kind, and considerate.

Some of the evidence of the Spirit's renewal and training is immediate in the new convert. But not always. We never graduate
from this school. The Spirit's training is always active and present—
throughout our earthly pilgrimage. The Lord Jesus said, "My sheep
hear my voice, and I know them, and they follow me" (John. 10:27).

The following words, written by a Scottish minister by the
name of Horatius Bonar (1808-1889), have spoken to my soul for
many years.

> *I was a wandering sheep,*
> *I did not love the fold;*
> *I did not love my Shepherd's voice,*
> *I would not be controlled.*

After the author leads the reader through his personal conversion to Christ, the ninth stanza of the hymn reads:

> *No more a wandering sheep,*
> *I love to be controlled;*
> *I love my tender Shepherd's voice,*
> *I love the peaceful fold.**

The Christian never graduates from the Spirit's training school:
"For the grace of God has appeared, bringing salvation for all people, training us ... to live godly lives in the present age."

July 9

Dying to Self-Centeredness

*"Take your son, your only son Isaac, whom you love,
and go to the land of Moriah, and offer him there as a burnt
offering on one of the mountains of which I shall tell you."*
Genesis 22:2

One of the masters in spiritual theology in the nineteenth century was the devout Lutheran minister George Steinberger (1865-1904). In a little volume, that is considered a classic by many who have read it—*In the Footprints of the Lamb*—this perceptive student of God's ways with men said this about man's essential problem: "The fall of our first parents was a result of their making themselves the center of life. The soul who does this today will learn that spiritual darkness and death, separation from and enmity toward God, are the consequences. In all that is selfish, the power of Satan is active. In the selfish heart there burns the hidden fire of Hell. As long as we cherish our own lives, we keep ourselves under God's curse; for on the cross God has cursed all that is selfish. To live for one's self is to be against God." Steinberger then adds: "Flesh [in the moral sense, as used by Paul] is ingrown selfness."* Intrinsic to total consecration to God is *death*—a deep death to one's sinful self-interest and every inordinate human attachment.

In offering his son Isaac to Yahweh, Abraham first experienced a deep, inner personal death to his own preferences, affections, and desires. Jesus said such is the case for anyone who would be one of his authentic disciples: "If anyone would come after me, let him deny himself and take up his cross and follow me" (Mark 8:34). Our Lord taught that one cannot be his disciple while making his own self-centered choices.

Abraham's pilgrimage with Yahweh reached a critical turning point with respect to his love for Isaac, his son. Two loves and loyalties were in danger of competing, with one canceling out the other. Yahweh, Abraham's covenant God, devised a plan whereby the patriarch would offer that which was most precious to him as a gift to his LORD. God asked for the gift of Abraham's son, which, in essence, was the giving of Abraham himself in total consecration to Yahweh.

God allows for no competitors.

Our Body the Lord's

Present your bodies as a living sacrifice, holy and acceptable to God.
Romans 12:1

The use of the word "holy" (*hagian*) in one's presentation/ consecration of the body to God indicates that Paul is addressing authentic Christian believers and not unbelievers. A non-Christian cannot make a presentation of a holy body to God. We must ask then, "How is it that a Christian can make an offering of a 'holy body' to God?" In this way: because the Christian has already been "set apart" (sanctified in Christ Jesus) to live a holy life" (see 1 Cor. 1:2).

Since the believer has been definitively sanctified (set apart to live a holy life) in Christ when he was justified and regenerated, he subsequently is called to make that sanctification complete by a giving himself in total consecration to the Lord Jesus Christ. On this matter, John Murray (1898-1975) commented: "Holiness is contrasted here with the defilement which characterizes the body of sin and with all sensual lust. Holiness is the fundamental essence as to what it means to be well-pleasing ['acceptable'] to God, the governing principle of a believer. These qualities have reference to his body as well as to his spirit and show how ethical character belongs to the body and to its functions. No terms could certify this fact more than 'holy' and 'well-pleasing to God.'"*

Holiness consists of more than God's setting one apart to live a holy life. The Christian must offer *himself* in total consecration to God, and separate himself from all moral evil: "let us cleanse ourselves from every defilement of the body and spirit, bringing holiness to completion in the fear of God" (2 Cor. 7:1).

How little the average Christian knows of total consecration and total sanctification. The apostle asked the Corinthians, "Do you not know that your body is a temple of the Holy Spirit within you, whom you have from God?" Then he declares, "You are not your own, for you were bought with a price. So glorify God in your body" (1 Cor. 6:19-20).

Are you totally the Lord's?

Walking in the Light

*But if we walk in the light, as he is in the light, we have fellowship with
one another, and the blood of Jesus his Son cleanses us from all sin.*
1 John 1:7

F. B. Meyer (1847-1929) was an able exponent of the Word of God.
He excelled in the pulpit and had earned a reputation for being a
godly, Spirit-filled Christian and preacher. He exhorted multitudes
of believers to holy living, and earnestly endeavored to lead a careful life himself. However, at the height of his ministry, he had a jolt-
ing experience.

Once, when preaching to immense crowds in a convention,
there arrived on the grounds a younger preacher and Bible teacher
who was gaining considerable attention. Most of the crowds left
Meyer's meetings and began attending the services of Dr. G. Campbell Morgan (1863-1949). For the first time in Meyer's ministerial
career he felt professional jealousy. He confessed such to a group of
friends and said, "The only way I can conquer my feeling is to pray
for him daily, which I do."*

The mightily used-of-God Scottish revivalist, Duncan Campbell
(1898-1972), once said, "Nowhere does the Word of God promise a
once-for-all cleansing. We are to walk in the light if we are to know
continuous cleansing. Let this be clearly understood, and then we
shall not fall into the error of trying to live today on the cleansing of
yesterday."**

The Bible does not condone a *sinning religion*. What the Bible
does teach is this: God desires to give each of his people a pure
heart, and it is only by walking in the light of God that he keeps
clean what he first purified.

Be assured, God is both able to cleanse the heart and keep it
clean, as we walk in the purity of his holiness. However, remember
when we have failed, God can and will cleanse what we have confessed.

*Lord, it is not enough for me to have
  been cleansed once from sin and its pollution;
I need You each moment to keep me pure,
  as I humbly confess my condition.*

Refining Fire

"Many will be purified, made spotless and refined."
Daniel 12:10

Do we really believe the promises of God's Word for a deep inner, moral cleansing, or do we try to explain them away? Have our ears grown accustomed to those teachers who insist that Christians cannot live a single day without lusting, coveting, evil thoughts, getting angry, causing dissension, committing immorality, lying and cheating, stealing and fornicating, committing adultery, worshiping mammon, and idolizing the forbidden?

Such teachers don't have the answer to these questions. They have explained away God's provision for such a deliverance, and have reduced the biblical passages which address these issues to only goals to be sought, ideals never to be reached, and a reality left for the next world, when one receives a glorified body. Some answers!

I like the answer that Baptist pastor A. J. Gordon (1836-1895) gave to those who said such teaching as the above espouses unbiblical perfectionism: "In regard to the doctrine of *sinless perfection* as a heresy, we regard contentment with *sinful imperfection* as a greater heresy. And we gravely fear that many Christians make the apostle's words, 'If we say we have no sin we deceive ourselves,' the unconscious justification for a low standard of Christian living."* No, we should not advocate "sinless perfectionism"; neither should we accept "sinful imperfectionism."

This promised purity for God's people is symbolically linked to three purifying agents: water (Ezek. 36:25), soap (Mal. 3:2-3), and fire (Matt. 3:11). God is saying that what these cleansers can accomplish in the physical world, I will accomplish through the Cross and Pentecost, through my beloved Son and the mighty infusion of my Spirit in the hearts of my thirsty-hearted disciples. Let our prayer be that of Charles Wesley (1707-1788):

Refining fire, go through my heart,
Illuminate my soul;
Scatter Thy life through every part,
*And sanctify the whole.***

"Touched by a Loving Heart"

Put on ... compassionate hearts.
Colossians 3:12

It was Dr. Bob Pierce (1914-1978), founder of the World Vision humanitarian agency, who used to say often, "Let my heart break with the things that break the heart of God." That's a compassionate heart. We won't get a heart like that from drinking at this world's well of selfishness and hardness.

Fanny Crosby (1820-1915), the blind hymn writer of another generation, who was a things-above-seeker, had it right when she wrote,

Down in the human heart, crushed by the tempter,
Feelings lie buried that grace can restore;
Touched by a loving heart, wakened by kindness,
Chords that are broken will vibrate once more. *

Crosby could pen those words because she was familiar with the transforming power of a compassionate heart. With a compassionate heart, the Christian will be moved by the spiritual lostness of the crowd, the hunger and pain of humanity, and the sorrow and hurts of others. How the church needs this grace. How I need this grace. It is found in Christ, the Man at God's right hand.

The Lord Jesus is the Christian's perfect example of what it means to *feel* not only compassion toward another, but to be *moved* with compassion. Repeatedly in the Gospel accounts, Jesus was moved to act when he felt compassion. For example, when the leper implored Jesus for healing, saying, "If you will, you can make me clean." Mark records that Jesus "Moved with pity ... stretched out his hand and touched him and said to him, 'I will; be clean'" (Mark 1:40-41). Again, before Jesus provided for the hungry crowd on one occasion, the compassionate Son of Man said, "I have compassion on the crowd because they have been with me now three days and have nothing to eat" (Matt. 15:32).

The Spirit of God exhorts believers, "Put on ... compassionate hearts" (Col. 3:12).

How we need an abundance of this Christian grace!

July 14

Conviction of Sin

"And when he comes, he will convict the world concerning sin."
John 16:8

Jesus said of the Holy Spirit, "And when he comes, he will convict the world concerning sin ..." It is impossible for a sinner to trust Christ as Lord and Savior without this prerequisite conviction of sin.

"I've been reading a friend of yours," said a young man to theologian J. I. Packer leaving church one Sunday morning. "I think he knows me."

"Who is it?" asked Packer.

"John Owen. He seems to know exactly what's going on inside me ..."*

John Owen (1616-1683) embodied the best of Puritan devotion: the awe of God, humility, wisdom, and an awareness of God's grace. He also dealt with the nature of sinful humanity as few writers have done as keenly or thoroughly. Of course, it is the Holy Spirit who really knows what is going on inside of us, not John Owen (though God uses human instruments in Spirit-conviction): "And no creature is hidden from his sight, but all are naked and exposed to the eyes of him to whom we must give account" (Heb. 4:13).

As a sixteen-year-old boy, kneeling at an altar of prayer, it was the Holy Spirit who uncovered layers of transgressions in my sinful, broken heart. He reminded me of the grapes I had stolen from a produce counter in the local A & P grocery store; of Cokes I took unlawfully from a soda machine; of the many unkindnesses I committed against my step-mother; and of the moral impurities of my wicked heart. But fundamentally, he showed me that I had sinned against him, a holy God.

Webster's dictionary won't help us understand what conviction of sin is all about, but all who have experienced the persuasive influence of the Holy Spirit indicting one's own conscience of unacceptable behavior (sin)—these know what conviction of sin is. One cannot be converted to Christ without it.

You broke my bleeding heart, O God.
You alone revealed my need.

July 15

More Than Words

*Our gospel came to you not only in word, but also in
power and in the Holy Spirit and with full conviction.*
1 Thessalonians 1:5

Without the Holy Spirit, all our Bible studies, sermons, seminars, prayers, songs, lovely sanctuaries, degrees, choirs and orchestras, are absolutely worthless—worthless. One of the greatest needs in our churches is Holy Spirit conviction—conviction of sin that awakens the sinner and disturbs the careless Christian.

Has the church forgotten how to do God's work in God's way? Listen to the late Times Square Church pastor David Wilkerson's (1931-2011) assessment of our dilemma: "We constantly hear awful exaggerations about the numbers of people who come to Jesus through various ministries. Christians report scores of people were saved as they preached in prisons, schools, tribal meetings. They say, "Everybody in the place gave his heart to Jesus. When I finished preaching, they came forward for salvation.

"No—that is a tragic exaggeration! All too often, what actually happens is that everyone simply repeats a prayer. They merely pray what they're told to pray—and few of them grasp what they're saying. Then most of them go back to their heathen ways!" Then Wilkerson adds: "I believe the church has even taken the feeling out of conviction. Think about it—you hardly ever see tears on the cheeks of those who are being saved anymore. Of course, I know tears don't save anyone. But God made us all human, with very real feelings. And any hell-bound sinner who has been moved by the Holy Spirit naturally feels a profound sorrow over the ways he has grieved the Lord."*

Alcibiades once said to Socrates: "Socrates, I hate you; for every time I see you, you show me what I am." And so it is with God; he strips us of all the veneer, facade and pretense. Then he shows us what we are and who we are. If we will listen, if we will bow down low enough, if we will stay on our face long enough, God will tenderly show us who we really are—then apply the remedy.

*Come in power, O Spirit of God,
Lest we be content with mere words!*

July 16

A Praying Prophet

*"Fill your horn with oil, and go. I will send you to Jesse the
Bethlehemite, for I have provided for myself a king among his sons."*
1 Samuel 16:1

Answers to our prayers do not come with a guarantee. Just because God gave us a certain leader in answer to prayer does not mean that person will always be God's person for that place for all time. Sometimes people fail, leaders fall, but God's work goes on. Thus, God turns to Samuel and says, "How long will you grieve over Saul, since I have rejected him from being king over Israel? Fill your horn with oil, and go. I will send you to Jesse the Bethlehemite, for I have provided for myself a king among his sons" (1 Sam. 16:1). Once again, as a result of prayerful communion with God, Samuel is told who Israel's next leader is to be.

Israel was blessed to have Samuel to pray for them. May the same God be pleased in our day to raise up many after his kind in the church. We are desperately in need of praying people—praying prophets—men and women who will pray for God to intervene, to give deliverance; people who will pray for God's choice for leadership. O *Lord, give us in our own day such people!*

We need a few men and women, who may be quite ordinary and yet exceptional like Thomas Haire, who became known as the praying plumber from Lisburn, Ireland. Haire once said to A. W. Tozer (1897-1963), "Praying is working along with God in the fulfillment of the divine plan. Praying is fighting close up front where the sharp deciding action is taking place. Prayer takes into account what the devil is trying to accomplish and where he is working, and attacks him at that strategic point."*

Samuel was that kind of intercessor; he was that kind of prophet. He was a praying prophet. May God in his mercy be pleased to give the church more praying Samuels in order that we might have more devout Davids.

As to men of old, you spoke, O God,
Raise up men in our own day—
Men who listen and obey your voice,
Standing firmly, come what may.

The Thirsty

"If anyone thirsts, let him come to me and drink. Whoever believes in me,
as the Scripture has said, 'Out of his heart will flow rivers of living water'"
John 7:37-38

The occasion on which Jesus spoke these words was the Jewish Feast of Tabernacles. Thousands of worshipers gathered annually in Jerusalem in the month of either September or October, to celebrate the harvest and offer thanks to God. This festive event memorialized Israel's journey from Egypt to Canaan, and served as a reminder of God's benevolent provision during difficult times.

Each day of the feast, at the time of the morning sacrifice, a priest brought into the forecourt of the temple a golden vessel, filled with water, drawn from the springs of Shiloh. The water was poured—mingled with sacrificial wine—into two bowls, which stood upon the altar. During this sacred rite, the priests sounded trumpets, clashed symbols, and then the words of Isaiah 12:3 were recited: "With joy you will draw water from the wells of salvation."

This feast lasted for seven days, with a closing assembly on the eighth day, "the great day" (John 7:37). It was on this day the Lord Jesus was compelled by the Spirit to make such a startling prophetic announcement. He promised that when the age of the Spirit was inaugurated (see John 7:39), it would be the privilege of every thirsty-hearted disciple to become a cataract of blessing.

Where is the person, born of the Spirit of God, who does not desire a life of effective fruitfulness to the glory of God? Surely every believer reading these words has such aspirations. Take heart, thirsty Christian! These words of Jesus hold the key to a life of fruitful service. Jesus says, "rivers of living water" will flow from the depths of one's inner being ("heart") on one condition: "If anyone thirsts"!

Wherever there has been a thirsty-hearted follower of the Man with the Golden Pitcher, there has been an infusion of the Holy Spirit with subsequent "rivers of living water."

Are you thirsty?

Obedience is Not Optional

"If anyone serves me, he must follow me."
John 12:26

The Christian is called to be a slave of the Lord Jesus Christ. This suggests he has voluntarily submitted himself, and all that he is and has, to be a faithful love-slave of the King of kings and Lord of lords. This is not a servile, slavish task. It is a calling, the highest of privileges.

The master Teacher knew there would always be those who would nominally identify with him and his teaching, but who rejected his lordship. The courageous Lutheran pastor-theologian, Dietrich Bonhoeffer (1906-1945), called this "cheap grace"—a kind of grace, which is divorced from a corresponding obedience to Christ.

Living four hundred years after Martin Luther and the Reformation movement, Bonhoeffer witnessed firsthand the absence of a living faith among the religious throng. As a voice in the wilderness, this man, who would soon be martyred at the hands of Nazi despots, challenged the church of his day: "When he spoke of grace, Luther always implied as a corollary that it cost him his own life, the life which was now for the first time subjected to the absolute obedience to Christ." Then Bonhoeffer pronounced this indictment, which could be applied to much of the church of our day: "Judged by the standard of Luther's doctrine, that of his followers was unassailable, and yet their orthodoxy spelt the end and destruction of the Reformation as a revelation on earth of the costly grace of God. *The justification of the sinner in the world degenerated into the justification of sin and the world. Costly grace was turned into cheap grace without discipleship."*

Nineteen hundred years before Bonehoeffer wrote those words, our Lord joined grace and obedience, justification and sanctification, faith and discipleship: "If anyone serves me, he must follow me." In other words, for every person wishing to be, or professing to be, a servant of Jesus, our Lord says following him is not optional. Obedience is inherent in discipleship.

Seeing the Glory of God

Jesus said to her, "Did I not tell you that if you
believed you would see the glory of God?"
John 11:40

Lazarus, a friend of Jesus and brother of Mary and Martha, was dead. Both sisters had enough confidence in Jesus that had he been present when their brother became seriously ill, Jesus could have healed him (see John 11:21, 32). However, they did not have faith that Jesus could raise their brother from death.

Jesus had previously assured Martha that her brother would rise again (see John 11:23). However, she took that to mean at the last resurrection. Martha believed that Jesus was the promised Messiah and the Son of God (see John 11:27), but she had no confidence that he could do what all thought to be impossible—raise the dead in the here and now.

Our Lord assured Martha that the "glory of God" would be revealed if she only believed. As used in this context, the "glory of God" means a demonstration of God's power, a God-event; it is a supernatural operation of the Spirit of God that is manifested here on earth, to the glory and praise of the Lord Jesus. God's glory cannot be dictated or manipulated. When experienced or seen, it changes lives, churches and communities.

Is this not one of the church's crying needs—to see repeated demonstrations of God's glory? Not the particular miracle which Christ performed outside little Bethany many years ago, but spiritual resurrections and transformations in the lives of those who are dead in trespasses and in sins.

The glory of God—a God-event—cannot be manufactured or programmed. It does not come from below but is sent from above. Man can't produce a God-event. Only God can produce God-events. Only God can raise the spiritually dead; only God can make saints out of sinners; only God can breathe life into a corpse; only God can give a "beautiful headdress instead of ashes, the oil of gladness instead of mourning, the garment of praise instead of a faint spirit" (Isa. 61:3).

Let us hear the words of the Lord Jesus: "Did I not tell you that if you believed you would see the glory of God?"

More Than John's Baptism

Apollos ... had been instructed in the way of the Lord. And being fervent in spirit, he spoke and taught accurately the things concerning Jesus, though he knew only the baptism of John.
Acts 18:24-25

The church has relied too long on academic credentials, ecclesiastical machinery, and the efforts and ingenuity of the flesh instead of the blessed Holy Spirit. And the results? A skilled, professional clergy that knows only John's baptism. And since the pastor cannot lead his people where he has not traveled, our pews become populated, for the most part, with sincere people who may have been born from above, but who know nothing of the power of the Holy Spirit.

Many churches are content to have an Apollos as their preacher—one who knows only the baptism of John. Why do I say that? Because—and let's be candid here—this is the present pathetic state of the average church. There is a famine of Spirit-filled preachers.

What is our greatest lack? The Holy Spirit. What is our greatest need? The Holy Spirit. Who is the missing Presence? The Holy Spirit. Oh, for preachers like the venerable Baptist, Charles Spurgeon (1834-1892), who, when ascending to his pulpit every Sunday morning and evening, prayed at each of the fifteen steps, "I believe in the Holy Ghost." Is it any wonder the Lord honored his ministry, as he preached in the power of the Spirit to London's masses?

Listen to what Martyn Lloyd-Jones (1899-1981), the late renowned pastor of London's Westminster Chapel, had to say on this subject: "The church has fallen into the error of thinking that a man can get this knowledge by academic teaching and learning. I am not here to decry these things; [he was a medical doctor when God called him to preach].... But they are not all-important, and the tragedy of the last hundred years has been to put a premium on such things, men boasting of their degrees and diplomas ... and so on. That is all very well, but it is not the way to know God more fully. It is through the Spirit, through the baptism of the Spirit that one comes to this fuller knowledge."*

It takes more than John's baptism to make a preacher!

Power from on High

"You shall receive power when the Holy Spirit has come upon you."
Acts 1:8

Dwight L. Moody (1837-1899) was a pastor and evangelist who founded what later came to be known as The Moody Memorial Church in Chicago. Though many thought this converted shoe salesman was quite successful as a pastor in the early years of his ministry, there were two saintly ladies who discerned a noticeable lack in this zealot for Christ. I'll allow his biographers to tell the story. "Occasionally after some of his meetings in Chicago, two Free Methodist women would say to him, 'Mr. Moody, we are praying that you may receive the enduement of the Holy Spirit.' This irritated Moody who believed they should rather pray for the people. But they persistently prayed that he would 'get the power.' Moody did not know exactly what they meant. Finally won over by their godly concern, he asked them to show him in the Scriptures the truth they insisted upon, and he even prayed with them for this power. Over months, as Moody gave himself to prayer, he realized the state his heart was in. 'I found I was ambitious; I was not preaching Christ; I was preaching for ambition. I found everything in my heart that ought not be there. For four months, a wrestling went on within me, and I was a miserable man.'"*

The anointing for which he prayed finally came when Moody was on a trip to New York, to raise funds to rebuild his church following the Great Chicago Fire. One day while he walked along Wall Street, Moody was so overcome with God's power that he had to find a friend's home to get alone to pray. The sense of God's presence was so great that he asked the Lord to withhold his hand, lest he die on the spot. That experience, Moody later said, marked a turning point in his life. From then on, he didn't preach different sermons but the response was greater than ever before.

What Priscilla and Aquila were to Apollos (see Acts 18:26), those two Free Methodist women were to Dwight Moody.

Spiritual Understanding

We have not ceased to pray for you, asking that you may be filled with
the knowledge of his will in all spiritual wisdom and understanding, so as
to walk in a manner worthy of the Lord, fully pleasing to him, bearing
fruit in every good work and increasing in the knowledge of God.
Colossians 1:9-10

Thomas Aquinas (1225-1274) was one of the Roman Catholic Church's greatest theologians. In 1879, he was officially proclaimed to be, in effect, the theologian and teacher of the entire "Holy Catholic Church." His famous theological work, *The Summa Theologica*, has been regarded ever since the twelfth century the standard work of the Roman Catholic Church. Aquinas was considered a renowned thinker and philosopher. And yet, he taught that it was impossible for a mortal man to have any kind of direct experience with God. After spending his entire life teaching that man could not have contact with immaterial reality, shortly before his death, Aquinas experienced a definitive visitation from God until he could no longer write theology. In responding to a friend who urged him to finish his great work, *The Summa Theologica*, he replied, "I can do no more; such things have been revealed to me that all that I have written seems as straw, and I now await the end of my life."[*]

Amazing! Here was a man who had written volumes of theology, and was recognized by his church as being its foremost theologian and teacher, but upon having a personal divine encounter with the Spirit of God he laid his pen aside, confessing that everything prior to this experience was like "straw"!

We should never disparage those who pursue higher education. A Christian should pursue knowledge and receive the highest formal education he and she can—in the will of God. However, too many Bible scholars and preachers have a full *head* and a cold *heart*. God wants to enlighten our minds, until we think his thoughts; he wants to warm our hearts with his presence, until he can use our minds to his glory and the good of the church and humanity.

Keeping Focused

And he took the blind man by the hand and led him out of the village, and when he had spit on his eyes and laid his hands on him, he asked him, "Do you see anything?" And he looked up and said, "I see people, but they look like trees, walking." Then Jesus laid his hands on his eyes again; and he opened his eyes, his sight was restored, and he saw everything clearly.
Mark 8:23-25

Many of us are living without clarity and focus. We resemble the blind man, who when asked by Jesus what he saw after the Master had touched his eyes, replied, "I see men, but they look like trees, walking." He saw, but everything was distorted, out of focus. Following Christ's second touch, "he saw everything clearly."

The devout Christian and Quaker Thomas Kelly (1893-1941) once observed, "The outer distractions of our interests reflect an inner lack of integration in our own selves. We are trying to be several selves at once without all our selves being organized by a single, mastering Life within us."*

These are arresting words, spoken by a man who did more than write. He thought. He pondered. He meditated. Then he wrote. And he wrote because he had something to say. Can we say that we are "being organized by a single, mastering Life within us"?

Addressing the great pressure the modern world exerts on the Christian, Evangelical author and conference speaker Os Guinness writes that unless believers learn to cope successfully with what he terms "pluralization," we cannot expect to live the Christian life successfully with confidence. Guinness defines pluralization as "the process by which the proliferation of choice rapidly multiplies the number of options." He continues, "This affects the private sphere of modern society at all levels, from consumer goods to relationships to worldviews and faiths."**

Our inner eyes will require the deft touch of Jesus if we are to live with a true focus, keeping our concentration on him—regardless of where our calling and daily duties take us.

Is life a *blur* to you? Come to Jesus; allow him to "touch" your inner eyes—once more.

July 24

The Discipline of Elimination

Let us lay aside every weight, and the sin which clings so closely.
Hebrews 12:1

Neither the Lord Jesus Christ, the Apostles, nor the first-century Christians could live a successful and faithful life without eliminating everything and anything that might hinder their calling. Thus Jesus warned his followers: "If your hand or your foot causes you to sin, cut it off and throw it away. It is better for you to enter life maimed or crippled than to have two hands or two feet and be thrown into eternal fire. And if your eye causes you to sin, gouge it out and throw it away. It is better for you to enter life with one eye than to have two eyes and be thrown into the fire of hell" (Matt. 18:8-9).

Again, concerned with the fleshly impediments that he knew would prevent them from growing in the grace and knowledge of God as they should, the inspired writer of the Book of Hebrews wrote these words to languishing believers: "Let us lay aside every weight, and the sin which clings so closely" (Heb. 12:1).

I well remember hearing the news as a young boy in 1954, that the four-minute mile barrier was broken. Olympic runner Roger Bannister broke the tape in record time—3:59.4. How did he do it? Every notable athlete competes successfully by eliminating everything that prevents him from his calling and goal. One can't go everywhere, do everything, enjoy every food, stay up all hours of the night, and set a record like Bannister did.

Jerome (342-420) was a master of classical learning—his age's best Latin writer, some have said. He had a passion for scholarship and devoured the works of pagan thinkers. As a Christian, Jerome was troubled by his failure to implement worthwhile priorities. Historians say he preferred the cultured style of Cicero and other rhetoricians to the plain, and—what he considered to be—clumsy style of the language of the Bible. However, a transforming event changed Jerome. One historian records: "In Antioch, he had a feverish dream in which Christ scourged him and accused him, 'You are a Ciceronian, and not a Christian.' Jerome vowed not to study pagan books again."*

What do you need to eliminate from your life?

Are You Looking Back?

"No one who puts his hand to the plow
and looks back is fit for the kingdom of God."
Luke 9:62

One cannot stay true to his Lord and his calling without remaining passionately in love with the Lord Jesus Christ. When our love for Christ grows cold, our faithfulness to Christ and our calling become dim—and eventually will die if we fail to be renewed by the Spirit.

A careless, passionate Christian is an oxymoron. One cannot live a careless Christian life and be totally surrendered to Christ. Too many Christians are living a double-minded existence. They are neither comfortable in the world nor in the church. And they are a spiritual drag on both. Are you looking back? Have you fallen in love with the world again?

As a teenager, helping my brother-in-law Joe on his farm, I well remember how he first taught me to plow a straight furrow with the tractor. Going out into a large field in springtime, he told me to point the front of the tractor at a distant object. By keeping the tractor pointed toward that object, I would be able to plow the first furrow straight, thereby assuring that all the following would be straight as well.

Being the young kid I was, after Joe left me in the field, I performed an experiment. I thought as I was plowing that first furrow, I should occasionally look behind to see how I was doing. Well, as I'm sure you know, every time I looked back, I created a *dogleg* in the furrow.

Jesus knew about farming and he knew people. He knew his followers could not be faithful disciples while looking back—back to Sodom, as Lot's wife did; back to the world, as Demas did.

What about you? Are you completely surrendered to the Lord Jesus Christ? Or are you looking back? You have a choice, you know. You will never fulfill your calling to belong exclusively to Jesus Christ, or be faithful in your vocational calling, whatever that may be, without making and maintaining a total surrender to our Lord and Teacher.

We are either looking back or looking to Jesus—which will it be?

In the Strength of God

"Apart from me you can do nothing."
John 15:5

Maybe you haven't heard of Charlie Riggs (1916-2008). Charlie served for many years as the crusade director for Billy Graham. He got the job in 1952 on the eve of the famous New York City crusade at Madison Square Garden when the director had to be replaced.

Billy Graham later said of Charlie, "I didn't think he could do it. But I had this peace—that Charlie so depended on the Holy Spirit that I knew the Lord could do it through Charlie."

Charlie had little formal training. When asked how he could handle the crusade logistics so well and for so many years, he said with typical humility, "I always asked the Lord to put me in over my head. That way, when I had a job to do, either the Lord had to help me, or I was sunk." God was delighted to help Charlie again and again.*

When the Lord puts us in over our head—which he often does—what is our recourse? Do we resort to the old way of doing things—doing things in our own strength? Or do we rely on his strength? Whether we perceive to be over our heads or not, we are to live in total dependence on Christ: "Apart from me you can do nothing."

Jesus spoke these words to the Twelve, just hours before his death. For over three years, our Lord had walked and lived among those men. He *knew* them! He *knows* us as well. Fallen man—even *Christian* people—often strive to live the Christian life and accomplish the purposes of God in one's own strength. We do this because we either are not *completely* his, or we *forget* whose we are. We either are living in *reliance* on ourselves or upon the Lord.

When Asa, Judah's king, once chose to rely on his own thinking instead of God's, the Lord sent the prophet Hanani to rebuke him. He reminded the king, "For the eyes of the Lord move to and fro throughout the earth that He may strongly support those whose heart is completely His" (2 Chron. 16:9 NASB).

Are you completely his?

Forgiveness

"Father, forgive them."
Luke 23:34

Jesus is our model for forgiveness. Our Teacher not only taught this truth with his lips, he movingly underscored it with his life during some of his darkest days on earth. What he admonished his disciples to do toward their offenders—at least seventy-times-seven (meaning as often as necessary)—he himself practiced the same toward his enemies: "Father, forgive them, for they know not what they do" (Luke 23:34).

Since Jesus extended forgiveness to his enemies while dying on the cross, we too are to follow in his steps by forgiving all those who have ever wronged us, regardless of how deeply we may have been wounded.

Forgiveness does not always come easy. It has been more than forty years ago now that I was standing on a church campground following an afternoon service. As I was visiting with two friends, a woman approached, addressing me with these words, "Brother Tilley, are you still living with your wife? I saw you drive out of a motel parking lot the other day." Then she turned and left. Her poisonous inference was obvious—she insinuated I was having an affair.

I told my friends I had no idea what she was talking about. However, it occurred to me later in the day that she had seen me leave a motel, where I had inquired about a room for some of my family who would be visiting us. This woman, who had turned against me and left our church, had determined to poison two of my leaders against their pastor. Gratefully, these men had the highest confidence in their pastor and were not shaken by her slanderous remark.

But how was I to react? Was I offended? Yes. She did me a great injustice. Could I forgive her? Yes. Was it easy? No. How could I forgive? Because I knew that I had been forgiven far more by a merciful God.

We can forgive others because we have been forgiven ourselves. Though Jesus never had to be forgiven, yet he forgave. What a model he is for us!

Steadfastness

*Therefore, my beloved brothers, be steadfast, immovable,
always abounding in the work of the Lord, knowing
that in the Lord your labor is not in vain.*
1 Corinthians 15:58

God has called his people to steadfast faithfulness. He has marked out a course for each of us to run, and we can either run the course faithfully to the finish, or we can fail and even drop out. Life can be hard, but God is good.

As he was sitting in the open-air one dreadful day in a Russian gulag, Alexsandr Solzhenitsyn (1918-2008) felt despair and gloom settling over him. This brilliant Christian writer was sentenced to serve years in a Siberian prison by an oppressive, despotic system. He didn't know if he could survive the cruelties of this tormenting nightmare. While feeling his own pain and despair, a man seated next to him picked up a stick and drew the sign of the cross in the dirt. Suddenly, Solzhenitsyn gained a renewed perspective. He got up, picked up his shovel, and went back to work. Knowing what Christ, as the innocent God-man had suffered for him, his will was infused with a new energy to persevere until the end—regardless.

Just before the patriarch Jacob went to his eternal reward, he gathered all his sons around him in order to bestow on each his farewell blessing. Coming to Joseph, he said, "With bitterness archers attacked [you]; they shot at [you] with hostility. But [your] bow remained steady, [your] strong arms stayed limber, because of the hand of the Mighty One of Jacob, because of the Shepherd, the Rock of Israel" (Gen. 49:23-24). Jacob said Joseph remained "steady"—persevered—in the face of extreme difficulties, which he had.

Jesus is our model for perseverance and steadfastness. He faithfully followed the will of the Father for his life to the very end of his earthly sojourn. He came to help you and me do the same.

*The will to be faithful to my God
Is more than I have in myself to give.
Thus, I need his strength for every day
To energize me with his life to live.*

July 29 is the header

Perfecting Holiness

Therefore, having these promises, beloved, let us cleanse ourselves from all defilement of flesh and spirit, perfecting holiness in the fear of God.
2 Corinthians 7:1 NASB

It would not be an exaggeration to say that the average professing Christian is more concerned about retaining his defiling habits than he is about living a life that pleases God. As long as we can go through the common religious rituals and still enjoy our sinful practices, all is well—or so we think. The modern Christian's unwitting mantra is, "Come weal or come woe my status is quo."

Who among us, after hearing the Word of God preached, goes home saying, "I have to get rid of _____." Or, "I must quit doing _____." A genuine Christian is indwelt by the Holy Spirit. The Holy Spirit calls every disciple of Jesus to take decisive and surgical action against every defiling thing. What is defiling your body and spirit? What unclean thing are you embracing, enjoying, indulging in, and practicing? What unholy attitude contaminates your heart, your tongue, and your thoughts? Our holy God calls us to take action, engage our will: "cleanse ourselves from all defilement of flesh and spirit." Clean house!

I well remember when Will came to church for the first time and knelt at the altar to receive Christ. I went to his home that afternoon to pay a visit. His lovely, but then unconverted wife, Penny, met me at the door. She said, "Oh, Pastor Tilley, something's wrong with Will. He's been reading the Bible ever since we came home from church!" What I found out later was that Will went home from church and immediately destroyed his pornography and poured his liquor down the kitchen-sink drain. And he didn't hear the pastor say anything that Sunday morning about either!

We perfect holiness "in the fear of God," not in the fear of what others think. To perfect holiness means to agree with what God says about our body and spirit, and then act on it. Holiness cannot be perfected without a cleansing. While the cleansing is decisive, with a resultant perfecting, God will reveal other needs in the Christian's life as he continues in his walk. However, once God reveals an unclean matter, the Holy Spirit will keep his finger there until we take action, or we will cause the Spirit to grieve (Eph. 4:30).

Stay Awake!

For you are all children of light, children of the day.
We are not of the night or of the darkness. So then let us not
sleep, as others do, but let us keep awake and be sober.
1 Thessalonians 5:5-6

The story is told that Napoleon Bonaparte made a surprise visit one night to his troops on the battlefield. As the French leader moved along in the gray light of the early morning, one sentry after another immediately challenged him. Finally, the crafty warrior stole up to a strategic spot, and there was no guard present to challenge Bonaparte. Moving closer, the general saw a pair of boots sticking out from under a shock of corn and a rifle propped up beside. He made no comment. He picked up the rifle and stood guard himself, waiting for the snoozing soldier to wake up. Eventually the corn stirred, and up jumped the guilty soldier. Can you imagine his surprise? Caught sleeping by Napoleon Bonaparte—what a tragedy!

There is a greater tragedy: a sleeping church, a sleeping disciple. When Jesus agonized in Gethsemane, his disciples were sleeping. In the parable of the ten virgins, when the bridegroom delayed his coming, all ten "became drowsy and slept" (Matt. 25:5). In the parable of the weeds, Jesus said the farmer sowed the good seed in his field. However, after the good seed was sown, his laborers were irresponsible: "but while his men were sleeping, his enemy came and sowed weeds among the wheat and went away" (Matt. 13:25).

Paul taught the Thessalonian believers about the imminent return of the Lord Jesus; therefore, they should not be taken by surprise at Christ's return. However, knowing the tendency for even children of light to become spiritually drowsy, he exhorts them to stay awake and keep alert: "So then let us not sleep, as others do, but let us keep awake and be sober." "Others" were sleeping two thousand years ago; "others" have fallen asleep today.

Christian, stay awake, lest your Lord finds you sleeping.

When Jesus comes to reward His servants,
Whether it be noon or night,
Faithful to Him will He find us watching,
*With our lamps all trimmed and bright?**

Burning Hearts

They said to each other, "Did not our hearts burn within us while he talked to us on the road, while he opened to us the Scriptures?"
Luke 24:32

When was the last time you experienced a "burning heart"?

It was the first Easter. Two disciples of the Lord Jesus were walking toward Emmaus, very likely returning home following their pilgrimage to observe Passover in Jerusalem. They were heartbroken, as they discussed what happened while there. A *Stranger* suddenly appears, joining the couple in their journey. The man listens as the two express their regret and sorrow about the one whom they had hoped would be Israel's Savior was instead killed. Furthermore, they said the word was circulating that this Jesus was now alive.

After the *Stranger* patiently listened to their woeful story, he carefully explained it all: "beginning with Moses and all the Prophets, he interpreted to them in all the Scriptures the things concerning himself" (Luke 24:27). After they arrived home, the three dined together. The Stranger "took the bread and blessed and broke it and gave it to them. And their eyes were opened, and they recognized him. And he vanished from their sight" (24:30-31). It was then we read, "Did not our hearts burn within us while he talked to us on the road, while he opened to us the Scriptures?" (24: 32).

As important as it is to read the Word of God, it is more consequential that we *understand* what we read. The risen Christ did not merely *quote* the appropriate Scripture to the two distraught travelers; he "opened" the Word, explaining God's truth. What a lesson here for preachers and Bible teachers. Such have a responsibility to explain to their hearers the Word of God. Moreover, teachers have the awesome task to expound the Scriptures as they relate to the Lord Jesus Christ. When a capable teacher and eager disciples come together, hearts will inevitably "burn" when the Spirit gives an understanding of God's truth.

The Christian's Advocates (part 1)

We have an Advocate with the Father, Jesus Christ the righteous.
1 John 2:1

According to the Word of God, the Christian has two Advocates. The one is the Lord Jesus Christ, who is presently seated at the right hand of God the Father: "We have an Advocate with the Father, Jesus Christ the righteous" (1 John 2:1); the other is the Holy Spirit, who indwells every believer, "And I will ask the Father, and he will give you another Advocate" (John 14:16 RIT).

The Greek word in these two texts, translated as "Advocate," is variously rendered by Bible translators: Advocate, Helper, Comforter, Counselor. The word means "one who comes to a person's aid; one who speaks in someone's defense."

The believer's Advocate seated at the Father's right hand is none other than the crucified, risen, ascended Lord Jesus Christ. He serves as the Christian's mediator and intercessor. The benefits of what God in Christ meritoriously wrought on the Cross, is administered through Christ's high priestly ministry. In the words of Charles Wesley (1707-1788):

He ever lives above,
For me to intercede;
His all redeeming love,
*His precious blood to plead.**

Centuries before the Word was made flesh, died, arose, and ascended to the Father's side to serve as the believer's Advocate, the suffering Job was given a glimpse of such an intercessor: "Even now my witness is in heaven; my *advocate* is on high; my intercessor is my friend" (Job 16:19-20 NIV). Unlike many of our Lord's distressed followers today, this Old Testament believer had the overwhelming confidence that his Advocate was also his Friend.

Take heart, dear follower of Christ, when you have failed in your walk with your Father-God—and who among us has not—your Advocate on high is *for* you, not against you. Your Advocate is face-to-face with the Father. Your Advocate is also your Friend!

The Christian's Advocates (part 2)

"I will ask the Father, and he will give you another Advocate."
John 14:16 RIT

We can only imagine the disappointment and sadness which overcame the Twelve when these words were first spoken. When Jesus
confided in the disciples that he would be leaving, but another
would come to be with them, they were unprepared to hear it:
"because I have said these things to you, sorrow has filled your
heart" (John 16:6). After all, the Lord Jesus had proven to be an
Advocate and Helper *par excellent*. But Jesus was about to finish
his ministry among men in the flesh. He would soon be leaving his
followers. Then what? Jesus graciously informed the Twelve about
the Advocate to come.

The next Advocate and Helper would indwell Christ's disciples:
"And I will ask the Father, and he will give you another Advocate....
You know him, for he dwells with you and will be in you" (John
14:16-17). While on earth, the Lord Jesus was confined to a human
body. However, he ascended to heaven and sent the Holy Spirit, so
that the Spirit would indwell every disciple. He promised not to
leave his followers as orphans. He kept that commitment, for on the
day of Pentecost, the Holy Spirit was poured out on his people.

The next Advocate and Helper would be with Christ's disciples
forever. "And I will ask the Father, and he will give you another Advocate, to be with you forever" (John 14:16). Forever! He
would not be here today and gone tomorrow. But every day, every
moment, in every circumstance of life, the Spirit, the Advocate,
would be present—forever!

The next Advocate and Helper would empower Christ's followers to live the Christian life victoriously and be effective witnesses in
this world. Just before his ascension into heaven, Jesus charged his
disciples: "And behold, I am sending the promise of my Father upon you. But stay in the city until you are clothed with power from on
high" (Luke 24:49). "But you will receive power when the Holy Spirit has come upon you, and you will be my witnesses in Jerusalem
and in all Judea and Samaria, and to the end of the earth" (Acts
1:8).

The Struggle (part 1)

Epaphras, who is one of you, a servant of Christ Jesus,
greets you, always struggling on your behalf in his prayers.
Colossians 4:12

Bible teachers who suggest there should not be any struggle in the life of the Christian evidently misunderstand what the Word of God says about the matter.

While the biblical concept of "struggle" is much broader than the occurrences of the word itself (or its synonyms), the contexts in which this word is found in the New Testament reveal the kinds of struggles a Christian does (should?) experience. The Greek word *agōna* (and its derivatives) is variously rendered: race, agony, struggle, fight, conflict (and more). In this and the following meditation, we will note four kinds of struggle mentioned in the New Testament.

The struggle of an endurance race. Interestingly enough, the Greek word for "race" in Hebrews 12:1 is *agōna*: "Therefore, since we are surrounded by so great a cloud of witnesses, let us also lay aside every weight, and sin which clings so closely, and let us run with endurance the *race* [struggle] that is set before us ..."

From beginning to end, this race for the Christian—this endurance run—is a conflict against the world, the flesh, and the Devil. It could be described as an agony, a struggle. There is no better treatise on this subject, outside biblical literature, than Bunyan's *Pilgrim's Progress*. From the City of Destruction to the Celestial City, Christian was engaged in a battle. So it is with every believer. It is a good fight of faith; nevertheless, it is a fight.

The struggle of intercessory prayer. Jesus knew this struggle as no one else when he prayed in Gethsemane: "And being in *agony* he prayed more earnestly; and his sweat became like drops of blood falling down to the ground" (Luke 22:44). Paul references one of his companions in the gospel who experienced the struggle of intercessory prayer: "Epaphras, who is one of you, a servant of Christ Jesus, greets you, always *struggling* on your behalf in his prayers, that you may stand mature and fully assured in all the will of God" (Col. 4:12). Prayer is often a struggle. It is a struggle, because we have an Adversary who opposes us every step of the way.

The Struggle (part 2)

*In your struggle against sin you have not yet
resisted to the point of shedding your blood.*
Hebrews 12:4

In continuing our thoughts on this subject of the Christian's struggles, note the additional "struggles" mentioned in the New Testament.

The struggle against sin. Because of the benefits flowing from the cross and the indwelling Spirit, we experience a peace and joy that accompany a fully surrendered life to the Lord Jesus Christ. Nevertheless, there remains a struggle, a fight against sin. Hebrews notes: "In your *struggle* against sin you have not yet resisted to the point of shedding your blood" (Heb. 12:4). To fight against temptation is to struggle against sin. This struggle won't cease until we leave this world.

> *Fight the good fight with all thy might;*
> *Christ is thy Strength, and Christ thy Right;*
> *Lay hold on life, and it shall be*
> *Thy joy and crown eternally.**

The good struggle. My wife Emily used to sing a song titled "Life is Hard but God is Good." Life can be difficult, really difficult, but God is good—always! Our merciful Father has invested everything necessary for us to win in this struggle. His Son died and arose; the Holy Spirit has been given to empower us. Jesus said, "In the world you will have tribulation. But take heart; I have overcome the world" (John 16:33). By God's grace, may we be able to say with the holy apostle at the end of our earthly sojourn, "I have fought the good fight ..." (2 Tim. 4:7).

> *Sure I must fight, if I would reign;*
> *increase my courage, Lord.*
> *I'll bear the toil, endure the pain,*
> *supported by thy word.***

Yes, the Christian life is often a struggle, but we are not left to fight this battle alone: "for he who is in you is greater than he who is in the world" (1 John 4:4).

We Need to Be Reminded

*Therefore I intend always to remind you of these qualities, though you
know them and are established in the truth that you have. I think it
right, as long as I am in this body, to stir you up by way of reminder.*
2 Peter 1:12-13

Each of us possesses a natural tendency to forgetfulness. Lest Israel
forgot Yahweh's mighty deeds done on her behalf, the people were
instructed to observe three principal feasts throughout their life-
time: Passover, Pentecost, and Tabernacles. The feast of Passover
reminded God's people of their miraculous deliverance from Egypt,
when the angel of death passed over every home that had blood
sprinkled on their respective door posts and lintels; where there was
no blood, the first-born was struck dead. The feast of Pentecost, or
Harvest, was observed to give thanks for God's faithfulness in
providing for his people. The third feast, Tabernacles, served as a
reminder when the people of Israel dwelled in tents during their
forty years in the wilderness.

Christians need constant reminders. One of the reasons our
Lord instituted the Eucharist was that God never wanted us to forget the importance of his Son's death: "This is my body, which is
given for you. Do this in *remembrance* of me" (Luke 22:19).

We need to read, and have read to us, the Scriptures repeatedly
in public worship, in private devotions, because we need to be reminded of the *whole* counsel of God.

The Apostle Peter knew this. He recognized that Christ's followers were prone to forget the importance of vital Christian truth and
qualities: Thus, he penned two letters—lest they forget: "I intend always to remind you ..."

*Sing them over again to me, wonderful words of life,
Let me more of their beauty see, wonderful words of life;
Words of life and beauty teach me faith and duty.
Beautiful words, wonderful words, wonderful words of life,
Beautiful words, wonderful words, wonderful words of life.**

Christians should never tire of being reminded of God's truth.

Courtesy

Remind them to ... show perfect courtesy toward all people.
Titus 3:2-3

Being disciples of the Lord Jesus, we should expect the world to behave like sinners. After all, the world is the world! But God expects his people to behave differently. Granted, all change—from unacceptable to acceptable behavior—does not occur at the moment of one's conversion to Christ. Much change comes to the Christian as he *learns* what God expects of him. It is one thing for saving grace to be believed and received; it is quite another thing to learn how this grace is to be *lived*.

Titus was appointed by the Apostle Paul to serve as an overseer in the church on the island of Crete. We catch a glimpse from his instructions to this church leader, of the kind of pagan culture these converts were raised in and surrounded by. Polygamy, gluttony, debauchery, drunkenness, greed, narcissism, fleshly indulgence, lying and stealing, and laziness—all of these sins, and so many more, characterized these degenerate people. However, Titus was God's appointed man to instruct these converts in how to live-out the Christian life in a pagan environment. God's grace not only saves us; God's grace trains us (see Titus 2:11). God is not content to leave us in the condition he first finds us; he is always teaching and correcting his people.

One way God's grace trains us is in how we should treat other people. The Cretans were evidently naturally *rude* people, lacking a proper respect for the rights and feelings of others. Sin does that to people, for sin is self-centered.

There are times, as Christians, when God must remind us how he wants us to treat others. One Sunday morning, sitting in our pew waiting for the service to begin, I was reading Titus, chapter 3. Soon afterward, someone approached me, who I was *naturally* disinclined to be friendly toward. Immediately, the Holy Spirit reminded me of what I had just read: "show perfect courtesy toward all people."

"Remind them," Paul wrote. I need this constant reminder when I interact with saints and sinners alike: "show perfect courtesy toward all people."

The Descent of Man

*For although they knew God, they did not honor him as
God or give thanks to him, but they became futile in their
thinking, and their foolish hearts were darkened.*
Romans 1:21

Man's descent began in the Garden of Eden, and continues to this day. The depths and extent to which man has fallen are delineated in Romans 1, and affirmed in the lives of countless people in contemporary society.

Adam and Eve were created to live face to face with their Creator-God. Interestingly enough, the Greek word for man (*anthropos*), literally means "upper-looking one." Man was created to look up, to look up to God, to commune with his Creator and Father. This was indeed Paradise—holy, unadulterated fellowship between the creature and the Creator.

However, when man chose his own way instead of pursuing God's way, he turned inward, when he was made to look upward. God's original image of himself within man became soiled, obscuring man's vision of God. Though fallen man has a conscience, that conscience has become damaged, warped, and misguided: "And since they did not see fit to acknowledge God, God gave them up to a debased mind to do what ought not to be done" (Rom. 1:28). The history of the human race, absent God, is found in Romans 1:18 -32. Man without God has plunged to a never-ending abyss of thanklessness, futility, foolishness, idolatry, shamelessness, homosexuality, filled with all manner of unrighteousness, evil, covetousness, malice. They are full of envy, murder, strife, deceit, maliciousness. They are gossips, slanderers, haters of God, insolent, haughty, boastful, inventors of evil, disobedient to parents, foolish, faithless, heartless, ruthless" (1:29-31). Furthermore, "Though they know God's righteous decree that those who practice such things deserve to die, they not only do them but give approval to those who practice them" (1:32).

It is by kneeling at the cross of Christ that man's final downward spiral into Hell can be averted. Only in looking to the Lord Jesus Christ will our *descent* be transformed into an *ascent*—an ascent to Heaven.

What Are We Reading?

When you come, bring the cloak that I left with Carpus at
Troas, also the books, and above all the parchments.
2 Timothy 4:13

The Apostle Paul's Second Letter to Timothy is most likely his final epistle. At this writing, Paul is in Rome; it is his second imprisonment. Farewell instructions are given to his son in the gospel, who has been one of his closest companions through years of tireless labors for the Lord Jesus.

Paul believes his life and ministry are coming to an end: "For I am already being poured out as a drink offering, and the time of my departure has come" (4:6). At this writing, some colleagues had abandoned both the Lord and Paul; others were engaged in ministry elsewhere. While Luke was present with him, he longed to have Timothy's fellowship: "Do your best to come to me soon" (4:9). And when Timothy did travel to Rome, Paul desired that he come become winter (4:21), thus the request for the cloak.

However, the imprisoned apostle and evangelist of the Lord Jesus wanted more than a coat to keep him warm; he asked Timothy to bring with him "the books, and above all the parchments." Paul never quit reading—even in prison. What were the books and parchments he referred to? We're not certain, but more than likely they consisted of portions of Scripture and additional excellent reading material. His mind and heart must be fed.

I'm convinced our pulpits would fare much better, and the people in the pews would be healthier, if God's servants spent more time in the Word and regularly read books worth reading. A good cure for so much sameness, lameness, and tameness in the ministry, is the Word of God and excellent books.

Paul pursued excellence all his Christian life and ministry, including his reading. Most of us are merely reading what's popular and the latest—hardly a good recipe for mature thinking. Sitting in prison, Paul was not interested in reading fluff and the recent "How to Market the Church" books. He needed meat for the mature—the Word of God, excellent books! "Bring the books, above all the parchments"!

The Whole Counsel of God

"For I did not shrink from declaring to you the whole counsel of God."
Acts 20:27

Ministers of the Lord Jesus Christ experience an ongoing challenge—the challenge to be faithful to God and his revealed Word in their preaching and teaching ministries. The only word ministers are called to declare is the Word of God. But our Adversary relentlessly attacks God's messengers, inviting them to preach a *soft* gospel a *diluted* gospel, a *different* gospel.

More than one God-called servant of Christ has chosen—ever so slightly to begin with—to delete unpopular truths from his sermons. He wants to make his people feel good, to like him, to congratulate him on his fine sermon when they leave the sanctuary. He may believe the *old* truth is *outdated* truth. Such a person has inadvertently fallen into one of Satan's deadliest snares: choosing to please people over choosing to please God.

After being chosen by Christ to be an apostle and teacher of the Word, the Apostle Paul had no desire to impress others with his learning: "plausible words of wisdom" (1 Cor. 2:4); nor did he speak "to please man," use "flattery," or "seek glory from people" (1 Thess. 2:4-6). He knew he had been called by God, and that he must give a final account to him.

Returning from another missionary trip, making his way to a final visit to Jerusalem, the ship Paul is sailing on harbors at Miletus. From there, Paul sends word to Ephesus that he wishes to meet with the church's elders. When the elders arrive, the beloved apostle reminded these men how he had both lived and ministered among them. He said he did not preach a partial gospel in Ephesus, a fragmented Word of God. When many others were "shrinking" from faithfully declaring the entire truth of God's revealed Word, Paul testifies, "I am innocent of the blood of all, for I did not shrink from declaring to you the whole counsel of God" (Acts 20:26-27).

Pray for your pastor. Pray that he will be a gentle person. Pray that he will speak the truth in love. And pray that he will faithfully and boldly declare "the whole counsel of God," as did the Apostle Paul.

Idolatry (part 1)

Little children, keep yourselves from idols.
1 John 5:21

The beloved apostle's final words to his children in the faith were a warning against the insidious and deadly sin of idolatry. Man was made to worship, and he was destined to find something to concentrate his passions and pleasures on; he can't live without a god of some form, an idol—no matter its shape.

The allure of idolatry is both real and persistent. Satan is a master of disguise and deception. He never confronts us with what appalls, only with what appeals. The Christian must remain vigilant. We must not avert our gaze from the true Reality, and begin to give our attention to a *representation* of what is true, righteous, holy, and pure. The Adversary doesn't mind if we give lip service to God, on the one hand, but on the other hand give our natural affection and loyalty to things temporal.

Whatever is supreme in our life is our idol. Idolatry takes many forms in the Western world—forms which present a constant snare to the Christian.

Food. What God created for us to enjoy and use to maintain healthy bodies can inordinately control us. One of the fruits of the Spirit is self-control (Gal. 5:23). We must not use in excess what God has called us to use in moderation. Paul writes of those whose "god is their belly" (Phil. 3:19). Obesity is epidemic in America; it shouldn't be among Christians.

Pleasure. Our Father-God "richly provides us with everything to enjoy" (1 Tim. 6:17). However, whenever we accept God's pleasing gifts, allowing them to control us, they have assumed a place of importance that dishonors God and enslaves us. Before our conversion, God says, "we were ... slaves to various passions and pleasures" (Titus 3:3). A Christian cannot be a slave to pleasure and a slave to Jesus Christ. Paul says one of the things that will characterize humanity in the last days is they will be "lovers of pleasure rather than lovers of God" (2 Tim. 3:4).

"Little children, keep yourselves from idols."

Idolatry (part 2)

Little children, keep yourselves from idols.
1 John 5:21

Mammon. The Lord Jesus and the apostles spoke and wrote about the danger of mammon displacing one's love for God. Jesus said either mammon or God will be our master: "No one can serve two masters, for either he will hate the one and love the other, or he will be devoted to the one and despise the other. You cannot serve God and money" (Matt. 6:24). The word rendered "money" by the ESV is broader than money; it has to do with the entire spectrum of what we possess, or wish to possess. We either possess our possessions or they possess us. We are either a slave to what we call our *own*, or we are a slave of the Lord Jesus Christ. In the words of the beloved apostle, "For the love of money is a root of all kinds of evils. It is through this craving that some have wandered away from the faith and pierced themselves with many pangs" (1 Tim. 6:10). This holds true for the pulpit as well as the pew. Thus, Paul warned church leaders that they should not be "a lover of money" (1 Tim. 3:3). We are supposed to earn, in order that we may provide for our family and contribute to the work of God and care for the needy. We must take care that we not turn God's gifts—money and possessions—into idols.

We can only be kept free from an idolatrous heart and lifestyle by loving God with our all: "You shall love the Lord your God with all your heart and with all your soul and with all your mind" (Matt. 22:37). Love, God's love—"love divine, all loves excelling"—is our protection against making an idol out of food, pleasure, mammon, or anything else. Those in whom God's love fills the heart and controls the mind will be safe from idolatry. However, whenever God's love is in declension, idolatry will fill the vacuum.

When God spoke the words, "You shall have no other gods before me" (Ex. 20:3), he was not speaking to pagans; he was addressing believers. When the apostle wrote, "Little children, keep yourselves from idols (1 John 5:21), his readers were Christians.

Allow God to speak to you about this ever-present danger—the danger of idolatry.

We're on the Winning Side

"Do not be afraid, for those who are with
us are more than those who are with them."
2 Kings 6:16

The Bible informs us there are forces in the spirit world which stand opposed to the people of God. These enemies of God and his children are unseen to the human eye, but nonetheless real. The Apostle Paul identifies these evil spirits as rulers, authorities, cosmic powers, and spiritual forces of evil (see Eph. 6:10-12). Their number is legion, and their leader is Satan, the god of this world.

These spiritual forces of evil align themselves with wicked men and institutions, which are in a campaign against righteousness and godliness on a local, regional, and worldwide level. These forces seek to control key leaders at every level of society, including the political, economic, judicial, entertainment, cultural, and ecclesiastical. What Satan failed to accomplish at Golgotha and the Empty Tomb two thousand years ago, he has since been tirelessly working with his demonic minions to achieve: the overthrow of God's kingdom; the defeat of Christ's church.

Satan's tactics in the pursuit of his ultimate goal are many and varied. When he fails to execute his plans by overt means, he approaches the church through covert operations: "for even Satan disguises himself as an angel of light. So it is no surprise if his servants [false teachers], also, disguise themselves as servants of righteousness" (2 Cor. 11:14-15).

We are told in 2 Kings 6 that God's people were under siege. When Elisha's servant rose early one morning, he reported to the prophet what he had seen: "an army with horses and chariots was all around the city" (6:15). Elisha knew there was a presence greater than the enemy; he saw it, but he wanted his servant to be convinced as well. So he prayed: "O Lord, please open his eyes that he may see" (6:17). The Lord heard his prayer: "So the Lord opened the eyes of the young man, and he saw, and behold, the mountain was full of horses and chariots of fire all around Elisha" (6:17).

The enemy only had horses and chariots. God had multitudes of horses and chariots of fire.

Fear not, child of God, we're on the winning side!

Bearing Fruit During Drought

"Blessed is the man who trusts in the Lord, whose trust is the Lord. He is like a tree planted by water, that sends out its roots by the stream, and does not fear when heat comes, for its leaves remain green, and is not anxious in the year of drought, for it does not cease to bear fruit."
Jeremiah 17:7-8

Regardless of life's providences—whether friendly or unfriendly—God's servants can produce fruit. They do so, because they are vitally connected to the Vine; they do so, because grace has enabled them to sink their roots deep into God's life, holiness, and love. When life's scorching sun bears down on them—day after day, month after month—they bear fruit for God. When all the "leaves" and "shrubs" about them shrivel and dry up, these men and women of God are like trees, sinking their roots even deeper, drawing upon God's preserving grace and goodness.

Jerusalem and Judah, during Jeremiah's time, became faithless followers of Yahweh. Repeatedly, Yahweh sent the faithful prophet bearing God's words, but they would not listen; they clung to their evil ways. These backsliders turned away from Yahweh, seeking help from fallen man. Of such, the Lord said, "He is like a shrub in the desert, and shall not see any good come. He shall dwell in the parched places of the wilderness, in an uninhabited salt land" (Jer. 17:6).

This world is a parched place in the wilderness; and like Judah of old, who were Yahweh's covenant people, much of the modern church is beset by drought and barrenness—from God's perspective. Judah remained religious, but was like a sleepwalker, monotonously performing her required rites. Yahweh rebuked them: "they have forsaken me, the fountain of living waters, and hewed out cisterns for themselves, broken cisterns that can hold no water" (Jer. 2:13).

Changing the metaphors from fountains and cisterns, God speaks of shrubs and trees and heat and green leaves in Jeremiah 17. How are we responding to the oppressive heat and drought in our culture, and possibly within our church? God says even during such seasons, it is possible to bear fruit to his glory.

August 14

Vain Worship

*"This people draw near with their mouth and honor me
with their lips, while their hearts are far from me."*
Isaiah 29:13

The very ceremonies and worship Yahweh designed, instituted, and
called his people to observe, at times became abhorrent to him.
Why? Because these rituals were performed by people with unclean
hands and stubborn hearts, who often rendered service to a foreign
god in addition to regularly appearing before Yahweh. Religious
ritual absent obedience is defiled worship, unacceptable worship.

Throughout Israel's history, Yahweh repeatedly rebuked his
covenant people because they rejected him, even though they proceeded to offer lip service to him. Note some of the ways in which
the Lord took issue with his people.

Circumcision. "Behold, the days are coming, declares the Lord,
when I will punish all those who are circumcised merely in the
flesh" (Jer. 9:25).

Sacrifices. "Oh that there were one among you who would shut
the doors, that you might not kindle fire on my altar in vain! I have
no pleasure in you, says the Lord of hosts, and I will not accept an
offering from your hand" (Mal. 1:10).

Sabbath Observance. "He has laid waste his booth like a garden, laid in ruins his meeting place; the Lord has made Zion forget
festival and Sabbath, and in his fierce indignation has spurned king
and priest" (Lam. 2:6).

Fasting. "Behold, you fast only to quarrel and to fight and to hit
with a wicked fist. Fasting like yours this day will not make your
voice to be heard on high" (Isa. 58:4).

These were all forms of worship the Lord had directed his people to observe and practice. Even so, when the worshipers' hearts
were not right before God, their worship became a stench and were
detestable to God.

When we kneel before the Lord, when we gather with the people of God, let us make sure that our hearts are right before God,
otherwise, it is an empty exercise, and it is vain worship.

The King Who Would Not Listen

As Jehudi read three or four columns, the king would cut them
off with a knife and throw them into the fire in the fire pot, until the
entire scroll was consumed in the fire that was in the fire pot.
Jeremiah 36:23

When one is a king, it can be very unpleasant to be told you need to amend your ways. After all, kings give commands, directing others what they should do; no one tells them what to do. Nevertheless, God is not partial to kings. God's words hold true for the beggar at the gate as well as for a king on his throne.

When the people heard the ominous word of the Lord from Jeremiah the prophet, calling them to turn from their evil ways and return to the Lord, they declared a fast. When King Jehoiakim learned about the scroll of God, he called a man by the name of Jehudi to bring the scroll and read it to him. What was the king's reaction to hearing God's words? "As Jehudi read three or four columns, the king would cut them off with a knife and throw them into the fire in the fire pot, until the entire scroll was consumed in the fire that was in the fire pot. Yet neither the king nor any of his servants who heard all these words were afraid, nor did they tear their garments" (Jer. 36:23-24).

Unless we keep a tender heart before the Lord, the longer we live and the further we climb in our careers, the less inclined we are to accept God's warnings and pleadings. Having grown accustomed to having our own way and doing our own thing, we don't want to be told by God how we should change our ways. We may not take a knife, cutting away God's unpleasant words to us. All we have to do is simply turn a deaf ear to the Word each time we hear it—column by column our conscience becomes seared.

Burning the Word in the fire does not destroy it. What we thought was final and finished, God revives, taking his Word to people who will hear: "The grass withers, the flower fades, but the word of our God will stand forever" (Isa. 40:8).

Every time we read and hear it read, let us embrace the Word of God, asking the Lord to enable us to obey it.

Where Shall We Minister Next?

*And when they had come up to Mysia, they attempted to go
into Bithynia, but the Spirit of Jesus did not allow them.*
Acts 16:7

In the normal course of decision-making in the church, our Lord usually works through sanctified minds as they ponder future ministry plans. In discussing the apparent possibilities and problems of one plan over another, prayerful saints conclude, under God, that a specific course of action should be taken. These deliberations may take an evening, or they may take days and months.

On the Apostle Paul's second missionary journey, his travels take him to Lystra, where he adds Timothy as a companion. The two traveled from city to city, teaching disciples as well as making additional converts. While they were on this mission, the Holy Spirit revealed they should not minister in Asia. So, they changed their plans; and upon coming to Mysia, they intended to travel into Bithynia, "but the Spirit of Jesus did not allow them." Thus, they proceeded to Troas, where Paul received a vison concerning his next phase of ministry.

What might we learn from this special leading of the Spirit in the ministry of Paul?

• Paul zealously pursued his calling as an apostle, teacher, and evangelist. He was eager to preach the gospel—anywhere and everywhere. He attempted to go into Asia and Bithynia, believing it was the right course of action. This seemed to be God's will.

• Knowing Paul as we do, we can be assured he prayerfully and carefully planned each phase of his mission. Everywhere he went, lives were changed by the power of God, sometimes many, sometimes few.

• Even though Paul had prayerfully believed he should pursue a mission in a particular location, it is apparent he was open to the Holy Spirit to change his mind, as is indicated in Acts 16.

• In making ministry plans, church leaders must lead with crucified egos, relying on the Holy Spirit to guide them, and be willing to change a previous plan to pursue a new direction, just as the apostle did.

Are you being led by the Holy Spirit?

An Improbable Choice

*"I was no prophet, nor a prophet's son, but I was a herdsman and
a dresser of sycamore figs. But the Lord took me from following the
flock, and the Lord said to me, 'Go, prophesy to my people Israel.'"*
Amos 7:14-15

The résumé of the prophet Amos would have been summarily discarded by most modern-day pulpit search committees (Of course, he wouldn't have submitted one to begin with; prophets don't submit résumés). Amos didn't possess proper credentials: He never went to college or seminary; he was not a polished speaker; he had only been "a herdsman and a dresser of sycamore figs." What did qualify him to be a prophet was simply this: "the Lord took me from following the flock, and the Lord said to me, 'Go, prophesy to my people Israel.'"

We should not conclude, however, that because Amos was a *nonprofessional*, he was uneducated and unlearned in the ways of God. Just as David had been schooled by the Lord for some years before he was called by God to lead Israel, we may rightfully assume that Amos got to know God and his ways as he tended livestock and cared for sycamore figs at Tekoa. Formal education for prospective ministers should neither be despised, nor should it be made a god. Previous generations were guilty of the former; this generation is guilty of the latter. The average American pulpit would not accept as their pastor a Charles Spurgeon, Dwight L. Moody, or an A. W. Tozer—each having no formal ministerial training.

Now, this is no polemic for an untrained ministry—Spurgeon himself established a school for ministerial training. And if a minister has not had a formal education, he surely shouldn't *glory* in that fact. However, we must insist that behind every vocational minister should be God's personal call: "the Lord said to me ..." God prepares the person before he calls; and God continues to educate a person after he calls. God may lead his servant to a Bible college, or to a seminary, or he may lead to neither. That's God's business. However God chooses to lead a person, God will use that man or woman for his sovereign purposes.

We should never disdain a person's background, nor question the means God has chosen to educate his respective servants.

August 18

The Precious Blood of Christ

*You were ransomed ... not with perishable things
such as silver or gold, but with the precious blood of
Christ, like that of a lamb without blemish or spot.*
1 Peter 1:18-19

When the Apostle Peter writes of our Lord's sacrificial, atoning death, he speaks of "the precious blood of Christ." Oh, the wonder of it all—Christ died for sinners; Christ died for us. The blood Christ shed is *precious*! Why was it that Peter said Christ's blood was precious? Consider the following:

• The blood of Christ is precious because it is the blood of the Son of God. "He entered once for all into the holy places, not by means of the blood of goats and calves but by means of his own blood, thus securing an eternal redemption" (Heb. 9:12).

• The blood of Christ is precious because without it there is no forgiveness of sins. "Without the shedding of blood there is no forgiveness of sins" (Heb. 9:22).

• The blood of Christ is precious because by it we are justified before God. "Since, therefore, we have now been justified by his blood, much more shall we be saved by him from the wrath of God" (Rom. 5:9).

• The blood of Christ is precious because by Christ's sacrifice we can draw near to God. "Therefore, brothers, since we have confidence to enter the holy places by the blood of Jesus ..." (Heb. 10:19).

• The blood of Christ is precious because by it we are cleansed from all sin. "But if we walk in the light, as he is in the light, we have fellowship with one another, and the blood of Jesus his Son cleanses us from all sin" (1 John 1:7).

• The blood of Christ is precious because by it we overcome our Adversary. "And they have conquered him by the blood of the Lamb and by the word of their testimony" (Rev. 12:11).

Precious! The precious blood of Christ!

*There is a fountain filled with blood drawn from Emmanuel's veins;
And sinners plunged beneath that flood lose all their guilty stains.
Lose all their guilty stains, lose all their guilty stains;
And sinners plunged beneath that flood lose all their guilty stains.**

True Greatness

"If you know these things, blessed are you if you do them."
John 13:17

In order to impress upon the consciousness of the Twelve how they were to relate to one another, Jesus used his Last Meal with the disciples as the occasion to demonstrate his view of genuine leadership: "Jesus, knowing that the Father had given all things into his hands, and that he had come from God and was going back to God, rose from supper. He laid aside his outer garments, and taking a towel, tied it around his waist. Then he poured water into a basin and began to wash the disciples' feet and to wipe them with the towel that was wrapped around him" (John. 13:3-5).

To reinforce the truth of what he had just done, Jesus says to the Twelve: "Do you understand what I have done to you? You call me Teacher and Lord, and you are right, for so I am. If I then, your Lord and Teacher, have washed your feet, you also ought to wash one another's feet. For I have given you an example, that you also should do just as I have done to you. Truly, truly, I say to you, a servant is not greater than his master, nor is a messenger greater than the one who sent him. If you know these things, blessed are you if you do them" (John. 13:12-17).

Jesus showed the way to true greatness—true greatness consists in serving others, giving oneself to others. How could the disciples ever forget this lesson? How can we?

In the words of Philip Greenslade, Jesus "is our example of leadership. Secure in our sonship we will not need to strive for position in order to prove who we are. We will not use our leadership opportunities to find emotional wholeness but to express it. In this security, we will be able to lay down our reputation as leaders in order to fulfill our calling."*

To listen to Jesus was to listen to the *Servant* of the Lord; to watch Jesus was to see the *Servant* of the Lord.

Ask the Lord to give you a *servant's* heart.

August 20

Our Heritage

Contend for the faith that was once for all delivered to the saints.
Jude 1:3

In every generation God has faithful, thirsty-hearted followers whose lives are singularly marked with a passion for Christ. These men and women are not content to know God in theory, neither do they settle for a mere creedal form of religion.

The constant refrain which characterizes each of these towers of godliness and good works, can be summed up in the prayer of David: "As the deer pants for the water brooks. So my soul pants for You, O God. My soul thirsts for the living God" (Psa. 42:1-2a NASB).

These men and women were God-thirsty men and women, who passionately loved, obeyed, and served their Lord. This was true of David and Daniel, Isaiah and Ezekiel, Hannah and Deborah, Joseph and Joshua, Caleb and Gideon. It was also true of Simeon and Anna, Elizabeth and Mary, Peter and Paul, Andrew and Timothy and a host of many other Old and New Testament worthies. It is no less true of a myriad of others over the last two thousand years of church history. To echo Hebrews 11:32f: And what more shall I say? For the time would fail me to tell of Ignatius of Antioch, John Chrysostom, Augustine of Hippo, Bernard of Clairvoix, Francis of Assisi, Thomas Aquinas, John Hus, Martin Luther, William Tyndale, John Calvin, John Knox, Teresa of Avila, Blaise Pascal, John Bunyan, Jonathan Edwards, George Mueller, John and Charles Wesley, George Whitefield, Francis Asbury, Jonathan Edwards, Charles Spurgeon, William Carey, Hudson Taylor, Dietrich Bonhoeffer, A. W. Tozer, C. S. Lewis—who demonstrated an indefatigable passion for Christ by defending the faith once for all delivered to the saints, cared for widows and orphans, and traveled the world with the Good News of Jesus Christ. These men and women expressed and practiced their passion for Christ before kings and apostate leaders. Some edified Christ's church by writing extensively; others rejoiced in the face of unbelievable trials and humanly insurmountable difficulties. For some, their testimonies were sealed with their own blood; many others remain known to God alone.

Let us thank God for such men and women. We are debtors!

The Bride of Christ

Let us rejoice and exult and give him the glory, for the marriage
of the Lamb has come, and his Bride has made herself ready.
Revelation 19:7

When we honor and acknowledge God's created order for mankind and the human family, we honor our Creator-God. What God has made uniquely different, we are not to confuse: "So God created man in his own image, in the image of God he created him; male and female he created them" (Gen. 1:27). Likewise, by honoring and supporting heterosexual marriage, we rightfully acknowledge our Father-God's design for perpetuating the human race: "Therefore a man shall leave his father and his mother and hold fast to his wife, and they shall become one flesh" (Gen. 2:24).

It should not be a surprise to God's people that what God has ordained should be under attack by the enemies of God. Since the fall of man, Satan has sought to destroy everything God created and ordained: "The thief comes only to steal and kill and destroy" (John 10:10). Those who seek to destroy what God has instituted are enemies of righteousness in need of the saving grace of the Lord Jesus Christ.

God is a God of life and order, not the God of death and confusion. Jesus said, "I came that they may have life and have it abundantly" (John 10:10). Those who advocate the destruction of the unborn, heterosexual marriage, and the uniqueness of the sexes, are instruments of darkness and death, destruction and disintegration.

May the people of God be shinning lights of righteousness, peace and joy in the Holy Spirit. May our marriages be a perpetual tribute to the love and mercy of God. Let us not only speak against the evil pervading our society, but let us take the light of Jesus everywhere we go, living out and speaking the truth in love.

I have many reasons to be grateful on this day, August 21, for it was on this day that Ruth Emily Voyles and I entered into God's ordained covenant of marriage. We were young in age and young in the faith at the time; now we are older, but more in love than ever. We have endeavored to honor God in our home, and God has wonderfully honored us in return—many times over. In a culture of death, let us be living epistles of life—the very life that Jesus gives.

August 22

A Hot and Cold Disciple

Peter said to him, "Even if I must die with you, I will not deny you!"
Matthew 26:35

For all the Apostle Peter's natural abilities, his natural *liabilities* were not only apparent to his contemporaries (and to us), but they were painfully obvious to the Lord Jesus. He was, indeed, "unstable as water" (Gen. 49:4).

Possessing an explosive and often intemperate personality, Peter is a study in contradictions—particularly as we see him in the Gospels. While, on the one hand, he readily answered Christ's call to discipleship when his brother Andrew introduced him to Jesus; on the other hand, his repeated failures in faith were glaringly real. One minute, this apostle was walking on water; the next minute, he was crying out, "Lord, save me!" (Matt. 14:30). One day, Peter confesses that Jesus is the "Christ, the Son of the living God"; another day, after learning that his Lord would eventually suffer terrible rejection and be killed, Peter thoughtlessly rebukes Christ: "Far be it from you, Lord! This shall never happen to you" (Matt. 16:16, 22).

Such a show of bravado brought a stern rebuke from Christ: "Get behind me, Satan! For you are not setting your mind on the things of God, but on the things of man" (Mark 8:33). Dennis F. Kinlaw says of Christ's rejoinder: "I now consider Jesus' reprimand of Peter to be the prime biblical text for holiness of heart.... The Greek literally means, 'You are not minded as God is minded.' 'You do not think as God thinks.'"* And then, of course, there was Peter's egotistical boast that though every other disciple would forsake his Lord, under no circumstance would he: "Though they all fall away because of you, I will never fall away.... Even if I must die with you, I will not deny you!" (Matt. 26:33, 35).

However, on the day of Pentecost, something took place within Peter's heart that substantially changed him. I wonder if what Peter experienced on that day needs to happen in the hearts of all vacillating disciples of Christ? The answer is obvious.

reath of God

He breathed on them and said to them, "Receive the Holy Spirit."
John 20:22

Writing over a century ago, while serving as a Baptist pastor in the city of Boston, Dr. A. J. Gordon (1836-1895) noted: "The Spirit is the breath of God in the body of his church. While that divine body survives and must, multitudes of churches have so shut out the Spirit from rule and authority and supremacy in the midst of them that the ascended Lord can only say to them: 'Thou hast a name to live and art dead' (Rev. 3:1). In a word, so vital and indispensable is the ministry of the Spirit, that without it nothing else will avail.... The body may be as to its organs perfect and entire, lacking nothing; but simply because the Spirit has been withdrawn from it, it has passed from a church into a corpse."*

Less than fifty years after Gordon, the Methodist president of Cliff College, England, Samuel Chadwick (1860-1932), wrote: "The church that is man-managed instead of God-governed is doomed to failure. A ministry that is college-trained but not Spirit-filled works no miracles. The church that multiplies committees and neglects prayer may be fussy, noisy, enterprising, but it labours in vain and spends its strength for nought. It is possible to excel in mechanics and fail in dynamic. There is a superabundance of machinery; what is lacking is power. To run an organization needs no God. Man can supply the energy, enterprise, and enthusiasm for things human. The real work of a church depends upon the power of the Spirit."*

Lamenting the desperate lack of the manifest presence of the Holy Spirit in our midst, while unwittingly depending on human resources, present-day minister and writer Frances Chan observes: "The church becomes irrelevant when it becomes a purely human creation. We are not all we were meant to be when everything in our lives and churches can be explained apart from the work and presence of the Spirit of God."**

A church without the Spirit is a corpse. A church with the Spirit is a thriving organism, fulfilling its God-intended purpose.

August 24

Inadequate Disciples

*"Truly, truly, I say to you, whoever believes in me will
also do the works that I do; and greater works than these
will he do, because I am going to the Father."*
John 14:12

The disciples were anything but prepared to proclaim faithfully the gospel of the Lord Jesus following his ascension. Jesus knew this. That is why he spent so much time in his final days speaking about the promised Paraclete in John 14 and 16.

The spiritual state of these men prior to Pentecost was not dissimilar to that of another group of believers in the early eighteenth century. Of the Herrnhut, German Moravians, under the leadership of Count Zinzendorf (1700-1760), it was said: "Differences of opinion and heated controversy on doctrinal questions threatened to disrupt the congregation. The majority were members of the Ancient Moravian Church of the Brethren. But other believers had also been attracted to Herrnhut. Lutherans, Reformed Baptists, etc., had joined the community. Questions of predestination, holiness, the meaning and mode of baptism, etc., seemed likely to divide the believers into a number of small and belligerent sects."*

Of these inadequate, failing saints, the Scottish hymn writer James Montgomery (1771-1854), who was raised in a Moravian Church manse, would later write:

They walked with God in Peace and Love,
But failed with one another;
While sternly for the Faith they strove,
Brother fell out with brother.
But He in whom they put their trust,
Who knew their frames that they were dust,
*Pitied and healed their weakness.***

These Moravian believers, as well as Christ's disciples, were to later discover a spiritual power and cleansing for their pronounced inadequacies. Yes, he ...

Who knew their frames that they were dust,
Pitied and healed their weakness.

Fullness of Joy

And the disciples were filled with joy and with the Holy Spirit.
Acts 13:52

Throughout both biblical and church history, we have plentiful examples of those whose lives and ministries were deepened by a fuller revelation of the Spirit's work in them. These men and women were servants of Christ, often ministers of the gospel, who came to a crisis point. Their respective religious backgrounds and experiences were wide-ranging, but the inner need was strikingly similar: They were forgiven people who came to the realization their egos needed crucifying and their hearts required a deep cleansing. Many of these saints were not seeking, necessarily, any heightened experience with God, but did possess a clear lack in their hearts and service for Christ.

Blaise Pascal (1623-1662) was a seventeenth-century Roman Catholic native of France, and one of the world's most remarkable men of his time. In the year 1654, he recorded (just for his own eyes) a life-changing revelation of the love of God in Christ Jesus, which resulted in a glorious effusion of joy. Following his death, it was discovered he had carried with him for some years a piece of paper sewn inside his coat pocket following that event. On this paper he preserved the memory of that Spirit-changing encounter.

This year of grace 1654.
Monday, 23 November, feast of Saint Clement, Pope and Martyr, and of others in the Martyrology.
Eve of Saint Chrysogonus, Martyr and others.
From about half past ten in the evening until half past midnight.
Fire!
"God of Abraham, God of Isaac, God of Jacob, not of philosophers and scholars.
Certainty, certainty, heartfelt, joy, peace.
God of Jesus Christ.
God of Jesus Christ ...
Joy, joy, joy, tears of joy."*

God leads each of his children differently, yet similarly. He desires to fill each of us with a fullness of his love and joy.

August 26

Love and Prayer

We give thanks to God always for all of you, constantly mentioning you in our prayers, 3 remembering before our God and Father your work of faith and labor of love and steadfastness of hope in our Lord Jesus Christ.
1 Thessalonians 1:2-3

A missionary was laboring in the country of India. After being on the field for some time, problems began to arise between the missionary and his fellow workers. The situation eventually became so serious that the district supervisor was called to help resolve the conflict.

After the supervisor had listened to all parties involved in the tensions, he suggested to the missionary that the two of them go for a walk. They walked from behind the missionary's house down an overgrown path. And then they stopped. Whereupon the supervisor turned to the missionary with these words of counsel: "You know, Brother, as long as your predecessor was here, this path was free of grass. That was his prayer path that led to his place of prayer. I recommend that you start wearing these weeds down and then watch what God will do."

There arose some severe relational problems between an American missionary and his native converts. Several meetings were held in order to arrive at some resolution. Nothing worked; the division grew wider. Finally, a godly and wise field superintendent was called to attempt to settle the dispute. The Africans were adamant; they insisted on the missionary's leaving.

Then the superintendent took the missionary aside, telling him of the natives' wishes. The man was crestfallen; he had prepared much of his life to go to Africa; thousands of dollars were invested by others; he didn't want to go home a failure. After hearing his brother's plea, the superintendent offered this solution: "If you wish to stay and continue laboring with these people, and you want to gain their hearts, I'm going to require that you read the love chapter of the Bible [1 Cor. 13] every day for the next six months, on your knees." It worked. He stayed and gained the hearts of the people.

Sometimes our greatest problem in the work of God is trying to do God's work in our own strength. God's love working in and through us, and believing prayer, can achieve wonderful results to the glory of God.

Abstaining from Evil

Abstain from every form of evil.
1 Thessalonians 5:22

No serious-minded Christian would dispute the existence of evil in this present world: "We know that we are from God, and the whole world lies in the power of the evil one." (1 John 5:19).

When Christians recognize the presence of evil, they must avoid it in all its forms. As the Spirit cautioned the early believers, so he warns us: "Abstain from every form of evil."

It is important to understand what this text does and does not say. D. Edmond Hiebert (1928-1995) correctly observed: "The rendering 'all appearance of evil' (KJV) must not be interpreted to mean that they are to avoid that which looks wicked to those who see it, although it may not be so. The term does not denote semblance as opposed to reality.... While believers should abstain from actions which will knowingly offend others, it is not always possible to abstain from everything which may appear evil to a narrow and foolish judgment. In contemporary Greek usage the term 'form' was also used to mean 'sort, kind, species.' This gives the best meaning here."*

Vance Havner (1901-1986) used to tell the story about how he and a friend once entered a semi-dark Chicago restaurant. Havner says, "I stumbled into the dimly-lit cavern, fumbled for a chair, and mumbled that I needed a flashlight in order to read the menu.... Gradually, however, I began to make out objects a little more clearly. My host said, 'Funny, isn't it how we get used to the dark?'"**

Havner went on to observe that getting used to moral evil in one's life is not a "funny" matter to God, nor should it be to the Christian.

The Lord is saying to every believer through this text: "Regardless of the form evil may take, you must abstain from it! Whether the evil is popularly accepted; whether it is entertained in private or practiced in public—evil must be off-limits to the believer."

"Abstain from every form of evil."

August 28

Frowning Providences

*Their father Jacob said to them, "You have bereaved me of
my children: Joseph is no more, and Simeon is no more, and
you would take Benjamin; all these things are against me."*
Genesis 42:36 NASB

*God moves in a mysterious way
His wonders to perform;
He plants His footsteps in the sea
And rides upon the storm.*

*Deep in unfathomable mines
Of never failing skill
He treasures up His bright designs
And works His sovereign will.*

*Ye fearful saints, fresh courage take;
The clouds ye so much dread
Are big with mercy and shall break
In blessings on your head.*

*Judge not the Lord by feeble sense,
But trust Him for His grace;
Behind a frowning providence
He hides a smiling face.*

*His purposes will ripen fast,
Unfolding every hour;
The bud may have a bitter taste,
But sweet will be the flower.*

*Blind unbelief is sure to err
And scan His work in vain;
God is His own interpreter,
And He will make it plain.**

Grieving the Spirit

*And do not grieve the Holy Spirit of God, by whom
you were sealed for the day of redemption.*
Ephesians 4:30

Duncan Campbell (1898-1972) was a Scottish evangelist who spent a good many years in useful service to the Lord in revival power, and then strangely entered a seventeen-year-period of barrenness. Looking back over those wilderness years, he lamented, "Here I was—a lovely congregation, and now proud of the fact that I was being asked to address conventions. You see, I was *Campbell of the Mid Argyll Revival*.... Oh, this heart of mine began to swell."

The Spirit of God used both his daughter and a young minister to bring conviction to his proud heart. Listening to the minister speaking one evening, Campbell's heart was powerfully convicted of its waywardness. Campbell recalled, "As he spoke, conviction deepened and gripped me until I felt utterly unworthy to hold the Bible in my hands. I said to my wife and daughter, 'I'm going to my study, and I do not wish to be disturbed. I want to face God with honesty and sincerity.'"

Campbell reports of that rendezvous with God: "So I went to my study. I fell on my face and confessed my backsliding. I confessed how I had drifted into modernism. I confessed how the evil heart of unbelief had gripped me." He left that room a revived, renewed, humbled preacher.

It is possible for Christians to grieve the Holy Spirit (after all, he is a Person) with our words, attitudes, and conduct. Duncan Campbell did so, and so can we.

Through the inspiration of the Holy Spirit, the Apostle Paul exhorted the Ephesian Church: "And do not grieve the Holy Spirit of God, by whom you were sealed for the day of redemption." One look at the Ephesians 4 context will inform us of the kind of attitudes and behavior that grieve the Spirit: sinful anger, unwholesome words, bitterness, unkindness, unforgiveness, etc.

As a Christian who is indwelt by the Spirit, we must take care that we don't grieve him by our carelessness. When we do, he will faithfully let us know, then we must take necessary action in order for the peace of God to return.

Walk as Children of Light

For at one time you were darkness, but now
you are light in the Lord. Walk as children of light.
Ephesians 5:8

The inspired New Testament writers use the word "run" when addressing the issue of Christian perseverance and endurance. For example: "Let us run with endurance the race that is set before us" (Heb. 12:1). However, anytime the writers use the word "walk" in their ethical imperatives, they use it as a figurative term, having to do with a way of life, behavior, conduct.

Ephesians 5:8-9a reads: "for at one time you were darkness, but now you are light in the Lord. Walk as children of light." "Darkness" and "light" are biblical metaphors representing evil and righteousness, wickedness and godliness, sin and holiness. Darkness and light are pervasive conditions—darkness in the unrighteous and light in the righteous. Paul says of these Ephesians, their lives before coming to Christ was not simply a matter of their being *in* darkness, but they themselves were essentially darkness ("you were darkness"). Everything about these converts prior to their life-changing encounter with the Lord Jesus was darkness itself—evil, wicked, ungodly, unrighteous. There was no light in them—not even a "spark of divinity."

However, these believers are no longer "darkness," says Paul, "but now you are light in the Lord." They are "light," but he qualifies it: "in the Lord."

I'm reminded here of the similar great transference taking place among the Colossian converts; Paul makes the same contrast in addressing them: "He has delivered us from the domain of darkness and transferred us to the kingdom of his beloved Son, in whom we have redemption, the forgiveness of sins" (Col. 1:13-14).

In every adult conversion to Christ, there is an observable contrast in the life of the convert to all who knew him or her before and after. The contrast is evident to those who have lived in close proximity to the new believer, as well as to some of those on the fringe of his or her relationships. It's inevitable, because they *walk* differently.

Sound Words

*If anyone teaches a different doctrine and does not agree with the
sound words of our Lord Jesus Christ and the teaching that accords with
godliness, he is puffed up with conceit and understands nothing. He has
an unhealthy craving for controversy and for quarrels about words ...*
1 Timothy 6:3-4

We cannot read the written Word of God without reading *words*. A
preacher uses *words* when proclaiming and explaining the gospel of
the Lord Jesus Christ. When we discuss the Word of God, we are
talking about *words*.

A pastor recently related to me an unfortunate incident which
occurred—of all places—in a local church prayer service. The pastor
was sharing a Bible study from the Book of Hebrews, addressing the
subject of sanctification. A minister in the service took issue with
the pastor over his interpretation of a particular passage. Following
some discussion, the attendee stormed out of the church. Amazing!
Both men had a PhD in theology; both believed in the biblical doctrine of sanctification and holiness, but one became quarrelsome—
damaging his Christian witness. The pastor may not have had the
correct view on the subject (that I don't know), but the angry man
certainly didn't behave in a sanctified manner.

The church is to speak with one voice concerning "the
sound words of our Lord Jesus Christ and the teaching that accords
with godliness." The fact of the matter is, the church isn't and hasn't
spoken with one voice on these matters since the first century. This
should make us weep. God has called leaders "to contend for the
faith that was once for all delivered to the saints" (Jude 1:3). However, God has also called us to contend for the faith without becoming *contentious*. It is possible for some of us to have "an unhealthy
craving for controversy and for quarrels about words." "Orthodoxy
in matters of belief," noted David Wells, "is not a substitute for holiness of life, either for the individual or for the church, because orthodoxy in biblical terms includes the moral outcome of that right
belief."*

Orthodoxy is important. Just as important is orthopraxy—
putting into practice the teaching of "sound words." Only as we are
controlled by the Word and Spirit will we achieve this symmetry.

Doing God's Work in God's Way

"Because you did not carry it the first time, the Lord our God broke out against us, because we did not seek him according to the rule."
1 Chronicles 15:13

Many of us fail in our walk with God and the ministry we engage in, not because we are not personally surrendered and devoted to God, but because we have failed to consult God. We are doing the work of the Lord; we are fully committed to him, and we are filled with zeal and enthusiasm to see God's work succeed. We are ready to volunteer in the church for a task that needs to be done; we love being involved in Kingdom ministry—it's our very life; it is who we are. But there's a problem: We are doing God's work, but often not in God's way. To do the work of God, without doing his work in his way, will eventually end in failure, possibly disaster; it may even bring personal embarrassment.

The Ark of the Covenant was the symbol of God's presence among Israel, and under the reign of Saul it had been long neglected. After David became king, the decision was made to transfer the ark from Kiriath-jearim to Jerusalem. While it was being transported on a cart, pulled by oxen (as the Philistines had done when it was in their possession), suddenly the animals stumbled. Instinctively, "Uzzah put out his hand to take hold of the ark" (1 Chron. 13:9). Immediately God struck Uzzah, for the ark was not to be touched by man's hands. David was angry with the Lord for striking Uzzah. In that moment, the king's human sympathy overcame his regard for God's holiness. The ark never moved for three months.

David finally righted his wrong. He appointed Levites to carry the ark, and they bore it with poles, as God had instructed Moses years before. David confessed his error to the Levites: "Because you did not carry it the first time, the Lord our God broke out against us, because we did not seek him according to the rule.... And the Levites carried the ark of God on their shoulders with the poles, as Moses had commanded according to the word of the Lord" (1 Chron. 15:13, 15).

It is a critical question: Are we doing the work of God in God's way or our way?

Restoring a Wandering Sinner

*My brothers, if anyone among you wanders from the
truth and someone brings him back, let him know that
whoever brings back a sinner from his wandering will save
his soul from death and will cover a multitude of sins.*
James 5:19-20

Of all the words that have been spoken and written about the Letter of James, the above text may be the least popular verses. Just the same, they are Spirit-inspired words, written by the holy apostle; they are the final words in his epistle.

James was concerned about the possibility of a believer, who either strays from believing correct doctrine, or who no longer conducts himself according to the teachings of Christ—or both. He identifies this person as one who "wanders from the truth" and as "a sinner." Clearly, this person was once vitally connected to the church; he was a believer and follower of Christ. Otherwise, James would not have twice mentioned about bringing such a person "back." You cannot be brought "back" to something to which you never *belonged*.

God does not want us to simply "write off" people who once walked with him and with whom we enjoyed fellowship. Jesus wants us to seek those who have wandered from the fold: "What man of you, having a hundred sheep, if he has lost one of them, does not leave the ninety-nine in the open country, and go after the one that is lost, until he finds it?" (Luke 15:4).

Occasionally, the Spirit will prompt some of us to seek out someone who has wandered from the truth. God will give you a prayer-burden for a particular person, and you will keep in contact with him or her until they return. I have seen that happen in my own life. I prayed and kept in touch for years with Fred until he came "Home" (I'm sure I was not the only one who cared).

Hear what the Lord has said of those who are instrumental in bringing back those who have wandered from the truth: "Let him know that whoever brings back a sinner from his wandering will save his soul from death and will cover a multitude of sins."

Is there someone the Spirit is talking to you about? Does the Lord want to use you to bring this person back?

"The Book That Would Understand Me"

For the word of God is living and active, sharper than any two-edged sword, piercing to the division of soul and of spirit, of joints and of marrow, and discerning the thoughts and intentions of the heart.
Hebrews 4:12

Emile Caillet (1984-1981) served as a professor for many years at Princeton Seminary. He was born in France and received an education that had no place for God. He was 23 years of age before he saw his first Bible.

While a soldier in WWI, Caillet was wounded and spent nine months in a hospital. Afterward, he returned to reading, "but they were no longer the same books. Neither was my motivation the same motivation. Reading in literature and philosophy, I found myself probing in depth for meaning. During long night watches in the foxholes, I had in a strange way been longing—I must say it, however queer it may sound—for a book that would understand me."

However, Caillet said he knew of no such book, so he began to write one for his own use. During his reading, whenever he read something that spoke to his inner condition, he would copy it in a leather-bound book that he always carried with him. He said, "The day came when I put the finishing touch to 'the book that would understand me,' speak to my condition, and help me through life's happenings. A beautiful, sunny day it was. I went out, sat under a tree, and opened my precious anthology. As I went on reading, however, a growing disappointment came over me. Instead of speaking to my condition, the various passages reminded me of their context, of the circumstances of my labor over their selection."

One day, his wife was given a Bible, and she gave it to her husband—a book he before had refused to have in their home. "I literally grabbed the book and rushed to my study with it. I opened and 'chanced' upon the Beatitudes! I read, and read, and read—now aloud with an indescribable warmth surging within. I could not find words to express my awe and wonder. And suddenly the realization dawned upon me: this was the book that would understand me!"

He prayed to the God of the Book that night, and said, "The God who answered was the same God of whom it was spoken in the book."*

September 4

Sodom's Sins

*Behold, this was the guilt of your sister Sodom: she and her
daughters had pride, excess of food, and prosperous ease, but did
not aid the poor and needy. They were haughty and did an
abomination before me. So I removed them, when I saw it.*
Ezekiel 16:49-50

In Ezekiel 16, God is not addressing the *world*; he is speaking through the prophet to *Jerusalem*—the holy city, the very citadel of Yahweh's covenant people. It is a sad history. God's chosen people have turned away, lusting after other gods. Their wickedness exceeds that of the surrounding pagan culture. They have sunk so low that God calls them Sodom's sister. The comparison is striking. When we observe Sodom's sins, we get a glimpse of Israel's.

"Pride." Yahweh said of fallen Israel: "But you trusted in your beauty and played the whore because of your renown and lavished your whorings on any passerby; your beauty became his" (v. 15). The root of all sin is pride—asserting our independence.

"Excess of food." God had prospered his people; they had trusted and obeyed his covenant laws. However, in their prosperity they forgot God, the source of their abundance. In seeking material security, Israel kept building bigger and bigger granaries.

"Prosperous ease." Prosperity inevitably brings with it added leisure. We have more time to entertain ourselves. We become self-absorbed, intoxicated with things: "lovers of pleasure rather than lovers of God" (2 Tim. 3:4). We can't wait to retire, so we can indulge even more in the desires of the flesh.

"Did not aid the poor and needy." Consumed with their cravings and insatiable desires, Israel became unconcerned with the less fortunate. Her heart was hardened; her eyes blinded—by the lust of the flesh, the lust of the eyes, and the pride of life.

"They were haughty and did an abomination before me." In the depths of asserting their autonomy, they abandoned their natural appetites, with men lusting after men and women lusting after women.

There is always a progression to sin. It happened to God's covenant people; it can happen to us.

By Faith Alone?

You see that a person is justified by works and not by faith alone.
James 2:24

Yes, that is precisely what James wrote: "You see that a person is justified by works and not by faith alone." What about the Apostle Paul? Doesn't what James said contradict the foremost apologist of the doctrine of justification by faith? Interestingly enough—at least to us—James did not quote Paul when discussing the subject of faith and works. However, both he and Paul cited Abraham as an example in shaping their respective arguments.

Paul said Abraham was not justified by works: "For if Abraham was justified by works, he has something to boast about, but not before God" (Rom. 4:2). Paul says Abraham's faith (in believing God would deliver on his promise to give him a son in his old age) was "counted to him as righteousness" (Rom. 4:22).

On the other hand, James asks the question, "Was not Abraham our father justified by works when he offered up his son Isaac on the altar?" (James 2:1). Immediately, James follows the question by joining with Paul in the matter. James said of Abraham, "You see that faith was active along with his works, and faith was completed by his works" (James 2:2).

In addressing his Jewish readers, those who trusted in their works of righteousness, Paul said, "For by works of the law no human being will be justified in his sight, since through the law comes knowledge of sin" (Rom. 3:20). For those who overemphasized *sola fide* (by faith alone), James' corrective was, "faith by itself, if it does not have works, is dead" (James 2:17).

An overemphasis on "faith alone" produces carelessness, if not lawlessness (living without regard to the law of God). Additionally, an overemphasis on "works alone" causes people to trust in their own righteousness, which makes the cross of Christ unnecessary. C. S. Lewis (1898-1963) likened the relationship between faith and works to a pair of scissors, of which both blades are necessary.

Trust and obey, for there's no other way
*To be happy in Jesus, but to trust and obey.**

Difficult Times in the Church

*But understand this, that in the last days
there will come times of difficulty.*
2 Timothy 3:1

Strictly speaking, the "last days" consist of that span of time from Pentecost to the return of the Lord Jesus Christ (see Acts 2:17). God informs us that during this era "there will come times of difficulty."

God's people have always experienced opposition, ridicule, rejection, and persecution—from without. However, the "difficult times" Paul writes about in 2 Timothy 3:1-9 is a prophecy of what an element in Christ's church will look like in the "last days." The apostle is not writing about what the "world" will look like in the "last days"; he is drawing a picture of what much of the church will look like. We can deduce this from the end of the previous chapter, where Paul charges Timothy to correct his opponents in the hope that they will repent and "come to their senses" (see 1 Tim. 2:23-26).

Note what many in the church will look like in the last days (2 Tim. 3:2-7).

• "For people will be lovers of self, lovers of money." Instead of loving God with their all and their neighbor as themselves, their love turns inward. And when we focus on ourselves, money soon becomes our god.

• "For people will be ... proud, arrogant, abusive, disobedient to their parents, ungrateful, unholy, heartless, unappeasable, slanderous, without self-control, brutal, not loving good, treacherous, reckless, swollen with conceit, lovers of pleasure rather than lovers of God." In the absence of the Spirit of God controlling our lives, the church soon descends to the level of the world; one cannot be distinguished from the other.

• "For people will [have] the appearance of godliness, but denying its power." Here is a clear reference to the audience Paul addresses. From the outside, many will look like godly people; however, such will refuse to be controlled by the Spirit's power.

Christian, pray that you will escape such evil. Pray to be daily filled with the Spirit's holy love and power. Pray that your local church will be the antithesis of 2 Timothy 3:1-9.

September 7

Diotrephes and Demetrius

I have written something to the church, but Diotrephes, who likes to put himself first, does not acknowledge our authority.... Demetrius has received a good testimony from everyone, and from the truth itself.
3 John 1:9, 11

It is a tragic blight within the church when an ego-driven person arrogates to himself arbitrary power to control others. Such an individual is controlled by the flesh and demonic powers. They often leave one local church for another because some of God's people refuse their manipulative, arrogant authority.

The Apostle John writes of this kind of person in his Third Letter. In the ancient church, there were itinerant ministers, sent by God to travel among the churches. Repeatedly, the apostles encouraged believers to welcome these men. A man by the name of Diotrephes refused to accept these traveling ministers: "he refuses to welcome the brothers"; furthermore, he "stops those who want to [welcome the brothers] and puts them out of the church" (v. 10). In fifty years of ministry, I have only seen one person like Diotrephes in a church, and I told him so at the time. He liked to put himself first, and would not acknowledge God-ordained leadership. He once said, "I'll board this church up before it's organized." It was a new-church plant, and had yet to be formally organized.

How unlike Diotrephes was Demetrius. John contrasted Diotrephes and Demetrius when he wrote, "Beloved, do not imitate evil but imitate good. Whoever does good is from God; whoever does evil has not seen God" (v. 11). Diotrephes was "evil"; Demetrius was "good." The fact is, "Demetrius has received a good testimony from everyone, and from the truth itself." Then Paul endorses Demetrius himself: "We also add our testimony, and you know that our testimony is true" (v. 12).

A Diotrephes in the local body must be confronted: "So if I come, I will bring up what he is doing, talking wicked nonsense against us" (v. 10). A Demetrius should be welcomed in every church and commended.

May the Lord help us to remove the one and be pleased to multiply the other. Purpose to be a Demetrius—a good servant of the Lord Jesus.

September 8

A Rogue Wave

And have mercy on those who doubt; save others by snatching
them out of the fire; to others show mercy with fear,
hating even the garment stained by the flesh.
Jude 1:22-23

I have recently learned about ocean phenomena called "rogue waves." Rogue waves are waves of an unusual height. While we don't have an explanation for all of their occurrences, they are usually formed when strong winds and extremely high currents merge to create an exceptionally large wave. Often rogue waves have resulted in capsized ships and lost lives.

I thought of Jude 1:22-23 one day in light of these rogue waves. I have known a few believers through the years who were suddenly struck by a "rogue wave." They were almost destroyed by it, if not for the mercy of the Lord and a few discerning and caring Christians. From all appearances, these people, including some ministers, were "sailing along" quite comfortably. To their church family, all seemed to be well. Then suddenly, it appeared from nowhere: they were hit by a "rogue wave"; they were overcome by sin. In the language of Jude, they had fallen into "the fire," "the garment stained by the flesh."

What should we do when we see one of our brothers and sisters "capsized" by a rogue wave? The Lord provides us with counsel: "Brothers, if anyone is caught in any transgression, you who are spiritual should restore him in a spirit of gentleness" (Gal. 6:1). The word "restore" is from the same word-group that is found in Mark 1:19, where it is said that Jesus saw James and John "in their boat mending [restoring] the nets." Spiritually mature believers are called to come alongside the one who has been hit by a "rogue wave" and carefully bring that injured believer to a safe place.

We might say, "Well, it is his fault!" Be careful! None of us is immune from being struck by a "rogue wave." One of the godliest men I know came alongside a brother, who was internationally renowned for his Christian integrity and scholarship, but was struck by a "rogue wave." This dear man was used by God to "mend" the brokenness in his brother. What a brother! What a friend!

We are called to be servants of mercy. I pray you are one.

September 9

A Glimpse of Heaven

*Then I saw a new heaven and a new earth, for the first heaven
and the first earth had passed away, and the sea was no more.*
Revelation 21:1

The Bible does not provide us with a full picture of what Heaven
looks like. However, though it may not furnish us with enough information to satisfy our curiosity, it gives us sufficient information
that God thought adequate for our finite understanding. And we
should be content for now to savor what the written revelation says
about Heaven, without reading or watching a movie about a believer's near-death experience!

What does the Bible say about Heaven?

• Heaven will be a prepared place for a prepared people. Jesus
said to his disciples before his departure, "I go to prepare a place for
you" (John 14:2).

• Heaven will be an enjoyable habitation for God's people because of those who will be absent: "But as for the cowardly, the
faithless, the detestable, as for murderers, the sexually immoral,
sorcerers, idolaters, and all liars, their portion will be in the lake
that burns with fire and sulfur, which is the second death" (Rev.
21:8).

• Heaven will be a delightful place for God's people because of
what will be missing: "He will wipe away every tear from their eyes,
and death shall be no more, neither shall there be mourning, nor
crying, nor pain anymore, for the former things have passed
away" (Rev. 21:4).

• Heaven will be Heaven because of who will be there—Jesus:
"They will see his face, and his name will be on their foreheads" (Rev. 22:4). Every overcoming believer will also be present:
"The one who conquers will have this heritage, and I will be his God
and he will be my son" (Rev. 21:7).

*Thro' the gates to the city in a robe of spotless white,
He will lead me where no tears will ever fall;
In the glad song of ages I shall mingle with delight,
But I long to meet my Savior first of all.**

Are you living like Heaven is your destination?

September 10

Words, Words, Words

Our gospel came to you not only in word, but also in
power and in the Holy Spirit and with full conviction.
1 Thessalonians 1:5

I recently entered my seventh decade. A few months following my sixteenth birthday, I preached my first sermon. Many sermons have been given since then, and I have listened to many other preachers across the years. Of all the observations I've made of preachers and preaching for over half a century, the one essential I see necessary—and too often lacking—is this: bringing a sense of the presence of Christ into the congregation, and leading the congregation into the same presence.

The Scottish New Testament Greek scholar William Barclay (1907-1978) was once an assistant to Duncan Blair, a Glasgow pastor. Barclay said of Blair, "The people loved him, for they never came out of the church without feeling that God had been there, and to this day they talk of him."*

To his own admission, the Apostle Paul was neither an orator nor a polished speaker. Instead, he preached with the power of the Holy Spirit sent down from heaven, and thus preached with "full conviction." Listeners always heard truth when Paul preached; they heard about Christ and the cross, for Christ was central to the apostle's preaching. But Paul did not only preach truth, he brought with him an aura of Christ's presence when he stood before his hearers; the Holy Spirit was manifestly present.

So much preaching is merely words, words, words. The words spoken may be true to the text; the words may be well thought-out and delivered in an interesting if not entertaining way, but they are only words.

Martyn Lloyd-Jones' (1899-1981) wife said of her husband: "Many people only knew him as a great preacher; I knew him as a man of prayer." When a preacher's head is full, without his heart being filled with the presence of Christ—fueled by prayer—people go home still hungry. Congregants need to hear more than words; they need to experience the living Christ coming through the preacher—week after week. Words alone kill; the presence of the Spirit gives life.

Jesus is Lord

No one can say "Jesus is Lord" except in the Holy Spirit.
1 Corinthians 12:3

The above text appears within the context of the subject of spiritual gifts. Paul assures his readers that no one "speaking in the Spirit of God ever says 'Jesus is accursed!'" (12:3). It could be some in the church were concerned that they may mistakenly say, "Jesus is accursed" when speaking in an ecstatic language. Paul rebuts that possibility: "no one can say 'Jesus is Lord' except by the Holy Spirit" (12:3). This is the affirmation we are concerned with here.

Someone may say, "It is easy to repeat, 'Jesus is Lord.' Why does one need the help of the Holy Spirit to make such a declaration?" Because no one can say, "Jesus is Lord" and mean it, without the Holy Spirit enabling one to make such an affirmation.

To confess that "Jesus Christ is Lord" is to acknowledge that I am Christ's willing subject. It involves more than praying a sinner's prayer, or going forward at the end of a worship service. To say, "Jesus is Lord" means that I have renounced every right to rule my own life; it means I have relinquished to Christ's control all that I am and have and hope to be. Knowing there were those who claimed to be identified with him but failed to obey him, Jesus said, "Not everyone who says to me, 'Lord, Lord,' will enter the kingdom of heaven, but the one who does the will of my Father who is in heaven" (Matt. 7:21). The lordship of Christ involves more than words, even words in the form of prayers.

After serving more than fifty years as a missionary in India, E. Stanley Jones (1884-1973) came to the conclusion that for converts to confess "Jesus is Lord" reduced many complexities into one simplicity. Some may believe this is too simplistic. Not so with the Apostle Paul, for he wrote, "If you confess with your mouth Jesus as Lord, and believe in your heart that God raised Him from the dead, you will be saved" (Rom. 10:9).

Such a confession should not be confined to a one-time event. The Christian should repeat it often: "Jesus is Lord! Jesus is Lord!" Then go out and live like it.

Is Jesus your Lord?

Purity and Evangelism

*And I heard the voice of the Lord saying, "Whom shall I send,
and who will go for us?" Then I said, "Here I am! Send me."*
Isaiah 6:8

Some disciples of the Lord Jesus are so consumed by their own
whiteness, that they fail to enter the Lord's harvest, reaping precious sheaves for the kingdom of God. On the other hand, there are
servants of Christ, who are so eager to evangelize, they neglect to
give themselves to heart-preparation. Isaiah 6 provides us with the
balance between heart-preparation and harvesting, holiness and
evangelism.

God knows best; he knows unless the heart is purified, all our
efforts will be tainted with *self*: self-exaltation, self-congratulation,
self-promotion, and a host of additional self-hyphenated attitudes.
It is an abominable, ugly sight, to listen to a person speak the words
of Christ and at the same time promote himself. The *way* we talk
about our ministry and good works, our statistics and goals, our
labors and travels, our facilities and results, our successes and accomplishments—are more of a commentary on *who* we are than
what we have done. "Jesus has more to do in us than through us,"
wrote the former principal of Regent College, James Houston. "Our
inner changes of heart become much more important than the
things we may achieve in front of other people."*

Isaiah would have been a failed prophet—in God's estimation—
unless he first submitted to a radical, definitive cleansing. A "Woe is
me" must always precede God's "Go." Unless the prophet had experienced the "burning coal," and seen "the King, the LORD of hosts,"
receiving a vision of God's holiness, his ministry may have impressed men, but he would have experienced God's censure.

The same men and women whom God calls to a vocational ministry, he first qualifies with a fiery cleansing. There is no Holy Spirit
power without a clean heart. To minister to others without adequate
heart-preparation is to restrict the flow of God's Spirit through us.
We have no right to speak of God to men in public, unless we first
do business with God in private.

September 13

Encouragement

Blessed be the God and Father of our Lord Jesus Christ,
the Father of mercies and God of all kinds of encouragement,
who encourages us in all our affliction, so that we may be
able to encourage those who are in any affliction, with the
encouragement with which we ourselves are encouraged by God.
2 Corinthians 1:3-5 RIT

The *English Standard Version of the Bible,* in keeping with some other versions, has chosen to translate the Greek word *parakleseōs* as "comfort," or one of its forms, in 2 Corinthians 1:3-7. The word "comfort" (or "comforts" and "comforted") occurs ten times in this passage. I have chosen to render the Greek word as "encourage." I do so because when we typically think of "comfort," we have in mind some form of consolation. While the word includes consolation, it is much broader than that. As an example, in Acts 4:36, Barnabas is called (as translated in the ESV) "the son of encouragement." The word "encouragement" in Acts 4:36 is the same Greek word rendered "comfort" in 2 Corinthians 1:3, and elsewhere. With that in the background, consider what Paul says about this matter of encouragement.

• God is the "God of all kinds of encouragement." God will use people and his ordered providences, to bring his people encouragement. Encouragement comes to us in "all shapes and sizes," as it were—often unexpectedly.

• God does not want us merely to receive his encouragement; he wants us to pass it on: "so that we may be able to encourage those who are in any affliction, with the encouragement with which we ourselves are encouraged by God." Some Christians remain wrapped up in their affliction. God doesn't want us to be only receivers; he wants us to be givers: "This is how the Lord helped me."

• Paul says an amazing thing about affliction and encouragement in 1:6: "If we are encouraged, it is for your encouragement and deliverance; and if we are encouraged, it is for your encouragement." Think about that! We are members of the body of Christ. If we are suffering and receiving God's encouragement, it is for the purpose of encouraging others.

Be encouraged! Encourage others!

What Causes God to Marvel

When Jesus heard this, he marveled and said to those who followed him, "Truly, I tell you, with no one in Israel have I found such faith."
Matthew 8:10

What causes men to *marvel* and what causes God to *marvel* is usually not one and the same. During the ministry of our Lord on earth, his disciples marveled that Jesus could calm a storm (Matt. 8:27); the crowds marveled when they saw Jesus cast out demons (Matt. 9:33); the Pharisees marveled at Jesus' sagacious reply to their question regarding who they should pay taxes to (Matt. 22:22); people marveled when Jesus cast out demons from the man who lived among tombs (Mark 5:20). And there were many other occasions when people marveled at the teaching and works of our Lord.

But what caused Jesus to *marvel* when he ministered here on earth?

First, Jesus marveled at unexpected faith. When Jesus traveled to the city of Capernaum, a military leader approached the Lord, pleading for him to intervene on behalf of his paralyzed servant whom he had left at home. When Jesus told the centurion that he would go to his home and heal his servant, he responded with amazing humility (Matt. 8:8-9). Jesus marveled at this Gentile's faith and said to the crowd: "Truly, I tell you, with no one in Israel have I found such faith" (Matt. 8:10).

Next, Jesus marveled at the unbelief of those who should have believed. Jesus was ministering one Sabbath in his hometown of Nazareth. When he finished, the hearers were incredulous. They questioned his credentials and authority; they wondered at his teaching and source of his wisdom—after all, Jesus was a hometown boy: "Is not this the carpenter, the son of Mary and brother of James and Joses and Judas and Simon? And are not his sisters here with us?" (Mark 6:3). Jesus "could do no mighty work there.... And he marveled because of their unbelief" (Mark 6:5-6).

Jesus marveled when faith was exercised from an unexpected source. Jesus marveled at the unbelief of people; he expected a different response.

What about you and me?

A Gospel for All People

*Who desires all people to be saved and to come to the knowledge
of the truth.... Who gave himself as a ransom for all.*
1 Timothy 2:6-7

The Scriptures plainly teach that because God loved the entire fallen race of mankind, he sent and gave his unique Son to die an atoning death on the Cross. God did not send his Son for only some people; he sent his Son for *all people*. Those who received his Son would be saved: "For God so loved the *world*, that he gave his only Son, that whoever believes in him should not perish but have eternal life" (John 3:16).

Occasionally one hears of a person excusing himself for not being a Christian by saying, "I have never felt God call me; I don't think I'm one of the *chosen*." The truth is, Jesus said, "And I, when I am lifted up from the earth, will draw *all people* to myself" (John 12:32). When Jesus said, "all people," we can be assured he meant "all people." Jesus said by means of his death on the Cross ("lifted up from the earth"), he would cause "all people" to sense their need for him. The degree to which each person may sense that need varies, but we must believe the words of Jesus.

After he urges that "supplications, prayers, intercessions, and thanksgivings be made for all people," including people in "high positions," Paul says, "This is good, and it is pleasing in the sight of God our Savior, who desires *all people* to be saved and to come to the knowledge of the truth. For there is one God, and there is one mediator between God and men, the man Christ Jesus, who gave himself as a ransom for *all*, which is the testimony given at the proper time" (1 Tim. 2:3-6). Furthermore, the Apostle John wrote of Christ's death for all people: "He is the propitiation for our sins, and not for ours only but also for the sins of the *whole world*.

How can some say that God wishes for *some people* to be saved when the Scriptures plainly teach that he "desires *all people* to be saved"? Oh, the man-made doctrines of men!

For me, I would rather side with what Jesus, Paul, and John said about a gospel for all people, than what some relative latecomers have said about the matter.

Sober Self-Appraisal

For by the grace given to me I say to everyone among you not to think of himself more highly than he ought to think, but to think with sober judgment, each according to the measure of faith that God has assigned.
Romans 12:3

There are at least two possibilities whenever we take a look at ourselves regarding our giftedness: either we become conceited or we discredit our gifts (which can be pride inverted). In Romans 12:3, Paul addresses the former—the temptation for a believer to think of himself "more highly than he ought to think." The apostle wrote these words in the context of dealing with the subject of spiritual gifts (12:4-8).

Clearly, Paul recognized the danger in the body of Christ for believers to compare their gifts with those of others. If Satan fails to prevent our conversion, he will work tirelessly within the body of Christ to create conflict and tension after our conversion. One strategy our adversary uses is to cause us to think our giftedness is superior to others. It has often been said that the most difficult instrument to play in an orchestra is "second violin." We all want to be the "first violinist" because we think we are the best violinist.

It is a revolutionary freeing day when we come to the realization that God has uniquely gifted each one of us "according to the grace given to us" (Rom. 12:6). No two preachers are alike, nor singers or teachers, or artists, or fathers and mothers, or students, or administrators, etc. Every person is to strive to be all that God wants him to be. We should call on God repeatedly to help us use the gifts he has given us—to the utmost, for his glory.

Charles Spurgeon (1834-1892) said, "Gaze at Jesus; glance at people." That's a timeless aphorism! Thank God for the gifts he has given you. Don't compare your gifts with those of others. Thank God for the gifts he has given your brothers and sisters in Christ; don't envy them. Use your gifts with humility, in the fear of God. Remember, they are gifts—something you have received by God's grace. Be a good steward of your gifts—use them wisely; use them faithfully.

September 17

Godly Discernment (part 1)

*But solid food is for the mature, for those who have their powers of
discernment trained by constant practice to distinguish good from evil.*
Hebrews 5:14

We should not think it unusual when the people of this world—be
they philosophers or politicians, broadcast commentators or enter-
tainers, cultural icons or professors—lack a moral compass, a spiritual center, godly wisdom. In the words of the apostle: "The natural
person does not accept the things of the Spirit of God, for they
are folly to him, and he is not able to understand them because they
are spiritually discerned" (1 Cor. 2:14).

However, unlike the common sinner, who does not possess the
light of God within, and gives no serious consideration to the revealed Word of God, our Lord has given his people the Holy Spirit
at the moment of their spiritual birth. That being said, no one is
given a complete *bundle* of spiritual wisdom at conversion. The
writer of Hebrews addresses this matter. He says godly discernment
is acquired from God as the "mature" believer ingests "solid food"—
that is, the deeper truth in God's Word. Such believers' consciences
have been "trained by constant practice": they are daily in the
Word, and are sensitive to the Holy Spirit. These believers have the
God-given, God-acquired ability to "distinguish good from evil."

Some young converts are given, at the time of their conversion,
exception moral insight. Following his conversion at a Billy Graham
Crusade in 1949, WWII veteran Louis Zamperini (1917-2014) went
home, poured his alcoholic drinks into the kitchen sink, destroyed
his pornography, and quit smoking. The scoffers may laugh at such
behavior, but evidently God was pleased.

One of the saddest commentaries on the twenty-first century's
church leadership is that it often is being led by men and women
who have not allowed God to educate their consciences "to distinguish good from evil." Thus, we have the untrained leading the untrained; the blind leading the blind. *Ditches* are inevitable.

Pray this will not be the case with you. And if you are among the
"mature," wear the mantle humbly, and lead others gently and patiently—just as Christ has led you.

Godly Discernment (part 2)

*"Give your servant therefore an understanding mind to
govern your people, that I may discern between good and
evil, for who is able to govern this your great people?"*
1 Kings 3:9

All of God's people are in need of moral discernment—the ability to distinguish between good and evil. This ability was intuitive with our first parents; however, when sin entered, everything became a moral blur: man lost his capacity to judge between right and wrong.

To those who have confused good and evil, God says through the prophet, "Woe to those who call evil good and good evil, who put darkness for light and light for darkness, who put bitter for sweet and sweet for bitter!" (Isa. 5:20). These words were first spoken to God's covenant people, Israel, a people whose light had become darkness.

Solomon, David's successor to the throne of Israel, knew from listening to and observing his father through the years, the importance of godly discernment. Therefore, when he became king, his primary concern was that he might possess the ability to discern good from evil. That concern was at the top of his prayer requests when he prayed; he knew only God could give man such ability.

Christians will walk through this world making unwise choices, if not damaging ones, if they don't have godly discernment. Every Christian needs it. The Apostle knew this well; consequently, he prayed for the Philippian believers: "And it is my prayer that your love may abound more and more, with knowledge and all discernment, so that you may approve what is excellent, and so be pure and blameless for the day of Christ" (Phil. 1:9).

A believer can only be equipped to make keen moral judgments if he has given himself totally to God. In doing so, the result will be "a spiritual transformation through the renewal of the mind, so that by testing he may discern what the will of God is, what is good and acceptable and perfect" (Rom. 12:2).

Led by wise leaders and surrounded by a core of godly believers, living in the Word and walking in the Spirit, God will lead his child in a safe moral path, giving him the ability to distinguish truth from error, good from evil.

September 19

Love-Slaves

"I love my master, my wife, and my children; I will not go out free."
Exodus 21:5

In Exodus 21, God provides Israel with laws regarding their treatment of slaves. In verses 2-6, we find the obligation of owners toward purchased slaves: after serving for six years, the slave is given the option of freedom. If the slave was purchased when single, he was to leave single; if he was purchased while married, he could leave with his wife; if he married and had children after being purchased, his wife and children became his master's property; and if he chose freedom, he must leave without them. However, "if the slave plainly says, 'I love my master, my wife, and my children; I will not go out free,' then his master shall bring him to God, and he shall bring him to the door or the doorpost. And his master shall bore his ear through with an awl, and he shall be his slave forever" (Ex. 21:5-6).

The slave who chose to stay with his master, because of his love for him, as well as for his wife and children, is a beautiful description of what motivates the believer to offer himself—without reservation—as a love-slave to the Lord Jesus Christ. The Christian's Master is a good, benevolent Person, without fault. We need never fear being mistreated or taken advantage of; and he compensates his love-slaves well—with every spiritual blessing in Christ, and with every good and perfect gift from above. Furthermore, this Master's love-slaves have been promised an inheritance as a son, for his love-slaves will reign as co-heirs with him forever.

Love-slaves of the Lord Jesus Christ serve him because they love him. They know their Master, and they seek to please him in all things. Because they belong to their Master, they know their Master will faithfully provide for them, protect them, instruct them, and when necessary, discipline them. These love-slaves know they could leave at any time, but they choose not to; they have committed themselves to serve their Master—forever.

These love-slaves live like sons—which they are: "for in Christ Jesus you are all sons of God, through faith" (Gal. 3:26). To paraphrase the beloved apostle: "We love our Master because he first loved us" (1 John 4:19).

September 20

When Bewildered

"For we are powerless against this great horde that is coming against us. We do not know what to do, but our eyes are on you."
2 Chronicles 20:12

There are times in the work of the Lord when we simply do not know the course of action we should take in regard to a particular matter. We may have discussed the subject at hand at great length. All the pros and cons which come to mind have been identified. There appears to be any number of options we could take—each seeming to be a reasonable one—but we remain uncertain. What should one do?

Jehoshaphat was one of Judah's good kings, and he once faced a perplexing situation. Three kings joined forces against him and Judah; his army was far outnumbered. What could he do? What course of action should he take? He prayed. Prayer is often our last resort; after we have tried everything else, we pray. Often critical decisions can be made with our sanctified, prayerful deliberations. But there are times—even after considerable prayer—when we do not have an answer. What should we do in such circumstances? Do what Jehoshaphat did—tell God we don't know the answer: "For we are powerless against this great horde that is coming against us. We do not know what to do, but our eyes are on you."

Our Father in Heaven loves honest prayers; after all, honest prayers are the only prayers he answers. True praying requires transparency before the all-seeing God. Let's not pretend we know the answers when we don't. Pride will insist it knows the course of action we should take; but if taken, it will surely result in disaster.

Judah was blessed to have a leader who prayed with an honest heart in the presence of all the assembled people: it was a prayer of urgency; it was a prayer of humility. As powerful as he was as a king, he acknowledged his powerlessness before Yahweh.

For Judah and their king, the answer was not long in coming. The Spirit of God gave them direction from a man of God by the name of Jahaziel. When facing a dilemma, God often provides the answer in a way we least expect. We don't know how or when the answer may come, but it will—if we express a resolute dependence upon our merciful Father.

September 21

Loving God and Loving People

"You shall love the Lord your God with all your heart and with all your soul and with all your mind.... You shall love your neighbor as yourself."
Matthew 22:37, 39

The God of love gave to Frank Laubach (1884-1970) a large capacity to both love God and love people. A former editor of *The Wesleyan Advocate* once heard Frank tell his story.

"Frank Laubach was a Methodist missionary in Mindanao, Philippines and was trying his best to serve Christ and the Methodist Church. One day, he realized that he could not minister to the people because he did not love them. During a spiritual retreat, Frank knew that he must receive love for these people, or he might as well leave.

"One night after evening vespers Frank retreated to a spot on the mountain alone. He agonizingly confessed to God that his ministry was a failure, that he simply did not love the people. And the Spirit led him to pray, 'Lord, I will not leave this mountain until You give me love for these people.' The hours passed. He was desperate enough to pray earnestly and hopeful enough to pray on. Perhaps at three or four o'clock in the morning, God's love for men was 'shed abroad in his heart.'

"For a few minutes, Frank lingered to enjoy the inrush of love; then he was constrained to leave the mountain, to travel the paths where men walked, and tell them he loved them. He met some Catholic friars, and he paused to tell them he loved them. Then he met some Buddhist monks. He found himself warmly greeting them as friends, and they surprised him by returning courtesies of love. He told the farmers, the women, the children—he told everyone he loved them. From that day, God opened their hearts to the gospel of God's love as Frank preached it. They believed that God loved because they knew that Frank Laubach loved.*

Everywhere the Son of Man walked, he demonstrated a genuine *agape* love for people, because he was filled with the very love of his Father in Heaven. Jesus loved people because he loved God.

God's love must be renewed in us regularly, lest we live diminished lives. Could it be we are in need of a *baptism of love*, as Frank Laubach experienced, and as did the disciples of old?

September 22

The Water of Salvation

"Everyone who drinks of this water will be thirsty again, but whoever drinks of the water that I will give him will never be thirsty again."
John 4:13-14

Man without God is thirsty—always thirsty. When David was on one of his flights from King Saul, some distance from Bethlehem, one day he suddenly thought of how he enjoyed the water from the well in that city. As far as he was concerned, there was no other water quite like it. In the presence of some of his mighty men, "David said longingly, 'Oh, that someone would give me water to drink from the well of Bethlehem that is by the gate'" (2 Sam. 23:15).

One day at noon, Jesus and his disciples came to a famous well while traveling through Samaria. Jesus sat on the edge of Jacob's well while his disciples went to buy lunch. A woman—thirsty in body and in soul—came to the well to draw water. She had not the slightest idea when she left home that day what and who was on her near horizon. She often drew water from the well, yet she always returned home with her jars full, but her heart empty, dissatisfied—always thirsting.

However, this day was different from all preceding days for this thirsty-hearted woman! This day she would meet one who was greater than Jacob, one who provided for man's spirit as well as man's body, one who wouldn't quibble over theological minutia, one who gave the quality of water, that when received, would satisfy her forever: "whoever drinks of the water that I will give him will never be thirsty again." Only Jesus satisfies!

Hallelujah! I have found Him
Whom my soul so long has craved!
Jesus satisfies my longings;
*Through His blood I now am saved.**

When one has discovered the Water of Life, others are inevitably drawn to Jesus through our witness: "Many Samaritans from that town believed in him because of the woman's testimony" (John 4:39).

September 23

Receiving from Christ's Fullness

For from his fullness we have all received, grace upon grace.
John 1:16

Whatever we have received as believers, it is always channeled by our Father through his Son, the Lord Jesus Christ, and communicated to us by the blessed Holy Spirit.

The Lord Jesus was a "full" Person. For those who may have questioned whether or not this One who claimed to be sent from God was uniquely divine, the Apostle Paul wrote, "For in him all the fullness of God was pleased to dwell" and "For in him the whole fullness of deity dwells bodily" (Col. 1:19; 2:9). Writing at the end of the first century, the Apostle John says of Jesus that he was "full of grace and truth," and that "from his fullness we have all received, grace upon grace" (John 1:14, 16). The inspired writers say Jesus was fully God, full of grace, and full of truth; and it is from Christ's fullness believers draw upon.

When the children of Israel were wandering in the wilderness forty years, they were provided morning and evening meals—manna and quail. That was grace—God's gift to undeserving people. Likewise, Israel was covered with a cloud by day and a fiery pillar by night—signs of the manifest presence of God; this was *reality*. For you see, the same word for truth in the Scriptures is also to be understood as "reality." When the Word came in the flesh, he was full of grace and the reality of God's presence. Everywhere Jesus went the reality of God was present.

It is from Christ's fullness—a fullness of grace and reality—that "we have all received grace upon grace." We need grace; we need reality. Both are found in Christ. I love F. F. Bruce's (1910-1990) remark on this: "What the followers of Christ draw from the ocean of divine fullness is grace upon grace—one wave of grace being constantly replaced by a fresh one."*

What is your need today? Whatever it is, you may freely draw from the fullness of the Lord Jesus Christ. We are undeserving, thus we receive grace; we are surrounded by pretense and shadows, therefore we need the reality of his abiding Presence.

Guarding the Sacrifice

And when birds of prey came down on the
carcasses, Abram drove them away.
Genesis 15:11

The Christian journey is one continuous sacrifice unto the Lord. When we initially came to Christ, we heard him say, "If anyone would come after me, let him deny himself and take up his cross daily and follow me" (Luke 9:23). Sometime later, we hear the voice of the Lord saying to us, "Present your bodies as a living sacrifice, holy and acceptable to God, which is your spiritual worship" (Rom. 12:1). The first call is a call to self-renunciation, cross-bearing, and obedience. The second call doesn't abrogate the first call but supersedes it; it is a call to complete consecration of our bodies—a "living sacrifice." In responding to the first call, we leave our sins to follow Christ; in responding to the second call, we give our bodies completely in consecration to Christ.

The devout, consecrated follower of the Lord Jesus will be under constant attack from his Adversary. Once we have made a complete offering of ourselves to God—a living sacrifice—the sacrifice will be contested by Satan. The "birds of prey" will come down—again and again—in an effort to steal away our sacrifice to God, our total consecration.

What did Abram do whenever his sacrifice to God was assaulted? He aggressively and relentlessly "drove them away." No one else knew that Abram's offering to God was being contested. And no one else knows when our consecration to God is under assault. But we know, and only we can take the initiative to guard our sacrifice, our consecration to God.

Abram was unwilling to allow one piece of his consecrated offering to God to be stolen by predators. What about you? Have you given yourself totally to the Lord, but have since *rationalized* away your offering? Get alone with God soon; renew your consecration to the Lord today.

September 25

The Saint's Daily Vocabulary

"Amen. Hallelujah!"
Revelation 19:4
"Father, I thank you ..."
John 11:41

I made a wonderful discovery some years ago: The language of the twenty-four elders and the four living creatures in Revelation 19, and the words of Jesus in John 11, reflect the Spirit's vocabulary of one whose heart is in Heaven. The language of the saints is a heavenly language, one given by the Spirit of God.

"Amen." The word is often spoken thoughtlessly, no doubt, at the conclusion of both public and private prayers; it serves more or less as a *period* at the end of a sentence. However, when prayed and spoken sincerely, "amen" means the pray-er and worshiper are in agreement with what has previously been prayed or spoken. There should be in the hearts of saints a continual "amen" upon hearing and reading the Word of God. We should always agree with what God has said, and then live out his word in the power of the Spirit.

"Hallelujah." This word is a transliteration of two Hebrew words, meaning "praise Yahweh," or "praise the Lord." Heaven is filled with praise—by angels, living creatures, elders, and a great multitude. The Psalms are filled with "hallelujahs," usually rendered as "praise the Lord." Though we see the people of God praising him throughout the Scripture, Revelation 19 alone records the actual word "hallelujah." There, a great multitude, twenty-four elders, and four living creatures, spontaneously burst forth with praises to God for his salvation, power, judgments, and the reign of God.

"Thank you." The Lord Jesus gave thanks for his Father's provisions (Mark 8:6), answered prayers (John 11:41), his Father's wisdom (Matt. 11:25), and during difficult circumstances (1 Cor. 11:23-24).

The language of Heaven and Jesus should characterize those who claim to be his followers. When God speaks, we say "Amen"; when God works, we say, "Hallelujah"; when God gives, we say, "Thank you."

This is the saint's daily vocabulary.

Consulting the Lord

Woe to those who go down to Egypt for help and rely on horses, who trust in chariots because they are many and in horsemen because they are very strong, but do not look to the Holy One of Israel or consult the Lord!
Isaiah 31:1

I was sitting in a conference session some years ago, where a church leader outlined his proposal for church growth. Immediately after the leader concluded, a dear elderly saint, seated next to me, whispered, "He didn't say a thing about prayer." I once attended a church growth seminar in the Midwest. All the pastors present were eager to learn what this world-renowned "expert" had to say on the subject. Following his lengthy presentation, the speaker began mingling with the conferees. I overheard a pastor ask the dear brother, "Dr. _____, we heard nothing about prayer in your presentation. What place does prayer have in the growth of the church?" The man's response was anemic, to say the least.

We are either living God-dependent lives, or making our decisions without taking time to consult the Lord. Too often, we pay only lip service to prayer. The Christian and the church are waging war "against the authorities, against the cosmic powers over this present darkness, against the spiritual forces of evil in the heavenly places" (Eph. 6:12), and we go blithely on our way without acknowledging the Head of the church about how we should minister. Flush from a resounding victory, Joshua proceeds to Ai after taking Jericho. Sending only a few soldiers to take Ai, Israel was soundly defeated. Why? Was it because of the sin of Achan? Yes, but something more. After the defeat at Ai, Joshua fell on his face before the Lord, and the Lord revealed to him Achan's sin. We have no record that Israel went into battle against Ai *after* Joshua consulted the Lord. If he had, we have reason to believe the Lord would have spared Israel's failure.

How much time does your church give to concentrated prayer sessions? If our prayer times were as lengthy as some of our business meetings, churches would be known for their victories instead of their defeats.

We are either trusting in God or ourselves. Prayer—real prayer—is a heartfelt expression of our dependence upon God.

September 27

Uncelebrated Saints

Of whom the world was not worthy.
Hebrews 11:38

It has been over fifty years ago that I purchased a book, authored by a professor at Greenville College. I've never forgotten a story Dr. Mary Alice Tenney (1889-1971) shared in her book, illustrating the undo importance we place on appearances.

She wrote about a stranger who had come to stay in a community for several days. A neighbor of Dr. Tenney's asked her one day, "Who is that grey-haired man in the unpressed suit who has been in town the last two days?"

Tenney's reply was, "Did you notice his face?"

"Not particularly," the neighbor answered.

Dr. Tenney notes, "I didn't say it, but this is what I wanted to say: 'You have seen in the last two days one of the greatest men in the world. A saint has visited this town, and you saw only an unpressed suit.'"*

After recording several Old Testament giants of faith at the end of Hebrews 11—Gideon, Barak, Samson, Jepththah, David, Samuel, as well as the many exploits wrought by men and women of faith— the Holy Spirit didn't want us to forget about the anonymous saints, whose faith was just as great as those mentioned. "Others suffered mocking and flogging, and even chains and imprisonment. They were stoned, they were sawn in two, they were killed with the sword. They went about in skins of sheep and goats, destitute, afflicted, mistreated—of whom the world was not worthy—wandering about in deserts and mountains, and in dens and caves of the earth" (Heb. 11:36-38).

God says the world doesn't deserve to have the saints mentioned in Hebrews 11 living among them. Why do we model before our children the importance we attach to cultural celebrities and the world's icons? This world's values are not God's. Jesus' adversaries acknowledged that he was not "swayed by appearances" (Mark 12:14). Why are we? Could it be because we are too much like the world? Who do we esteem—the godly or the godless? Our children and grandchildren will notice the difference.

The Presence of the King

Then King David went in and sat before the Lord and said, "Who am I, O Lord God, and what is my house, that you have brought me thus far?"
2 Samuel 7:18

It was 1974 when I read for the first time the book authored by V. Raymond Edman (1900-1967), *They Found the Secret*. Now, over forty years later, this book is bound with a rubber band, because of much use; and I have given many copies away.

Dr. Edman was the fourth president of Wheaton College and later its chancellor. The last time he spoke in the college chapel, he suffered a fatal heart attack. The title of his sermon that day was "The Presence of the King." In that message, Edman related his visit to the country of Ethiopia, at the invitation of King Haile Selassie the First. He shared how he was told to observe the proper protocol for entering the king's presence. After his name was called by an attendant, he was to approach the throne room entrance, where he should stop and bow, asking quietly if he could approach. Whereupon, the king would grant permission.

After telling his experience of being in the presence of the king, Edman proceeded to talk to the students and faculty about another King. "But I speak primarily of another King. This chapel is the house of the King. Chapel is designed to be a meeting on your part with the King of kings and the Lord of lords Himself. To that end, chapel is designed for the purpose of worship. Over these years, going back to Jonathan Blanchard, Charles Blanchard, J. Oliver Buswell, myself, and now to President Armerding, there has been this same basic objective—that chapel is to be a time of worship, not a lecture, not an entertainment, but a time of meeting the King. Coming in, sit down and wait in silence before the Lord. In so doing, you will prepare your own hearts to hear the Lord, to meet with the King. Your heart will learn to cultivate what the Scripture says, 'Be still and know that I am God.' Over these years, I have learned the immense value of that deep, inner silence as David, the king, sat in God's presence to hear from him."*

A few minutes later, one of Wheaton's greatest presidents was ushered into the presence of the King of kings and Lord of lords.

Jesus' Food

Jesus said to them, "My food is to do the will of
him who sent me and to accomplish his work."
John 4:34

The ultimate purpose of Jesus' mission on earth was to provide an atoning sacrifice for the sins of the world. However, from the beginning of his ministry to its end, he continually modeled a sacrificial lifestyle—pouring out his days in service to the glory of his Father in Heaven.

No matter his audience, the Lord Jesus always elevated the conversation; he lifted the eyes of those about him to true realities. Whenever he saw and heard people placing undo importance on the things of this life, it became a teaching moment for our Lord.

The journey had been long, and the sun undoubtedly was quite hot that day when our Lord was traveling along the Samaritan road with his disciples. Approaching the city of Sychar, he comes to Jacob's well and takes a seat. He was tired and thirsty. As his disciples go to town to buy lunch, a woman comes to draw water from the well, whom Jesus engages in conversation. She came for water; Jesus used the opportunity to elevate the conversation: "Everyone who drinks of this water will be thirsty again, but whoever drinks of the water that I will give him will never be thirsty again" (John 4:14).

While Jesus ministers to the sinful woman, the disciples return with lunch. Their cultural sensibilities were shocked to see Jesus talking with this woman, but they held their peace. After the woman left, the disciples "were urging him, saying, 'Rabbi, eat'" (4:31).

Now for another teaching moment: "I have food to eat that you do not know about" (4:32). The disciples thought Jesus was referring to material food and wondered if he had already eaten. He had. However, not the kind of food they had in mind: "Jesus said to them, 'My food is to do the will of him who sent me and to accomplish his work'" (4:34).

The will and work of God for Jesus was to minister to the spiritual needs of lost sheep; to be engaged in pointing people to the way to Heaven—that's why Jesus came. "Look, I tell you, lift up your eyes, and see that the fields are white for harvest" (4:35).

September 30

Beholding the Face

And we all, with unveiled face, beholding the glory of the Lord,
are being transformed into the same image from one degree of
glory to another. For this comes from the Lord who is the Spirit.
2 Corinthians 3:18

One early morning I was sitting in a local restaurant, reading the
Word and drinking a cup of coffee. I was taken by a man seated a
short distance from me. Periodically, he looked at a photo on his
phone, and after that, leaned back, with eyes closed. In a little while,
he would lean forward again, look at the photo, and resume his rev-
erie. I could easily see the photo was of a lovely woman (his wife?
girlfriend?). Presumably, he was on the road, looking at and thinking about his lover.

As Christians, we should be constantly looking into the face of
our crucified, risen Lord. No, we don't see him with the naked eye,
but "though [we] do not now see him, [we] believe in him and rejoice with joy that is inexpressible and filled with glory" (1 Pet. 1:8).
Unlike the man in the restaurant, gazing at his absent lover, there is
a wonderful, mysterious change occurring in a Christian as he be-
holds the face of Jesus, in Word and Spirit—he is being changed
into the image of Jesus. Glory begets glory. The more we concentrate on the Man at God's right hand, the more we become like him.
"For God, who said, 'Let light shine out of darkness,' has shone in
our hearts to give the light of the knowledge of the glory of God in
the face of Jesus Christ" (2 Cor. 4:6).

It has been my privilege through the years to catch a glimpse of
God's glory in the lives of some of his intimate followers. I saw it in
a young Anglican pastor on the continent of Africa. I saw it in the
life and death of a much-esteemed theologian. I saw it in my mother, when she sang solos in our local church. I saw it again this week,
as I traveled a distance to visit three hours with a ninety-two- year-
old retired professor and college president.

John was given a vision of those who are to inhabit the City of
God: "They will see his face, and his name will be on their foreheads" (Rev. 22:4). They saw the "face" of the Lamb; his likeness
("name") was visibly apparent "on their foreheads"—on their countenance and in their character.

October 1

The Tie That Binds

And above all these put on love, which binds
everything together in perfect harmony.
Colossians 3:14

John Fawcett (1740-1817), the author of the following hymn, was converted at the age of sixteen under the ministry of George White-field (1714-1770). While pastoring a small Baptist Church in Wainsgate, England, he accepted a call to pastor a considerably larger church in London. When all his family's earthly goods were being loaded for the move to London, many of the Fawcett's parishioners were in tears. His wife went to her husband and lamented, "John, I cannot bear this." "Neither can I," responded her husband. Turning to the movers, he said, "Unload the wagons and put everything as it was before."* With this episode in mind, Fawcett later wrote the following words.

Blest be the tie that binds
Our hearts in Christian love;
The fellowship of kindred minds
Is like to that above.

Before our Father's throne
We pour our ardent prayers;
Our fears, our hopes, our aims are one
Our comforts and our cares.

We share each other's woes,
Our mutual burdens bear;
And often for each other flows
The sympathizing tear.

When we asunder part,
It gives us inward pain;
But we shall still be joined in heart,
*And hope to meet again.***

Some seventeen-hundred years before John Fawcett penned the above words, the Apostle John wrote to first-century believers: "We know that we have passed out of death into life, because we love the brothers." There is nothing that *oils* the church's machinery more than *agape* love for our brothers and sisters in Christ. Love "binds everything together in perfect harmony."

Serving with Humility

Shepherd the flock of God that is among you,
exercising oversight, ... not domineering over those
in your charge, but being examples to the flock.
1 Peter 5:2-3

Depending on the personality and culture of the church leader, some leaders may insist on their proposals being accepted by the group in a crude and aggressive manner, while other personalities may be more subtle in asserting their will over others. Either way, the "ark of God" often stalls because a dominant, self-willed leader insists on having it his way or no way.

This was Diotrephes' problem—he insisted on having his own way. The Apostle John had to say about him: "I wrote to the church, but Diotrephes, who loves to be first, will have nothing to do with us" (3 John 9 NIV). Pride rejects God-led leadership because it loves to assert itself, it wants to control others.

Realizing leaders would be subject to great temptation in this matter of administering God's work with humility, the Apostle Peter exhorts the leaders of his day to exercise their ministry without "domineering" the members of Christ's body. If the lordship of Jesus Christ is to be honored in his churches, then the humility of Christ must characterize its leaders.

In his Introduction to 2 Corinthians in *The Message*, Eugene Peterson wisely remarks how the Apostle Paul handled his leadership role among the churches. "Because leadership is necessarily an exercise of authority, it easily shifts into an exercise of power. But the minute it does that, it begins to inflict damage on both the leader and the led. Paul, studying Jesus, had learned a kind of leadership in which he managed to stay out of the way so that others could deal with God without having to go through him."*

We should constantly pray for our church leaders, that they would have a heart to lead Christ's flock with true humility.

To God Be the Glory

*The seventy-two returned with joy, saying, "Lord, even the demons
are subject to us in your name!" And he said to them,
"I saw Satan fall like lightning from heaven."*
Luke 10:17-18

Can God trust you to give him all the glory?
When the Methodist evangelist John R. Church (1899-1994)
was a young, aspiring preacher, he was invited to give the commencement address at Asbury College in the 1930s. Later in recounting that event with Dr. Dennis F. Kinlaw, Church related the
following account. "The place was packed. Excitement was high.
God was with me, and I soared. I thought, I have this audience in
the palm of my hand. I can do anything I want with them. Suddenly,
a cold chill moved over me. I closed the service immediately, went
to my room, and got on my knees. I said, 'God, if you'll forgive me,
I'll never be guilty of that again.'
"For years afterward, I met people who said, 'Dr. Church, do
you remember when you were at Asbury for commencement?' It
happened so many times that I knew what was coming. They would
say, 'You know, I have never heard such oratory.'
"I would ask, 'What did I preach about?'
"I never met a person who could recall the text or the topic I
had preached about," Dr. Church said. "All they remembered was
the oratory."**
Knowing the deadly sin of pride would prove to be his downfall
unless avoided, George Whitefield (1714-1770), who was preparing
to be ordained as an Anglican minister, prayed this prayer: "Dearest
Redeemer, make me humble, prepare me for Thy future mercies;
and whenever Thou seest me in danger of being exalted above
measure, graciously send a thorn in the flesh, so that Thy blessings
may not prove to be my ruin."*
When Johann Sebastian Bach (1685-1750) began a new composition, he would write, "*Jesu Juva*" ("Jesus, help"). When finished,
he would write, "*Soli Deo Gloria*" ("To God alone be the Glory").*
Unless we take our pride to the Cross, it will crucify us, no matter how much our service for Christ may *glitter*.

October 4

The Wonder of It All

*The heavens declare the glory of God, and
the sky above proclaims his handiwork.*
Psalm 19:1

I remember reading the conversion story of the Church of the Nazarene evangelist Bud Robinson (1860-1942). After leaving a West Texas Methodist camp meeting altar, where he experienced God's saving grace, Bud recounts: "The Lord marched out all the stars of heaven on a dress parade for my special benefit, and the stars leaped and hopped and skipped and jumped and turned somersaults and clapped their hands and laughed all night. The Lord showed me that it was all at his expense and did not cost me one nickel. I just lay [down] and laughed all night."

Having spent the night following his conversion sleeping under an ox wagon (he was poor and the times were primitive), Bud writes, "The next morning, as day was beginning to break, I crawled from under the ox wagon and went out on the camp ground. I watched the sun rise in all its grandeur and glory. The whole heavens were lighted up. I would look in one direction, and it would appear to be like mountains of oranges; in another direction, like tons of strawberries, and I'd look in another direction and it was like tons of ice cream. It seemed to me that the angels were having strawberries and ice cream for breakfast. I turned and looked at a great flock of clouds in another direction and it had the appearance of a great flock of sheep with their wool on fire. Just about that time heaven came down to the earth and I was so blest that soon I was leaping up and down, clapping my hands and praising God as loud as I could shout."*

Of course, we know the heavens always declare the glory of God, but newly converted Bud Robinson only had his eyes recently opened to it and was giving God glory along with the heavens.

When grace enters our lives, we almost involuntarily lift our eyes to the Lord and join the heavens in giving him glory.

We should never lose the wonder of God's grace; we should neve fail to give God all the glory.

Serving in Jesus' Name

*Whatever you do in word or deed, do all in the name of the
Lord Jesus, giving thanks through him to God the Father.*
Colossians 3:17

It was A. W. Tozer (1897-1963) who once wrote: "It is not what a
man does that determines whether his work is sacred or secular; it
is *why* he does it. The motive is everything. Let a man sanctify the
Lord God in his heart and he can thereafter do no common act. All
he does is good and acceptable to God through Jesus Christ. For
such a man, living itself will be sacramental and the whole world a
sanctuary."*

The Apostle Paul wrote to the Colossian Church: "Whatever you
do in word or deed, do all in the name of the Lord Jesus, giving
thanks through him to God the Father." To act and speak in Jesus'
name is to acknowledge the lordship of Jesus Christ in whatever we
say and do. It is to live out even the so-called mundane tasks of
life—eating and drinking—"to the glory of God" (see 1 Cor. 10:31).

Some years ago, my wife Emily and I were parked outside a local ice cream store. As we were enjoying our cones and time together, softly in the background one of our instrumental CD hymns was
playing "Just as I Am." While listening to this classic hymn, I said,
"You know, Charlotte Elliott (1789-1881) had no idea when she
penned those words the extent to which God would use them."
Then, after Emily and I thought about that for a moment, we both
agreed that God's Word affirms that any and everything done or
said in Jesus' name has a lasting quality to it—it will never die. It
will never die because it was done in Jesus' name.

Another hymn writer, by the name of Frances Havergal (1836-
1879), spent much of her life writing hymns in Jesus' name. Her
remarkable usefulness began when she consecrated herself fully to
the Lord Jesus Christ. Her complete devotion was strikingly expressed by her own hand:

Take my will, and make it Thine; it shall be no longer mine.
Take my heart, it is Thine own; it shall be Thy royal throne.
Take my love, my Lord, I pour at Thy feet its treasure store.
*Take myself, and I will be ever, only, all for Thee.***

October 6

Our Body, God's Temple

Your body is the temple of the Holy Spirit.
1 Thessalonians 4:3

When the inspired apostle reminded the immature Thessalonian believers, "For this is the will of God, your sanctification," he did so within the context of addressing the subject of sexual behavior. Some of these converts had fallen into sinful conduct following their confession of faith, or had never broken with their licentious lifestyle. God says to such through Paul's pen: "abstain from sexual immorality.... For God has not called us for the purpose of impurity but in sanctification" (1 Thess. 4:1-8).

In his first letter to the Corinthian Church, Paul exhorts Christians to "flee immorality" (1 Cor. 6:18). Why? Because "your body is the temple of the Holy Spirit who is in you.... For you have been bought with a price: therefore glorify God in your body."

Just as we should never desecrate an earthly sanctuary that has been consecrated to God for sacred purposes, so the Christian is called by God to cleanse his consecrated temple—the body—"from all defilement of the flesh and spirit, perfecting holiness in the fear of God" (2 Cor. 7:1).

The disciple of Jesus who takes a flippant attitude about his sexual behavior, about what he eats and drinks (including the portions), what he views—everything he does with his body—and merely shrugs his shoulders and says, "It isn't anyone's business!"—is saying in effect, that it isn't God's "business" either.

God is concerned about the Christian's witness in the world and his influence in the church, but he is equally concerned with how we treat our bodies. Thus we are called by God to "present [our] bodies a living and holy sacrifice, acceptable to God, which is [our] spiritual service of worship" (Rom 12:1).

Our body is the temple of the Holy Spirit. How are we treating, or mistreating his temple?

October 7

Nameless Saints

Here we have no lasting city, but we seek the city that is to come.
Hebrews 13:14

Christian history and tradition inform us that Andrew preached the gospel in Macedonia, Scythia and Russia. Bartholomew preached Christ in many countries, but mostly in India and Armenia. James the Son of Zebedee is believed to be the first Christian missionary to Spain. John's travels took him throughout Asia Minor and the Island of Patmos. Thaddaeus preached in Mesopotamia and Persia. Matthew traveled to Egypt and Ethiopia. Peter evangelized throughout Pontus, Galatia, Bithynia, Cappadocia and Asia. Simon Zelotes preached in Egypt, Mauritania, Africa, Libya and Britain. Thomas ministered in India, and to the Parthians, Medes and Persians. We are told that all of these were martyred for their faith except for John, who died a natural death.

On the other hand, there are far more *nameless* saints who never engaged in the works of service the apostles did, but who, nonetheless, caught God's eye because they built with gold, silver and precious stones (see 1 Cor. 3:12-13). They are God-purified, holy followers. And wherever they live and serve, they are producing quality works to the glory of Christ. Most of these dear people don't stand behind a pulpit or sit on church boards. But their knees are calloused. Their hands are busy. Their feet are worn.

These select saints have a glow in their eye, a song on their lips, and a Presence in their hearts. They live on earth, but dwell in Heaven. They enjoy this life, but are living for the next. They go about their Father's business in this world: loving, giving, encouraging, serving, reaching, caring, worshiping, sharing, communing, learning and growing—in the purity and power of the Spirit.

These saints have caught a glimpse of the next world and can't be impressed with the tinsel of this one. They confess: "Here we have no lasting city, but we seek the city that is to come."

Lord, enlarge your church with more people like these!

The Judgment Seat of Christ

For we must all appear before the judgment seat of Christ.
2 Corinthians 5:10

Martha Snell Nicholson (1898-1953) was a bedridden invalid for most of her life, suffering from four incurable diseases. For over thirty-five years, pain was often her daily companion. Though her husband faithfully tended to her needs for many years, he died suddenly, leaving her with added challenges. However, through all of her suffering, she wrote some of the finest Christian poetry.

Louis T. Talbot (1889-1976), long-time president of the Bible Institute of Los Angeles (now Biola University), called Martha "one of the most amazing demonstrations of the grace of God that I have witnessed.... Out of her troubles were born the exquisite verses which have blessed and comforted thousands of Christians the world around."*

While this consecrated lady was confined much of her life to her home in Washington State, her God-glorifying poetry has ministered to Christians around the world for years. The following thought-provoking words are her thoughts on the Judgment Seat of Christ.

When I stand at the Judgment Seat of Christ
And He shows me His plan for me,
The plan of my life as it might have been,
Had He had His way; and I see
How I blocked Him here, and I checked Him there,
And I would not yield my will,
Will there be grief in my Saviour's eyes,
Grief though He loves me still?
He would have me rich, and I stand here poor,
Stripped of all but His grace,
While memory runs like a hunted thing
Down the paths I cannot retrace.
Then my desolate heart will well nigh break
With tears that I cannot shed;
I shall cover my face with my empty hands;
I shall bow my uncrowned head.
Lord of the years that are left to me,
I give them to Thy hand;
Take me and break me, mold me to
*The pattern Thou hast planned.***

October 9

Loving Christ Warmly

"But I have this against you, that you have
abandoned the love you had at first."
Revelation 2:4

Are you still relatively young, anticipating many more years? Then accept the challenge to sink your spiritual roots deeper into God's love. Are you more advanced in years? God is not finished with you; ask him to renew your spirit, and spread out your *wings* to climb to new horizons in faith.

More than fifty years ago, A. W. Tozer (1897-1963) wrote, "Perhaps the most serious charge that can be brought against modern Christians is that we are not sufficiently in love with Christ."* May such not be said of us. This is no time for sluggards in the church! Live for Christ! Know Christ! Love Christ! Serve Christ— passionately—in the power of the Holy Spirit!

Ray Palmer (1808-1887) served his Lord as a minister of the gospel and a hymn writer for many years in New England. Of the many beautiful hymns he authored, one of my favorites is "My Faith Looks Up to Thee." He wrote this hymn shortly after his graduation from Yale University, while teaching at a school in New York. He basically kept the poem to himself until meeting his friend Lowell Mason on a street one day in the city of Boston. Mason inquired of Palmer if he could write something new for a hymnal he was compiling. Palmer passed on to Mason the lyrics of "My Faith Looks Up to Thee," which he had kept for the previous two years. After taking the poem home and setting it to music, Mason told Palmer several days later, "You may live many years and do many good things, but I think you will be best known to posterity as the author of "My Faith Looks Up to Thee." The Lord has used one stanza of that hymn to speak to me repeatedly through the years:

May Thy rich grace impart
Strength to my fainting heart, my zeal inspire!
As Thou hast died for me, O may my love to Thee,
Pure warm, and changeless be, a living fire!

The Assurance of Salvation

*The Spirit himself bears witness with our
spirit that we are children of God.*
Romans 8:16

Believing that he should serve God and the Church of England as a missionary in the state of Georgia, John Wesley (1703-1791) and his brother Charles (1707-1788) sailed to the American colony in the fall of 1735. His brief ministry of approximately two years in this foreign land was a failure, according to his own testimony. In his February, 1738, journal entry, Wesley laments his shortcomings: "It is now two years and almost four months since I left my native country, in order to teach the Georgian Indian the nature of Christianity: But what have I learned myself in the meantime? Why, (what I least of all suspected) that I who went to America to convert others was never myself converted to God [later editing his *Journal*, he noted: 'I am not sure of this']. I am not mad, though I thus speak; but I speak the words of truth and soberness, if haply some of those who still dream may awake, and see, that as I am, so are they."*

It was not until May 24, 1738, that John Wesley came to an experiential knowledge and assurance that Christ was his Lord and Savior. God used some devout Moravian Christians and Luther's *Commentary on Romans* to lead Wesley to an evangelical faith in Christ. In writing about this transformational experience, he entered into his diary, "In the evening, I went very unwillingly to a society in Aldersgate Street, where one was reading Luther's Preface to the Epistle to the Romans. About a quarter before nine, while he was describing the change which God works in the heart through faith in Christ, I felt my heart strangely warmed. I felt I did trust in Christ, Christ alone for salvation: And an assurance was given me, that he had taken away my sins, even mine, and saved me from the law of sin and death."*

It is possible to be an ordained minister of the gospel, a missionary to a foreign country, and to be zealous for the cause of God, without being saved and having the assurance of one's salvation.

Do you *know* the Lord Jesus as your Savior?

October 11

Heart Knowledge

That Christ may dwell in your hearts through faith.
Ephesians 3:17

One cannot cultivate and express a passionate love for Christ without knowing Christ, and to know Christ is to experience Christ in our hearts. In addressing this issue, Oxford University professor and author Alister McGrath recalls a conversation he had with a previous Archbishop of Canterbury. "I vividly remember a conversation some years ago with Donald Coggan, a former archbishop of Canterbury. We were discussing some of the challenges to theological education, and had ended by sharing our concerns over people who left theological education knowing a lot more about God but seemingly loving God rather less than when they came in. Coggan turned to me sadly and remarked: 'The journey from head to heart is one of the longest and most difficult that we know.'"*

Such a journey is only possible for a sincere seeker after God, inviting Christ to take full possession of one's heart.

This was a prayer burden the Apostle Paul carried for the Ephesian Church. His prayer for them was "that Christ may *dwell* in your hearts through faith" (Eph. 3:17). Among the several concerns he expressed in this prayer were particular petitions about two things: That the Ephesians would have more than a head knowledge of Christ ("that Christ may dwell in your *hearts*"); secondly, that Christ would make his home in their hearts ("that Christ may *dwell* in your hearts").

As an apostle, evangelist, and teacher, Paul was not content with merely a *cerebral* Christianity. He knew Christ personally and experientially and desired the same for all to whom he ministered.

Every pastor should reflect Paul's concern for his own flock. Church membership, water baptism, and confirmation, do not make one a Christian. It takes Christ coming *inside* one's heart to do that.

More than a historical figure,
More than a word on paper,
More than a tradition to savor—
I long to know you, O Christ!

October 12

Resurrection Power

That I may know him and the power of his resurrection.
Philippians 3:10

In making a comparison between the love of God and the power of God in the salvation events, F. F. Bruce (1910-1990) says, "If the love of God is supremely demonstrated in the death of Christ ['but God shows his love for us in that while we were yet sinners, Christ died for us,' Rom. 5:8], his power is supremely demonstrated in the resurrection of Christ, and those who are united by faith with the risen Christ have this power imparted to them." It is this power, says Bruce, that "enables the believer to ignore the dictates or enticements of sin and to lead a life of holiness which pleases God."* New Testament Greek scholar Marvin Vincent (1834-1922) concurs with this interpretation: "The resurrection is viewed, not only as something which Paul hopes to experience after death, nor as a historical experience of Christ, which is a subject of grateful and inspiring remembrance, but as a present, continuously active force in his Christian development."*

Speaking pastorally on this subject, the late long-time pastor of Westminster Chapel, Martyn Lloyd-Jones (1899-1981), asks rhetorically, "But what about the man or woman who comes to me and says, 'Here am I in my weakness, conscious of sin within me, temptation always around and about me, the whole world organized on the side of sin and Satan and evil. It is difficult enough to keep straight and moral at all in a world like this, and you are asking me to live the kind of life that Jesus of Nazareth lived on this earth—it is impossible.'" Lloyd-Jones says the answer to this dilemma lies in the truth contained within this text: "The answer to such a person is, 'the power of His resurrection.' He is risen, he has given a manifestation of His power, and that power is being offered to us. That is the power that can become ours, however weak we are; it can lift us and raise us up in newness of life, and enable us to walk with him."**

Are you experiencing Christ's resurrection power—the very life-giving energy which enables you to live this day to his glory?

October 13

Suffering for Christ

For I consider that the sufferings of this present time are not
worth comparing with the glory that is to be revealed to us.
Romans 8:18

Richard (1909-2001) and Sabina (1913-2000) Wurmbrand were
two devout Romanian Christians who suffered greatly at the hands
of the communists when Romania was under the rule of despots. A
Lutheran pastor, Richard and his wife courageously opposed atheis-
tic communism while ministering to the underground church in
their country. He eventually was arrested and imprisoned, serving
fourteen years in a concentration camp; Sabrina was incarcerated
for eleven years. This pastor and wife experienced unimaginable
abuse under the regime during those years. But, interestingly
enough, they had asked God for it!

Before their sufferings came, Wurmbrand writes, "My life as a
pastor, until this time, had been full of satisfaction. I had all I needed for my family. I had the trust and love of my parishioners. But I
was not at peace. Why was I allowed to live as usual, while a cruel
dictatorship was destroying everything, which was dear to me, and
while others were suffering for their faith?" Then he says something
that the Western Church knows very little about (including me):
"On many nights, Sabina and I prayed together, asking God to let us
bear a cross."*

God heard the prayers of this devout couple and laid heavy
crosses upon these valiant souls, which they were to bear for many
years. In the words of Karl Barth (1886-1968), "The way in which
the power of Christ's resurrection works powerfully in the apostle
is, that he is clothed with the shame of the Cross."* Glorious
"shame" at that!

Listening to the typical prayer request in the Western World,
one is struck by the dissimilarities with the Suffering Church. There
is no "cross" in our requests; there is no suffering for Jesus.

I wonder: Is it because of our timid witness?

Joy in Suffering

We rejoice in our sufferings.
Romans 5:3

As he witnessed the last days of the imprisonment of Lutheran pastor and theologian Dietrich Bonhoeffer (1906-1945), just before his execution at the hands of the German Nazis, an English military officer later wrote, "Bonhoeffer always seemed to me to spread an atmosphere of happiness and joy over the least incident and profound gratitude for the mere fact that he was alive.... He was one of the very few persons I have ever met for whom God was real and always near."*

Could it be that we would love Christ more if we knew Christ better? Could it be that Christ would be more real and near to me if I were bolder in my witness? Do I desire to know Christ intimately—enough to pray that he would allow me to more closely experience the fellowship of his sufferings, as Paul prayed (see Phil. 3:10)?

The Apostle Paul was from a rare *breed*. He actually rejoiced because he was suffering for the Lord Jesus Christ. He was not merely suffering for a cause; he was not suffering because of his self-willed foolishness; he wasn't suffering because he was trying to make a name for himself. He was suffering for Jesus—the Christ of the Damascus Road, the brutal Cross, and the Empty Tomb.

Following his powerful sermon and pointed indictment of those who had rejected Christ during his earthly ministry, Stephen's hearers became enraged, hurling stones at him. And what was Stephen's reaction? What did his persecutors see? Luke records, "And gazing at him, all who sat in the council saw that his face was like the face of an angel" (Acts 6:15).

When the pressure is on because of our identification with Christ, could an onlooker afterward say of us, "He was one of the very few persons I have ever met for whom God was real and always near"? Could anyone say, "His face was like the face of an angel"?

Are you rejoicing in your sufferings, or are you complaining?

October 15

"Do you love me?"

"Simon, son of John, do you love Me?"
John 21:17

When Jesus dialogued with Simon Peter following his resurrection, the one question he raised with this defeated disciple had nothing to do with what Peter's future ministerial goals might be. Our Lord went to the very heart of Peter's need because he knows what constitutes a dynamic, authentic relationship with himself. Thus, Jesus asked Peter three times, "Do you love me?" While myriad religious, worthwhile pursuits may captivate the attention of the twenty-first-century church, there is only one fundamental question our Lord asks us in the midst of our flurry of activities: "Do you love Me— right now, this very moment—are you passionately in love with ME?"

During his brief life, the Scottish pastor and evangelist, Robert Murray M'Cheyne (1813-1843), gained a reputation for personal piety and devotion to the Lord Jesus. Prior to his being taken suddenly ill, a visitor heard M'Cheyne preach one Sunday, what proved to be his last sermon, and sent him a note of appreciation. However, the godly pastor was unable to read the correspondence because of his grave condition. Following his death, the note was discovered and opened. It read: "I hope you will pardon a stranger for addressing to you a few lines. I heard you preach last Sabbath evening, and it pleased God to bless that sermon to my soul. It was not so much what you said, as your manner of speaking that struck me. I saw in you a beauty in holiness that I never saw before. You also said something in your prayer that struck me very much. It was, 'Thou knowest that we love Thee.' Oh, sir, what would I give that I could say to my blessed Saviour, 'Thou knowest that I love Thee!'"*

To know Christ is to love Christ. To love Christ is to follow Christ. Do you love Christ? Are you following Christ?

More love to Thee, O Christ, more love to Thee!
Hear Thou the prayer I make on bended knee.
This is my earnest plea: More love, O Christ, to Thee;
*More love to Thee, more love to Thee!***

Don't Be Ashamed (part 1)

*"For whoever is ashamed of me and of my words in this adulterous
and sinful generation, of him will the Son of Man also be ashamed
when he comes in the glory of his Father with the holy angels."*
Mark 8:38

It was to his disciples and the multitude that Jesus spoke the above
words. Some of those present were true followers of Jesus, and
some were contemplating becoming his disciples.

Jesus was always up-front with candidates for discipleship. He
never employed ruses to gain a following. The numbers' game was
out of the question: he wasn't on a campaign to see how many followers he could acquire. He wasn't in competition with the neighborhood rabbi.

Jesus' call to discipleship was demanding: it involved self-
denial, a personal cross, and obedience (Mark 8:34). In comparison
to their love for him, Jesus said whoever followed him must "hate"
every human relation—father, mother, wife, children, and siblings
(see Luke 14:26). To become a follower of Jesus, one must enter
through the "narrow gate" (Matt. 7:13).

Jesus knew that his call to an exclusive attachment to himself
would at times evoke fear among his followers, and they would be
tempted to be ashamed of being identified with him and the words
he spoke. Are you ashamed of Jesus? Are you ashamed of identifying with the truth he spoke? Peter denied his Lord three times in the
same night. Why? It was because he was ashamed. Fearing for their
own lives after Jesus was arrested, all of Christ's disciples "left him
and fled" (Mark 14:50).

When the pressure is on—in the office, with a group of the unsaved, in the classroom, with your employer, among your peers—
and moral issues are under discussion, do you equivocate, or do you
prayerfully ask the Spirit to help you to be "wise as a serpent and
innocent as a dove" (Matt. 10:16)? Or are you ashamed of being
identified with Jesus and his words?

Jesus said if we are ashamed of him in this world, he will be
ashamed of us when he returns.

Don't Be Ashamed (part 2)

"So everyone who acknowledges me before men, I also will acknowledge before my Father who is in heaven, but whoever denies me before men, I also will deny before my Father who is in heaven."
Matthew 10:32-33

The above saying of Jesus is the counterpoint to his words recorded in Mark 8:38. In the Mark text, Jesus' emphasis was on shame—a warning against being ashamed of him and his words. Here in the Matthew text, Jesus stresses the importance of confession and acknowledgement of him "before men." We will be rewarded, Jesus says, if we acknowledge him before men; on the other hand, if we fail to acknowledge him—deny him—he will deny us before his Father in heaven.

There are many ways we can acknowledge Jesus "among men." The Holy Spirit will lead us in this matter and use each of our unique personalities to be a humble witness for Christ. There are times our witness may offend the unsaved; leave that matter with the Lord. We should never ask the Lord to help us not to offend people over speaking the truth. The truth can be—and often is—very offensive; people stumble over God's truth. It is appropriate to pray for boldness in speaking the truth, as the apostles did (see Acts 4:23f).

Living in a pluralistic, secular culture as we do—"this adulterous and sinful generation"—Christians can unwittingly become tame and timid, reluctant and intimidated, in the presence of unbelievers. We should not be *abrasive* in confessing Christ before others, but we do need to be *bold* with a holy, Christlike boldness.

Let us regularly ask the Lord to help us to acknowledge our true identity—in the way we talk and walk, in the attitudes we display, and by prayerfully speaking truth as he opens the doors. Remember, the Spirit is speaking to people before we speak, he is leading the way. Let us walk through life's marketplace unafraid.

We do well to emulate the boldness of Peter and John, as they stood before the opponents of Christ: "we cannot but speak of what we have seen and heard" (Acts 4:20).

Ask the Lord how you can be a faithful witness—to acknowledge Jesus "before men."

October 18

Partings

"I shall go to him, but he will not return to me."
2 Samuel 12:23

Life is full of good-byes and separations. Many of these occur during the course of every-day-life. A husband and wife embrace before they part for work. Parents bid their children good-bye as they leave for school. To friends and family, as well as to casual acquaintances, leaving one another for a brief period of time—and sometimes longer—is a regular occurrence.

Partings often bring with them deep sorrow. When Jesus announced to his disciples and friends that he would soon be leaving them, he said, "Sorrow has filled your heart" (John 16:6). One of the most moving accounts in Scripture of members of the body of Christ bidding farewell to one another is when Paul met with the Ephesian elders for the last time: "And there was much weeping on the part of all; they embraced Paul and kissed him, being sorrowful most of all because of the word he had spoken, that they would not see his face again" (Acts 20:37-38). Death came to Bethany one day, taking away a much-loved brother; Mary and Martha were overcome with a painful separation. Partings can be excruciating.

My wife Emily and I recently traveled some distance to visit dear friends of more than fifty years. Not having seen one another for several years, we reminisced, laughed, and shed some tears. After finishing an enjoyable meal, the hostess took a photo of the four of us. Then we walked outside. While Emily and Miriam exchanged parting words, Tom and I did the same. We both had been engaged in Christian service all our lives; we had much in common. Finally, with our hands on each other's shoulders, Tom began to sing,

If we never meet again this side of Heaven,
As we struggle through this world and its strife—
There's another meeting place somewhere in Heaven,
*By the side of the river of life.**

For God's people, "good-byes" are never final. There is a Great Reunion on the horizon, with Jesus as the center of attention. What a Day that will be—with no more good-byes!

A Singing People (part 1)

Be filled with the Spirit, speaking to one another
in psalms and hymns and spiritual songs, singing
and making melody with your heart to the Lord.
Ephesians 5:18-19 NASB

A friend and I were on a subway train many years ago, returning to our motel room in downtown Boston. That evening we had attended a Billy Graham Crusade at Boston University's football stadium. Soon after taking our seats on the train, someone began to sing, and then several of us joined in:

Blessed assurance, Jesus is mine!
Oh, what a foretaste of glory divine!
Heir of salvation, purchase of God,
*Born of His Spirit, washed in His blood.**

Christians have always been a joyful, singing people—wherever they are!

The early Christians met regularly for worship, instruction, and mutual edification. Unlike many, if not most, church services in our contemporary culture today, there was considerable interaction among believers when they gathered in the first century (see 1 Corinthians). Today, this kind of interaction often occurs in small-group gatherings.

Paul suggests to the church that "psalms" (the Old Testament Psalter that Christian Gentiles would become increasingly familiar with); "hymns" (musical compositions of praise and worship directed toward and exalting God); "spiritual songs" (as opposed to pagan songs; these would include songs, which are more experiential in nature—testimony songs) be sung.

We are far more blessed in our day, than the first-century church was when it comes to the plethora of hymns and spiritual songs available to us. Every generation of Christians has had the Psalms, but more and more these are being set to music for the church's edification. And the hymns—how we should familiarize ourselves with, memorize, and sing the hymns—as well as spiritual songs.

A Singing People (part 2)

*Be filled with the Spirit, ... singing and making
melody with your heart to the Lord.*
Ephesians 5:18-19 NASB

I grew up with singing—Christian singing. My dear mother, who suddenly went to be with the Lord soon after I turned twelve years of age, was a singer. She did not have a trained voice, but she sang well—and in the Spirit; she was also the church pianist and played the accordion. Singing filled our home. More than once I was awakened in the morning by Mom softly playing, mostly familiar gospel songs. I can still hear her playing and singing,

*Showers of blessing,
Showers of blessing we need:
Mercy drops round us are falling,
But for the showers we plead.**

I've heard a lot of good voices through the years—in local churches, Bible conferences, seminars, camp meetings, colleges, etc. —singing Christian songs, but I have heard far fewer songs sung in the church from those who sing with heart-melody, those who are singing in the Spirit. What a difference the Spirit makes in our music!

A few years ago, I taught a two-week's concentrated course at a seminary in Lagos, Nigeria. Upon returning to our classroom following the chapel service one morning, where God showed up in a wonderful way, an Anglican pastor, asked, "Dr. Tilley, may I sing a song?" I replied, "You certainly can." Whereupon this ebony-skinned brother rose to his feet, and with a glow on his face, sang the song, of which the chorus follows:

*Heaven came down and glory filled my soul,
When at the cross the Savior made me whole;
My sins were washed away, and my night was turned to day,
Heaven came down and glory filled my soul!***

I never heard the song sung as well by anyone as I had that day. Christians are a joy-filled, singing people. Do you have a song in your heart?

October 21

"O to Be Like Thee"

*"A disciple is not above his teacher, nor a servant
above his master. It is enough for the disciple to be
like his teacher, and the servant like his master."*
Matthew 10:24-25

Thomas Chisholm (1866-1960) described himself as "just an old shoe." However, this "old shoe" authored over 1200 poems and hymns. Among the best known are "Great is Thy Faithfulness, "He Was Wounded for Our Transgressions," and "O To Be Like Thee," which follows.

*O to be like Thee! blessèd Redeemer,
This is my constant longing and prayer;
Gladly I'll forfeit all of earth's treasures,
Jesus, Thy perfect likeness to wear.*

*O to be like Thee! full of compassion,
Loving, forgiving, tender and kind,
Helping the helpless, cheering the fainting,
Seeking the wandering sinner to find.*

*O to be like Thee! lowly in spirit,
Holy and harmless, patient and brave;
Meekly enduring cruel reproaches,
Willing to suffer others to save.*

*O to be like Thee! Lord, I am coming
Now to receive anointing divine;
All that I am and have I am bringing,
Lord, from this moment all shall be Thine.*

*O to be like Thee! while I am pleading,
Pour out Thy Spirit, fill with Thy love;
Make me a temple meet for Thy dwelling,
Fit me for life and Heaven above.* *

What Chisholm expressed in this hymn is the heart-cry of every disciple of the Lord Jesus, and a cry that often comes from our lips. We are not made like Christ in the work of justification; it is only by the Spirit's work in us (sanctification) that we become increasingly like the Son.

"Awake My Soul When Sin is Nigh"

*"Watch and pray that you may not enter into temptation.
The spirit indeed is willing, but the flesh is weak."*
Mark 14:38

The last thing the disciple of the Lord Jesus wants to do is wound the blessed Spirit of God. But it can and does happen, as every honest Christian would confess. Because of our susceptibility to sin, Jesus repeatedly warned his disciples, "Watch and pray that you may not enter into temptation. The spirit indeed is willing, but the flesh is weak."

Because he personally had known failure and was informed in the strategies of Satan, the Apostle Peter alerted Christians to "Be sober-minded; be watchful. Your adversary the devil prowls around like a roaring lion, seeking someone to devour (1 Pet. 5:8).

Being zealous to please his Lord, and not wanting to grieve the indwelling Spirit, Charles Wesley (1707-1788) cried out to God in prayer:

I want a principle within
of watchful, godly fear,
A sensibility of sin,
a pain to feel it near.

I want the first approach to feel
of pride or wrong desire,
To catch the wandering of my will,
and quench the kindling fire.

From Thee that I no more may stray,
no more Thy goodness grieve,
Grant me the filial awe, I pray, the
tender conscience give.

Quick as the apple of an eye,
O God, my conscience make;
Awake my soul when sin is nigh,
and keep it still awake. *

Do you want a "sensibility to sin"? Is this your prayer: "Quick as the apple of an eye, O God, my conscience make"?

Christ is Glorified in His Disciples

"Father ... all mine are yours, and yours are
mine, and I am glorified in them."
John 17:10

The Spirit glorifies Jesus through Christ's followers. That's amazing! On the very night of his betrayal, the Twelve heard Jesus pray, "Father ... all mine are yours, and yours are mine, and I am glorified in them."

When I read and pause to think on these amazing, poignant words, prayed by our Lord for those who were present, as well as for all future followers, several things come to mind.

First, I am humbled. Humbled to think the Spirit can take a sinner, clean him up, and then use him to be a temple of praise to the Lord Jesus.

Second, I'm challenged by this prayer—challenged to live in the power of the Spirit that he would be pleased to use me—an unprofitable servant—to bring some measure of glory to him who loved me and gave himself for me.

Third, I'm led to confess—confess the multitude of times I have failed to bring glory to the Lord Jesus by my words, thoughts, and deeds.

Think of it, the blessed Holy Spirit—the Spirit of truth—indwells the disciples individually and the church collectively—to glorify the Father's Son, the sinner's Savior, the bride's Bridegroom, the servant's Master, the creature's Creator, the subject's Sovereign, the Lord of lords, and the King of kings.

The Lord Jesus taught us to say, "When you have done all that you were commanded, say, 'We are unworthy servants; we have only done what was our duty'" (Luke 17:10).

He takes unworthy servants, and somehow brings glory to the Father through us.

I am so wondrously saved from sin,
Jesus so sweetly abides within,
There at the cross where He took me in;
Glory to His Name!*

Welcome Home

So that Christ may dwell in your hearts through faith.
Ephesians 3:17

When Paul prays for believers to be strengthened by the Spirit "that Christ may dwell in your hearts through faith," one might logically ask a series of questions: Wasn't Paul writing to Christians? Doesn't Christ dwell in the hearts of all Christians? Why would he pray that Christ would dwell in their hearts if Christ dwells in the hearts of all Christians?

The key word in all this is the word "dwell." What does it mean? The Greek word translated "dwell" occurs, with its cognates, some forty-one times in the New Testament. The word is used in both a physical and spiritual sense. An example of a physical sense is used in Matthew 2:23, where it is said of Joseph (including Mary and the child Jesus), he "came and lived in a city called Nazareth." The word for "lived" is the same Greek root word rendered "dwell" in Ephesians 3:17. Another example, in addition to our text, of this word used in a spiritual sense is located in Colossians 1:19, where Paul says of Christ, "For in him all the fullness of God was pleased to dwell."

Paul's prayer burden for these believers is that they might receive such a mighty strengthening of the Holy Spirit in their lives, until they allow Christ to make his *home* in their hearts.

Ephesians 3:17 sounds very similar to the words of Jesus in John 14:23: "If anyone loves me, he will keep my word, and my Father will love him, and we will come to him and make our home with him."

Have you welcomed the Father and the Son to make your heart their home, by keeping Christ's words?

Not a brief glance I beg, a passing word;
But, as thou dwell'st with thy disciples, Lord,
Familiar, condescending, patient, free,
Come, not to sojourn, but abide with me!*

October 25

Seeing Christ in His Followers

The love of every one of you for one another is increasing.
2 Thessalonians 1:3

The Thessalonian Christians became known for their faith in God and their love for one another. Paul, the church's founder, says to them, "we ... give thanks to God for you, brothers, as is right, because your faith is growing abundantly, and the love of every one of you for one another is increasing."

Clearly, the love of Christ was shining through these early believers. Haven't you noticed the same, in those whose walk with Christ is a close one? Christians shouldn't put on "airs"; however, Christ's love, abiding in the hearts of his people, can be observed by others.

Beatrice Clelland (1912-1997) was acquainted with this kind of Christian when she penned these words:

Not merely in the words you say,
Not only in the deeds confessed,
But in the most unconscious way,
Is Christ expressed.

Is it a beatific smile,
A holy light upon the brow?
Oh no, I felt His presence while
You laughed just now.

For me, 'twas not the truth you taught,
To you so clear to me so dim,
But when you came to me you brought
A sense of Him.

And from your life He beckons me,
And from your heart His love is shed,
Till I lose sight of you and see
The Christ instead.

Pray often that your love for Christ and his people would increase. A love-filled person is winsome and magnetic. Pray that God's love will flow through you without obstruction.

October 26

Love Which Excels

That according to the riches of his glory he may grant you ...
to know the love of Christ that surpasses knowledge.
Ephesians 3:16, 19

Paul prays that these believers may "know the love of Christ which surpasses knowledge." What an oxymoron—apparently. Is Paul actually praying that we might "know" the unknowable? Not really. This word rendered "surpasses" could more correctly be rendered "excels." Paul prays that these believers may experience such a heart-knowledge of Christ's very own love, a love which excels all other loves. It is this quality of *agape* love that Methodism's prolific hymn writer wrote about:

Love divine, all loves excelling,
joy of heav'n to earth come down;
Fix in us Thy humble dwelling;
all Thy faithful mercies crown.
Jesus, Thou art all compassion,
pure, unbounded love Thou art;
Visit us with Thy salvation;
*enter ev'ry trembling heart.**

You can't know the love of Christ by reading about it alone, by taking a course in it, by attending a seminar about it. This love is not an exercise of the head as much as it is an experience of the heart. It is the love of Christ, the love which originates with Christ and that flows into our hearts from Christ by his Spirit. It is Christ's very own love.

We know and experience this love by knowing Christ, by becoming intimately acquainted with Christ, by walking with Christ, by conversing with Christ, by delighting in Christ's presence, by communing with Christ—through the Word and Spirit. Frederick Faber (1814-1863) was so filled with this love of Christ that one day he wrote:

I love Thee so, I know not how
My transports to control;
Thy love is like a burning fire
*Within my very soul.**

Listening Prayer

And Samuel said, "Speak, for your servant hears."
1 Samuel 3:10

Much that is said and written about prayer fails to note the importance of *listening*—listening to the voice of the Good Shepherd during the quiet time.

Prayer is many things. Prayer includes offering praise and thanksgiving to God; it often takes the form of supplication and intercession. Prayer intercedes before God with upraised hands while the Joshuas are on the fields of battle, warring against the enemy (Ex. 17:8-13). There are also times when prayer consists of no more than groans being poured out before a merciful God, groans incapable of articulating one's petitions (Rom. 8:26-27).

Prayer is also *listening*—listening to hear the voice of the Spirit coming through the written Word of God, listening to hear the voice of the Spirit speaking in order to apply the Word of God to one's particular circumstances.

Daily listening prayer takes time—unhurried, uncluttered, all alone, quietness—time. Time spent in solitude with God, with his Word. Bible reading should be a devotional exercise which is done while praying, meditating, and contemplating. The maturing disciple of the Lord Jesus is learning to listen to the voice of the Shepherd as he reads Spirit-inspired truth.

It is possible to read the written Word of God without hearing the voice of God, just as people often heard the voice of Jesus two millennia ago with their physical ears, but never embraced his spoken truth. Hence, we hear the Lord Jesus repeatedly ending his messages with the exhortation: "He who has an ear to hear, let him hear."

If you do not already practice listening prayer as you read God's sacred Word, try doing so the next time. Moreover, when leaving the place of daily solitude, learn to cultivate the spiritual exercise of listening to the Voice throughout the day.

God is speaking; are we listening?

The Futility of Self-Effort

*He saved us, not on the basis of deeds which we have done
in righteousness, but according to His mercy, by the washing
of regeneration and renewing by the Holy Spirit.*
Titus 3:5

With the Fall came both death and distance. Where life had reigned before, physical and spiritual death were to become commonplace afterward. A severe fissure occurred in man's relation to God. Suddenly, where there had been sweet and constant communion, there were now alienation and isolation. Man was severed from his Creator. Instead of facing God, he runs from God. Instead of walking in open transparency with his Father, he seeks to hide from him.

There is now rebellion against God, rationalization of his sin, malice toward his companion, and a dreadful fear of Elohim. "To complete all," says Adam Clarke (1760-1832), "the garden of pleasure is interdicted, and this man, who was made after the image of God, and who would be like him, [was] shamefully expelled from a place where pure spirits alone could dwell."* Life on earth was radically altered for Adam and Eve, and for all their progeny.

After the Fall, man began the futile journey of trying to reach God through his own ingenuity and will-power, and redeem himself through self-effort. Fig leaves were the symbolic moral attempt to cover his gross iniquity.

But God would have none of it. Man was incapable of initiating and engineering his salvation. He had dug himself into a deep, dark hole by choosing his own way—turning inward instead of gazing upward and outward. God must take the initiative if man is to be saved from himself. Man sought to cover himself; God chose to shed blood that man would be effectively and adequately covered.

Man had reached for what he wanted and got it—so he originally thought. That is what sin is, according to Dr. Dennis Kinlaw: "Sin is simply turning your eyes away from God and reaching for what you want."**

Are you reaching for God or for sin?

October 29

Keeper of the Springs

Keep your heart with all vigilance, for from it flow the springs of life.
Proverbs 4:23

While attending a conference in the city of Boston, many years ago, I heard evangelist Dr. John Wesley White share how there had been times during the course of his Christian journey when he had run, as it were, on *empty*. I grieve when I think of this; for I, too, have done the same. Nevertheless, we are in keeping with the Scriptures when we say God desires all of his children to walk in the Spirit's fullness—daily, moment-by-moment. This is my aspiration; this is my desire. Only one thing can keep you and me from this—sin. We must allow the gracious Spirit of Christ to keep our hearts clean if we are to live *full* lives.

Many years ago, so the legend goes, a little town began to grow at the base of a mountain. To ensure that all the springs that supplied its water were kept clean, the city fathers hired a ranger. With painstaking dedication, he daily patrolled the hills situated above the community, cleaning up every spring and pool he found, removing silt, leaves, and mud, so that the water ran down clean, cold, and pure.

One day, however, a dramatic change occurred when a group of foolish, stingy businessmen took over the administration of the city council. Scanning the budget for any possible waste, they concluded that paying a salary to the Keeper of the Springs could be dispensed with. They fired him.

It wasn't long before the citizens were overcome with sickness and death. An investigation ensued. The problem? The springs had become contaminated.

The open secret to living in the Spirit's fullness is to daily surrender to the Spirit's cleansing. God only fills those whom he first cleanses. Do we want to walk in the Spirit's fullness? Let us invite the "Keeper of the Springs" to keep our hearts pure. Let us always be seeking the gracious Giver of every good and perfect gift to fill us daily, and on special occasions, with his fullness—with himself!

October 30

God's Ability

*Now to him who is able to do far more abundantly than all that
we ask or think, according to the power at work within us.*
Ephesians 3:20

The British Methodist preacher, educator and author, Thomas Cook (1859-1912), remarked beautifully about the promises of God: "Every promise of God is supported by four pillars, each one as strong as the pillars of heaven—God's justice or holiness, which will not suffer Him to deceive; His grace and goodness, which will not permit Him to forget; His truth, which will not permit Him to change; and His power which makes Him able to accomplish."*

Dear, struggling Christian, do you often despair as to whether you can live a life which is pleasing to God? Do you wonder whether you will ever become a loving, established believer? Have you grown weary of a life of defeat? Then this prayer and promise in Ephesians 3:14-21) is for you. Take heart; God is able, for God has promised.

Note the apostle said, "God is able"; not, "*You* are able." Man's ability must flow from God's ability. Man can only act effectively after God has first acted within man. Paul had no confidence in the flesh—in his natural giftedness and abilities. He once did. He once boasted of his own righteousness and religious exploits. Previously, he was a zealous, fervent, self-righteous fanatic. He struggled and worked feverishly to earn God's righteousness, God's approval—all in vain. However, following his Damascus Road revelation of the living Christ, and subsequent filling of the Spirit, Paul viewed all his former works as rubbish. After Christ was revealed both to him and in him, the apostle knew it was God's ability working in him that was the moving cause behind all he was and did and accomplished.

God is able. God possesses the ability to do and perform in the hearts and lives of every one of his followers all that is consistent with his will. And in the context of Ephesians 3:14-21, Paul says God possesses the ability to make every believer strong in his or her interior life. He says God can establish every believer in love. He says God can fill every believer out of his very own fullness.

Are you thirsty?

A Clean Conscience

Let us draw near with a true heart in full assurance of faith,
with our hearts sprinkled clean from an evil conscience.
Hebrews 10:22

Our Evangelical ears are often shocked whenever we hear the word "perfect," with respect to anything having to do with God's work in us. And yet we dare not construe God's inspired words to mean anything less than what God spoke.

Hebrews 10:1 reads: "For since the law was but a shadow of the good things to come instead of the true form of these realities, it can never, by the same sacrifices that are continually offered every year, *make perfect* those who draw near." The inference, which is explicated later in this passage, is that through the New Covenant, a perfect conscience will be possible.

The Greek verb (*teleiosai*) in this passage is translated "make perfect" by four of today's major Bible versions (NASB, NRSV NIV, ESV). A good synonym for the word is "complete," meaning here, "lacking nothing essential for the whole."*

In Hebrews 10, the writer is contrasting the two covenants. He says the Old Covenant worshipers could never be perfected through their many sacrifices. And then he asks: "Otherwise, would they not have ceased to be offered, since the worshipers, having once been cleansed, would no longer have any *consciousness* of sins?" (Heb. 10:2). The obvious answer to his question is, Yes, if the Old Covenant worshipers had, indeed, experienced an inner moral cleansing of sin, they, consequently, would not have been burdened with a continual consciousness of sin.

Through the blood of the everlasting covenant, through the once-for-all offering of the body of God's Son, a clean conscience became a reality: "Therefore, brothers, since we have confidence to enter the holy places by the blood of Jesus, by the new and living way that he opened for us through the curtain, that is, through his flesh, and since we have a great priest over the house of God, let us draw near with a true heart in full assurance of faith, with our hearts sprinkled clean from an evil conscience."

Yes, the New Covenant believer is privileged to "no longer have any consciousness of sins."

When a Christian Sins

My little children, I am writing these things to you so that
you may not sin. But if anyone does sin, we have an advocate
with the Father, Jesus Christ the righteous. He is the propitiation for
our sins, and not for ours only but also for the sins of the whole world.
1 John 2:1-2

What should a Christian do when he fails in his walk with God? Despair? Rationalize his failure? Hide behind the mask of perfectionism? No! What is the advice of the inspired writer? "My little children, I am writing these things to you so that you may not sin. But if anyone does sin, we have an advocate with the Father, Jesus Christ the righteous. He is the propitiation for our sins, and not for ours only but also for the sins of the whole world." John says Christ is the "propitiation for *our* sins." And again, "If we confess *our* sins, he is faithful and just to forgive us *our* sins and to cleanse *us* from all unrighteousness" (1 John 1:7).

Dr. Dennis Kinlaw observes, "There are some days when I know that I have not acted as I ought, when I have been more like the forlorn disciples on Easter night than I would like to admit. I can almost hear the heavenly Father ask Jesus, 'Son, how did that Kinlaw guy do today?' I hear the Son respond, 'Well, Father, he did not do so well today ...'" Kinlaw proceeds, "Then I hear the Father say, 'Shall we give up on him?' But then my spirit leaps ... when, in my imagination, I see Jesus lift two scarred hands to the Father and say, 'No, Father. We have a substantial investment in him. We are not going to give up on him.'"*

There are times in which the Christian may tend to despair when he has failed ... again. The interceding Lord Jesus, our Advocate with the Father, never despairs over our failures.

Take heart, Christian, we have an Advocate with the Father!

He ever lives above, for me to intercede;
His all redeeming love, His precious blood, to plead:
His blood atoned for all our race,
*And sprinkles now the throne of grace.***

November 2

A Sympathetic High Priest

For we do not have a high priest who is unable to
sympathize with our weaknesses, but one who in every
respect has been tempted as we are, yet without sin.
Hebrews 4:15

One of the qualifications for a person to be a high priest under the Levitical law was that he should possess the capacity to deal sympathetically with the worshipers: "He can deal gently with the ignorant and wayward, since he himself is beset with weakness" (Heb. 5:2).

The priests did not always live up to their high calling. New Testament scholar F. F. Bruce noted, "From the fall of the house of Zadok [171 B.C.] to the destruction of the temple [70 A.D.] two hundred and forty years later, there were very few high priests in Israel, who manifested the personal qualities so indispensable to their sacred office."*

The author of Hebrews says the priests under the Old Covenant were compelled to deal sympathetically with the people because they themselves were "beset with weakness." However, Jesus sympathizes with our weakness—not because he himself was weak—he wasn't—but because he underwent temptation, just like we do.

The reading audience of the Book of Hebrews was weakened in their faith because of opposition; they were vulnerable; they were tempted to turn back. What a welcome word of encouragement they heard when this letter was read in their meetings: "For we do not have a high priest who is unable to sympathize with our weaknesses, but one who in every respect has been tempted as we are, yet without sin."

The writer did not write, "For *we did not have* a high priest who is unable to sympathize with our weaknesses, but one ..." No, he wrote quite the contrary: "For *we do not have* a high priest who is unable to sympathize with our weaknesses, *but one* who in every respect has been tempted as we are, yet without sin."

Their High Priest is alive—and sympathetic! He overcame temptation—so can they, with his help! And this High Priest still lives at the right hand of the Majesty on High; he is our High Priest, the Lord Jesus Christ.

November 3

Words for Distressed Believers

Do not throw away your confidence, which has a great reward.
Hebrews 10:35

I wonder what prayer-request-time sounded like in a first-century prayer meeting. I have an idea it was unlike many of ours. These early believers faced death; often their houses were ransacked. Some were tortured, and others lost employment. Many relatives and friends had begun to shun these Christ-followers. The people of the Way no longer sacrificed at the temple; they did not observe the same rituals they once had. Christians often faced mocking, beatings, slander, ridicule, and imprisonment.

I imagine a typical house-church prayer request in the first century went something like this: "Brothers and sisters, Naomi needs our prayers. She was beaten on her way home from working in the harvest fields last evening. That's why you don't see her here tonight. As you know, we were excommunicated from the synagogue last week, because of our public confession of faith in Jesus as our risen Lord and Savior. Our young children are grievously distraught by what happened to their mother. To compound their plight, they have lost all their friends at the synagogue. I hate to burden you with more, but I was informed three days ago, by my employer, that he will dismiss me from a position I have held for more than fifteen years if I don't publicly renounce Jesus Christ as Lord."

Some of these shaken saints were on the verge of turning back to their former ways. Many were sorely distressed and afflicted. By the day, they were growing weaker in the faith.

There are words of encouragement to such believers in the Word of God: "Do not throw away your confidence, which has a great reward. For you have need of endurance, so that when you have done the will of God you may receive what is promised" (Heb. 10:35-36).

The cross is not greater than His grace,
The storm cannot hide His blessèd face;
I am satisfied to know
That with Jesus here below,
I can conquer every foe.*

November 4

One Man's Passion

Fan into flame the gift of God.
2 Timothy 1:6

I have been blessed, times without number, in reading the biographies and journals of Christian men and women of God. My heart is warmed by the Spirit repeatedly as I read the *Journals of George Whitfield* (1714-1770), an English evangelist who sailed often to America to preach the gospel. Here are a few selections from his Journals.

• "Spent the morning agreeably in conversation, intercession for all friends and all mankind, walking on the seashore."

• "O that the Lord would open our understandings! for they are but a dead letter without the illumination of His Holy Spirit."

• "Was much strengthened in my present undertaking, by reading the story of Ezra, and joined in intercession with those who set apart this day as a day of fasting and prayer for the sins of the nation to which we belong."

• On board ship: "This afternoon, about 4 o'clock, as I was in secret, humbling myself before God, interceding for my friends, and had been praying for a fair wind, and assistance in the great work lying before me, news was brought that the wind was fair; which put me in mind of the angel's being sent to Daniel, to tell him his prayer was heard, when he was humbling his soul with fasting, and praying for the peace and restoration of Jerusalem."

• On board ship: "I have besought the Lord many times to send us a fair wind; but now I see He does not think fit to answer me. I am wholly resigned, knowing that His grace will be sufficient for me, and that His time is best. Our ship is much out of repair, and our food by no means enough to support nature in an ordinary way, being of the most indifferent kind, too—an ounce or two of salt-beef, a pint of muddy water, and a cake made of flour and skimmings of the pot. I think often on Him who preserved Moses in the ark of the bulrushes. So long as I look upwards my faith will not fail."

• "Oh that I knew how to be thankful! Oh that Heaven and earth would join with me in praising God!"

Devotion like this should stimulate our faith.

November 5

"Always"

Rejoice in the Lord always; again I will say, rejoice.
Philippians 4:4

Often in my devotional times through the years, I have found it a rewarding exercise to perform a search on a particular word in the Bible. Here are some selections from the New Testament of the word "always." Let your heart be refreshed by the Spirit as mine has been in performing such an exercise.

"Teaching them to observe all that I have commanded you. And behold, I am with you *always*, to the end of the age" (Matt. 28:20).

"And he told them a parable to the effect that they ought *always* to pray and not lose heart" (Luke 18:1).

"I knew that you *always* hear me, but I said this on account of the people standing around, that they may believe that you sent me" (John 11:42).

"So I *always* take pains to have a clear conscience toward both God and man" (Acts 24:16).

"Therefore, my beloved brothers, be steadfast, immovable, *always* abounding in the work of the Lord, knowing that in the Lord your labor is not in vain" (1 Cor. 15:58).

"Giving thanks *always* and for everything to God the Father in the name of our Lord Jesus Christ" (Eph. 5:20).

"Rejoice in the Lord *always*; again I will say, rejoice" (Phil. 4:4).

"Let your speech *always* be gracious, seasoned with salt, so that you may know how you ought to answer each person" (Col. 4:6).

"Then we who are alive, who are left, will be caught up together with them in the clouds to meet the Lord in the air, and so we will *always* be with the Lord" (1 Thess. 4:17).

"To this end we *always* pray for you, that our God may make you worthy of his calling and may fulfill every resolve for good and every work of faith by his power" (2 Thess. 1:11).

Kingdom Identifiers

For the kingdom of God is not a matter of eating and drinking
but of righteousness and peace and joy in the Holy Spirit.
Romans 14:17

Several years ago, the brakes on my wife Emily's vehicle began making an abnormal noise. The company's laboratory in Texas discovered the local mechanic had added transmission fluid to the brake system instead of brake fluid; they could make such a determination because their fluids contained special "identifiers."

The Apostle Paul wrote about kingdom "identifiers" which mark the people of God. There were those in the Roman Church who had been exulting in their personal dietary regulations and religious observances: "One person believes he may eat anything, while the weak person eats only vegetables" (Rom. 14:2); "One person esteems one day as better than another, while another esteems all days alike" (Rom. 14:5). Paul corrected those who insisted that others should practice inconsequential religious rituals and regulations: "For the kingdom of God is not a matter of eating and drinking" (Rom. 14:7).

It is wrong to elevate religious practices that are fundamentally indifferent, and make them essentially important. One can do many religious things without the Spirit's help. However, God's kingdom is not of this world; his rule is not a matter of ceremonial observances and bodily regulations. These are *shadows*, not *substance*.

From the earliest time, Christians have often fallen into superficial exercises of spirituality, which they have interpreted as necessary to their faith. However, they have not been content to keep these practices to themselves; they have insisted their fellow believers observe what they practice.

Paul says those in God's kingdom have special "identifiers" which set them apart from those who practice legal righteousness. God's kingdom *identifiers* are "righteousness and peace and joy in the Holy Spirit," in contrast to man-made standards of righteousness. Where the Spirit is present and active, these identifiers will be readily observable. Where the Spirit is not actively present, there exists merely the shell of spiritual reality and freedom.

A Holy Trilogy

*Rejoice always, pray without ceasing, give thanks in all
circumstances; for this is the will of God in Christ Jesus for you.*
1 Thessalonians 5:16-17

At first glance, whenever the disciple of the Lord Jesus first reads
the above exhortations (or reads them for the hundredth time), he
may react with disbelief, asking, *How can this be? How can any
person be always rejoicing, always praying, always giving
thanks? That's just not natural,* so he reasons.

He's right. It is not *natural.*

What is *natural?* Complaining, grumbling, questioning, ingratitude, sporadic prayers, and attempting to live without reference to
God. What is supernatural is joy, ceaseless prayer, gratitude—in all
circumstances.

The people of God are Spirit-people, not flesh-driven people.
We are people who have changed kingdoms: "He has delivered us
from the domain of darkness and transferred us to the kingdom
of his beloved Son" (Col. 1:13). We are people who are indwelt by
the Lord Jesus Christ himself: "Christ in you, the hope of glory" (Col. 1:27).

Joy. Joy is a product of the Spirit (Gal. 5:22). Where the Spirit
of God is present and active, there is an abundance of joy. The first
Christians were a joyful people because they were a full-of-the-
Spirit people: "And the disciples were filled with joy and with the
Holy Spirit" (Acts 13:52).

Prayer. "Prayer is the Christian's native air," to quote James
Montgomery (1771-1854).* The Christian does not merely pray at
stated times—he lives in an atmosphere of prayer. He is constantly
lifting his heart to God. This is learned behavior; this becomes the
new normal for the wholehearted believer.

Thankfulness. There is so much ingratitude in the world; this
should not be characteristic of Christ-followers. No matter the circumstance, the Christian will discern some reason to give thanks to
God.

In practicing this holy trilogy, Paul says, "this is the will of God
in Christ Jesus for you." Are you learning to practice God's will in
this regard?

November 8

The Making of a Name

*"I will bless you and make your name
great, so that you will be a blessing."*
Genesis 12:2

I was astonished in my Bible reading one day, by the contrast recorded in Genesis 11:4 and Genesis 12:2. In Genesis 11, we have the record of people who purposed to "build a city and tower with its top in the heavens" (v. 4). They said they would accomplish this "ourselves" (v. 4). These ancient pagan leaders weren't timid in why they wanted to construct such an edifice: "let us make a name for ourselves, lest we be dispersed over the face of the whole earth" (v. 4).

By contrast, look at God's call and promise to Abram in Genesis 12:2: "And I will make of you a great nation, and I will bless you and make your name great, so that you will be a blessing" (v. 2).

In Genesis 11, we have people who set out to make "a name for ourselves." In Genesis 12, we have a man of whom God said, "I will make your name great."

Those who strive for greatness strive in the flesh. Self-chosen greatness inevitably ends in confusion and disaster, as it did for those who attempted to reach into the heavens by their own effort. Much of the history of the world and the church is a record of ego-driven men and women who made a wreck of themselves and others because they were motivated to make a name for themselves. Such ambition dominates others and destroys anyone who gets in its way.

Conversely, those chosen by God, whom God wishes to make great, are measured by his estimate of true greatness. For this reason, God often selects the obscure, as was Abram and David; the humble, as was Jeremiah; the teachable, as was Timothy.

The pagans in Genesis 11 were neither thinking about their accountability to God nor wanting to be a blessing to others. How unlike the man from Ur of the Chaldeans, who walked in obedience to the God who said, "I will bless you and make your name great, so that you will be a blessing."

"Humble yourselves before the Lord, and he will exalt you" (James 4:10).

November 9

Noah's Faith

*By faith Noah, being warned by God concerning events
as yet unseen, in reverent fear constructed an ark for the
saving of his household. By this he condemned the world and
became an heir of the righteousness that comes by faith.*
Hebrews 11:7

Noah appears among the great men and women of faith in Hebrews 11, because he exercised faith in an era that was darker than any other.

Noah alone served God in his generation. Think of it! We believe we have it rough—remember Noah. What a man! What a man of faith! Noah had no Bible. He never attended a Bible study. He never attended a seminar on "How to Live a Godly Life." He had no fellowship with other believers—outside of his family. Noah simply walked with God, listened to God, obeyed God—when no one else did.

*He walked with God when everyone else
  was only thinking evilly
  and behaving wickedly.
He was showered with the grace of God,
  and God saw he was blameless
  and righteous, unlike others.
He listened to God's voice carefully,
  when no one else listened or
  cared what God had plainly said.
He built the Ark because God told him
  to, and because he wanted
  to see his family saved.
He is noteworthy because of whom
  he believed in, and because
  he lived out his faith with fear.
We should imitate such faith as his,
  for today is similar.
But who will listen; who cares?**

November 10

Serving as a Priest

To him who loves us and has freed us from our sins by his
blood and made us ... priests to his God and Father.
Revelation 1:5-6

The primary function of the priest under the Old Covenant was to come into the presence of God on behalf of the people of Israel. Because he alone could enter the second compartment of the temple—the Holy of Holies—God required these priests to wear special garments, garments which were both beautiful and symbolic.

Beginning with Aaron, each high priest wore an ephod, with two shoulder pieces consisting of an onyx stone on each shoulder. On these stones were engraved the names of the twelve tribes of Israel—six names on each shoulder. Furthermore, the high priest wore a breastpiece made of gold, blue, purple, and scarlet yarns and fine linen. On this breastpiece were placed a variety of twelve precious stones; these stones were set in gold filigree, with the names of the respective twelve tribes of Israel.

For centuries, each time the high priest entered the Holy Places to offer sacrifices and sprinkle blood over the mercy seat, he did so carrying Israel on his shoulders and over his heart. He was God's mediatorial representative on behalf of the people. He never entered the Holy Places without making intercession for God's people.

Forty days following his death on the cross and resurrection from the grave, our Great High Priest, the Lord Jesus Christ, "entered, not into holy places made with hands, which are copies of the true things, but into heaven itself, now to appear in the presence of God on our behalf" (Heb. 9:24).

But here is an amazing fact: Not only is our High Priest forever interceding for the saints, but Christians are designated as priests as well, called to intercede for others: Christ has "made us ... priests to his God and Father."

For whom have you been serving and interceding as a priest? One of the most sacred exercises a Christian can perform is that of praying for another person. We are called to exercise this privilege and responsibility faithfully.

November 11

A Study in Contrasts

"Therefore the leprosy of Naaman shall cling to you and to your descendants forever." So he went out from his presence a leper, like snow.
2 Kings 5:27

Recorded in 2 Kings 5 are the accounts of two primary events: the healing of a military commander by the name of Naaman, under the ministry of Elisha the prophet; and Elisha's attendant, Gehazi, being struck with the dreaded disease of leprosy

Naaman was a valiant soldier who suffered from leprosy. Through the mediation of his wife's Israelite maid, Naaman learned about the healing ministry of Elisha, traveled to Samaria, and after a struggle with pride was healed by God of his leprosy.

Filled with gratitude for Elisha's role in his healing, Naaman wanted to reward the prophet with a gift, but Elisha refused, saying, "As the Lord lives, before whom I stand, I will receive none" (5:16). The writer of 2 Kings immediately added: "And he urged him to take it, but he refused." The man of God would not make merchandise of his calling. He was no charlatan; he was no hireling. Elijah learned well from his mentor Elijah. God had called, gifted, and anointed him for special service; he would not be bought.

On the other hand, Elisha's servant Gehazi dropped his guard. Having overheard his master's refusal of Naaman's offer, Gehazi was overcome with a covetous and greedy spirit. He tracked down the commander and told him a lie in order to obtain the gift for himself. God revealed to Elisha Gehazi's duplicity, and Elisha confronted his servant about his sin and announced God's discipline: "'The leprosy of Naaman shall cling to you and to your descendants forever.' So he went out from his presence a leper, like snow" (5:21).

Servants of God are called to a high and holy office. They must not be seen as men and women who take advantage of their position to accumulate wealth. At all costs, the peril of a greedy disposition is to be avoided. Elisha passed the test; Gehazi didn't.

There is a graphic contrast depicted in this passage: Naaman, a pagan, was healed of leprosy because he believed God's prophet. Gehazi, an Israelite, succumbed to greed and was struck with leprosy. The one returned home clean; the other returned stained.

November 12

Discouragement (part 1)

And he asked that he might die, saying, "It is enough; now,
O Lord, take away my life, for I am no better than my fathers."
1 Kings 19:4

One of church's foremost hymnists was William Cowper (1731-1800). As with many artists, Cowper battled his entire life against depression and spiritual discouragement. His was more than an occasional bout with mental torment. Depression eventually sent him to a mental institution for a time, and more than once tempted him to take his own life. Most of us know nothing of the depth of Cowper's personal afflictions; however, we have experienced forms of discouragement—with ourselves and with God's providences.

The prophet Elijah was a man of great passion. Having defeated the prophets of Baal on Mount Carmel, and being used by God to call down rain following a devastating absence of both rain and dew for some three years, this fearless prophet flees for his life, after being threatened by Queen Jezebel. Following a day's journey, the prophet sits down under a tree and informs God he is *resigning*: "It is enough; now, O Lord, take away my life, for I am no better than my fathers."

Elijah reacted to discouragement and depression like many: he simply wanted to sleep, and so he did. Sleep is often a coping mechanism, an escape mechanism, for the depressed. Seeing no solutions, having no hope—the tortured soul turns to sleeping.

However, God does not sleep; he always cares for his wounded servants. In Elijah's case, God sends an angel to waken him and provides him with a meal—twice. After eating the second meal, the prophet "went in the strength of that food forty days and forty nights to Horeb," where he is given a new mission from God.

Our God is our merciful Father in Heaven: "For he knows our frame; he remembers that we are dust" (Psa. 103:14). He's a God who lifts us up when we are *down*. As difficult as it sometimes becomes, while walking through our valley of discouragement, if we simply allow God to awaken us from our *sleep*, and *eat* the Word he has prepared for us, we will discover refreshment and renewal and rejuvenation. Then, we can go forth being used once again in the Lord's service.

Discouragement (part 2)

*Now when John heard in prison about the deeds of the
Christ, he sent word by his disciples and said to him, "Are
you the one who is to come, or shall we look for another?"*
Matthew 11:2-3

John the Baptist was given one of the highest privileges ever afforded a prophet: to proclaim to the Jewish people and the world the arrival of the long-expected Messiah. His message was both direct and radical: "I am the voice of one crying out in the wilderness, 'Make straight the way of the Lord,' as the prophet Isaiah said" (John 1:23). In his unique role, John knew his place and kept it with humility: "I baptize with water, but among you stands one you do not know, even he who comes after me, the strap of whose sandal I am not worthy to untie" (John 1:26-27).

However, John's ministry was brief. After all, when you confront royalty about its sexual immorality, you're soon destined to lose your head! John was arrested; he sits in prison, and he begins to wonder about the mission he was given. Was he mistaken? Had he really been called by God to be his messenger? Was this Jesus of Nazareth truly the promised Messiah? Or was it all a mere fantasy, spawned by an overactive imagination? He wants confirmation; he needs reassurance.

So, John sends his disciples to Jesus, asking the primary question, "Are you the one who is to come, or shall we look for another?" The messengers return to prison with Jesus' words: "Go and tell John what you hear and see: the blind receive their sight and the lame walk, lepers are cleansed and the deaf hear, and the dead are raised up, and the poor have good news preached to them. And blessed is the one who is not offended by me" (Matt. 11:4-6).

Whenever we begin to question God, as we walk through the "Slough of Despond," it is the Word of God, and his Word alone, which can reassure the besieged soul. At times like this, we need to take up the shield of faith and the sword of the Spirit (Eph. 6:16-17). In the words of Martin Luther (1483-1546): "One little word shall fell him."* That "little word" is the Word of God.

If discouraged, go to Jesus; listen to the words of God coming through his written revelation.

Manna

*When the people of Israel saw it, they said to one another,
"What is it?" For they did not know what it was. And Moses said
to them, "It is the bread that the Lord has given you to eat."*
Exodus 16:15

The patience, longsuffering, and generosity of God are something to behold. Having delivered his elect people from servitude and shame, where they lived in exile for some 400 years, these Hebrews began to grumble about their lack of provision within a month of crossing the Red Sea. They left Egypt, but they carried *Egypt* with them; they had changed geographical locations, but their hearts were unchanged.

How soon fallen man forgets his Benefactor and his benevolences: "Would that we had died by the hand of the Lord in the land of Egypt, when we sat by the meat pots and ate bread to the full, for you have brought us out into this wilderness to kill this whole assembly with hunger," so complained the people (Ex. 16:3). And Yahweh responded in mercy and grace. He announced he would provide them bread in the morning and meat in the evening. When the people went out early in the morning to gather the promised food, they exclaimed, "What is it?"—which in Hebrew is *man hu*, from which the term "manna" is derived. What observations can we make of God's wonderful provision for his people in the wilderness?

• The manna was a gift from God. It was given by a generous, benevolent, caring Yahweh, just as Jesus was the gift of Bread sent from heaven (John 6:41).

• The manna was provided to undeserving people. Although Israel was an elect people, they were needy. We, likewise, are undeserving people: "For by grace you have been saved through faith. And this is not your own doing; it is the gift of God" (Eph. 2:8).

• Though given by God, the people had to appropriate the food. If left, the manna spoiled. We too must actively receive God's grace. Jesus said, "Whoever comes to me shall not hunger." We must "come"—and keep coming; this also is of grace.

• The manna was to be gathered daily. Likewise, if our inner self is to be renewed day by day (2 Cor. 4:16), we must take daily measures to keep renewed. The health of our soul depends on it.

Day by Day

Then Haggai, the messenger of the Lord, spoke to the people
with the Lord's message, "I am with you, declares the Lord."
Haggai 1:13

Two of my favorite hymns were authored by Karolina Sandell-Berg (1832-1903). Sandell-Berg's native country was Sweden, and she was the daughter of a Lutheran pastor. History reports she was accompanying her father on a trip across a lake one day, and her father fell overboard, drowning. Out of the depths of this sorrow, she began to write some of her first hymns.

Oscar Ahnfelt (1813-1882) took on the joyful responsibility of setting many of Sandell-Berg's verse to music, and sang them across Sweden as he played a ten-string guitar. Both artists were considered "pietists" in their day (would that all of God's people were pietists!). Their state church disapproved of their hymns, and they were ordered to appear before the king and sing. After listening to them, King Karl XV announced, "You may sing as much as you desire in both of my kingdoms."* Not only were her hymns sung in the king's kingdoms, they have been sung around the world by Christians ever since. The following verses are selections from "Day by Day" and "Children of the Heavenly Father."

Day by day, and with each passing moment,
Strength I find to meet my trials here;
Trusting in my Father's wise bestowment,
I've no cause for worry or for fear.
He, whose heart is kind beyond all measure,
Gives unto each day what He deems best,
Lovingly its part of pain and pleasure,
*Mingling toil with peace and rest.***

* * *

Children of the heav'nly Father
Safely in His bosom gather;
Nestling bird nor star in Heaven
Such a refuge e'er was given.

God His own doth tend and nourish;
In His holy courts they flourish;
From all evil things He spares them;
*In His mighty arms He bears them.****

November 16

The Old and the New

"You ... shall clear out the old to make way for the new."
Leviticus 26:10

While reading recently in Leviticus, I was struck by the above text and began thinking of similar passages, which speak of the "old" and the "new."

In Leviticus 26, Yahweh reminds Israel of the bountiful blessing that will be theirs upon entering their long-awaited inheritance, the Land of Promise. Yahweh promises rain in due season; plentiful harvests; protection from enemies; subdued wild animals; and victory everywhere they went. All of this is contingent upon their obedience. God says Israel's produce will be so abundant, that they will need to "clear out the old to make way for the new." This is an apt metaphor for the need for regular spiritual renewal. Previous blessings do not last forever; make room for new ones.

Furthermore, addressing the transition from the Old Covenant to the New, Jesus compared the old to rigid wineskins and the new to fresh wine: "No one puts new wine into old wineskins. If he does, the wine will burst the skins—and the wine is destroyed, and so are the skins. But new wine is for fresh wineskins" (Mark 2:22). While Jesus did not abolish the old, he and his teachings fulfilled and superseded it. Christ bursts the crusty wineskin, bringing in the fresh wine of the Spirit.

Additionally, Jesus taught that a well-informed teacher should be able to draw from and understand the connection between the old and the new: "Therefore every scribe who has been trained for the kingdom of heaven is like a master of a house, who brings out of his treasure what is new and what is old."

As students of both the Word and ways of God among men throughout history, we learn from the past so that we might adequately minister in the present. The Spirit reminds us: "For whatever was written in former days was written for our instruction, that through endurance and through the encouragement of the Scriptures we might have hope" (Rom. 15:4).

In our making "way for the new," let us take care we don't discard what God intends for us to keep.

Numbers, Numbers, Numbers

*But David's heart struck him after he had numbered the people. And
David said to the Lord, "I have sinned greatly in what I have done."*
2 Samuel 24:10

There is something in talking about our ministry statistics that engenders pride.

When I became the pastor of a church in upstate New York, the attendance began to decline. The church had an attendance board in the sanctuary, and it became increasingly painful for me to look at the numbers. One day, I walked over to the board, took it off the wall, and was about to place it in a closet, when I heard a voice, "Tilley, you're not as dead to *self* as you thought, are you?" I put it back.

Over the next few years, the Lord began to move powerfully among us, and the attendance grew by leaps and bounds. What did I do? I created a graph in my study, showing the impressive gains. One day, I heard the voice again, "Why did you make that chart for all to see who enter your study?" I took it down.

King David got himself into serious trouble with the Lord for taking the initiative to number his forces. There is no military reason as to why he did this. However, because of God's reaction to David's action, we know David did what he did because of a prideful heart. Joab, his commander, tried to dissuade him; David insisted.

God sent the prophet Gad to confront David, and the king confessed his sin and accepted God's discipline. He and the people suffered from his prideful action.

2 Samuel 24:1 says the LORD "incited David against them, saying, 'Go, number Israel and Judah.'" We read in 1 Chronicles 21:1 that "Satan stood against Israel and incited David to number Israel." How can we reconcile this paradox? In this way: God is never the author of evil, though he sometimes allows Satan to accomplish his purposes.

We can grieve the Holy Spirit in the way we report what he is doing through us. By keeping the attention on the Lord of glory, we will be spared from self-glorying. By walking in the Spirit, we can be kept from boasting in our accomplishments.

November 18

Temptation

*So when the woman saw that the tree was good for food,
and that it was a delight to the eyes, and that the tree was to be
desired to make one wise, she took of its fruit and ate, and she
also gave some to her husband who was with her, and he ate.*
Genesis 3:6

Temptation is a strong desire to act contrary to what we know to be the will of God. To be tempted is not to sin. It is only when our will gives consent to the temptation, that sin has been committed.

Among all the trees in Eden's garden were the tree of life and the tree of the knowledge of good and evil. Since God had made Adam the garden's caretaker, he may have seen both trees often. However, the one tree was forbidden: "And the Lord God commanded the man, saying, 'You may surely eat of every tree of the garden, but of the tree of the knowledge of good and evil you shall not eat, for in the day that you eat of it you shall surely die'" (Gen. 2:16-17). God never intended for man to experience sin.

However, being in the presence of forbidden fruit day after day can be overwhelming at times, unless we stay vitally connected to the Vine. One cannot always remove himself from the sources of temptation; hence, we must make sure that our interior life remains renewed, lest we succumb to external pressures.

There was nothing inherently evil in Eve's *looking*, though one could argue she got too close to the "tree," the object of temptation. Be that as it may, when she began to entertain the question of the veracity of God's Word—"Did God actually say?"—she suddenly became easy prey for Satan's snare.

All Christians have their weaker moments, when they are more vulnerable to sinful enticements. One must learn his or her vulnerabilities, lest we fail our Lord in temptation's hour. On this subject, I like the prayer Scottish minister and theologian John Baillie (1886-1960) once prayed: "O God, do Thou enable me so to discipline my will that in hours of stress I may honestly seek after those things for which I have prayed in hours of peace."* Let all God's people say, "Amen."

November 19

Watch and Pray

*"Watch and pray that you may not enter into temptation.
The spirit indeed is willing, but the flesh is weak."*
Matthew 26:41

Jesus took with him into Gethsemane Simon Peter, James and John, the three apostles who were brought into his confidence more often than others. There in the garden, the Son of Man was sorely tested. The cross lay before him, the sin of the world was upon him, and weak disciples were about him. He prayed. He prayed earnestly; he prayed agonizingly. He brought with him the chosen three to share his load. They failed.

The three were invited by Jesus to "watch with me" (26:38). Each time he returned from offering his supplications to the Father, they were sleeping. He asked Peter, "So, could you not watch with me one hour?" (26:40). Then he said to the three, "Watch and pray that you may not enter into temptation. The spirit indeed is willing, but the flesh is weak" (26:41). They failed to stay alert, not realizing their Adversary was on the prowl—even when their Lord was nearby. They failed to pray, at least as earnestly as they should have. They slept.

The three, with the nine, did enter into temptation. They all forsook their Lord during his and their hour of trial. We still read of those failures. Are we any better? Are we failing to meet temptation triumphantly? Are we alert, watchful disciples of Jesus? Are we willing in spirit but weak as they were? Has not our Lord told us the secret of overcoming in the hour of trial and temptation?

It is an axiom of the Kingdom: Those who pray well live well; and those who live well, pray well. Let us confess our weakness, but let us also confess God's strength, and receive his divine energy to enable us to watch and to pray. Our weakness joined with his strength equals victory.

*Help me to watch and pray,
And on thyself rely,
Assured, if I my trust betray,
I shall forever die.**

Look and Live

*And the Lord said to Moses, "Make a fiery serpent and set it on
a pole, and everyone who is bitten, when he sees it, shall live."*
Numbers 21:8

It was the nature of God's covenant people to murmur and complain. In Numbers 21, they are complaining because of the type of food God furnished them—manna in the morning and quail in the evening.

Our Father-God does not approve of our complaints about his provisions. He sent "fiery serpents among the people, and they bit the people, so that many people of Israel died" (21:6). When in trouble, Israel was quick to repent, as they did on this occasion. Ever the faithful intercessor, Moses sought God for an answer. He was instructed to manufacture a "fiery serpent and set it on a pole." "So Moses made a bronze serpent and set it on a pole. And if a serpent bit anyone, he would look at the bronze serpent and live" (21:9).

In speaking to the inquiring Nicodemus one night, Jesus drew upon this Old Testament account: "And as Moses lifted up the serpent in the wilderness, so must the Son of Man be lifted up, that whoever believes in him may have eternal life" (John 3:14-15). How is it that incident in the wilderness is analogous to Christ's death and the eternal life he gives?

• We have all been "bitten" by sin, and sin is a deadly poison (Rom. 3:23; 6:23).

• The remedy for our "bite" (sin) was lifted up on a piece of wood, a cross (Phil. 2:8).

• Since the Hebrew word for bronze can also be translated copper, this figure may have been made from copper, since we know this mineral was mined in that region. Copper is a reddish substance; "the blood of Christ cleanses from all sin" (1 John 1:7).

• The poisoned people were saved when they looked at the serpent; we are saved when we look to Christ (John 3:15).

"Look and live," my brother, live,
Look to Jesus now, and live;
'Tis recorded in His word, hallelujah!
It is only that you "look and live."*

Sojourners

"Hear my prayer, O Lord, and give ear to my cry; hold not your peace at my tears! For I am a sojourner with you, a guest, like all my fathers."
Psalm 39:12

Are we sincerely able to identify with the psalmist? He says, "I am a sojourner with you." Sojourners are Christians in transit; the country in which they reside is not their true home. With the apostle, they often confess, "Our citizenship is in heaven, and from it we await a Savior, the Lord Jesus Christ" (Phil. 3:20).

When the people of Israel entered their land of promise, they were informed by Yahweh they should consider themselves as essentially tenants of the land of their inheritance. For this reason, they were directed not to sell the land, for the land was the Lord's: "The land shall not be sold in perpetuity, for the land is mine. For you are strangers and sojourners with me" (Lev. 25:23).

Nowhere under the New Covenant does our Lord disallow property ownership. However, the practice of God's people viewing themselves as sojourners is clearly expressed in the New Testament. In urging Christians to "abstain from the passions of the flesh," Peter called them "sojourners and exiles" (1 Pet. 2:11). Do you consider yourself a permanent dweller in this world, or are you living as a Christian sojourner, someone who is on a journey "to the city that has foundations, whose designer and builder is God" (Heb. 11:10)?

A Christian sojourner's conduct in this world will be reflected in how he manages time ... uses money ... treats the body ... cares for the soul ... relates to others ... employs one's gifts. The sojourner lives joyfully in the present, but always keeps an eye on the Prize—our victorious Lord.

Peter Kreeft shares a good test, as to whether or not we are real sojourners or just pretenders, by asking ourselves a question: "Have you done or avoided or given up a single thing today solely because you believed that God wanted you to?"*

Many of us will weep because of *what* we leave behind! Instead, let's identify with the saints of old who freely confessed: "For here we have no lasting city, but we seek the city that is to come" (Heb. 13:14).

Saved by Blood

*"The blood shall be a sign for you, on the houses where you are.
And when I see the blood, I will pass over you, and no plague
will befall you to destroy you, when I strike the land of Egypt."*
Exodus 12:13

After living in Egypt for centuries, and with Pharaoh's tyranny increasingly oppressive, God mercifully responds to the cry of his children. Moses was anointed to lead them out of bondage; however, Pharaoh's heart was hardened following every agreement to release the Hebrews, no matter the plague. Finally, Yahweh issues his ultimatum—the shedding of blood.

Every head of a household was directed by Yahweh to fetch a lamb on the tenth of the month; the selected lamb was to have no physical defects ("without blemish"). Four days later, the chosen lamb was to be slaughtered. Some of the lamb's blood was to be applied to the door posts and lintel, in each house where the sacrificed lamb was eaten. Yahweh informed them how the lamb should be eaten: "with your belt fastened, your sandals on your feet, and your staff in your hand. And you shall eat it in haste" (12:11). It was called "the LORD'S Passover." It was called such, because as the Lord passed over Egypt that night, every house which had the blood applied to its door would be spared the death of the firstborn: "when I see the blood, I will pass over you."

Christ is our Passover: "Christ, our Passover lamb, has been sacrificed" (1 Cor. 5:7). For each repentant, believing sinner who obediently appropriates God's atoning Lamb, death is averted; eternal life is given, and hope springs eternal.

It was a dreadful night, that night in Egypt, for throughout the vast country, fathers and mothers and sons and daughters were grieving over the loss of the firstborn child—all, that is, except in the homes where a lamb's blood had been applied.

Judgment is coming, all will be there,
Each one receiving justly his due;
Hide in the saving sin-cleansing blood,
*And I will pass, will pass over you.**

Is Christ your Passover Lamb?

The Father's Lamb

*Abraham said, "God will provide for himself
the lamb for a burnt offering, my son."*
Genesis 22:8

While there were many kinds of animals offered in Israel's long sacrificial system, the lamb became God's primary symbol, representing the future self-sacrificial offering of his Son in mankind's redemption. Multiple thousands, if not millions, of lambs were slain by Jewish priests through the centuries on the prescribed bronze altar of sacrifice.

The first explicit occurrence in the Old Testament of a lamb being offered in sacrifice is found in the Genesis 22 narrative. Abraham, at Yahweh's instruction, was providentially given a lamb as a substitute for the life of Isaac his son. Isaac needs not to die, for Yahweh provided a lamb.

The next instance of a lamb being offered in sacrifice to the Lord is located in Exodus 12. The Hebrew people are on the cusp of leaving Egyptian bondage, but not before the shedding of a lamb's blood—undoubtedly thousands of lambs. Because Pharaoh repeatedly refused to release the Hebrew people to Moses' care, God designed a final and perfect measure. Lambs were to be slain; their blood would be shed. The head of each household was to select carefully the appropriate lamb: "Your lamb shall be without blemish" (12:5). Just as these lambs were to have no physical defects, the Father's Lamb had no moral defects; he was perfect in every respect: "holy, innocent, unstained, separated from sinners" (Heb. 7:26).

When John saw Jesus walking along one of Palestine's dusty roads one day, he immediately recognized the Father's Lamb. The prophet cried out, "Behold, the Lamb of God ..." This was not just any lamb; this was God's Lamb, the Father's Lamb! However, John did not stop with that. He cried out for all to hear, "Behold, the Lamb of God who *takes away the sin of the world!*" (John 1:29).

Yes, God the Father provided for fallen mankind a Lamb! When the Lamb was offered that dreadful and glorious day on Golgotha's brow, it was the Father's Lamb, the Father's atoning substitutionary Sacrifice for the sins of the world—even yours, even mine!

A Changed Man

And they came to Jesus and saw the demon-possessed
man, the one who had had the legion, sitting there,
clothed and in his right mind, and they were afraid.
Mark 5:15

While browsing through a used-book store in January, 1971, I came across a biography of Henry Milans (1861-1946). It is an amazing story of a life almost destroyed, but one remarkably transformed by the power of God.

When his father returned from the Civil War, the family moved from Pennsylvania to the nation's capital. As a young man, Henry began working in a printer's shop, where he fell in love with ink and type, and also developed an appetite for alcohol. By age 20, Henry was an alcoholic. Nevertheless, he steadily rose through the newspaper business until he became managing editor of the *New York Daily Mirror*.

It was said that Henry had mastered his profession but failed to master himself; alcohol consumed him. Eventually, he entered Bellevue Hospital. A visiting professor from Cornell University told his class in Henry's presence, "This is a case of hopeless alcoholism. He cannot be cured. He must die drunk."

Fired from his job, unable to maintain employment anywhere, Henry ended up a drunken bum. On a Thanksgiving morning, 1910, Milans awakened under a warehouse loading platform. Almost frozen to death, he looked into the eyes of a sweet girl; she was dressed in a Salvation Army uniform. She invited him to a service. For a week, Henry attended services until he surrendered fully to the claims of the Lord Jesus Christ. What science and social programs cannot do, the power of God can!

His life was transformed. For the rest of his life, he never touched a drop of alcohol, and testified that God had miraculously taken the appetite away. Dr. Wilbur Chapman—the "Billy Graham" of his day—featured Milans in his crusades. Chapman once said, "I know all the famous converts in America, but Milans is the greatest of them all."* As with the transformed demon-possessed man in Mark 5, Milans spent the remainder of his life telling "how much Jesus had done for him" (5:20).

The Mission of Jesus

"Behold, I have come to do your will, O God."
Hebrews 10:7

I wonder how many of the earth's population knows where they came from, why they are here, and where they are going. The Son of Man, who was also the Son of God, knew the answer to all three questions. From Jesus' own self-testimony, observe what he said about where he came from, why he was here, and where he was going.

• Jesus knew both his place of origin and his destination. "I know where I came from and where I am going" (John 8:14).
• Jesus came to do the will of his Father. "Behold, I have come to do your will, O God" (Heb. 10:7).
• Jesus came to fulfill the Law of God. "Do not think that I have come to abolish the Law or the Prophets; I have not come to abolish them but to fulfill them" (Matt. 5:17).
• Jesus came to serve others. "The Son of Man came not to be served but to serve" (Matt. 20:28).
• Jesus came to impart the very life of God to believing people. "I came that they may have life and have it abundantly" (John 10:10).
• Jesus came to teach the truth of God, which resulted in opposition and persecution. "I came to cast fire on the earth, and would that it were already kindled!" (Luke 12:49).
• Jesus came to find lost people. "For the Son of Man came to seek and to save the lost" (Luke 19:10).
• Jesus came to lay down his life as an atoning sacrifice for sin. "The Son of Man came ... to give his life as a ransom for many (Matt. 20:28).

Will you rejoice just now, that the Lord Jesus *came*?!

Man of sorrows what a name
for the Son of God, who came
ruined sinners to reclaim:
Hallelujah, what a Savior!*

November 26

Judgment and Judgmentalism

For what have I to do with judging outsiders? Is it not those
inside the church whom you are to judge? God judges
those outside. "Purge the evil person from among you."
1 Corinthians 5:12

Contrary to popular belief, there is a type of judgment God approves, as well as an attitude of judgmentalism he disapproves. Living in the miasma of tolerance and moral ambiguity that we are, it has become increasingly unpopular for the saints to vocalize God's truth with regard to socially acceptable sins. Christians have become timid in the marketplace, as well as in much of the church.

In the 1 Corinthians 5 narrative, the Apostle Paul rebukes the church's leadership for tolerating in their fellowship a man who is living in an incestuous relationship with his stepmother. The apostle said such conduct was not "tolerated even among pagans" (v. 1). The church turned a blind eye to immorality in their midst. Would Paul make a judgment? "For though absent in body, I am present in spirit; and as if present, I have already *pronounced judgment* on the one who did such a thing" (v. 3).

Paul made a judgment, and he called the church to do the same: "Let him who has done this be removed from among you" (v. 2)— excommunicate him! This sounds harsh to our ears, which have become desensitized to sin in the church. Paul's concern was that if overt sin was not confronted in the church, it would spread; others would begin to think it was acceptable behavior: "Do you not know that a little leaven leavens the whole lump? Cleanse out the old leaven that you may be a new lump, as you really are unleavened" (vv. 6 -7). To underscore his point, Paul adds, "I am writing to you not to associate with anyone who bears the name of *brother* if he is guilty of sexual immorality or greed, or is an idolater, reviler, drunkard, or swindler—not even to eat with such a one" (v. 11). Then note who is responsible for making these kinds of judgments: "For what have I to do with judging outsiders? Is it not those *inside* the church whom you are to judge? God judges those *outside*" (vv. 12-13).

There you have it: the church is to judge insiders; God will judge the outsiders.

Calling Sinners to Repentance

Jesus said to her, "Go, call your husband, and come here." The woman answered him, "I have no husband." Jesus said to her, "You are right in saying, 'I have no husband'; for you have had five husbands, and the one you now have is not your husband. What you have said is true."
John 4:16-18

Since Paul says the church is to judge insiders and God is to judge outsiders (1 Cor. 5:12-13), how does this relate to calling sinners to repentance? Should pastors and teachers call sin for what it is—from the pulpit and in Bible study groups? Should witnesses for Christ be silent about sinful behavior?

In a Bible study class some years ago, the issue of homosexuality was discussed, and defended as an acceptable Christian lifestyle by one of the class members. Following the study, that member's wife asked a minister who was present, "Then what message does the church have for those in our community who are living a homosexual lifestyle if you say their behavior is sinful?" The response given was: "The same message John the Baptist and Jesus gave to sinners in their day: 'Repent and believe the gospel'" (Mark 1:15; Matt. 4:17). The silence was almost deafening.

The Lord Jesus was never brash in calling sinners to repentance, but neither was he timid. He loved the sinner; he was the sinner's friend, and he died for sinners. He tactfully and discerningly shared truth with his listeners; he lovingly revealed to them their hearts. Jesus knew that unless a person was willing to forsake their sin, they could not embrace his grace and holiness. Thus, he discreetly informed the thirsty-hearted Samaritan woman that he was quite aware of her sinful lifestyle: "You are right in saying, 'I have no husband'; for you have had five husbands, and the one you now have is not your husband. What you have said is true."

Jesus' voice was not *shrill* in calling this sin-burdened woman to repentance. He knew that once she tasted the "water" he offered she would be forever changed. This woman never resented that Jesus revealed her sins (some will, of course). No, she went back home and announced: "He told me all that I ever did" (John 4:39).

Calling people to repent requires wisdom as well as humble boldness. The Spirit will teach us if we will listen.

November 28

Relinquishing Control

*"Truly, truly, I say to you, when you were young, you used to
dress yourself and walk wherever you wanted, but when
you are old, you will stretch out your hands, and another
will dress you and carry you where you do not want to go."*
John 21:18

Simon Peter was accustomed to being in control. As a self-employed businessman, he fished when and where he chose. It was always his decision on which side of the boat to cast his net; and he decided when to call it a night. He was not easily persuaded to change his mind, even by his Lord.

Each of us is born with a twisted need to be in control of our time, career, schedule, space, and a plethora of assorted self-centered activities. We came into this world believing it revolved around us. Then comes the clash of wills—ours and God's. Jesus calls, "If anyone would come after me, let him deny himself" (Mark 8:34). Immediately, we face our autonomous selves. Who will win this war of wills? Who will control?

Since we can't control God, we attempt to control others: our children after they leave home, our spouse, our little environment, even those in authority over us. The more out of control we are, the more we try to control others.

Slowly, Simon Peter learned the lessons about who should rightfully control his life. Nevertheless, he repeatedly attempted to force himself upon others and his Lord. From his attempt to dissuade Jesus from dying on the cross—"Peter took him aside and began to rebuke him" (Mark. 8:32)—to his meddlesome inquiry—"Lord, what about this man?" (John 21:21)—Simon Peter tried to control others, as well as his destiny. However, Peter's life was fundamentally changed at Pentecost. For there he received a pure heart (Acts 15:9). When the heart is cleansed, one no longer needs to be in control; he now joyfully loves to be controlled by his Shepherd.

When it came his time to die, Peter could peacefully "stretch out [his] hands, and [allow another to] dress [him] and carry [him] where [he did] not want to go." How could he do that? Because he followed the footsteps of his Lord, who prayed, "Not as I will, but as you will" (Matt. 26:39).

Heavenly Wisdom

But the wisdom from above is first pure, then peaceable, gentle, open to reason, full of mercy and good fruits, impartial and sincere.
James 3:17

The Christian and local churches are always making decisions. How, what, and why we decide issues, which have moral and ethical implications, will depend upon the spiritual condition of the heart. If the heart is right before God, informed by his Word, and keeping step with the Holy Spirit, then we are in an excellent position to make critical decisions.

God has informed us why some are *incapable* of making wise decisions in the body of Christ: "you have bitter jealousy and selfish ambition in your hearts" (James 3:14). These people are looking out for themselves; they are self-centered, and proud. The counsel such people offer, says James, "is earthly, unspiritual, demonic" (3:15). Where this kind of "wisdom" prevails, "there will be disorder and every vile practice" (3:16).

What does heavenly wisdom look like—"the wisdom from above" (3:17)? God tells us in James 1:17.

"Pure." God will never lead his people to have impure motives or engage in impure conduct. God is holy; he calls his people to walk in righteousness and true holiness.

"Peaceable." God's people should be peace-loving people. When contending for the truth, they are not to be contentious. In arguing for the right, they are not to be argumentative.

"Gentle." Gentleness is a product of the Spirit (Gal. 5:23); it is the opposite of harshness. To be gentle is to exercise the kindness of God under provocation.

"Open to reason." This is a willingness to yield. A Christian is to be strong in heart, not strong headed. In matters indifferent, we should be reasonable people.

"Full." We are to be "full of mercy" toward those who fail; we are to be full of "good fruits," not evil works.

"Impartial and sincere." Our judgments should be without prejudice; our lives should be lived without pretense.

Ask often for God to grant you this kind of wisdom. It only comes from above.

Suffering Saints

Weep with those who weep.
Romans 12:15

As I pen these words, many followers of the Lamb are suffering; and a great number have sealed their testimony with their blood. Suffering and death for the cause of God are not new phenomena. In addressing the religious elite one day, Jesus said, "from the blood of righteous Abel to the blood of Zechariah the son of Barachiah," God's people have died for the faith (Matt. 23:35). John the Baptist was killed because he spoke truth. Stephen was the church's first martyr. Of the twelve apostles, tradition informs us that except for John, each was killed because of his allegiance to the Lord Jesus.

In the Apostle Paul's personal greetings throughout his letters, he identifies many who suffered for Jesus' sake. For example, in Romans 16, he writes of Prisca and Aquila, "who risked their necks for my life"; of Andronicus and Junia, he said they were "my fellow prisoners." Addressing the Thessalonian believers, Paul noted they had "received the word in much affliction" (1 Thess. 1:6). Of course, Paul himself suffered greatly for Christ (e.g., see 2 Cor. 11:23-27). And Jesus himself was the foremost sufferer.

We should remember those who are suffering for Christ. We may not know them personally, but we can still faithfully offer them to the Lord in prayer. It was said of some first-century Christians, "you had compassion on those in prison." Those believers were encouraged to "Remember those who are in prison, as though in prison with them, and those who are mistreated, since you also are in the body" (Heb. 10:34; 13:3). They were in prison because they would not deny Jesus.

It has frequently been said that more Christians have suffered and died for their faith in the last and the beginning of this century than the first nineteen centuries. Whether they are Catholic or Orthodox, Protestant or Coptic, if they have confessed Jesus is Lord by the Holy Spirit, they are our brothers and sisters in Christ, and we have been called to "weep with those who weep" (Rom. 12:14).

Remember, O Lord, your suffering saints, we pray.

The Presence (part 1)

And he said, "My presence will go with you, and I will give you rest."
Exodus 33:14

The children of Israel were privileged people; they were repeatedly the unworthy recipients of God's merciful grace. For Israel, Yahweh raised up Moses, a God-fearing man; delivered his chosen people from Egypt; met their physical needs day by day; and gave Israel the Law.

However, these were stiff-necked and often defiant people. Before Moses descended from the Mount, where the Law was given, the erring multitude had constructed an idol, with Aaron's passive permission. God was angry, and so was Moses. Through Moses' intercession, God spares the people, though three thousand lost their lives.

Following the golden calf debacle, Yahweh directs Moses to resume the journey; however, he informs him, "but I will not go with you" (Ex. 33:3). Yahweh told Moses that even though he would no longer be present among the people, he would send an angel and drive out the pagan nations. Moses would have none of it; he had to get alone with Yahweh, and talk the matter over.

It was in the Tent of Meeting that Moses bared his soul before Yahweh. Whenever Moses entered this tent, "the pillar of cloud would descend and stand at the entrance of the tent, and the Lord would speak with Moses" (33:9). It was in this tent that "the Lord used to speak to Moses face to face, as a man speaks to his friend" (33:11).

Moses had to settle the issue: Was Yahweh going with him and Israel on their journey to Canaan or not? Yahweh relents: "My presence will go with you, and I will give you rest" (33:14). Moses' response? "If your presence will not go with me, do not bring us up from here" (33:14).

We should never take for granted that God is "with" us, as we seek to fulfill his assigned missions and tasks. I sometimes wonder: How many church members would know it if the Holy Spirit suddenly absented himself from their gatherings? Would the "show" just go on?

The Presence (part 2)

*"For how shall it be known that I have found favor in your sight, I
and your people? Is it not in your going with us, so that we are distinct,
I and your people, from every other people on the face of the earth?"*
Exodus 33:16

Moses learned his lesson. There was a time when he endeavored to
do the work of God on his own initiative and in his own strength.
He was a born leader, who had an intuitive sense of justice. While
still a young man, Moses saw an Egyptian beating one of his fellow
Hebrews; he immediately saw the injustice and killed the man.
However, Moses' ways were not Yahweh's ways. Thus, the sovereign
Lord sent Moses into the wilderness to be schooled and disciplined
by him. It was in the wilderness where Moses learned the ways of
Yahweh; it was there he experienced the revealed presence of the "I
Am."

Israel was special to Yahweh. To Israel was given the Law, the
tabernacle and later the temple—the unique dwelling places of God.
God also gave to his people a special identifying sign, the sign of
circumcision. To Israel was given a unique day, the Sabbath, as well
as many feasts and ceremonies.

However, when Moses is imploring God for help and reassurance, his reliance is not upon Israel's history and past victories; he
does not boast about Israel's unique signs, rituals, and ceremonies.
No, Moses fully understood what made Israel "Israel": "Is it not in
your going with us, so that we are distinct, I and your people, from
every other people on the face of the earth?"

We are so presumptuous, assuming God will bless our efforts.
However, Moses knew differently. Following Israel's refusal to enter
Canaan at Kadesh-Barnea, and God's announced discipline for their
disobedience, a delegation said they would go anyway. Moses
warned them that Yahweh would not be with them: "But they *pre-
sumed* to go up to the heights of the hill country, although neither the ark of the covenant of the Lord nor Moses departed out of
the camp. Then the Amalekites and the Canaanites who lived in that
hill country came down and defeated them ..." (Num. 14:44-45).

God's manifest presence is what distinguishes his people from
all other people. Are we convinced of this?

December 3

The Presence (part 3)

And he said, "My presence will go with you, and I will give you rest."
Exodus 33:14

Moses would settle for no substitutes. Neither an angel, nor successful military campaigns alone would satisfy this leader of God's people. He must know that God was in the midst of his people. Moses knew God personally; he encountered and pleaded with God. He was not content to go another step without knowing Yahweh would continue the journey with him and the people: "Please show me your glory" (Ex. 33:18). God heard the cry of his servant.

For New Covenant Christians, "God's glory has shone in our hearts to give the light of the knowledge of the glory of God in the face of Jesus Christ" (2 Cor. 4:6). Are we gazing on Jesus?

The Spirit himself, indwelling us, is God with us—Immanuel. The Holy Spirit is God's presence, Christ's presence with us. We must settle for no substitutes, and we should not *assume* he is blessing *our* efforts and *our* ministries. Moses assumed nothing! In the words of David, "Seek the LORD and his strength; seek his presence continually" (1 Chron. 16:11).

More than a way out of my darkness,
  more than joy in my distress;
More than a remedy for sickness—
  I need Christ himself!

More than relief from a bad conscience,
  more than smiling Providence;
More than a signal of his presence—
  I need Christ himself!

More than mere feelings without measure,
  more than blessings I treasure;
More than passing sentient pleasure—
  I need Christ himself!

More than titillating sensation,
  more than a revelation;
More than a brilliant visitation—
  I need Christ himself!

All of these gifts absent the Giver,
  leave the heart like a pauper;
Let me trust in only the Savior—
  then I'll have Christ himself!

December 4

The Presence (part 4)

"And the name of the city from that time on shall be, 'The LORD is There.'"
Ezekiel 48:35

While pastoring in the city of Chicago, the Lord was pleased to prosper the ministry of his servant, Dwight L. Moody (1837-1899). A poor little boy used to travel some distance to Moody's church Sunday after Sunday. A neighborhood police officer took note of the lad making his weekly trips to the church. Curious as to why the boy would walk by himself to go to church so far removed from his own community, the officer asked him one Sunday morning, "Son, why do you go to Mr. Moody's church?" The boy was quick to reply, "Because they love a fella down there."

It was my privilege, many years ago, to pastor one of God's choice saints. As with all of God's special people, Grandma Berg was a bit quaint. Up in years at the time, she traveled several miles to our church. One day, she said to me, "Brother Tilley, I was talking to the Lord recently and asked him a question. I said, 'Lord, there is a church right across the street from where I am living; why should I travel such a distance to the church I attend?'" Then Grandma Berg's face lit up. "Pastor, do you know what the Lord answered?" I shook my head. She said the Lord told her (and believe me, she and the Lord were on speaking terms), "Because I am present in that church and not in the one across the street."

What will make Heaven special will be the presence of God: "And I saw no temple in the city, for its temple is the Lord God the Almighty and the Lamb. And the city has no need of sun or moon to shine on it, for the glory of God gives it light, and its lamp is the Lamb" (Rev. 21:23). What makes a local church an authentic church is the manifest presence of the Holy One meeting with his people; it is a place where the holy love and presence of Jesus caused a little boy and a Grandma Berg to travel a distance to attend.

It requires more than stained-glass windows and a pipe organ and a traditional liturgy and an ornate structure and an orator in the pulpit to make a church. A church is not a church unless the Lord Jesus is welcomed in the person of the Holy Spirit. God's thirsty-hearted people will travel a distance to attend a church like that.

December 5

Coming Down from the Mountain

*While Moses went up to God. The Lord called to him
out of the mountain, saying, "Thus you shall say to the
house of Jacob, and tell the people of Israel: ..."*
Exodus 19:3

In the Scriptures, the "mountain" is often the place where God reveals himself and his will to a person. Following such a revelation,
the person was to go down the mountain and begin to implement
God's revealed plan. Such was the case with the man Moses. God
revealed himself to Moses on Mount Sinai. In that revelation, God
gave to his servant his holy Law, which in turn was to be delivered
to the people in the valley.

What we do after our experiences on the *Mount* will determine
our life in the *valley*. God brings us near to himself through the
preached or read Word of God. We see his truth; the Spirit of God
reveals to us a course of action we should take. As we delight in the
wonderful truth and presence of God, we aspire to do his will. What
happens next? We descend the *mountain*, (leaving a church service,
or concluding our quiet time with the Lord). We walk out into life's
plains and *valleys* forgetting and failing to follow through with what
the Spirit revealed to us on the *mountain*. Thus, we return to our
idols, our disobedience, our neglect, our powerlessness.

Three disciples once came down from a mountain one day after
experiencing a wonderful revelation of the Lord Jesus. However,
when they returned to the valley, they were powerless. They were
powerless because they failed to translate their time with Jesus into
actions of faith.

Let us care what we do after God reveals himself to us. See to it
that you fulfill your tasks "through hours of gloom." Matthew Arnold (1822-1888) said it well:

> We cannot kindle when we will
> The fire that in the heart resides,
> The Spirit bloweth and is still,
> In mystery our soul abides;
> But tasks, in hours of insight willed,
> Can be through hours of gloom fulfilled.*

December 6

Others

"I must preach the good news of the kingdom of God to the other towns as well; for I was sent for this purpose."
Luke 4:43

The Lord Jesus Christ was the most selfless person who ever walked on the face of this earth. Never did the Son of Man act selfishly. He always did those things that pleased his Father, and in pleasing his Father, his human interactions were others-oriented.

Jesus came to serve others; he came to seek and to save the lost. To the blind and lame, the diseased and demon possessed, the hungry and grieving, the poor and troubled—everywhere Jesus went he was lifting burdens, proclaiming liberty, healing the sick and showing compassion and mercy. Where he found sinners, Jesus showed them the way to the Father; where he discovered ignorance, Jesus taught the truth of God; where he saw hypocrisy, he exposed the lie. Jesus invested his life in reaching out to others.

In serving and seeking others, our Lord's self-interests were always subordinated to the will of his Father. Jesus was never motivated by *sinful* self-interests. As the Son of Man, he made daily choices, whether he would allow even legitimate interests to interfere with the Father's interests for him. As a man, Jesus had physical needs and family concerns like any person. However, he did not allow the necessities of life to detract from his daily mission and ultimate calling.

"Let each of us please his neighbor for his good, to build him up. For Christ did not please himself, but as it is written, 'The reproaches of those who reproached you fell on me'" (Rom. 15:2-3). Self-pleasing is not the way of Jesus; the Cross is the ultimate proof of that.

Each of us has a unique calling in life, but whatever our calling is, it must center in pleasing the Father and serving others to the glory of God. One Christmas the founder of the Salvation Army, William Booth (1829-1912), sent a one-word greeting to his officers around the world. His message was "OTHERS."

In the home, in the church, in life's marketplace, the disciple of Jesus, who is walking in God's light, will be thinking more of others than himself.

No Little People

"She has done what she could."
Mark 14:8

H. C. Morrison (1857-1942) twice served as president of Asbury College (now University), and was the founder of Asbury Theological Seminary; he also served the Methodist Church as a pastor and evangelist.

When Morrison was appointed to his first church in Stanford, Kentucky, he immediately began to get acquainted with the area pastors and inquired about the needs of the community. The Baptist pastor told him, "The spiritual life here is none too good. We need a revival. There is a wonderful woman down here at the toll gate on the Crab Orchard Pike. Her name is Mary McAfee [1844-1902]. She is a very remarkable Christian; a little peculiar in her views, but wonderfully filled with the Spirit. If we had more like her, the churches would be in much better condition. She is a member of your church." Morrison asked the same question of the Presbyterian Church pastor, and his reply was, "Have you met Mary McAfee? She is a member of your congregation. She keeps the toll gate down here on the Crab Orchard Pike, something more than half a mile out. You must call to see her. She is a remarkable saint, has some queer notions, but has a wonderful experience. She claims an experience of full salvation, and she certainly lives very close to her Lord." Everywhere the new pastor went he heard about Mary McAfee. In time, a reporter from the Courier-Journal newspaper (Louisville, Ky.) learned about Mary and wrote an article, "Mary McAfee: The Sanctified Tollgate Keeper."

Years later, Dr. Morrison returned to Stanford to speak at Mary McAfee's funeral. He wrote afterward: "As I stood by the plain coffin and looked at her quiet, saintly face that seemed to tell of a soul that had entered into eternal rest, I hadn't a doubt but directly and indirectly a hundred thousand souls had been touched for good through the holy life and the beautiful testimony of a little maiden woman who kept the toll gate on the Crab Orchard Turnpike in the outskirts of Stanford, Kentucky."*

Mary simply did what she could—in the power of the Spirit.

December 8

The Allure of the Sirens

And your ears shall hear a word behind you, saying, "This is the way,
walk in it," when you turn to the right or when you turn to the left.
Isaiah 30:21

In Greek mythology, the Sirens were beautiful but seductive female creatures. These fantasy figures loved to entice sailors with their enchanting music, hoping to lure them to their shore, making shipwreck.

Odysseus long desired to hear the songs of the Sirens, but he knew if he ever succumbed to their alluring sounds, he would lose all rational thought. Thus, upon approaching the shore one day, he put wax in the ears of his own sailors, and had them tie him to the ship's mast, so he might not yield to the temptation to jump into the sea, joining the Sirens. Nearing the shore, the Sirens began to sing their tempting music; however, though he wanted to join them, his men kept Odysseus safe.

There are times in one's Christian pilgrimage, when the Sirens of temptation become almost irresistible. In those moments, the cross of Christ is our only safety; we must *tie ourselves* to the cross, lest we yield to the sounds of the "Sirens." In the cross of Christ, we find the power to overcome.

> *Yield not to temptation, for yielding is sin;*
> *Each victory will help you some other to win;*
> *Fight manfully onward, dark passions subdue,*
> *Look ever to Jesus, He'll carry you through.*
>
> Refrain
> *Ask the Savior to help you,*
> *Comfort, strengthen and keep you;*
> *He is willing to aid you,*
> *He will carry you through.* *

The prophet Isaiah foresaw a day when a Teacher would appear in the world, who would instruct his followers through the Holy Spirit. When tempted to lose one's way, the promise is, "And your ears shall hear a word behind you, saying, 'This is the way, walk in it,' when you turn to the right or when you turn to the left" (Isa. 30:21). Christ is our safety; the Spirit is our enabler.

December 9

"I Kissed My Mule"

And Zacchaeus stood and said to the Lord, "Behold, Lord, the half of my goods I give to the poor. And if I have defrauded anyone of anything, I restore it fourfold." And Jesus said to him, "Today salvation has come to this house, since he also is a son of Abraham."
Luke 19:8-9

I once pastored a church in which a dear sister in Christ told me a remarkable story regarding her husband's conversion to Christ. By the time I arrived at the church, her husband had gone to be with the Lord. After relating his conversion account, she handed me a little gospel tract he had written, recounting his story.

Joe immigrated to America in 1903. He had worked in the coal mines in France, and upon traveling to Illinois, found employment doing the same. He was raised in a nominal Christian family, but had never heard prayer offered by either parent. He lived a hard, sinful life, and much of his time was spent in the local tavern.

Joe loved baseball. One Sunday, as he was on his way to a game, he saw some people gathered on the street corner. Curious, he went over to listen. He never went to the ball game. The two following Sundays, he did the same thing; he wanted to hear what these people were talking about. Following the meeting on the third Sunday, Joe went home and prayed, "Lord, have mercy on me!" He said, "The room seemed to light up. I knew I was a new creature in Christ."

On the third day following his conversion, Joe was getting ready to leave home for the mine; he was a mule driver. He said, "As I threw the whip over my shoulder, a voice spoke to me, 'Joe, what are you going to do?'" Joe said, "I knew it was the voice of God; I had used that whip on my poor mule until his body was scarred all over."

When he arrived at the mine, Joe walked over to his mule. Putting his arm around the mule, he asked for his forgiveness. "I told him I had been mean to him, and wasn't going to use a whip on him anymore. I pulled his head to my face and kissed him on the nose."

As it was with Zacchaeus, so it was with Joe. When Jesus enters one's life, wonderful changes occur—even in how we treat animals!

Serving the Saints

For God is not unjust so as to overlook your work and the love that you have shown for his name in serving the saints, as you still do.
Hebrews 6:10

Samuel Brengle (1860-1936) was born into poverty in southern Indiana. In the providence of God, he was converted and called to preach at an early age. Observing his giftedness and devotion to Christ, the Lord touched the hearts of people with means to provide for his education. Brengle graduated with honors from DePauw University; while there, he frequently preached in local churches.

He was encouraged to pursue his studies further and enrolled at Boston University, where he also excelled. While studying under Dr. Daniel Steele, Brengle experienced a powerful enduement of the Spirit, which prepared him for future ministry. Before he graduated, he had received invitations to pastor some of the largest Methodist churches. However, while listening to William Booth (1829-1912), the founder of the Salvation Army, preach one day, Brengle felt called of God to join this zealous evangelistic organization.

Brengle was required to travel to London for training. Though General Booth thought Brengle was unfit for the Army, because of his extensive education, Brengle assured the general that God had called him.

Brengle's training began in a dark cellar. His biographer relates the following. "He found himself with eighteen pairs of muddy boots, a can of blacking, and a sharp temptation. Remembering the Lord's story of the man who buried his talent, he prayed, 'Lord God, am I burying my talent? Is this the best they can do for me in the Salvation Army? Am I a fool? Have I followed my own fancy 3,000 miles to come here to black boots?'" Then the Lord reminded Brengle that he himself had washed the feet of his disciples. Brengle replied, "Dear Lord, Thou didst wash their feet; I will black their boots." Years later, Brengle wrote, "I had fellowship with Jesus every morning for a week while in that cellar I blacked boots. My new prayer was, 'Dear Lord, let me serve the servants of Jesus. That is sufficient for me.'"*

Are you serving any of God's saints? If not, ask the Lord to show you the saints you might serve—with joy.

The Twice-Born

"One thing I do know, that though I was blind, now I see."
John 9:25

The testimony of the healed blind man in John's Gospel is the evangelical mantra of every adult convert of the Lord Jesus Christ. Millions of men and women through the centuries have spoken of a past and present, a before and after, a death to life, a night and day, a lost and found, a blindness and sight. These changed people were transformed by a Power outside of themselves. That power was the saving gospel of God, made possible by the atoning death of Jesus Christ, and graciously communicated to repentant souls by the blessed Holy Spirit.

> *Amazing grace! How sweet the sound*
> *That saved a wretch like me!*
> *I once was lost, but now am found;*
> *Was blind, but now I see.**

A copy of *Twice-Born Men* by Harold Begbie (1871-1929) has graced a shelf in my library for over thirty years. In this volume of biographical accounts of Christian conversion, this Anglican writer was fascinated by those who underwent an observable transformation. He concluded, "There is no medicine, no Act of Parliament, no moral treatise, and no invention of philanthropy, which can transform a man radically bad into a man radically good."** Before coming to Christ, regardless of one's position in society, we were each "radically bad" in our heart if not always in our behavior. We were lost sheep: "All we like sheep have gone astray; we have turned—every one—to his own way; ..." (Isa. 53:6).

All conversions are not Damascus Road experiences; they are as varied as the convert. However, all twice-born people are given a consciousness, coming from Above, that they are now at peace with God, indwelt by the love of God, and experience the joy of God. In the beginning, they may not be able to explain it; they can only describe it. But they know; they see. They can say with the blind man, "One thing I do know, that though I was blind, now I see."

I, too, know. Whereas I was born for the first time on this date, December 11, I was born again some sixteen years later. By the wonderful grace of God, I am a twice-born man. All glory to God!

Loyal to the Father's Truth

"But because I tell the truth, you do not believe me."
John 8:45

Jesus Christ was neither hated nor crucified because he was *nice*. Jesus did not stir up opposition against himself, raising the ire of many onlookers, because of a particular miracle he performed. As long as Jesus fed the famished multitudes and quietly taught his disciples privately, the prevailing religious authorities would never have been disturbed.

What got Jesus in trouble was *truth*—divine truth. If Jesus had only walked among religious leaders, diplomatically establishing winsome relationships, teaching in an abstract, philosophical way, encouraging everyone to get along, all would have admired him; he would have been awarded the "Nobel Peace Prize." But Jesus did not come to gain admirers; he was sent by the Father to speak the truth into the hearts of people, and to die for the sins of the world.

Why did the message of Jesus create such animosity in so many who heard him?

• Because Jesus claimed to be the eternal Son of God. "Truly, truly, I say to you, before Abraham was, I am" (John 8:58).

• Because Jesus claimed to be the very source of truth and reality, the exclusive path to the Father. "I am the way, and the truth, and the life. No one comes to the Father except through me" (John 14:6).

• Because Jesus exercised authority given him by his Father, instead of bowing to man-made traditions. "But the ruler of the synagogue, indignant because Jesus had healed on the Sabbath ..." (Luke 13:14).

• Because Jesus uncovered the hypocrisy of the self-righteous. "So you also outwardly appear righteous to others, but within you are full of hypocrisy and lawlessness" (Matt. 23:28).

• Because Jesus fearlessly and faithfully spoke truth. "But because I tell the truth, you do not believe me" (John 8:45).

This world would never have had a crucified Jesus if he had not been a truth-speaking Jesus. Satan pays no attention to a benign preacher.

December 13

The Final Judgment

It is appointed for man to die once, and after that comes judgment.
Hebrews 9:27

There is a designated Judgment Day, when the God of creation and redemption will call every person to give an account to him. The Scriptures are clear on this matter. The just God of all the earth has embedded in man's conscience the concept of justice, as well as revealing his standard of justice more definitively through his revealed Word. He is the God of righteousness, who requires righteousness in all people.

For those who are trusting in God's Sin-Bearer, the Lamb of God who takes away the sins of the world, their sins have been judged on the cross. These believers will escape final condemnation because God is "just and the justifier of the one who has faith in Jesus" (Rom. 3:26). "There is therefore now no condemnation for those who are in Christ Jesus" (Rom. 8:1). However, believers will still be judged on the basis of the quality of their works. "For we must all appear before the judgment seat of Christ, so that each one may be recompensed for his deeds in the body, according to what he has done, whether good or bad" (2 Cor. 5:10 NASB).

For those who are not trusting in Christ, and have not been clothed with his righteousness, these will be openly condemned by the just God on that great and awful Day. "Then I saw a great white throne and him who was seated on it. From his presence earth and sky fled away, and no place was found for them. And I saw the dead, great and small, standing before the throne, and books were opened.... And if anyone's name was not found written in the book of life, he was thrown into the lake of fire" (Rev. 20:11-12, 15).

This is a most sobering truth. The Father sent the Son into this world to offer himself as the atoning sacrifice for sin, so that all people may experience eternal life (John 3:16). Without Christ's life, there is nothing left but everlasting death. "Whoever believes in him is not condemned, but whoever does not believe is condemned already, because he has not believed in the name of the only Son of God" (John 3:18).

Are you *trusting* in Christ alone for your salvation? Not "trusted," but "trusting"!

December 14

Doing the Will of God

"Your will be done, on earth as it is in heaven."
Matthew 6:10

Someone has said the most important words in the world are, "Your will be done." Only a child of God can pray those words to his Father in Heaven. For only a person walking in intimacy with the heavenly Father desires the will of God to be done more than anything else in his life. The one who has surrendered his will to the will of God can honestly pray, "Your will be done, on earth as it is in heaven." As long as we insist on our *own* will, we can never pray, "*Your* will be done."

How should the will of God be done by us as it is done in heaven?

• *Delightfully.* What parent takes joy in a child obeying, but obeying without joy? The apostle says we are "to keep God's commandments and do what pleases him" (1 John 3:22). We may be assured that each heavenly being performs his duties with pleasure, delighting to do the will of God. We too should do the will of God with delight.

• *Eagerly.* To demonstrate an earnest and urgent desire and an interest in the performance of an assignment are commendable human qualities. Do we believe the angels Michael and Gabriel were reluctant messengers of the Lord? God's people should long to do God's will, however difficult or unpopular it may be?

• *Diligently.* A teacher remarked about a student, "He certainly is diligent in his studies." Can our Father in heaven say that about you? Are we diligent in the pursuit of a sanctified life in the power of the Spirit?

• *Single-mindedly.* The cherubim in Ezekiel's vision "went straight forward, without turning as they went" (Ezek. 1:9). Similarly, should the will of God be done by each of us. It is not our concern how others may or may not be doing the will of God; our gaze must be on Jesus, not others.

• *Obediently.* When the heart is in tune with God, his servants desire to obey him. When the heart is contaminated, the will of God becomes a drudgery an impossibility. To know God is to embrace his will and to walk with him in humble obedience.

Nourished by the Word

*And he said to me, "Son of man, feed your belly with this
scroll that I give you and fill your stomach with it." Then
I ate it, and it was in my mouth as sweet as honey.*
Ezekiel 3:3

Soon after the Iron Curtain fell in 1990, I traveled twice with ministry teams into the heart of Russia. Following each evening evangelistic service, we gave Bibles in the Russian language to the people. Thousands of copies were distributed to those who had mostly been deprived of having a personal copy of the entire Word of God.

One evening after service, an elderly lady approached me with outstretched hands, begging for a copy of God's Word. As I placed a Bible in her withered hands, she immediately clutched it to her breast, effusively expressing her gratitude, then hurried away, protecting it from anyone who might try snatching it away.

God's written Word should not be thought of as a kind of talisman, possessing some mysterious *magical* power. Nor should it be thought of a sort of religious idol to be worshiped. God's inspired and authoritative words have been preserved for his people to be built up in the most Holy Faith. In referring to the Old Testament Scriptures, Paul wrote, "For whatever was written in former days was written for our instruction, that through endurance and through the encouragement of the Scriptures we might have hope" (Rom. 15:4). This is how all Scripture should be viewed.

The Word of God informs the mind, convicts the conscience, warms the heart, leads us in paths of righteousness, and tells us the truth about God, the Adversary, this world, the future and ourselves. It is like water for the thirsty, meat for the hungry, and an oasis for the weary. What is true of the written Word is true of the Living Word of God. For the written Word will unerringly lead us to the Living Word. To feast on one is to feast on both. "I am the living bread that came down from heaven. If anyone eats of this bread, he will live forever" (John 6:51).

Are you being nourished by the Word, by the Bread from Heaven?

December 16

The Language of Redemption

In him we have redemption through his blood, the forgiveness
of our trespasses, according to the riches of his grace.
Ephesians 1:7

We cannot appreciate what God has revealed in his Word, without having a basic understanding of language. This is true, for example, in the use of prepositions. A preposition is a word governing another word or element in a clause. There are over 150 prepositions in the English language (three are used in the opening sentence of this paragraph). It can be an enlightening and heartwarming study as we read the Word of God, to note how the inspired writers used prepositions concerning what Christ has done for us. In demonstrating this, look briefly at Ephesians 1:3-13, selecting only one preposition, the preposition "in" (italics added), which is used twelve times by the Apostle Paul, denoting our relation to God the Father and the Lord Jesus Christ.

1:3. God has "blessed us *in* Christ ... *in* the heavenly places."

1:4. God "chose us *in* [Christ] before the foundation of the world, that we should be holy and blameless before him."

1:4-5. *In* love he predestined us for adoption as sons through Jesus Christ."

1:6. God has "blessed us *in* the Beloved."

1:7. "*In* [Christ] we have redemption through his blood, the forgiveness of our trespasses."

1:7-8. God's redemption and forgiveness were "lavished upon us, *in* all wisdom and insight."

1:9. God made "known to us the mystery of his will, according to his purpose, which he set forth *in* Christ."

1:10. God's plan is to eventually "unite all things *in* [Christ], things in heaven and things on earth."

1:11. "*In* [Christ] we have obtained an inheritance."

1:12. "*In* [Christ] you also, when you heard the word of truth, the gospel of your salvation, and believed *in* him, were sealed with the promised Holy Spirit."

Dear believer, our merciful God and Father has devised a wonderful plan of redemption *in* Christ, his Son. Let the saints of God be ever filled with joyful gratitude!

God's Plans for His People

*"For I know the plans I have for you, declares the LORD, plans
for welfare and not for evil, to give you a future and a hope."*
Jeremiah 29:11

I experienced a difficult period in pastoral ministry many years ago.
Filled with disappointment and discouragement, a dear sister in
Christ spoke the above words to me one evening, just before she and
her husband left our house. The Spirit took those words, which were
his words, and wrote them on my heart. Soon afterward, I created a
plaque and mounted it on the wall of my study, adding verses 12
and 13. It has been on the wall of my study, above my desktop com-
puter, ever since.

These words (with many others) were first given by Yahweh to
the prophet Jeremiah, and thereafter hand-delivered to God's people in Babylon, by a man named Elasah. Israel was far removed
from the homeland, living as exiles in Babylon. No one enjoys being
away from home for long. Israel was absent from her homeland because of disobedience and defiance. She had forsaken Yahweh and
his Law; she had developed a stiff neck and a hard heart, turning to
idolatry and debauchery.

And yet God speaks to his covenant people in exile in their sins.
He promises to bring them home to Jerusalem, when their seventy
years away from home have been fulfilled: "I will visit you, and I will
fulfill to you my promise and bring you back to this place" (Jer.
29:10).

It could be someone is reading these words that has drifted
away from God's plans for his or her life. You are, as it were, living
in *exile*. Day after day, your mind is filled with a longing for a better
time—a time like you once experienced, as you walked in close intimacy with your Father. Today, don't harden your heart; instead,
listen to God's Word to you: "For I know the plans I have for you,
declares the Lord, plans for welfare and not for evil, to give you a
future and a hope. Then you will call upon me and come and pray to
me, and I will hear you. You will seek me and find me, when you
seek me with all your heart" (Jer. 29:11-13).

God has plans for you! Listen to him. Seek him with all your
heart.

How Much Has God Done for You?

*"Return to your home, and declare how much God has done
for you." And he went away, proclaiming throughout
the whole city how much Jesus had done for him.*
Luke 8:39

The demonized man in the Luke 8 narrative, after his healing and conversion, was a noticeably changed person. Following a prolonged period, when "he had worn no clothes, and he had not lived in a house but among the tombs" (v. 27), the Prophet of Nazareth, God's Son, spoke the word and many "demons came out of the man" (v. 33). Those who knew this man, were struck by his sudden transformation: "Then people went out to see what had happened, and they came to Jesus and found the man from whom the demons had gone, sitting at the feet of Jesus, clothed and in his right mind, and they were afraid" (v. 35).

The healed man was so overcome with joy and gratitude for what Jesus had done, he "begged that he might be with him" (v. 38). We might say he wanted to go into *full-time* Christian service. Jesus had other plans for him: "Return to your home, and declare how much God has done for you" (v. 39).

We were not all demonized prior to our conversion; however, we were all lost sinners. What did God do for you? Jesus says, "Declare how much God has done for you." Do you ever share it? Charles Wesley (1707-1788) did. The fact is he wished he had a thousand tongues to proclaim what God in Christ had done for him.

*O for a thousand tongues to sing
My great Redeemer's praise,
The glories of my God and King,
The triumphs of His grace!*

*My gracious Master and my God,
Assist me to proclaim,
To spread through all the earth abroad
The honors of Thy name.**

The transformed man acted on Jesus' word: "And he went away, proclaiming throughout the whole city how much Jesus had done for him" (v. 39). Shall we do less?

December 19

The Unpredictable Christ

And he looked around at them with anger, grieved
at their hardness of heart, and said to the man, "Stretch out
your hand." He stretched it out, and his hand was restored.
Mark 3:5

The church without the Spirit is very predictable; nothing ever happens that is not printed in the Sunday order of service. Congregants in the typical Western World church can easily predict what will occur in the next service. They can do so, because where the Spirit is absent, Jesus is absent; and when Jesus is absent there is no life, no freshness, and no newness. Everything is boringly predictable.

When the Lord Jesus ministered on earth, there was a spontaneity and an energy, an originality and authenticity, when he taught and labored among the people. There was always a magnetic freshness about Jesus—everywhere he went. That was so, because Jesus walked with his Father in holy intimacy, and ministered in the power of the Spirit.

It mattered not to Jesus that his detractors were invariably present—even in worship services. Jesus never felt intimidated. He lived to hear the approval of his Father; he feared no one. Jesus knew that people grumbled about his message and methods. He was well aware that the elite religionists and protectors of the Law and tradition disapproved of his ways and work. For Jesus, if he could meet a person's need, the venue was immaterial.

In the midst of teaching in the synagogue one Sabbath, Jesus suddenly stopped. He saw a man present with an afflicted hand. There were many needs in the congregation that day, one might well imagine, but here was a man who caught Jesus' attention. Jesus speaks to the man: "Stretch out your hand" (Mark 3:5). There was an immediate healing: "He stretched it out, and his hand was restored" (Mark 3:5).

We should not crave the phenomenal and spectacular. We should simply ask for the manifest presence of Jesus to be among his people. When Jesus is present—really present—one can never predict what may occur. Do you wonder at that? Ask the man who once had a withered hand.

December 20

"Behold, the Lamb of God"

"Behold, the Lamb of God, who takes away the sin of the world!"
John 1:29

From the beginning of his ministry to the very end, John the Baptist pointed all men and women to Messiah, the Lord Jesus Christ. Anytime anyone tried to make a celebrity of John, he was told by the prophet what his mission in life was all about—it was all about deflecting attention from himself and directing the eyes and hearts of his hearers to Jesus.

John hired no *slick* front men to go before him, announcing his arrival. No expensive advertisements and brochures, detailing his résumé and successes preceded his campaigns. Both his wardrobe and his diet were sparse, but his message was plain and clear: "Behold, the Lamb of God, who takes away the sin of the world!"

This forerunner of our Lord was a man with a mission and with a message. Before he ever went public, he soaked in the presence of God in the wilderness, clarifying his calling. He knew God. He knew why he was here and what he was about. He was not called to gain a following after himself. No! He made sure of that. "The next day again John was standing with two of his disciples, and he looked at Jesus as he walked by and said, 'Behold, the Lamb of God!' The two disciples heard him say this, and they followed Jesus" (John 1:35-37).

Most of us know John 3:16; we would do well to memorize John 3:30. Some troublemakers approached John one day, intending to cause division between him and Christ. They told John that Jesus was baptizing more people than John (though, as we read elsewhere, Jesus himself never performed baptisms). How would John react to that? Unfortunately, there is probably as much jealously among ministers as any other profession. John's response? "I am not the Christ, but I have been sent before him. The one who has the bride is the bridegroom. The friend of the bridegroom, who stands and hears him, rejoices greatly at the bridegroom's voice. Therefore this joy of mine is now complete. He must increase, but I must decrease" (John 3:28-30).

We either take the glory, or we deflect it to the Lord Jesus. Away with ministerial pride; point to Jesus!

December 21

Thirsting for the Spirit

"Blessed are those who hunger and thirst for
righteousness, for they shall be satisfied."
Matthew 5:6

Following his remarkable conversion to Christ, an African young man by the name of Samuel Morris (1873-1893) wanted to know more about God and his holiness and particularly more about the Holy Spirit than the missionaries could tell him. But the missionaries told Sammy if he could get to New York City, there was a man who lived there by the name of Stephen Merritt, who could tell him more about the Holy Spirit.

When Sammy arrived in New York City, he was graciously welcomed by Stephen and Mrs. Merritt. He was taken on a tour of the city and shown many of the attractions. Merritt was a busy man. He invited Sammy to go with him to a funeral where he was to speak. On their way, Sammy asked his new friend, "Did you ever pray while riding in a coach?" Merritt said he had not "formally" prayed in a coach. Sammy told him they should pray, and then Sammy prayed: "Father, I have been months coming to see Stephen Merritt so that I could talk to him about the Holy Ghost. Now that I am here, he shows me the harbor, the churches, the banks and other buildings, but does not say a word about this Spirit I am so anxious to know more about. Fill him with Thyself so that he will not think, or talk, or write, or preach about anything but Thee and the Holy Ghost."

Merritt later said that he had been in many religious meetings during his ministry in the church, but that he had "never experienced the burning presence of the Holy Spirit as he did while he was kneeling in that coach, beside Sammy Morris, who was penniless and clad in tattered garments."*

One's thirst for God and his holiness may be felt in multiple ways, depending on the particular need at the time. But however it may be experienced, it always leads to a greater knowledge and intimacy with God.

The more we want of God, the less we desire everything else. A young African knew this. What about you and me?

December 22

"Behold"

But as he considered these things, behold, an
angel of the Lord appeared to him in a dream.
Matthew 1:20

It recently dawned on me, when reading the Gospel narratives surrounding our Lord's birth, that one little word was repeated, a word I had hardly noticed before—the word "behold."

This six-letter word (four letters in Greek) is easy to miss, thereby overlooking its significance. We rarely hear it in contemporary English, but it was frequently used in the Bible—a total of 1069 occurrences. Matthew and Luke employed this word in their Gospels more than any other New Testament writers—40 and 39 respectively; of those 79 occurrences, a good many appear in the Birth-narratives. I'm confident the choice of this word was not by accident. God wanted the principal parties in the Incarnation Event to realize its eternal importance. So the word "behold" was employed to capture the people's attention. God was calling men and women's attention to see, to ponder, to consider attentively the subject at hand. Note the following sampling.

But as he considered these things, *behold*, an angel of the Lord appeared to him in a dream (Matt. 1:20).

"*Behold*, the virgin shall conceive and bear a son, and they shall call his name Immanuel" (which means, God with us)" (Matt. 1:23).

Behold, wise men from the east came to Jerusalem (Matt. 2:1).

"And *behold*, your relative Elizabeth in her old age has also conceived a son" (Luke 1:36).

"*Behold*, I am the servant of the Lord; let it be to me according to your word" (Luke 1:38).

And Simeon blessed them and said to Mary his mother, "*Behold*, this child is appointed for the fall and rising of many in Israel, and for a sign that is opposed" (Luke 2:34).

Clearly, God wants all people to take special notice in the birth of his Son. He didn't want anyone to escape the eternal importance of this Event!

Name Above All Names

*"She will bear a son, and you shall call his name
Jesus, for he will save his people from their sins."*
Matthew 1:21

The history of Old Testament Israel is a lamentable record of slavery and deliverance, bondage and freedom, and sinning and repenting. From the days when Jacob and his family traveled to Egypt and subsequently became slaves, to their epochal deliverance from Pharaoh's tyranny some four hundred years later under Moses, God's covenant people were in need of a deliverer, a savior.

Moses' successor Joshua was a true servant of the Lord and one of Israel's foremost military leaders. As Moses' assistant, he served for years faithfully at his mentor's side. Joshua's experiences and accomplishments were many: he witnessed the Red Sea miracle; was present at the giving of the Law on Sinai; he was among the twelve spies sent into the land of Canaan; he was privileged to enter Canaan at the Jordon River crossing; and following the death of Moses, he became Israel's leader, winning many victories.

The name "Joshua" occurs some thirty times in the Pentateuch. He was originally named *Hoshea*, which means "salvation." However, in Numbers 13:16, Moses changed his name to *Joshua*, which means "Yahweh saves."

When the angel of the Lord appeared to Joseph, announcing that Mary's conception was "from the Holy Spirit" (Matt. 1:20), that was a startling proclamation. In the same breath, the angel informed Joseph the child was to be named "Jesus" (the Greek counterpart to the Hebrew name "Joshua"). For the Jews, that name was replete with meaning.

However, this *Joshua* was to be so much greater than the Joshua of old. This Joshua is salvation itself: "you shall call his name Jesus, for he will save his people from their sins."

This is man's fundamental need now being met with God's perfect answer—Jesus, God's very own Son!

Have you welcomed Jesus to be your Savior—from your sins?

December 24

Preparation for Christ's Coming

For this is he who was spoken of by the prophet Isaiah
when he said, "The voice of one crying in the wilderness:
'Prepare the way of the Lord; make his paths straight.'"
Matthew 3:3

Just as soil requires adequate preparation before it can receive the farmer's seed, so the heart of man must be in a suitable condition before receiving Christ as Lord and Savior.

Repentance is the work of the Spirit of God in the depths of a man's being, producing a godly sorrow that leads to salvation (see 2 Cor. 7:10). Repentance is not salvation, any more than plowing soil is the equivalent of planting seed. However, without repentance, Christ cannot enter; without repentance, there is no eternal life.

Repentance is a *turning*—a turning from one's sin, then turning toward God. This language of *turning* was often used by the Old Testament prophets in calling people to repentance: "Repent and turn away from your idols, and *turn* away your faces from all your abominations" (Ezek. 14:6); "*Turn* now, every one of you, from his evil way and evil deeds" (Jer. 25:5). To repent is to undergo a change of mind and behavior with regards to God and sin; it cannot be manufactured or self-induced.

In the plan of God, John the Baptist prepared the way for people to receive the Messiah: "The voice of one crying in the wilderness: 'Prepare the way of the Lord; make his paths straight.'" Unless the plow of repentance cut deeply into the hearts of those Judean people, whether they were priests or Pharisees, farmers or tax collectors, they would be unable to receive the long-anticipated Savior. Have you experienced true repentance? Have you turned away from your sins?

Come, Thou long expected Jesus
Born to set Thy people free;
From our fears and sins release us,
Let us find our rest in Thee.
Israel's Strength and Consolation,
Hope of all the earth Thou art;
Dear Desire of every nation,
*Joy of every longing heart.**

God with Us

*"Behold, the virgin shall conceive and bear a son, and they
shall call his name Immanuel (which means, God with us)."*
Matthew 1:23

Say it slowly: "God with us." Say it again: "God with us." Repeat the Hebrew equivalent: "Immanuel." Does it have a familiar ring to it? Too familiar?

I'm amazed the Incarnation of the Lord Jesus Christ holds no more *wonder* to me than it does. When the angel announced to Mary that she would be the human vehicle by which Immanuel would enter this world, she was overcome with reverential fear and awe. The same held true for Joseph and the Judean shepherds: an unearthly sense of wonder, adoration, mystery, mixed with a deep feeling of humility that they were the privileged recipients of such knowledge. "Immanuel ... God with us"!

The God who did mighty and marvelous exploits among his people from the earliest times had now come among his people to be "with" them—God himself. The miracle of the Red Sea crossing pales in comparison to "Immanuel—God with us"! The thunderings and lightnings on Sinai, at the giving of the Law—what is that in view of Immanuel—God himself coming in the flesh to live "with" his people? After a history of tabernacle and temple worship, after listening to the prophets read week after week, after teaching their children faithfully about the coming Messiah—suddenly he is "with" them!

Interestingly enough, in the Matthew 1 narrative, Joseph is told by the angel to name the child "Jesus" (1:21). However, when it comes to his name "Immanuel," the text reads, "they shall call his name Immanuel" 1:23). In other words, whenever believing men and women looked upon the Word made flesh, "they" would say among themselves, "Immanuel—God is with us."

It is a historical fact that God took on himself human flesh some two thousand years ago—conceived by the Holy Spirit, laid in a manger, walked among men, was crucified, and on the third day arose from the grave. That's a fact.

The question: Is Immanuel now "with" you? If not, invite him to be "with" you today.

Christ as Prophet (part 1)

In these last days he has spoken to us by his Son.
Hebrews 1:2

The Lord Jesus Christ was, and is, the perfect and ultimate fulfillment of all three anointed offices in Old Testament history: prophet, priest, and king.

Prophets were anointed men; that is, they were set apart to be God's spokesmen. Faithful prophets did not speak their own words and deliver their own message. Prophets were God's voice, delivering God's message, without addition or subtraction. Prophets were God-called men; no one *decided* to become a prophet. Moses, Samuel, Jeremiah, Ezekiel, Amos, and a host others, were specially called and chosen by God.

Moses prophesied of a day when Israel's preeminent Prophet would appear: "The Lord your God will raise up for you a prophet like me from among you, from your brothers—it is to him you shall listen" (Deut. 18:15). The Apostle Peter saw this text fulfilled in Christ, and quoted it when he addressed the people in Acts 3, following the healing of the lame beggar. The opening words in the Book of Hebrews speak of the Lord Jesus as a prophet, and not just any prophet, but the Son of God: "Long ago, at many times and in many ways, God spoke to our fathers by the prophets, but in these last days he has spoken to us by his Son" (Heb. 1:1-2).

God's incarnate Son was a faithful prophet; he delivered the Father's words without fear or favor, and without alteration. The words he spoke, he received from the Father: "For he whom God has sent utters the words of God, for he gives the Spirit without measure" (John 3:34). Christ declared to both his adversaries and his followers: "The words that I say to you I do not speak on my own authority" (John 14:10).

As a prophet, everything Jesus said would occur came true, including his death and resurrection and the outpouring of the Holy Spirit. Much of what Christ prophesied is yet to occur, but be assured: the return for his Bride, the judgment of all peoples and nations, his earthly reign, and much more, will be fulfilled.

Jesus was a prophet—*the* Prophet. We can take him at his Word!

Christ as High Priest (part 2)

*We have a great high priest who has passed
through the heavens, Jesus, the Son of God.*
Hebrews 4:14

High priests under the Old Covenant represented the people to God;
they were mediators, bringing God and man together by means of
sacrifice. In the Lord Jesus Christ, we see the complete fulfillment
of the office of the Old Testament high priest, and the Book of Hebrews beautifully describes how Jesus is the better and perfect high
priest.

• The earthly high priest passed through a veil; Jesus passed
into the heavens: "we have a great high priest who has passed
through the heavens, Jesus, the Son of God" (4:14).

• All earthly high priests were flawed human beings, not so
with Jesus: "For it was indeed fitting that we should have such
a high priest, holy, innocent, unstained, separated from sinners, and
exalted above the heavens" (7:26).

• OT priests eventually died and were replaced by another man;
Jesus' priesthood is permanent: "The former priests were many in
number, because they were prevented by death from continuing in
office, but he holds his priesthood permanently, because he continues forever" (7:23-24).

• There was no chair in the OT temple; the high priest never sat
down, signifying his ministry was incomplete: "we have such a high
priest, one who is seated at the right hand of the throne of the Majesty in heaven" (8:1).

• The OT high priests entered the Holy of Holies many times,
though only once each year: "he [Christ] entered once for all into
the holy places" (9:12).

• Christ took his own blood into the Most Holy Place:
"he entered once for all into the holy places, not by means of the
blood of goats and calves but by means of his own blood, thus securing an eternal redemption" (9:12).

• Christ, as our heavenly High Priest, always lives to make intercession for the saints (see 7:25). Hallelujah!

Christ as King (part 3)

*"The time is fulfilled, and the kingdom of God is
at hand; repent and believe in the gospel."*
Mark 1:15

The prophets of old foretold a time when a King and kingdom would arrive on earth, superseding all other kings and kingdoms. Isaiah wrote, "For to us a child is born, to us a son is given; and the government shall be upon his shoulder" (9:6). He further prophesied this coming King would be the final successor to the throne of David, that he would rule in peace, and his would be an everlasting kingdom of justice and righteousness (see 9:7).

The forerunner of this King, John the Baptist, announced the coming of the King was imminent, and that in order to prepare for his coming people needed to repent: "Repent, for the kingdom of heaven is at hand" (Matt. 3:2). When a repentant sinner receives the Lord Jesus Christ, he receives the King and commits himself to live under his rule.

As the incarnate Son of God, the King came to live among men as a servant, taking the Jewish world by surprise. This King's kingdom would be different; he would not rule with conventional military weapons and political power: "My kingdom is not of this world. If my kingdom were of this world, my servants would have been fighting" (Matt. 18:36). This King's kingdom would be identified by "righteousness and peace and joy in the Holy Spirit" (Rom. 14:17).

Christ's Kingdom is both now, and not yet. When he came in the flesh, the kingdom of God was present in the person of Jesus; it became internal wherever the King was received. However, the full manifestation of Christ's reign is yet to be realized. For this reason, our Lord taught us to pray, "Your kingdom come, your will be done, on earth as it is in heaven" (Matt. 6:10). The will of God is done when the King's servants joyfully accept his rule.

There is a future Day, when the King will reign on earth and throughout his universe—forever. "Then the seventh angel blew his trumpet, and there were loud voices in heaven, saying, 'The kingdom of the world has become the kingdom of our Lord and of his Christ, and he shall reign forever and ever'" (Rev. 11:15).

My Heart—Christ's Home

"If anyone loves me, he will keep my word, and my Father will
love him, and we will come to him and make our home with him."
John 14:23

In 1954, a young Presbyterian pastor by the name of Robert Boyd
Munger (1911-2001) preached a sermon to his California congregation titled "My Heart, Christ's Home." In that sermon, Munger relates: "One evening I invited Jesus Christ into my heart.... He came
into the darkness of my heart and turned on the light. He built a fire
on the hearth and banished the chill. He started music where there
had been stillness, and He filled the emptiness with His own loving,
wonderful fellowship."

As the pastor continued, he describes the Lord Jesus Christ
wanting Munger to make his heart Christ's home. He figuratively
relates Christ entering, one by one, each room of his heart, asking a
variety of questions, as he entered his study, dining room, living
room, workroom, recreation room, bedroom, and hall closet. After
he and Christ had closely surveyed each room, Munger said to himself, "I have been trying to keep this heart of mine clean and available for Christ, but it is hard work. I start on one room, and no sooner have I cleaned it than I discover another room is dirty. I begin on
the second room, and the first one is already dusty again. I'm getting tired trying to maintain a clean heart and an obedient life. I just
am not up to it!" Then Munger asked, "Lord, is there a possibility
you would be willing to manage the whole house ... keeping my
heart what it ought to be and myself doing what I ought to be doing?" Munger said, "I could see his face light up as he replied, 'I'd
love to! This is exactly what I came to do. You can't live out the
Christian life in your own strength.'"*

There is nothing *automatic* in our Christian walk; every step
requires God's grace and our cooperation. That being said, the
Christian life is the easiest life to live, when we live in total surrender to the Lord Jesus Christ, allowing him to have complete access
to every area of our heart and life.

The Father and the Son desire to make your heart their home.
Are you willing?

Our Lord is Coming Soon

*He who testifies to these things says, "Surely I
am coming soon." Amen. Come, Lord Jesus!*
Revelation 22:20

The final book of the Bible accentuates the return of our Lord and Savior, Jesus Christ. The Old Testament prophets foretold the first and second advents of the Christ; the four Evangelists recorded our Savior's first appearance; and the apostles not only spoke of the Lord Jesus' first coming, but pointed their readers to his return.

Jesus is coming again!

Three times in the last chapter of the last book of the Bible, Jesus announced to the Apostle John that he was returning to earth. Each time he emphasizes the imminence of his return by using the word "soon": "Behold, I am coming soon"; "Behold, I am coming soon"; "Surely I am coming soon" (Rev. 22:7, 12, 20). Of course the word "soon" is a relative term; it has reference to time. Christians should not assume a nonchalant attitude because Jesus has not yet returned for his Bride. We must heed the words of Jesus: "Stay dressed for action and keep your lamps burning" (Luke 12:35).

Let these three texts serve as more than casual reminders; let them sink into the depths of your heart, and live each day in holy anticipation of our Lord's return.

"And behold, I am coming soon. Blessed is the one who keeps the words of the prophecy of this book" (Rev. 22:7).

"Behold, I am coming soon, bringing my recompense with me, to repay each one for what he has done" (Rev. 22:12).

"He who testifies to these things says, 'Surely I am coming soon'" (Rev. 22:20).

A little girl came home from Sunday school, and told her mother that she had learned Jesus was coming again. She asked her mother if he could come that very day. Her mother responded in the affirmative. Then the little child said to her mother, "Mommy, please comb my hair." She wanted to be ready.

Are you ready? Join with the Apostle John, saying from your heart, "Amen. Come, Lord Jesus!" (Rev. 22:20).

December 31

A Glorious Anticipation

*He will swallow up death forever; and the Lord God will wipe
away tears from all faces, and the reproach of his people
he will take away from all the earth, for the Lord has spoken.*
Isaiah 25:8

The Old Covenant was full of both longing and prophecy of a coming Messianic rule and reign. The prophets themselves did not have complete knowledge as to how this would all unfold: "Concerning this salvation, the prophets who prophesied about the grace that was to be yours searched and inquired carefully, inquiring what person or time the Spirit of Christ in them was indicating when he predicted the sufferings of Christ and the subsequent glories" (1 Pet. 1:10-11). They did not know when Messiah would appear the first time as the incarnate Son of God; they did not know precisely when he would appear the second time to reign on earth. But they knew he would come; they knew there would be a day in which Messiah would rule on earth in righteousness.

Christ has come; Christ will come again. This the Word declares; this the Christian believes; this is the Christian's hope. We know he has come; we know he is coming again. In his first coming, our salvation was purchased; atonement was made. In his second coming, Satan will be destroyed; the presence of sin will be banished, and the remnants of sin will be cleansed from the earth and our universe.

When Christ returns for the saints, everything that is painful and hurtful, sorrowful and grievous, sad and distressful, disappointing and discouraging—and so much more—will be cleansed finally and fully from our consciousness and from the universe. Then, we shall see the King, the Lord Jesus Christ, our Redeemer, and our Savior.

Hear God's promise of what the future of the saints will be: "Behold, the dwelling place of God is with man. He will dwell with them, and they will be his people, and God himself will be with them as their God. He will wipe away every tear from their eyes, and death shall be no more, neither shall there be mourning, nor crying, nor pain anymore, for the former things have passed away" (Rev. 21:3-4).

Scripture Index

Ref	Date
26:3	June 23
29:13	Aug. 14
30:21	Dec. 8
31:1	Sept. 26
40:31	Apr. 23
43:20	May 27
50:4-5	Feb. 17
64:1	Apr. 30

Jeremiah

Ref	Date
17:7-8	Aug. 13
23:6	Jan. 8
29:11	Dec. 17
36:23	Aug. 15

Ezekiel

Ref	Date
3:3	Dec. 15
16:49-50	Sept. 4
17:24	May 14
48:35	Dec. 4

Daniel

Ref	Date
6:10	June 15
12:10	July 12

Joel

Ref	Date
2:15	Apr. 25

Amos

Ref	Date
7:14-15	Aug. 17

Obadiah

Ref	Date
1:17	June 10

Habakkuk

Ref	Date
3:17-18	May 25

Haggai

Ref	Date
1:13	Nov. 15

Zechariah

Ref	Date
4:6	May 18
7:12	June 17

Malachi

Ref	Date
3:16	Mar. 4

Matthew

Ref	Date
1:20	Dec. 22
1:21	July 5, Dec. 24
1:23	Dec. 25
3:3	Dec. 23
5:6	Dec. 21
5:8	May 3
5:13	Feb. 22
6:10	Dec. 14
6:11	May 7
7:13-14	Feb. 11
8:10	Sept. 14
10:24-25	Oct. 21
10:25	Jan. 25
10:31	June 29
10:32-33	Oct. 17
11:2-3	Nov. 13
11:28	Jan. 10
11:29	Jan. 11
11:29-30	Jan. 12
12:34	July 6
12:41	Jan. 7
17:8	May 26
20:15-16	Jan. 15
22:37, 39	Sept. 21
23:33	Mar. 17
26:7	Feb. 14
26:10	June 14
26:35	Aug. 22
26:41	Nov. 19

Mark

Ref	Date
1:15	Dec. 28
3:5	Dec. 19
5:15	Nov. 24
5:19	May 2
6:31	Jan. 16
8:23-25	July 23
8:34	Mar. 29
8:38	Oct. 16
9:7	Apr. 1
9:23	June 18
10:21	Jan. 28
10:43-44	May 22
11:24	May 9, 10
12:30	Jan. 27
14:8	Dec. 7
14:32-33	Mar. 24
14:38	Oct. 22

Luke

Ref	Date
1:50	Jan. 5
1:68, 77-78	Mar. 23
4:43	Dec. 6
7:13	Feb. 13
8:18	Mar. 16
8:39	Dec. 18
9:62	July 25
10:2	June 25
10:17-18	Oct. 3
10:41-42	Mar. 14
11:1	Jan. 21
11:35	Apr. 19
16:15	Mar. 19
17:10	June 30

19:8-9	Dec. 9
19:10	May 17
23:24	July 27
24:32	July 31

John

1:1	Jan. 2
1:4	June 8
1:16	Sept. 23
1:29	Dec. 20
3:3	June 20
4:13-14	Sept. 22
4:16-18	Nov. 27
4:34	Sept. 29
7:37-38	May 12, July 17
8:45	Dec. 12
8:53	Jan. 6
9:25	Dec. 11
10:27	Feb. 20
11:40	July 19
11:41	Sept. 25
12:25	Jan. 26
13:14-15	Apr. 14
13:17	Aug. 19
13:23	Mar. 18
14:9	July 18
14:12	Aug. 24
14:15	Feb. 21
14:16-17	Jan. 13
14:17	Aug. 2
14:23	Dec. 29
15:2	May 16
15:5	Mar. 22, July 26
16:8	July 14
17:10	Oct. 23
17:14	April 24
20:22	Aug. 23
21:17	Jan. 24, Oct. 15
21:18	Nov. 28
21:21	May 28

Acts

1:8	July 21
2:2	May 21
2:43	Feb. 2
4:31	Mar. 2
5:11	Feb. 3
9:31	Feb. 4
13:52	Aug. 25
16:7	Aug. 16
18:24-25	July 20
20:27	Aug. 9
27:23	June 16

Romans

1:1	Feb 24
1:22	Aug. 7
5:3	Oct. 14
8:16	Oct. 10
8:18	Oct. 13
12:1	July 10
12:3	Sept. 16
12:15	Nov. 30
14:17	Nov. 6
15:13	Feb. 5

1 Corinthians

1:2	Mar. 30
1:17	Mar. 27
1:18	Mar. 25
5:12	Nov. 26
6:19	May 5
12:3	Sept. 11
13:13	June 19
15:58	July 28
16:13	May 30

2 Corinthians

1:3-5	Sept. 13
1:9	Jan. 31
2:15	May 1
3:18	Sept. 30
4:16	May 24
4:17	Feb. 16
5:10	Oct. 8
5:19	Mar. 26
7:1	July 29
12:7	Jan. 23, May 15

Galatians

1:15-16	July 4
2:20	May 23
3:3	Jan. 9
5:16	Mar. 6
5:22	Apr. 2-8
5:22, 23	Apr. 9-11
6:9	Feb. 27

Ephesians

1:7	Dec. 16
3:16	Oct. 26
3:17	Oct. 11, 24
3:19	Mar. 9, Oct. 26
3:20	Oct. 30
4:30	Aug. 29
5:8	Aug. 30
5:10	May 29
5:18-19	Oct. 19, 20
5:25	Feb. 15

Philippians

2:14-15	May 8
2:16	May 13
2:20	Apr. 21
3:8	Mar. 8

3:10	Mar. 3, Oct. 12
4:4	Nov. 5

Colossians

1:9-10	July 22
1:27	July 2, 3
3:12	July 13
3:14	Oct. 1
3:17	Oct. 5
4:2	Jan. 18
4:12	Aug. 3

1 Thessalonians

1:2-3	Aug. 26, Feb. 25
1:5	Sept. 10
1:6	July 15
4:3	Oct. 6
5:5-6	July 30
5:16-17	Nov. 7
5:22	Aug. 27
5:23	Mar. 31

2 Thessalonians

1:3	Oct. 25
1:11-12	Apr. 13

1 Timothy

2:6-7	Sept. 15
2:8-9	Mar. 15
6:3-4	Aug. 31

2 Timothy

1:6	Nov. 4
2:20-21	May 4
3:1	Sept. 6
4:7	Feb. 6
4:13	Aug. 8

Titus

2:13	Apr. 18
3:2-3	Aug. 6
3:4-6	Mar. 21
3:5	July 7, Oct. 28
3:11-12	July 8

Hebrews

1:2	Dec. 26
2:11	Mar. 5
4:9	May 20
4:12	Sept. 3
4:14	Dec. 27
4:15	Nov. 2
4:16	Jan. 4
5:14	Sept. 17
6:10	Dec. 10
9:24	Jan. 22
9:27	Dec. 13
10:7	Nov. 25
10:22	Oct. 31
10:24	June 6
10:35	Nov. 3
11:4	Jan. 29
11:7	Nov. 9
11:38	Sept. 27
12:1	July 24
12:2	Mar. 1
12:4	Aug. 4
13:7-8	Feb. 26
13:14	Oct. 7

James

2:24	Sept. 5
3:17	Nov. 29
5:16	Jan. 19
5:19-20	Sept. 2

1 Peter

1:15-16	Mar. 28
1:18-19	Aug. 18
2:4-5	Feb. 12
5:2-3	Oct. 2
5:5	Feb. 23
5:6	Feb. 28
5:8	June 9

2 Peter

1:12-13	Aug. 5

1 John

1:7	July 11
2:1	Aug. 1
2:1-2	Nov. 1
3:1	Mar. 10
5:11	June
7	
5:14	May
6	
5:21	Aug. 10, 11

3 John

1:3	Jan.
14	
1:9, 11	Sept. 7

Jude

1:3	Aug. 20
1:20	June
2	
1:21	June
3	
1:22-23	Sept.
8	
1:24	June
3	

Revelation

Endnotes

January 3.   Taken from "The Light of the World is Jesus" by Philip P. Bliss.

January 4.   The original source of this narrative is unknown to me.

January 12.   Taken from "Love Divine All Loves Excelling" by Charles Wesley.

January 13.   Daniel Steele, *The Gospel of the Comforter*, (Salem, OH: Schmul Publishing Co., 1960; reprinted from 1897 edition), 282-283.

January 16.   J. Sidlow Baxter, *Going Deeper*, (Grand Rapids: Zondervan, 1959), 133-134.
              Taken from "Take Time to Be Holy" by William D. Longstaff.

January 19.   Howard Taylor, *Hudson Taylor and the China Inland Mission* (London: The Religious Tract Society, 1921), 625.

January 22.   Andrew Bonar, *Robert Murray M'Cheyne* (London: The Banner of Truth Trust, reprinted 1962 from original 1844 edition), 179.

January 23.   Lettie Cowman, *Springs in the Valley* (Los Angeles: The Oriental Missionary Society, 1939), 62.

January 24.   The original source of this poem is unknown to me.

January 25.   Kari Torjesen Malcolm, *We Signed Our Lives Away* (Downers Grove, IL: IVP Press, 1990), 23-24.

January 26.   Rob Mackenzie, *David Livingstone: The Truth Behind the Legend* (Fearn, Scotland: Christian Focus Publications, 2000), 17. Used by permission of Christian Focus Publications.

January 28.   "All for Jesus" by Mary D. James.

January 29.   Roger Steer, *George Müller: Delighted in God* (Wheaton, IL: Harold Shaw Publishers, 1975), 182.

January 31.   Taken from "I Surrender All" by Judson W. Van DeVenter.

February 2.   Robert E. Coleman, *One Divine Moment* (Old Tappan, NJ: Fleming H. Revell Co., 1970), 100.

February 5.   Viktor Frankl, *Man's Search for Meaning*, rev. (New York: Washington Square Press, 1959), 28.

February 10.   C. S. Lewis, *Mere Christianity* (New York: Macmillan Publishing Co., 1952), 28.

February 11.   Taken from "Come, Jesus, Lord with Holy Fire" by Charles Wesley.

February 12.   C. S. Lewis, *Mere Christianity* (New York: Macmillan Publishing Co., 1952), 140.

February 15.   H. C. G. Moule, *The Epistle to the Ephesians*, Cambridge: University Press, 1893; reprint, *Studies in Ephesians* (Grand Rapids: Kregel Publications, 1977), 127.

February 16.   Retrieved from wholesomewords.org.
              Rob Mackenzie, *David Livingstone: The Truth Behind the Legend* (Fearn, Scotland: Christian Focus Publications, 2000), 172.
              Ibid., 181. Used by permission of Christian Focus Publications.

February 17.   Brother Lawrence, *The Practice of the Presence of God* (Westwood, NJ: Fleming H. Revell Co., 1958), 46.

February 18.   James Houston, *The Transforming Power of Prayer: Deepening Your Friendship With God* (Colorado Springs, CO: NavPress, 1996), 158-159.

February 19.   J. I. Packer, *A Quest for Godliness* (Wheaton, IL: Crossway Books, 1990), 86.

February 20.   Robert Elliott Speer, *The Master of the Heart* (New York: Fleming H. Revell, 1908), 50-51.
          Taken from "Lord, I Have Shut the Door" by William H. Runyan.

February 21.   Henry Scougal, *The Life of God in the Soul of Man* (originally published in 1677, Kindle e-book).
          C. S. Lewis, *Mere Christianity* (New York: Macmillan Publishing Co., 1952), 174.
          Dallas Willard, cited in *For All the Saints: Evangelical Theology and Christian Spirituality*, George, Timothy, Alister McGrath, ed. (Louisville, KY: Westminster John Knox Press, 2003), 40.

February 22.   William Law, *A Serious Call to a Devout and Holy Life*, John W. Meister, ed. (Philadelphia: The Westminster Press, 1975), 20.

February 23.   William Barclay, *In the Hands of God* (New York: Harper & Row Publishers, 1966), 88-89.
          Charles H. Spurgeon, *Spurgeon's Expository Encyclopedia*, Vol. XIII (Grand Rapids: Baker Book House, 1952), 286.

February 25.   Marvin Vincent, *Word Studies in the New Testament*, Vol. III (Grand Rapids: William B. Eerdmans Publishing Co., 1965), 2.
          Murray J. Harris, *Slave for Christ* (Downers Grove, IL: InterVarsity Press, 1999), 18.
          Calvin Miller, *The Empowered Leader: 10 Keys to Servant Leadership* (Nashville, TN: Broadman & Holman Publishers, 1995), 14.

February 26.   Jonathan Edwards, *David Brainerd: His Life and Diary* (Chicago: Moody Press, 1949), 245.

February 27.   Kenneth N. Taylor, *My Life: A Guided Tour* (Wheaton, IL: Tyndale House Publishers, 1991), 207. Used by permission of Tyndale House Publishers, Inc. All rights reserved.

February 28.   Frederick Bruner, *Matthew, A Commentary*. Vol. 2, rev. ed. (Grand Rapids: William B. Eerdmans Publishing Co., 2004), 326.

March 3.   A. W. Tozer, *The Pursuit of God* (Harrisburg, PA: Christian Publications, 1948),15.

March 4.   Taken from "Blest Be the Tie That Binds" by John Fawcett.

March 8.   J. I. Packer, *Knowing God* (Downers Grove, IL: InterVarsity Press, 1973), 20.

March 12.   Adam Clarke, *Clarke's Commentary*, Vol. III (Nashville, TN: Abingdon, n.d.), 283.

March 15.   Taken from "Let the Beauty of Jesus Be Seen in Me" by Albert Orsborn.

March 18.   "Near to the Heart of God" by Cleland B. McAfee.

March 19.   Taken from "All for Jesus" by Mary D. James.

March 21.   Retrieved from cyberhymnal.org.
          "Not What My Hands Have Done" by Horatius Bonar.

March 22.   "Dependence" by William Cowper.

March 24.   Taken from "Majestic Sweetness" by Samuel Stennett.
          Taken from "My God, My God! And Can It Be?" by Frederick W. Faber.

March 30.   Dallas Willard, *The Divine Conspiracy* (New York: HarperCollins, 1998), 36.

March 31.   D. Edmond Hiebert, *The Thessalonian Epistles* (Chicago: Moody, 1971), 250.

April 1.   Taken from "Sun of My Soul" by John Keble.

April 4.   Taken from "Oh, the Peace That Jesus Gives" by Haldor Lillenas.

April 6.	Francis A. Schaeffer, *The Mark of the Christian* (Downers Grove, IL: InterVarsity Press, 1970), 22-23.
April 8.	Quoted by John M. Drescher in *Spirit Fruit* (Scottdale, PA: Herald Press, 1974), 260. Used by permission.
April 9.	William Barclay, *Flesh and Spirit* (Grand Rapids: Baker, 1976), 113.
April 15.	Taken from "How Firm a Foundation" by John Rippon.
April 17.	Taken from "The Light of the World is Jesus" by Philip P. Bliss.
April 20.	Taken from "Father, of Jesus Christ, My Lord" by Charles Wesley.
April 24.	Taken from "Jesus, I My Cross Have Taken" by Henry Lyte.
April 29.	Taken from "Wonderful Words of Life" by Philip P. Bliss.
May 4.	Quoted by Thomas Cook in *New Testament Holiness* (London: The Epworth Press, 1958), 6.
May 9.	Charles G. Finney, *Charles G. Finney: An Autobiography* (Old Tappan, NJ: Fleming H. Revell Co., 1908), 10.
May 10.	Fred A. Hartley III, *Everything by Prayer* (Camp Hill PA: Christian Publications, 2003), 36.
May 12.	Taken from "Jesus, Thou Joy of Loving Hearts" by Bernard of Clairvaux.
May 13.	Søren Kierkegaard, *Purity of Heart is to Will One Thing* (New York: Harper & Row, 1948), 209-210.
May 14.	C. S. Lewis, *Mere Christianity* (New York: Macmillan Publishing Co., 1952), 111.
May 16.	Retrieved from ipm.iastate.edu.
May 19.	Duncan Campbell, *Duncan Campbell: The Story of a Soul Winner* (Hobe Sound, FL: H.S.B.C. Press, n.d.), 6.
May 22.	George MacDonald, *Knowing the Heart of God*, edited by Michael R. Phillips (Minneapolis, MN: Bethany House Publishers, 1990), 253.
May 26.	George MacDonald, *Knowing the Heart of God*, edited by Michael R. Phillips (Minneapolis, MN: Bethany House Publishers, 1990), 97.
May 30.	"Am I a Soldier of the Cross?" by Isaac Watts.
June 9.	"My Soul, Be on Your Guard" by George Heath.
June 11.	"There is Power in the Blood" by Lewis E. Jones.
June 14.	Taken from "Savior, Thy Dying Love" by S. Dryden Phelps.
June 23.	"Like a River Glorious" by Frances R. Havergal.
June 27.	Taken from "Take My Life and Let It Be" by Frances R. Havergal.
June 28.	Os Guinness & John Seel, *No God But God* (Chicago: Moody, 1992), 15.
July 1.	William Barclay, *The Letters to the Galatians and Ephesians, The Daily Study Bible Series*, rev. ed. (Philadelphia: The Westminster Press, 1976), 178.
July 2.	Retrieved from lovechapelhill.wordpress.com.
July 4.	Joe Brice, *Pentecost* (London: Hodder & Stoughton, 1936, reprinted by Convention Book Store, 1973), 25-26. Taken from "I Worship Thee, O Holy Ghost" by William Warren.
July 5.	Taken from "And Can It Be?" by Charles Wesley.
July 6.	E. Stanley Jones, *A Song of Ascents: A Spiritual Autobiography*, (Nashville: Abingdon, 1968), 34.
July 7.	Retrieved from "Startled Beyond Measure: How D. James Kennedy Came to Christ." Truth in Action Ministries.www.truthinaction. org.

July 8.	Taken from "I Was a Wandering Sheep" by Horatius Bonar.
July 9.	George Steinberger, *In the Footsteps of the Lamb,* edited by Ralph I. Tilley (Sellersburg, IN: LITS Books, 2015, reprinted from 1936 edition), 36-37.
July 10.	John Murray, *The Epistle to the Romans* (Grand Rapids: William B. Eerdmans Publishing Co., 1965), 149.
July 11.	W. E. Sangster, *The Path to Perfection* (New York: Abingdon-Cokesbury, 1943), 135.
	Retrieved from sermonindex.net.
	Andrew Bonar, *Robert Murray M'Cheyne* (London: The Banner of Truth Trust, 1962, reprint), 185.
July 12.	A. J. Gordon, *The Ministry of the Spirit* (Philadelphia: American Baptist Publication Society, 1896), 116-117.
	Taken from "My God, I Know, I Feel Thee Mine" by Charles Wesley.
July 13.	Taken from "Rescue the Perishing" by Fanny Crosby.
July 14.	John Owen, Introduction by J. I. Packer in *Triumph over Temptation,* James M. Houston, ed. (Colorado Springs, CO: Cook Communications, 2005), 21.
July 15.	David Wilkerson, "Times Square Church Pulpit Series," August 2, 1999.
July 16.	A. W. Tozer, *The Praying Plumber of Lisburn* (Harrisburg, PA: Christian Publications, n.d.), 24.
July 18.	Dietrich Bonhoeffer, *The Cost of Discipleship* (New York: Macmillan, 1966), 53, emphasis added.
July 20.	Martyn Lloyd-Jones, *Joy Unspeakable* (Wheaton, IL: Harold Shaw Publishers, 1985), 114.
July 21.	George and Donald Sweeting, *Lessons from the Life of Moody,* revised (Chicago: Moody Press, 2001), 96-97. Used by permission.
July 22.	Martyn Lloyd-Jones, *Joy Unspeakable* (Wheaton, IL: Harold Shaw Publishers, 1985), 113-114.
July 23.	Thomas Kelly, *A Testament of Devotion* (New York: Harper & Brothers, 1941), 80.
	Os Guinness, *The Call* (Nashville: Word, 2003), 164, 166.
July 24.	"Christian History" (Worchester, PA: Christian History Institute), 80:3.
July 26.	Quoted in "On the Father Front" by Ray Pritchard, Vol. 8, No. 2, 1995.
July 30.	Taken from "Will Jesus Find Us Watching?" by Fanny Crosby.
August 1.	Taken from "Arise My Soul, Arise?" by Charles Wesley.
August 4.	Taken from "Fight the Good Fight of Faith with All Thy Might" by John S. B. Monsell.
	Taken from "Am I a Soldier of the Cross?" by Isaac Watts.
August 5.	Taken from "Wonderful Words of Life" by Phillip P. Bliss.
August 18.	Taken from "There is a Fountain Filled with Blood" by William Cowper.
August 19.	Philip Greenslade, *Leadership, Greatness & Servanthood* (Minneapolis, MN: Bethany House Publishers, 1984), 102.
August 22.	Dennis F. Kinlaw, *The Mind of Christ* (Nappanee, IN: Evangel Publishing House, 1998), 60. Used by permission.
August 23.	A. J. Gordon, *The Ministry of the Spirit* (Philadelphia: American Baptist Publication Society, 1896), 141-142.
	Samuel Chadwick, *The Way to Pentecost* (Berne, IN: Light and Hope Publications, 1937), 12.

Francis Chan, (2009) *The Forgotten God* [Kindle iPad version]. Retrieved from amazon.com.

August 24. John Greenfield. *When the Spirit Came* (Minneapolis: Bethany Fellowship, 1976), 19.

Taken from "The God of Your Forefathers Praise" by James Montgomery.

August 25. Quoted by Peter Kreeft, *Christianity for Modern Pagans: Pascal's Pensées Edited, Outlined & Explained*, selections from Pascal's *Pensées* translated by A. J. Krailsheimer (San Francisco: Ignatius Press, 1993), 325.

August 27. D. Edmond Hiebert, *The Thessalonian Epistles* (Chicago: Moody Press, 1971), 248-249.

Vance Havner, *Why Not Just Be Christians?* (Westwood, NJ: Fleming H. Revell Co., 1964), 19.

August 28. Taken from "God Moves in a Mysterious Way" by William Cowper.

August 29. Duncan Campbell, *Duncan Campbell: The Story of a Soul Winner* (Hobe Sound, FL: H.S.B.C. Press, n.d.), 5-6.

August 31. David Wells, *God the Evangelist* (Crown Hill, UK: Authentic Media; 2nd edition, 2000), 58.

September 3. "The Book that Would Understand Me" triablogue.blogspot.com. This quote originally appeared in "Eternity Magazine, 1974.

September 5. Taken from "Trust and Obey" by John H. Sammis.

September 9. Taken from "My Savior First of All" by Fanny Crosby.

September 10. William Barclay, *Fishers of Men* (Philadelphia: The Westminster Press, 1966), 112.

September 12. James Houston, *The Transforming Power of Prayer* (Colorado Springs, CO: NavPress, 1998), 36.

September 21. I first read this in *The Wesleyan Advocate*; I have misplaced the complete reference data.

September 22. Taken from "Satisfied" by Clara Teare.

September 23. F. F. Bruce, *The Gospel of John* (Grand Rapids: Wm. B. Eerdmans, 1983), 43.

September 27. Mary Alice Tenney, *Living in Two Worlds* (Winona Lake, IN: Light and Life Press), 61.

September 28. Retrieved from Dr. V. Raymond Edman, "The Presence of the King," wheaton.edu.

October 1. Retrieved from "Blest Be the Tie That Binds," cyberhymnal.org.
"Blest Be the Tie That Binds" by John Fawcett.

October 2. Eugene Peterson, *The Message: The New Testament in Contemporary English* (Colorado Springs, CO: NavPress, 1993), 368. Used by permission of NavPress. All rights reserved. Represented by Tyndale House Publishers, Inc.

October 3. Dennis F. Kinlaw, *Preaching in the Spirit* (Grand Rapids: Zondervan, 1985), 46. Used by permission of Warner Press.

George Whitefield, *George Whitefield's Journals* (Carlisle, PA: The Banner of Truth Trust, reprint 1998), Nov. 29, 1739.

Quoted by Timothy George in "Delighted by Doctrine." Retrieved from beesondivinity.com.

October 4. Bud Robinson, *Sunshine and Smiles* (Kokomo, IN: Newby Book Room, n.d.), 44-45.

October 5. A. W. Tozer, *The Pursuit of God* (Harrisburg, PA: Christian Publications, 1948), 127.

Taken from "Take My Life and Let It Be" by Frances Havergal.

October 8.   Bernard R. DeRemer, "Martha Snell Nicholson: Pilgrimage of Pain," pulpithelps.com.
              Taken from "When I stand at the Judgment Seat of Christ" by Martha Snell Nicholson.

October 9.   A. W. Tozer, *That Incredible Christian* (Harrisburg, PA: Christian Publications, 1964), 129.

October 10.   Taken from "My Faith Looks Up to Thee" by Ray Palmer.

October 11.   Alister McGrath, *Knowing Christ* (New York: Random House, 2002), 41.

October 12.   F. F. Bruce, *Philippians, New International Biblical Commentary*, Vol. 11 (Peabody, Mass: Hendrickson Publishers, 1989), 115.
              Marvin R. Vincent, *A Critical and Exegetical Commentary on the Epistles to the Philippians and to Philemon, The International Critical Commentary* (Edinburgh, Scotland: T. & T. Clark, 1955), 104.
              Martyn Lloyd-Jones, *The Life of Joy and Peace: An Exposition of Philippians* (Grand Rapids: Baker Books, 1990), 308. Used by permission of Elizabeth Catherwood.

October 13.   Richard Wurmbrand, *In God's Underground*, Charles Foley, ed. (New York: Bantam Books, 1968), 25.
              Karl Barth, *The Epistle to the Philippians*, translated by James W. Leitch (Richmond, Va.: John Knox Press, 1962), 103.

October 14.   Dietrich Bonhoeffer, *Life Together*, translated by John W. Doberstein (New York: Harper & Row Publishers, 1954), 13.

October 15.   Andrew Bonar, *The Life of Robert Murray M'Chyne* (London: The Banner of Truth Trust, 1844), 186.
              Taken from "More Love to Thee, O Christ" by Elizabeth P. Prentiss.

October 18.   Taken from "If We Never Meet Again This Side of Heaven" by Albert Brumley.

October 19.   Taken from "Blessed Assurance" by Fanny Crosby.

October 20.   Taken from "There Shall Be Showers of Blessing" by Daniel W. Whittle.
              Taken from "Heaven Came Down" by John W. Peterson.

October 21.   "O to Be Like Thee" by Thomas Chisholm.

October 22.   "I Want a Principle Within" by Charles Wesley.

October 23.   Taken from "Down at the Cross" by Elisha A. Hoffman.

October 24.   Taken from "Abide with Me" by Henty F. Lyte.

October 25.   "Indwelt" by Beatrice Clelland.

October 26.   Taken from Love Divine, "All Loves Excelling" by Charles Wesley.
              Taken from "O Jesus, Jesus, Dearest Lord" by Frederick Faber.

October 28.   Adam Clarke, *Clarke's Commentaries* (Nashville: Abingdon Press, n.d.), 1:57.
              Dennis F. Kinlaw, *This Day With the Master* (Grand Rapids: Zondervan, 2002), November 16.

October 30.   Thomas Cook, *New Testament Holiness* (London: Epworth Press: 1902), 127.

October 31.   "The American Heritage Dictionary of the English Language." 4th ed. (New York: Houghton Mifflin Co., 2000), 1305.

November 1.   Dennis F. Kinlaw. *Preaching in the Spirit* (Grand Rapids: Zondervan, 1985), 116-117. Used by permission.
              Taken from "Arise, My Soul, Arise" by Charles Wesley.

November 2.   F. F. Bruce, *The Epistle to the Hebrews*. (Grand Rapids: Wm. B.

Eerdmans Co., 1964), 90.

November 3.   Taken from "The Cross is Not Greater" by Ballington Booth.

November 9.   Ralph I. Tilley, *Letters from Noah* (Sellersburg, IN: LITS Books, 2013), xv.

November 13. Taken from "A Mighty Fortress is Our God" by Martin Luther.

November 15. Retrieved from thecyberhymnal.org.
              Taken from "Day by Day" by Karolina Sandell-Berg.
              Taken from "Children of the Heavenly Father" by Karolina Sandell-Berg.

November 18. John Baillie, *A Diary of Private Prayer* (New York: Simon & Schuster, 1977), 135.

November 19. Taken from "A Charge to Keep I Have" by Charles Wesley.

November 20. Taken from "Look and Live" by William A. Ogden.

November 21. Peter Kreeft, *Christianity for Modern Pagans: Pascal's Penseés Edited, Outlined & Explained* (San Francisco: Ignatius Press, 1966), 234.

November 22. Taken from "When I See the Blood" by John G. Foote.

November 24. Clarence W. Hall, *Out of the Depths: The Life-Story of Henry F. Milans* (New York: The Salvation Army, 1935), 100, 118, 174.

November 25. Taken from "Man of Sorrows, What a Name" by Philip P. Bliss.

December 5.   "We Cannot Kindle When We Will" by Matthew Arnold.

December 7.   Retrieved from http://wesley.nnu.edu/wesleyctr/books.

December 8.   Taken from "Yield Not to Temptation" by Horatio R. Palmer.

December 10. Clarence W. Hall, *Samuel Logan Brengle: Portrait of a Prophet* ((New York: The Salvation Army, 1933), 74.

December 11. Taken from "Amazing Grace" by John Newton.
              Harold Begbie, *Twice-Born Men: A Clinic in Regeneration* (New York: Fleming H. Revell Co., 1909), 18.

December 18. Taken from "O for a Thousand Tongues to Sing" by Charles Wesley.

December 21. Lindley Baldwin, *Samuel Morris: The March of Faith* (Minneapolis, MN, 1942), 48.

December 24. Taken from "Come, Thou Long Expected Jesus" by Charles Wesley.

December 29. Robert Boyd Munger, *My Heart—Christ's Home* (Downers Grove, IL: InterVarsity Press, 1986), 26-27. Used by permission.

Unless quoted material is in the public domain, or falls under the "fair use" guideline for copyrighted publications, permission has been secured from the publisher/ author to use copyrighted material.

To the author's knowledge, all selections from hymns are "in the public domain."

65205670R00236

Made in the USA
Charleston, SC
23 December 2016